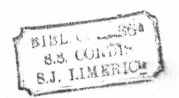

D1349873

Jerome Nadal, S.J.

Jerome Nadal, S.J.
1507–1580

Tracking the
First Generation of Jesuits

by

William V. Bangert, S.J.

edited and completed by
Thomas M. McCoog, S.J.

A Campion Book

Loyola University Press
Chicago

Loyola University Press
3441 North Ashland Avenue
Chicago, Illinois 60657

Library of Congress Cataloging-in-Publication Data

Bangert, William V.
    Jerome Nadal, S.J., 1507–1580: tracking the first generation of Jesuits / by
William V. Bangert, edited and completed by Thomas M. McCoog.
       p.   cm.
    Includes bibliographical references and index.
    ISBN 0-8294-0733-2
    1. Nadal, Gerónimo, 1507–1580. 2. Jesuits—Italy—Biography. I. McCoog,
Thomas M. II. Title.
BX4705.N17B36   1992
271'.5302—dc20
[B]   92–4955
                                               CIP

Cover design by Nancy Gruenke
Cover artwork by Ralph Creasman
Map artwork by Robert Voigts

Engravings of early Jesuits from P. Alfred Hamy, S.J., *Galerie Illustrée de la
Compagnie de Jésus* (Paris, 1893), courtesy of the rare book collection of the
library of Loyola University of Chicago.

To the Novices of the American Assistancy

Their hope is our future

Contents

Maps and Illustrations

Preface

Historians of the Society of Jesus have long been aware of the significance of Jerome Nadal. From the beginning, he was the recognized authentic interpreter of the Ignatian vision and spirituality. Juan de Polanco, the Society's first secretary and first historian, testified to Nadal's grasp of these ideals: "He knows our father Master Ignatius well because he had many dealings with him and he seems to have understood his spirit and comprehended our Institute as well as anyone I know in the Society."[1] Because of his grasp of the Institute, Nadal was sent by Ignatius to a large number of Jesuit communities throughout western Europe, where he promulgated and interpreted the Society's new *Constitutions*. In this, as Ignatius wrote, Nadal "altogether knows my mind and enjoys the same authority as myself."[2] In this work Nadal became "the greatest rover that his Order has probably ever known."[3] In the evaluation of James Brodrick, neither Francis Xavier nor Peter Canisius was as *perpetuum mobile* as Nadal. As he traveled from community to community and exhorted each to Ignatian ideals, Nadal was the man most responsible for the spiritual exultation that underlay the Society's activities during its first century.[4]

The absence of serious studies of Nadal has frequently been noted. The definitive national histories of the Jesuits in Italy, Spain, and Portugal by, respectively, Mario Scaduto, Antonio Astráin, and Francisco Rodrigues have delineated the role Nadal played in each of their countries. Through efforts of the Jesuit Historical Institute in Rome, most of Nadal's works have been published. Nonetheless, Miguel Nicolau's *Jerónimo Nadal: Obras y Doctrinas Espirituales* [5] is the only monograph, and it is more a

thematic study of Nadal's spirituality than a biography. Dennis
Pate's unpublished doctoral thesis was the first attempt in English
to chart Nadal's travels and to explain his role in the development of the Society of Jesus.[6] Unfortunately this work has not
been available to a wide public.

During the last decade of his life, Fr. William Bangert, S.J.,
visited many of the American Jesuit novitiates and lectured on
Jesuit history to the novices. Throughout his lectures on the
early Society, he emphasized the significance of Nadal in the
creation of the Society's constitutional and spiritual framework,
and he mourned the lack of an English study of this important
Jesuit. In the late 1970s as Fr. Bangert, for reasons of age and
health, reduced the number of novitiates visited annually, he
prepared to write that study. His dual biography of Claude Jay
and Alfonso Salmerón was with the publisher, and he was ready
to embark on another project.

I was one of the novices first introduced to the history of the
Society by Fr. Bangert. He communicated his enthusiasm to me
and encouraged me to pursue a doctorate in this field. Over the
years, we exchanged news and insights through frequent correspondence. In a letter dated April 7, 1983, Fr. Bangert informed
me that his work on Nadal continued steadily. He estimated
that the finished biography would be some twelve chapters, and
he had already written all but the first and last chapters. He
expected to send the finished chapters to a professional typist and
to have the final draft completed within a year. In a subsequent
letter, in response to my query about Pate's thesis, he wrote that
it was a "steady and reliable account" of Nadal's travels as visitor.
He complained, however, that it did "not go into theories of his
inner life (as related in his *Orationis observationes*)." Fr. Bangert
presumably intended in his biography to deal with both external
activity and internal development. Although, to my knowledge,
Fr. Bangert never used unpublished, archival material in his
works, his familiarity with Spanish, Portuguese, Italian, German, and French, along with the required Latin, allowed him
to read all the published material on Nadal.

Nearly two years later, the work was cut short for medical
reasons. In November 1984, Fr. Bangert was bothered by increasingly severe abdominal pains. In February he finally underwent a series of tests. On March 17, 1985, he was told that he
had cancer of the pancreas and liver, and possibly of a kidney. It

was too late for effective chemotherapy and Bill died on October 6. In our last telephone conversation, he asked me if I would accept his manuscript. He did not expect me to complete it, he assured me, but he would simply feel better if he knew that there was a chance that the biography would one day be published.

I made arrangements to visit him in the infirmary of Murray-Weigel Hall at Fordham University, to go over what he had completed. He died before that meeting. A few weeks later, I visited Murray-Weigel Hall and sought the manuscript. It had disappeared, and no one seemed to know where it had gone. For nearly two years I followed numerous leads in an attempt to ascertain its location. I finally located and collected it in May of 1987. Because of other obligations, I was not able to look at it until the autumn of 1988.

Bill had not finished the biography. The original twelve chapters had grown considerably, but the last fifteen years of Nadal's life still had not been treated. Yet even the truncated biography had considerable value. I photocopied the typescript and sent copies to Frs. John O'Malley, S.J., and Thomas Clancy, S.J., for their evaluation and opinion. Though they mourned the absence of the last fifteen years, both thought the biography as it stood was a valuable contribution to early Jesuit history and they encouraged me to see to its publication. It was, they agreed, "vintage Bangert." In a letter to Dr. Dennis Pate I asked him if he would be willing to write a concluding chapter. He was unable to do so because of other commitments and a change in his field of research. Drawing extensively on Pate's thesis, therefore, I undertook to write the concluding chapter.

With the typescript came a large number of loose notes and fragments, on incidents or ideas that Fr. Bangert hoped to include in later chapters. I inserted most of these in the text in proper chronological order; a few I discarded. I have added short summaries at the end of some chapters and references both to English translations of Nadal's works (whenever possible) and to recent historical works. I would like to thank Frs. Ted Cunnion, S.J., and Joseph Browne, S.J., of Murray-Weigel Hall at Fordham University for tracking down books from Fr. Bangert's collection that are currently in Murray-Weigel's library. With the cheerful assistance of the staffs at the Loyola-Notre Dame Library in Baltimore and the Woodstock Theological Library in Washington, D.C., I checked all Bill's footnotes. For the most part, however, I have allowed Bill's work to stand on its own merits.

I acknowledge, too, the tremendous assistance provided by Nancy Marshall, Marion Wielgosz, Melia Peisinger, and Carla Bundick of the Word Processing Center of Loyola College; they guided me through the labyrinth of word processing. Fr. Thomas R. Fitzgerald, S.J., of Loyola College provided ready aid in translating some of the more arcane Latin passages. I would also like to thank Fr. Bill Davish, S.J., of Loyola College, Baltimore, who painstakingly eliminated misspellings and grammatical errors from this manuscript and rendered the final product readable. Finally I wish to thank Erin Milnes at Loyola University Press for her careful and patient scrutiny of the manuscript. Her gentle prodding forced me to abandon a certain Jesuit myopia for a wider perspective. Despite a distance of seven time zones, we were able to smooth out all the rough spots thanks to thefacsimile machine, the telephone, and a good deal of determination.

In a conversation, Fr. Bangert mentioned that he had hoped to dedicate this work to the many Jesuit novices he had taught over the years; it was their hopeful enthusiasm that kept his own historical interests alive. It was his desire to inspire them with the zeal that animated the early Society through its history. The esteem and affection in which Bill's memory is held by so many of his past pupils is a testimony to his influence.

Thomas M. McCoog, S.J.
Loyola College, Baltimore

1

A Round of Universities

My thinking was this: I do not want to link myself with those fellows. Who knows but one day they will fall into the hands of the Inquisition. . . . Never again at Paris did I trouble myself with Ignatius and his friends.

Nadal's recollection of his rejection of
Ignatius' efforts to befriend him at Paris

There is no indication that in 1507 the people of Palma de Majorca celebrated the sixteen-hundred-and-thirtieth anniversary of the founding of their city by the Romans through the conquest of Majorca in 123 B.C. But among the small day-to-day incidents that were recorded was the birth on August 11, 1507, of a son to Antonio Nadal and Maria Morey, both natives of Majorca. The boy was named Jerome (Jerónimo). He was born in the family home, located on the street now called Calle de Padre Nadal, about a half-mile from the shore of the lovely, expansive, ten-mile-wide bay of Palma de Majorca. Antonio was an attorney by profession. Jerome had a younger brother, Esteban, and two sisters. Records of his childhood and early education do not exist.[1]

Nadal's next appearance in the deposition of history was as a nineteen-year-old student at the University of Alcalá de Henares. Slight in build, animated, intellectually alert, emotional, and religiously devout, he took his place among the students at the youngest of Spain's intellectual centers. From 1526, for possibly

Jerome Nadal

five or six years, he studied humanities there and acquired a good grasp of Latin, Greek, and Hebrew.[2]

Among the students, he came to know at least casually a few who in years to come would be closely tied to his life and vocation. One was Nicolás Alonso y Pérez (Nicolás Bobadilla), a blunt, argumentative, rough-edged native of Bobadilla del Camino in Old Castile, who had come to Alcalá four years earlier at the age of thirteen. Another was Diego Laínez, a slight, fifteen-year-old youth of quick wit and sharp tongue, who came to Alcalá in 1527, a year after Nadal, from Almazán in Old Castile. An even younger student was Alfonso Salmerón, strong in body and quick in mind, who at the age of thirteen was among the first students to enter the famous Trilingual College at Alcalá in 1528. The first fragile filaments of acquaintance bound these teenagers in a casual and loose amity. Unknown to them, those first ties were the prelude to the tighter cords of a fast and firm brotherhood of the future.

Another student at Alcalá, a thirty-five-year-old Basque named Ignatius Loyola (Iñigo de Loyola), came to the university in the same year as did Nadal. Nadal saw him but did not speak with him. And what he saw made him wary. Three times, on November 19, 1526, on March 6, 1527, and again on May 10, 1527, Ignatius faced ecclesiastical inquiries. He and three younger men had appeared in Alcalá dressed in pilgrim garb. They begged their daily bread. By spiritual counseling, catechesis, and exhortation, Ignatius attracted many people about himself, especially a group of some forty women. Some of the women swooned at his words, two disappeared on a pilgrimage, a third wanted to go and live in a desert. Ignatius became a curiosity in town. Strange stories about him made the rounds. At the instigation of the Inquisition, the vicar general investigated him on three occasions. Eventually he directed him to put aside the pilgrim's garb, to wear either lay or clerical dress, and to stop speaking on theological matters until he had finished his courses in theology. Restive under those restraints, Ignatius left Alcalá for the University of Salamanca in June of 1527. Nadal felt ill at ease about this strange student who had come and gone within some fourteen months.[3]

These episodes added a bit more fuzz to the confused spiritual climate that permeated certain areas of Spain even into the next century. In 1520, in the province of Guadalajara, a movement emerged that aroused memories of the positions taken by "the spirituals" of the medieval Church, and even by some heretics of the early Church. Claiming to have the key to true religious life in a Spanish form of illuminism, the *alumbrados* (the "Enlightened Ones") uncoupled that life from external posture and gesture and affixed it entirely to interior grace and the movements of the Holy Spirit. They did not make frontal attacks on the Church; nor did they withdraw from its official cult. Varying emphases among the *alumbrados* made the maze of their beliefs only the more elusive.[4]

Apart from the *alumbrados* there were loyal Catholics who carried on a debate that at times became quite clouded: how harmonize two theologies of different styles, the one scholastic, investigative, cognitive, and the other mystical, hidden, loving? When Loyola and Nadal were together at Alcalá, Francisco de Osuna, himself trained at Alcalá, published (in 1527) his popular *Tercer Abcedario Espiritual,* designed to show how the theology of the mind and the theology of the heart could aid each other. Osuna's work epitomized a debate that went on in Spain into the seventeenth century. This kind of inquiry, despite its merits, deepened the mist of uncertainty that surrounded religious life in Spain and that made clear and sound judgment difficult. Nadal saw Ignatius Loyola through that mist of uncertainty, and his memory of the strange happenings that surrounded Ignatius through fourteen months deepened his suspicions of the Basque. Some five years would pass before he would see him again. During that period his mistrust did not abate.[5]

At times Nadal's acquaintances quit Alcalá and went their diverse ways. Nicolás Bobadilla received his bachelor's degree in June of 1529 and went to Valladolid to continue his studies. Laínez earned his master's degree in the fall of 1532 and left for Paris, probably within a month or two. With him went Alfonso Salmerón. Within weeks of their departure, Nadal also left Alcalá. He too went to Paris. There he matriculated at the University on December 16, 1532. And there he felt the first stirrings of a vocation to the priesthood and started his study of theology. He also enrolled for courses in mathematics. In the Latin Quarter he soon recognized some of his former fellow students from Alcalá. Ignatius had been there for five years, Laínez and Salmerón a few weeks. Almost a year later, in the fall of 1533, Bobadilla appeared after almost four years of theological studies at Valladolid.[6]

One day Nadal met Ignatius in the Faubourg St. Jacques. Recently he had been sick and feared that he would die. He told Ignatius this. Ignatius took this as a cue to tease Nadal. He asked him a direct and personal question: "My dear man, why were you afraid to die?" Nadal countered with a personal question of his own, "Are you telling me that you have no fear of death, a fear that even Christ had?" Ignatius answered, "For fifteen years *1515* now, I have not been afraid to die." That was the first recorded tilt between the two men. There would be others, and Ignatius usually took the offensive.[7]

Nadal soon discovered that Ignatius had become the center of a group of students that included Laínez, Salmerón, and then Bobadilla. Each Sunday they gathered at the Charterhouse hidden behind high walls amid fields and vineyards close to the Porte St. Jacques. There they went to confession, attended Mass, and received Holy Communion. Nadal felt impelled to join them. He made his confession to Ignatius' confessor, the Portuguese Fr. Manuel Miona. Each Sunday he too went to the Charterhouse, where he met other students of Ignatius' group: Pierre Favre, then twenty-six years old, a Savoyard from the Alpine passes near Annecy; Francis Xavier (Francisco Javier), also twenty-six, a Navarrese nobleman who for three years had held aloof from Ignatius before changing and becoming one of his closest friends; and Simão Rodrigues, a twenty-three-year-old Portugese nobleman from the northern town of Vouzella.[8]

Ignatius had come to Paris in 1528, at age thirty-seven, after a series of unusual experiences. Courtier and army enlistee, this Basque gentleman fell in battle at the age of thirty at Pamplona in May of 1521 in a siege between defending Spanish forces and invading troops of France. During recuperation of nearly a year at his home in Loyola, he read and reflected long on two medieval books of devotion: the Carthusian Ludolph of Saxony's *Vita Christa* and a selection of the lives of the saints, *Flos sanctorum*, by Jacopo da Varazze. Gradually and gently he felt drawn to a life of severe penance and single-minded devotion in the service of Jesus Christ. In the small town of Manresa on the River Cardoner, amid rough and mountainous countryside under the shadow of the Benedictine Monastery of Montserrat, he prayed seven hours a day, fasted severely, and afflicted his body with harsh penances, endured a period of deep desolation, and then received extraordinary spiritual illumination of mind and heart.

From his experiences and his readings issued the core of the *Spiritual Exercises,* a small manual that he designed with a definite purpose: "the conquest of self and the regulation of one's life in such a way that no decision is made under the influence of any inordinate attachment."

The *Spiritual Exercises* became his *vade mecum* during a pilgrimage to the Holy Land, three years of Latin studies in Barcelona, a year of university studies at Alcalá, and a few months at Salamanca, before he went to Paris to continue the studies he had undertaken to fit him better to serve Christ in poverty and humility. In Paris, by conversation, spiritual counsel, and guidance through the steps of the Spiritual Exercises, he incited in other students a desire to share his spiritual aspirations. Gradually a loose and informal brotherhood formed.[9]

Nadal joined the devotions of this brotherhood at the Charterhouse for only a short time until they put him under spiritual siege. Nadal saw a purpose in this. It was Ignatius trying "to give me a push toward a devout life." Laínez led the way. One day he went to Nadal's lodging and found him reading a work of Theophylactus, an eleventh-century Byzantine scriptural exegete of lucid thought and expression who modeled himself on St. John Chrysostom and insisted on practical morality in his interpretation of the text. That gave Laínez his cue. He turned the conversation to the question of the spiritual interpretation of scripture. It left Nadal cold. "He didn't move me even a millimeter. What he was talking about went completely over my head." Pierre Favre was the next to try. He spoke about religious devotion. "He too got nowhere," recalled Nadal. Then his confessor, Fr. Manuel Miona, who was also Ignatius' confessor, made a visit. He pushed further, suggesting that Nadal become one of the group that was becoming known as "Iñigistas." Several times he advanced this idea and just as often Nadal turned the questions back on Miona. "You yourself are not an Iñigista. Why are you trying to make me one?"

Then Ignatius took the initiative. He had no more success than the others. One day the two men met near the Porte St. Jacques. Their conversation took a peculiar turn. Ignatius recalled his unpleasant three months in Salamanca in the summer of 1527, his detention by Dominicans in the convent of San Esteban, his imprisonment in a dungeon by the vicar general, the limits placed on his talk about spiritual subjects. This puzzled

Nadal. Why had Ignatius chosen that particular episode? Nadal wondered whether Ignatius feared that Nadal had heard about it and drew suspicious conclusions. "That was far from the truth," noted Nadal. Despite his disclaimer, though, a mist of doubt about Ignatius' orthodoxy had remained in his mind ever since the vicar general in Alcalá three times investigated Ignatius in an atmosphere charged with suspicion of the *alumbrados*. That memory made Nadal wary of being linked in any way to Ignatius.[10]

As they walked together that day, Ignatius led the way to the nearby chapel of Saint Étienne-des-Grés opposite the Dominican convent. In the chapel, Ignatius did something unusual. As he supported himself by leaning against the baptismal font, he read to Nadal a letter he had sent to a nephew in Spain. The point of the letter: leave the world and take up a more perfect way of life. He then suggested that Nadal make the Spiritual Exercises. Nadal raised his guard. He thought he perceived what Ignatius was up to; yet he was torn. He felt a repugnance toward Ignatius' suggestion, but he also felt an attraction. The repugnance won out, and strenuously indeed. The two men emerged from the chapel and stood for a while in front. There Nadal issued an edict. Pointing to a copy of the New Testament he was holding, he told Ignatius, "This is the book I intend to follow. Where you men are headed I do not know. Do not mention these things anymore. Forget about me." In a chronicle of his life that he dated from 1535, he made this entry: "My thinking was this: I do not want to link myself with those fellows. Who knows but one day they will fall into the hands of the Inquisition." It was an unpleasant episode. What started casually enough ended in angering Nadal. This may have been the last time Ignatius and Nadal spoke to each other in Paris.[11]

Deep in Nadal's spirit a serious concern for the purity of the Catholic faith had taken root. The mere possibility that Ignatius was tainted with illuminism made a break with him and his friends imperative. But there was another reason: he had his reputation in Majorca to protect. In Paris resided a highly respected Franciscan friar named Panades. Nadal feared that the friar might write home that Nadal was hobnobbing with a group suspected of unorthodox faith. "Never again at Paris did I trouble myself with Ignatius and his friends."[12] He had covered his flank.

August 15 in 1534 was a significant day—far more significant than they realized—for the "Iñigistas." Early that morning Ignatius, Francis Xavier, Pierre Favre, Diego Laínez, Alfonso Salmerón, Simão Rodrigues, and Nicolás Bobadilla left the Latin Quarter, crossed the Seine, and climbed the height of Montmartre to the small chapel of Saint Denis. In the crypt of the chapel, Pierre Favre, who had been ordained only three months before, offered Mass. At the Communion he turned to his kneeling friends and held the Host before them as each pronounced simple vows to follow Christ in poverty and chastity and to go to the Holy Land to labor for the conversion of the Turks. To the last vow they attached a qualification. Should it prove impossible to reach the Holy Land, they would go to Rome and ask the pope to choose the work they should do in the church. Forty-three years later, Simão Rodrigues still felt the inspiration of that day on Montmartre. "These Fathers," recalled Rodrigues, "vowed themselves to God with a genuine and unlimited spirit of dedication. They made their offering with a spontaneity, a surrender of self-will, a trust in the Divine Mercy, that whenever I think back on the occasion, as I have often done, I am filled with intense fervor, renewed with a growth of piety, and overtaken by wonder unspeakable." Nadal was not there. If things had happened as it seems Ignatius hoped, the original group of the future Society of Jesus would have numbered eight—including Nadal.[13]

Within two and a half years, the Iñigistas and Nadal quit Paris. In April or May of 1535 Ignatius traveled to his home at Loyola. A severe illness lingered until doctors resorted to the ultimate remedy of those days, a return to one's native air. Ignatius and his friends agreed to meet in Venice in the spring of 1537 and sail to the Holy Land. During 1536, the Paix des Dames of 1529 between France and Spain collapsed and the two countries again waged war. By the fall of 1536, feeling in Paris against the Spaniards attained such a pitch that the "Iñigistas" decided, for the sake of the Spaniards in their group, to reach Venice before the date they had planned. In mid-November they did so. Under the same anti-Spanish pressure, Nadal, too, decided to quit Paris. He left for the university in Avignon, still a papal enclave, where he could expect immunity from the French troops. There he hoped to finish his theological studies and master his grasp of the Hebrew language. As he left Paris he dropped a curtain on the Iñigistas. "I had absolutely no idea of what they planned. I did not think about them. I inquired no further about them."[14] The break was complete, he thought.

In Avignon, Nadal found a home away from home. Within that papal enclave, a sizable colony of Majorcan and Catalan bankers and businessmen conducted commercial dealings with Florentines, Genovese, and Piedmontese. Some Catalans opened their home to him. On March 16, 1537, he took a major step toward the priesthood: he was ordained subdeacon.[15]

During his first year at the university, Nadal gained a surer grasp of Hebrew. He found valuable help in one of the oldest elements of Avignon's life: "the pope's Jews," a colony that numbered some fifty families. Ever since Avignon had come under papal jurisdiction in the fourteenth century, the fortunes of the Jews fluctuated with the history of the popes. Ten years before Nadal arrived there, the Jews, by order of Pope Clement VII, had to wear, under penalty of a fine of a hundred gold ducats, a yellow hat as identification. Under the next pope, Paul III, whose personal physician was a Jew, they fared so well that the bishop of nearby Carpentras, Jacopo Sadoleto, complained that Paul preferred Jews to Christians.[16]

The Jews of Avignon never achieved distinction. Their rabbis and their schools never won the reputation for brilliance enjoyed by those in Spain, Alsace, and Poland. Neither did their doctors and lawyers. It was therefore a somewhat mediocre group to whom Nadal turned for help in mastering Hebrew, but he learned much: the intricacies and nuances of their scriptural literature and their interpretation of their holy books. He noted that he paid them well.[17]

One day his teachers startled him. A delegation from the entire Jewish community, eight or ten rabbis, approached him. Expressing admiration for his skill and wide learning in natural philosophy and theology, they invited him to be their spiritual leader and chief rabbi. For his services they offered him two to three scudi a year. Nadal exploded. "Out of my sight, you pigs, you heretics tied to the Mosaic law, a law you neither understand nor observe. What have you seen in me to make you imagine that I would leave the faith of Christ to become a Jew? On your way. And don't come back again."[18]

Nadal paid for that blast. The French monarch at that time, Francis I, troubled by inroads of Spanish forces into his realm, had decreed that all Spaniards should, under penalty of death, be out of France within fifteen days. The Jews went to the provost of Avignon, delated Nadal as a Spaniard who had violated the king's decree, and demanded his execution. They threatened the provost: unless he obeyed the royal decree, they would file a complaint against him with the king. They fortified their demand with a large amount of money. The provost summoned Nadal. He asked why he had disobeyed the royal decree and remained in Avignon. Nadal based his defense on two points: first, technically he was not a Spaniard because he was from Majorca, an island that, even though under the Spanish crown, was not part of the continental area called Spain; and second, the royal decree lacked force in papal territory. In his second argument Nadal was on solid legal ground. Both points, however, the provost brushed aside and lamented that, if he did not impose the supreme penalty, he himself would be condemned to death. Nadal lost the case.[19]

The provost acted swiftly. Soldiers escorted Nadal through the streets to the place of execution. Along the way the Jews taunted him. In their own tongue they prayed that God would punish him to the extent he deserved for his perfidy. They chided him for his infidelity to God. The rope was readied; it was fitted about his neck; the pyre to receive his corpse was burning. Nadal refused to die speechless. Loudly and in Hebrew he shouted, "You devilish spirits, you heretics stuck in the law of Moses, do you think that in death or in life I would desert the truth and the faith of Christ Jesus and become a Jew? If you do, you are making an unspeakable mistake like the blindness you have shown to the history of the Messiah. Out of the way, you traitors. I am ready to die for the Catholic faith."[20]

Nadal's riposte to the Jews in their own tongue dismayed the provost. It left him in serious doubt. How just was the sentence he had imposed? He wondered whether Nadal was not a Jew, a target of vengeful rabbis seeking to settle differences within their community. Amid the confusion of charge and counter-charge, all in Hebrew, he set Nadal free. Nadal returned to the center of the city, clinging to his copy of a Hebrew edition of the Pentateuch. A French soldier accosted him, grabbed him by the beard, and called him a dog of a Jew. Other soldiers stole his handsome mantle. He hid within the city until King Francis withdrew his troops from Avignon as the army of the Emperor Charles fell back into Italy.[21]

A little more than a year after receiving the subdiaconate, Nadal was ordained deacon on April 6, 1538. Two weeks later, on the twentieth, in the chapel of Santa Ana supra Ruppem de Danis on the imposing Rocher des Doms, he received the order of priesthood from Avignon's suffragan bishop, Simon de Podio. On May 11, he received his doctorate in theology under the tutelage of Pietro da Forli.[22]

These happy events occurred during an ebb in Nadal's physical and spiritual energies. He identified his sojourn in Avignon with a relentless siege of headaches and stomach distress. He almost died. A bitter and inexorable sickness of soul set in. He lost confidence in his scholarly endeavors and in his ability to preach. Mistrust of self made his soul a bog. Six years of interior ache and pain had begun.[23]

Some time after June of 1538, Nadal left Avignon for Nice, whence he planned to sail for Barcelona on his way home to Palma de Majorca. In Nice he stayed with Franciscans, who recently had hosted Pope Paul III during a tense conference held with the other two leaders of Christendom, Emperor Charles V and King Francis I.[24] Nadal has left us no reflections on the disappointing conclusions of those august meetings, which ended with no more solid commitment to a lasting peace than a truce of ten years. The rest of his life he would spend under the disillusioning spell of that failure to end the Habsburg-Valois rivalry. He often encountered troops on the march and more than once he almost lost his life to them along the roads of Europe.

Nadal had spent twelve years in three universities, yet the lines of his intellectual formation that those years limned are tantalizingly faint. At this stage of historical research, the sources have yielded a mere pittance. Nadal himself identified no professor under whom he studied. (His mentor at Avignon, Pietro da Forli, is known from the university's records, not Nadal's.) He mentioned no academic courses he attended. He revealed no author he read save Theophylactus. He identified no *collegium* where he lived.

For most of his future, Nadal was a man of ideas. He would work from a certain theology of history; he would make a clear choice between a theology of the mind and a theology of the heart; he would adopt an unusual schema of the spiritual life; he would extensively incorporate philology into his use of scripture. Perhaps he made all those intellectual positions his own while at the universities, but he brought them into the clear only as years passed. Save for the penchant for scriptural studies that his stay at Avignon clearly revealed, the universities he attended have to this day remained severely reticent about what they gave this student from Majorca. What must have been a rich period in his formative years remains aggravatingly in the dark to us.

2

The Long Way Round

Ignatius the general! Xavier in the Indies! A religious
order called the Society of Jesus! What an astonishing
turn of affairs! I will go to Rome to see Ignatius and
find out what's happening. And right away.

Nadal in his *Chronicon Natalis*, 1545

When Nadal returned to Majorca, he found awaiting him his
mother, his younger brother Esteban, his two sisters, and an
uncle. He had financial security in a beautiful country villa in
lovely Binibassi, miles from Palma de Majorca. He found generous friends among influential clerics of the island; he received
honorable recognition within the ecclesiastical structure of
Palma; he was invested with three benefices, one in the Church
of Santa Eulalia, the richest and most prestigious parish of
Majorca. These weathercocks of security and content, however,
belied the pain Nadal was to suffer through several miserable
years.[1]

In a few terse sentences he cast the setting of his life in
Majorca. He wrote that "not a day, not an hour—why do I speak
of days and hours—not a moment did I live without the keenest
anxiety, disgust, and bitterness of spirit. My head always throbbed,
my stomach was always upset. I was always in the throes of
melancholy. All my friends could not comprehend what was
going on. They surmised that I was turning into a misanthrope.
I was always under treatment of doctors and taking their medi-
cines. I was an out-and-out dragging burden on myself."[2]

Failure in several intellectual and spiritual ventures churned sullen seas within. While other priests were attaining recognition as fine preachers, he made little or no impression in the pulpit. The chapter of the cathedral invited him to give a series of lectures on St. Paul's Epistle to the Romans. The novelty of a new speaker drew large crowds. But the numbers dwindled away, and he had the embarrassment of having his lectures canceled. He made a fresh try. He opened a series of lectures on the canon of the Mass. Again his hearers vanished and the program was scratched. Family problems aggravated his misery. He did not get along with his uncle. Without asking his advice and even without informing him, his brother married. Still more, it was a marriage he did not approve of. Most distressing of all, his mother died. In his sorrow he endured in what he called a manner quite unbecoming. Amid that anguish, when he and others thought that all was lost, he yielded no quarter to the idea of giving up his priestly vocation.[3]

One of the best-known priests in Palma befriended Nadal and tried to relieve his pervasive depression. Generously he gave his time and care. Nicolás Montañans y Berard was a canon and sacristan of the cathedral, and from 1541 an inquisitor of the realm. Born into a family of jurists, he and his brother Jaime earned their doctorates in law. More and more he drew Nadal into the circle of his friends. He obtained for him an appointment as a member of the council of the Inquisition. Almost daily he invited him to dinner and supper at his suburban home. Occasionally he took him to dine at his brother Jaime's estate. At those meals Nadal met many of the leading men of the island.[4]

One guest was a priest, Dr. Jaime Palou. Palou became anxious about his host's sick and depressed friend. One day he took Nadal aside. With exquisite kindness he told him that he was puzzled that a man so nicely placed in life should be so sad and troubled. Nadal agreed. He too wondered about that. If it baffled Palou, it baffled him even more. He desired nothing more than that Palou, or anyone else, would come forward and locate the root of his melancholy.

One day Palou told Nadal that Elizabeth Cifra, a woman in her eighties, whose confessor he was, had founded a boarding school for girls of noble families known as de la Crianza. Stories abounded about her: she performed miracles; she had seen blood streaming from her crucifix; she had predicted the naval disaster that the Emperor Charles V suffered off the coast of Africa in October of 1541. Nadal perked up. He became interested in Elizabeth. Earnestly he asked Palou to request her prayers for relief from his affliction. Palou did so.

In May of 1542 Elizabeth died. Nadal was chosen, most likely by Palou, to be one of the four theologians who carried her bier at the funeral. Palou delivered the sermon, in which he gave an account of her life and good deeds. A wave of emotion swept through Nadal such as he had never before experienced. He completely broke down in tears. His friend Canon Antonio Torroella looked on in dismay. This experience, Nadal recalled, almost completely recast the state of his mind.[5]

Someone placed in his hands a small book about Elizabeth. Over and over he read it. From his avid reading he gathered several practices of devotion. One was to make the Sign of the Cross often over his heart while pronouncing the name of Jesus. One day during his reading he felt impelled to make a general confession of his life. He prepared most carefully. For several days he wrote his sins in a small book. The confession he spread over three days. At the end he burned the list of his sins while joyfully singing the *Cantemus Domino* of Moses. "I began to feel some of the weight lifted from me. I was not, however, completely free." Some thirty years later, he recorded that the memory of Elizabeth Cifra remained for him a rich source of spiritual joy.[6]

Jaime Pou, a cousin of Montañans, became an important influence in Nadal's life. When Pou's mother, Doña Práxeles Berard y Caulelles, died between 1500 and 1502, Jaime had been a child of three or four. He was taken to the home of his mother's sister Beatriz, the wife of Nicolás Montañans and mother of the future canon and Inquisitor, Nicolás. Until he was eighteen years old, he lived in the Montañans' household and studied at the cathedral school. He then left Majorca to study law at Bologna. With his legal studies he gradually mixed work in the Roman curia; later he finally joined the papal bureaucracy. In 1538, the year Nadal returned to Majorca from France, Pou returned from Italy. For both men the Montañans household was a natural haven. For Pou it was home; for Nadal it was an oasis of comfort amid his melancholy. There they became friends. Pou was then about forty; Nadal was ten years younger. In December 1540, Pou's legal expertise received recognition in his appointment as a canon of Palma's cathedral chapter, but by April 1542 he resigned from the chapter, since he had been called to Rome to be an auditor of the Rota. Nadal was to discover that the friend he found at the Montañans would be an important influence in his life.[7]

Some time in late 1542 or early 1543, Nadal's life took a notable turn. He ascribed the change to the intercession of Elizabeth Cifra. It took him to the northeastern coastal area of Majorca, a charming place called Miramar. Eighteen months before Elizabeth died, the expedition of Charles V against the Turks in North Africa met disaster—as Elizabeth had predicted—when mighty storms destroyed or scattered the ships across the western Mediterranean. A survivor, a soldier named Antonio Castañeda from Valladolid, found haven in Majorca and decided to stay. Earlier he had twice entered a Franciscan novitiate and left. A reawakened religious fervor after the wreck guided him to Miramar, where he adopted the life of a hermit thoroughly given to prayer and penance.

At first he lived in a cave near the sea. Talk about this soldier-turned-penitent spread widely. Canon Montañans y Berard approached him and made a suggestion. In that general area, the king had granted Montañans, in 1519, an estate on which stood a house and the Church of the Most Holy Trinity. He suggested to Castañeda that he move his residence to a cistern near the church and there continue his life of austerity. Castañeda did so. Montañans had a further suggestion: that Castañeda seek ordination to the priesthood and then assume the care of the church, which benefice Montañans would gladly yield to him. The hermit moved cautiously on that.[8]

Nadal heard stories about Castañeda, in ample form no doubt from Montañans. He moved to Miramar and took up residence on the Montañans' estate in the house next to the Church of the Most Holy Trinity. He introduced himself to Castañeda and promptly felt at ease with him as they discussed prayer and the life of the spirit. Nadal did not do all the visiting; at times Castañeda left his cistern and went to Nadal's dwelling. Nadal thought he was receiving a good grounding in prayer, and much of his interior distress dissipated. Traces of it remained, but the tenacity of its grip had been broken.

Nadal was delighted with what he found at Miramar. The winter of 1542–1543 was a stormy one, so he moved to a more protected house near the garden of the Charterhouse of Valldemosa. To enter the monastery to say Mass he used the back door. This move however, did not interrupt his meetings with Castañeda, since the distance between the hermit's cistern and the Carthusian monastery was no greater than the previous walk. Castañeda went to see Nadal at Valldemosa as often as he had done at the Most Holy Trinity.[9]

During this sojourn at Miramar, Nadal took up a serious study of the writings of the Pseudo-Dionysius. As he delved into the mystical theology of this thinker of the sixth century, he learned ideas and attitudes about the deification of the human through intimate union with the divine, the soul's growth in "unknowing" by the shedding of the intellect's reasoning and the senses' perceptions, and entry into that darkness that is illumined by divine rays. To the end of his days these ideas remained, ever vying for a regnant place in his personal life and shaping the way he taught others the principles of spiritual living. The Pseudo-Dionysius was the second—Theophylactus, it will be remembered, was the first—writer whom Nadal himself identified as an intellectual and spiritual guide during this period.[10]

Early in 1545, Nadal received two letters within a few weeks that gave a fresh turn to his life. Both letters came from Rome. The first came from Don Felipe de Cervallo, viceroy of Emperor Charles V in Majorca. With his own letter Cervallo included a copy of another he had received from Rome, one that had been sent to Ignatius Loyola—then in Rome some eight years—by Francis Xavier, who had been in the Far East three years. As Nadal read Xavier's account of the Church's expansion in the Indies and his expression of joy that the pope had given formal approval of the Society of Jesus, a bright flash of memory brought images of the Iñigistas he had known in Paris. He was stunned. It was, he said, like "waking from a long sleep." Profoundly shaken, he slammed the palm of his hand on the table and exclaimed, "Now this is something!" He likened the vehemence of his gesture to the force of his last tart words to Ignatius in Paris, "Forget about me!" What he learned from that letter startled him. "Ignatius the general! Xavier in the Indies! A religious order called the Society of Jesus! What an astonishing turn of affairs! I shall go to Rome to see Ignatius and find out what's happening. And right away."[11]

The second letter came from his friend in Rome, Jaime Pou. While working at the Rota, Pou was assigned to assist at the general council of the Church due to convene in December of 1545. He wrote Nadal to invite him to come to Rome and assist in that formidable enterprise. Nadal did not hesitate; to Rome he would go.

But second thoughts intruded. He hesitated about a move so grave. He reviewed his motives. Pou's invitation was compelling. The news about Ignatius and his friends was intriguing. And a desire to study law, stimulated no doubt by his close friendship with such professional ecclesiastical lawyers as Montañans and Pou, was stirring within him. Where better to study this discipline than at the center of the Church's legal organization and structure. All motives pointed to Rome. But he made one point eminently clear and wrote it into the record: he had no intent to change his status as a secular priest and become an "Iñigista." He then went to see hermit Antonio and related what had happened. Antonio enthusiastically backed his decision to go to Rome. The argument that most appealed to the hermit was the prospect of working at a general council of the Church. Nadal was elated that his friend had endorsed the move to Rome.[12]

To leave Majorca, Nadal sadly discovered, was not easy. He had to survive a family tempest. Since the family's inheritance was legally in his hands as the elder son, his uncle stormily objected to his absence from Majorca. Knowing that his uncle held Jaime Pou in great esteem, he pointed to Pou's invitation to join him at Rome and Trent. He won the support of his two brothers-in-law, but the uncle remained adamant in his resistance. Nadal, however, held to his purpose and entrusted the family estate to the immediate care of Esteban under the uncle's general supervision. On July 2, 1545, he set sail for Barcelona.[13] Never again would he see the wide graceful harbor of Palma.

On this quest abroad at age thirty-eight, Nadal resembled the distorted reflections of a building on troubled waters, the facade continually shifting and taking odd angles. There were the intense emotional outbursts at his mother's death and at the funeral of Elizabeth Cifra; the prolonged states of depression; the restlessness that drew him to the hermitage at Miramar; the impetuous, even violent, change of direction that swept him to

Rome. All suggested a temperament in which a calm and serene intellectual judgment might find it hard to survive. Those impulsive bursts of feeling were never to be far below the surface.

After a slow trip of over three months, Nadal arrived in Rome on October 10. Having checked his luggage and his mule at a hospice, he faced the question: whom should he call on first, his friend of Majorca, Jaime Pou, or Ignatius and his group? He went to the Jesuit house attached to the Church of Santa Maria della Strada. There he asked for Fr. Jerónimo Doménech, a native of Valencia who five years earlier had joined Ignatius and his friends in the religious community they called the Society of Jesus. With Doménech he felt a cultural affinity, especially in their common Catalan language. Quickly he explained to him his curiosity about the Society of Jesus. Doménech thought the best way for Nadal to get a reliable answer was to make the Spiritual Exercises for a month or so. He moved quickly, anxious lest his guest be caught up in the distractions of Rome at a time when the city was in a festal mood, celebrating the eleventh anniversary of the coronation of Pope Paul III.[14]

The two men went in search of Ignatius, who at the moment was at one of his favorite projects, the Casa Santa Martha, a home he had opened for the social and spiritual renewal of prostitutes.[15] On the street they met him returning. Ignatius greeted Nadal pleasantly and with a playful taunt, a replay of their encounters at Paris. Genially he suggested that what brought Nadal to Rome were the graces Ignatius had won for him. Nadal was not amused. "His remarks irked me," he recalled, "and I showed it."[16]

Doménech then hustled Nadal back to the hospice. They claimed Nadal's baggage and mule, and promptly headed for the home of a gentleman named Felipe Cassini. There Doménech planned to have Nadal make the Spiritual Exercises. Nadal wryly observed the haste of his Valencian host, who seemed anxious to get him behind the walls of Cassini's house "before I could even get a glimpse of the Roman scene." At Cassini's front door, however, Doménech's plan suddenly unraveled for there he and Nadal met two gentlemen of the household of Fr. Jaime Pou, who had been on the lookout for his Majorcan friend.[17]

Sometime in the late summer or early fall of 1545, Pou had received letters from Majorca alerting him that Nadal was on his

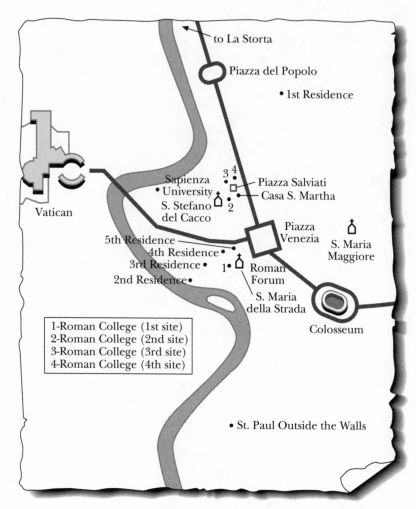

Sites in Rome especially familiar to the early Jesuits

Jesuit Residences
1st Residence (Nov. 1537–June 1538): formerly the villa of Quirino Garzoni
2nd Residence (summer 1538): near the Ponte Sisto
3rd Residence (Oct. 1538–Feb. 1541): now the Palazzo Delfini
4th Residence (Feb. 1541–Sept. 1544): now part of the Church of the Gesù
5th Residence (from Sept. 1544): became the General's residence after Ignatius' death
and is now part of the Residence of the Gesù

The Roman College
1st Site (1551–1553): near Santa Maria della Strada on Via Minerva
2nd Site (1553–1557): near Santo Stefano del Cacco
3rd Site (1557–1560): on the Piazza Salviati
4th Site (1560–the suppression of the Society in 1773): next to the 3rd Site

way to Rome. Since he wanted to open his home to his friend, he ordered his attendants to keep their eyes open for him in the city. Two of them spotted him as soon as he entered Rome and promptly informed their master. He sent them back to Nadal with the insistent invitation that he be guest at the Pou residence. The attendants overtook Nadal at the doorstep of the Cassini home and there Nadal had to make a quick decision: enter the residence and begin the Exercises, or join Pou's attendants. He decided to accept the invitation of his fellow Majorcan, assuring Doménech that in good time he would return to the Jesuit house to see him and Ignatius.

Nadal, not at all unhappy that the Exercises had been delayed, really welcomed the disruption of Doménech's plan. An attraction to the Society of Jesus he did admit. But he also felt an interior drag holding him back. For a little while at least he could forestall a final decision on entering the Society of Jesus. His comment: "And so the fish escaped his [Ignatius'] hook."[18]

For a month Nadal enjoyed Pou's hospitality. His host gave him a room nicely decorated with tapestries and showed him every courtesy. Nadal spent his days touring Rome, especially the ruins of the ancient city. For thirty days he did not offer Mass, quite in contrast to his daily practice in Majorca. He called that period a time of dissipation. He liked living in the Pou residence; he did not want to leave. Yet he was not at peace. The existence of the Society of Jesus lurked in a corner of his mind. Several times, on impulse, he dropped in to see Ignatius, who chatted with him quietly and affably but never raised the question whether he should enter the religious life. Now and then he invited him to dinner. On those occasions Doménech and Laínez were less reticent than Ignatius and repeatedly peppered Nadal with the suggestion that he get down to business and make the Exercises. Those suggestions he brushed aside.[19]

On one visit Nadal took Ignatius aside at dinner time and asked whether they might speak in private. Nadal told Ignatius: "Those other Fathers are stuffing me with a lot of talk about the Exercises. . . . I know what they are up to. They want me to leave my present station in life and join your group. There are, however, many reasons that seem to argue against my fitness to take on the way of life designed in your Institute. I want you to hear directly from me an account of those reasons." He recited a list of his failed enterprises; he described his bad health. His sins, however, he did not mention. Ignatius listened attentively. With a trace of a smile, he replied gently: "That's fine. If God should call you to the Society, there will be no dearth of work that you could handle."[20]

This conversation with Ignatius moved Nadal to think seriously about making the Exercises. He feared informing Pou but this he had to do. He explained to Pou that, since the precise date for the opening of the Council of Trent had yet to be announced, he had time on his hands that he would like to use by following for twenty-five or thirty days a program of prayer that Ignatius had devised. Pou raised no difficulty. Ignatius took special care that Nadal received congenial quarters. Apprehensive about Nadal's melancholic tendencies, he commissioned Fr. Pietro Sentino to find a room that looked on a garden. This took time. Nadal the foot-dragger suddenly became Nadal the eager beaver. He wanted to get moving. The delay irked him.[21]

The retreat began on November 5, 1545. Doménech was the director. Nadal plunged into this spiritual venture in high excitement. With the fierce ardor of a conquistador he set his heart on an El Dorado of extraordinary spiritual experience, a revelation or a vision. He fully expected a rich cache of mystical gold. As he meditated in the First Week of the Exercises on the malice of sin, the history of his personal sins, and the punishments of hell, he prayed for shame and confusion in view of the many times that he deserved eternal damnation, for intense sorrow, even tears, because of his sins, for a deep sense of the pains endured in hell, and for a fear of suffering that awful fate. He went through those exercises serenely sure that he had received their purifying graces. Ignatius, however, was troubled. Nadal's manner made him apprehensive. He confided to Doménech that Nadal worried him. "This fellow is going to be a problem for us. He carries a large dose of melancholy within him. You can see it in his eyes. I am afraid that, if God does not give him a vocation to the Society, he will slide into an out-and-out depression and lose his mind. Right now he wants to serve God. But he is really a crippled person."[22]

Nadal capped the First Week with a general confession of his life. This he made to Ignatius. After the confession, Ignatius gave him a terse bit of ascetical counsel: God was opening to him a new direction in his life; by his sins he had rejected God's grace and abused his faculties of mind and heart; with the grace he received in the sacrament of Penance, he should concentrate on the correction of those abuses.

This was Nadal's first formal lesson from Ignatius: no high-flown scheme for entering into mystic union with God, but an unadorned, down-to-earth regime of repentance and reform. Nadal never forgot that first lesson: Ignatius' insistence on the central role of sorrow and confession in the labor of breaking sinful habits and developing the habits of virtue. Forty years later, he still kept purification at the heart of all spiritual progress.[23]

Nadal entered the Second Week of the Exercises. Within the meditations on the life of Christ, he prayed that he might receive "an intimate knowledge of Our Lord, who has become man for me, that I may love him more and follow him more closely." He felt sure that unusual graces were coming to him. Two exercises especially held him: the one on the Kingdom of Christ, an introduction to the Second Week; the other on Two Standards, a key meditation at the core of the Second Week. In the first he meditated on Christ's call to all humankind to join him in his enterprise "to conquer the whole world and all my enemies, and thus to enter into the glory of my Father." He asked for the grace not to be deaf to this call but to be prompt and diligent to carry out Christ's will. As one who wished to distinguish himself in his response, he protested to Christ that he chose to imitate him in poverty, in bearing abuse, in suffering wrong, if this should be the divine will.[24]

No less did the second exercise put him on his mettle. He meditated on the awesome contest between Christ and Lucifer to win the minds and hearts of humankind. He looked on Lucifer, horrible and fearful, sending his demons through the world with a strategy of three steps: tempt humankind to covet riches, which ease their way in the quest of empty honors, and eventually bring them to high-flown pride. He turned and looked on Christ, beautiful and attractive, also sending his followers throughout the world with a strategy of three steps: attract humankind to the highest spiritual poverty, even actual poverty if God so wills, which leads them to a desire of insults and contempt in union with Christ condemned, and this in turn to humility. The two strategies stood against each other in stark contrast: poverty and riches; contempt and honor; humility and pride. Nadal prayed that it be granted him to follow Christ's strategy in order to imitate him the better. He had come to Rome to learn what the Ignatian group was about. At this point in the Second Week of the Exercises he learned. Doors opened on the Jesuit inner force: a quest for personal likeness to Christ in his poverty, his rejection by humankind, his humility, his laborious campaign to win all humankind to his Kingdom against the strategy of Lucifer. Nadal became *engagé*. Carried by the swift currents of his enthusiasm, he embraced the meditations on the Kingdom and the Two Standards.[25]

Then, with startling suddenness, everything went awry. To his pain Nadal discovered that his penetration of those key exercises reached no great depth. The practical implications in his life eluded him. His understanding was notional and superficial. The theory captivated him; the reality escaped him—but not for long. He reached that crucial point in the Exercises called Making a Choice of a Way of Life. Back in beautiful Binibassi he owned a lovely country estate. He held title to the family inheritance. He retained some benefices. If he elected the Jesuit way of life he must dispose of those possessions. Still more, since a Jesuit was open to assignment to any part of the world, he most likely would never again see his family, or the Montañans, or other friends in Majorca. He had to decide which would be to God's greater glory and his personal salvation: to retain or to dispose of his possessions.[26]

Ignatius had devised careful procedures to help a retreatant reach that choice. First, he described Three Times when a sound choice of a way of life may be made; Nadal had come to his point of decision during what Ignatius identified as the Third Time: "a time of tranquility, that is, a time when the soul is not agitated by different spirits, and has free and peaceful use of its natural powers." During the First and Second Weeks, Nadal had experienced no troubling opposition; he accepted all with delight. For use during this Third Time, Ignatius drew up two procedures to guide the retreatant to a sound decision. Nadal followed these procedures. He placed before him his holdings in Majorca. Carefully he wrote the advantages of keeping them in his quest for God's greater glory and his own salvation. Then he enumerated the disadvantages and dangers of retaining them. He pushed further. He listed the advantages of disposing of them; then the disadvantages and the dangers. The Exercises then directed the retreatant to make his decision not because of any sensual inclination but because of motives that most convinced his reason. But this Nadal found he could not do.[27]

The personal implications of entering the Society of Jesus finally struck him with frightening force. He went into a dither. His fervor dried up; he could not concentrate. Headaches and stomach pains drained him. His mind became clouded, his will obstinate and dry. He became stuck in a morass of indecision, buffeted by arguments pro and con. He tried other devices in the Exercises for reaching a decision: at the moment of death, and again at the moment of divine judgment, what decision would he then wish he had made; what advice would he give to another person in like circumstances? To no avail. The darkness did not lift. For days the pain and the anguish went on, yielding no answer. Doménech began to lose heart. Judging that Nadal had exhausted the possibility of reaching a sound decision, he advised him to move on through the Exercises and leave his election in abeyance.[28]

But Nadal asked Doménech for more time. He pleaded that he "wanted to make one last try that evening." Doménech consented. During that last try the darkness suddenly lifted. Nadal felt a rush of consolation sweep his whole being. He was confident that God had sent a special grace, impelling him to give himself to the Society of Jesus. The reasons he had arrayed against entering the Society suddenly dissolved into empty phrases. All had fallen, battle victims in his bitter internal conflict. Not one remained standing to resist his entrance into the Society. To his dismay he had been plunged into what Ignatius called the First Time of the Three Times when "a correct and good choice of a way of life may be made," a time when the Lord so intensely attracts a soul that there can be no hesitation in responding to the divine will. Lucidly he detected the forces behind his rationale for not entering the Society: his feelings of aversion, his desire for honor and esteem, his worries about the future, his warped will. He identified them for what they were: fusiliers ranged against the Kingdom of God. These were what had buffeted him, tormented him, darkened his spiritual vision. Even though a certain sensible repugnance hung on, he now saw it, in the glow of divine light, as an intensely compelling sign that God was calling him to the Society.

Nadal had begun the Exercises with surging ardor and the vehemence of a conquistador. During the night of November

23, that spirit poured into the throbbing words he then jotted: "Even should all the trials I have so far endured, or trials even more abundant than those, or the trials any man in the world has suffered, or the trials the devil is capable of loosing, even should all these fall on me, buffet me, withstand me, gainsay me, frighten me, I decide and resolve, in the name of the Holy Trinity, of Jesus Christ, and of the Holy Spirit, to follow the evangelical counsels as delineated by the vows of the Society of Jesus. I am ready to do whatever these vows entail, even though they [Ignatius and the Society] should wish me to make them immediately. In trembling I write this, with profound fear of Christ Jesus, our God and our Lord. As one who has known his supreme mercy, I make my promise with my whole soul, my whole will, my whole strength. To him be the glory. Amen. In the Year of the Lord 1545, the twenty-third of November, at five in the evening, my eighteenth day in the Exercises." What he called "indescribable consolation" penetrated his whole being, body and soul. A little later that evening he made another vow: even should the Society not accept him, he would nevertheless carry through and pronounce the vows of the religious state.[29]

The retreat continued. Nadal fell silent about his interior dispositions as he entered the Third Week of the Exercises, during which he contemplated various scenes in the passion and death of Christ, and prayed for sorrow and compassion and shame because of Christ's suffering for his sins. Then came the Fourth Week, when he contemplated the appearances of the Risen Lord and prayed for the grace to be glad and to rejoice intensely because of Christ's great joy and glory; and then came the crowning Contemplation to Attain Love of God. Not a peep did he make in his Chronicle about these contemplations. Yet he was not silent about his determination to make his entrance into the Society. On November 27 he assured Doménech that he was ready to dispose of his benefices and paternal inheritance whenever Ignatius would indicate that he should do so. Two days later, on the twenty-ninth, he capped his retreat by entering the novitiate of the Society of Jesus. He was thirty-eight years old.[30]

3

Learning the Ignatian Way

*May Ignatius write his life. . . . At this time he could
do nothing more worthwhile for us and the Society. . . .
The utterly pure spirit of Fr. Ignatius, raised to God
and united with him, is what enables the Society to
carry on and what earns God's favor. . . . Lord, grant
that I may have the spirit of Fr. Ignatius.*

Nadal in his *Orationis observationes*, 1546–1547

Nadal began his novitiate in the undistinguished way usual
for Jesuit novices. Ignatius told him that after two days he was to
go to the kitchen and help the cook. When unoccupied in the
kitchen he was to assist the gardener. After twenty-six days amid
the stoves and the kettles, the father minister directed him to
work in the dining room. He was happy. Despite low physical
energies, he felt that he was growing in his love for the Society.
There were little irritants. He was given a broom with the
brushwood cut short, deliberately designed to make sweeping
difficult. He found this fatiguing. Yet he insisted that this did
not diminish his delight.[1]

On the fringe of Nadal's content, however, lurked a vexing
spectre: the need to tell Jaime Pou of his decision to be a Jesuit.
He dreaded a nasty storm. Ignatius appreciated his fear and
advised him to put off the encounter in the hope that an
unforeseen solution of the problem would open. But the delay
could not continue indefinitely. One day Nadal went to Pou's

Ignatius Loyola

home and broke the news. As he had feared, Pou became very angry. But while his friend poured out his pique, Nadal detected the central reason for this display of ill-humor: Pou feared for his own reputation in Majorca; he cringed before the criticism he foresaw for his failure to stop Nadal from becoming a Jesuit. Pou then proposed a pact: Nadal should write his friends in Majorca—and these friends naturally included Pou's cousins, the Montañans—and explain the history and meaning of his calling to the Society of Jesus. If those friends made no fuss, Pou would drop his own complaint. No longer would he feel like a target of blame.

Nadal agreed. He wrote to Fr. Nicolás Montañans y Berard to describe the nature of his vocation and the settled peace he found in the Society of Jesus. Montañans spread the news among Nadal's other friends. They raised no dust. Pou was content, since his reputation remained unblemished. And he retained Nadal within the circle of his special friends.[2]

Ignatius was notably gentle toward the new novice. Occasionally he invited Nadal to eat with him in his private dining room. He often went to Nadal's room to chat or took him for a walk. Ignatius' first advice on spiritual reading reflected his own experience at Manresa. There he discovered the *Imitation of Christ*, at that time attributed by many to Jean Gerson, celebrated chancellor of the University of Paris in the fifteenth century. Thereafter Ignatius read a chapter a day, and in moments of leisure he often opened its pages at random. Never did he fail to find help. He advised Nadal to read the *Imitation* every day, to meditate upon its words, and, during sickness and other trials, to read any chance page. Nadal remembered that counsel. "He [Ignatius] had wonderful praise for that little book. He went so far as to say that whenever I opened Gerson in the future, I would find precisely the apt thought for that moment. This had been his own experience."[3]

Ignatius ordered Nadal not to fast. Nadal replied that he feared lest his failure to fast might scandalize some members of the community. Ignatius bridled. If Nadal would identify any such Jesuit, he declared, he would promptly dismiss that man from the Society. The subject of fasting sparked a silly scruple in Nadal's conscience. One day he felt acutely hungry, but he worried lest by eating he would be surrendering to his natural appetites. Ignatius asked him why he took food. "To stay alive to enable me to do penance for my sins and serve God," replied Nadal. With a gentle smile, Ignatius said simply, "Eat, my poor man."

After Nadal made his general confession during his retreat, Ignatius stressed compunction of heart. Penance now became Nadal's burning preoccupation. He complained to Ignatius that he had not imposed any. Ignatius refused to do so and said simply, "Don't worry about it." Nadal was puzzled. He wondered what Ignatius had in mind. He finally settled on this interpretation: Ignatius was trying to take the measure of a fragile and sensitive spirit and to carry it "in the arms of gentle courtesy."[4]

During those early days of Jesuit life, a surge of devotion swept Nadal into a vow-making spree. Unknown to Ignatius, he made vow after vow in quick succession, each nuancing a previous one. As we have seen, during the closing days of his retreat he vowed to pronounce the vows of the Society and, later the same day, he vowed to make the vows of religious life even if the Society refused to accept him. A week and a half later he bolstered these vows with another. On December 3 he made a promise to close the door on his freedom to choose another religious order unless the Society absolutely refused to accept him for even the meanest kind of work. The cascade did not stop there. Two weeks later, he shaded his last vow still more: if the Society did not receive him, he would pronounce the vows of religion in no other order save the one the Society would advise. The stream crested in early January 1546. He felt a void in his life because he had not yet pronounced the vows of the religious state. He had only vowed to make those vows. This was not enough. He saw a rich treasure of merit slipping from him.[5]

Yearning to staunch that loss, Nadal prayed and offered Masses. He used the Exercises' methods for making a choice. To him the result was clear: his intense desire to pronounce religious vows of poverty, chastity, and obedience in the Society of Jesus must be instantly honored. This yearning he brought to Ignatius. Ignatius assured him that he understood his aspirations. "But pay attention to what I am now telling you," he continued. "Because of your desire to make the vows of religion, you are earning merit before God. Remember this, though: there is another kind of merit, and that is *not* pronouncing those vows, precisely because I do not think that you should."[6]

Nadal yielded, but not for long. He examined Ignatius' reply. He asked himself: are you making your vows to Ignatius or to God? The conclusion he reached was clear: "By all means pronounce the vows. God so wills." He resolved to obey this inner answer to his question without informing Ignatius. Yet he held back. To pronounce vows amid a burst of religious fervor would not be an especially noble and chivalrous act. He sensed that a burst of repugnance for the religious life was lurking just around the corner. He chose to make his vows face to face with that repugnance; that would be a firmer affirmation of his resolve to be a Jesuit. He did not have to wait long, for one night, as he recited the *Te Deum* at Lauds, an overwhelming distaste for his venture enveloped him. He interrupted his recitation of the divine office and recited a formula that he himself had composed, since no form had yet been set by the Society. High elation followed this act.[7]

Nadal went to Ignatius to tell him of the fait accompli. Ignatius made no fuss. Quite simply he gave his approval. Ignatius' quiet assent to his highly unusual conduct puzzled Nadal. He did not know how to construe it. Finally he settled on what he called "an easy" interpretation: Ignatius really wanted him to pronounce the Society's vows but had been reluctant to take the initiative and tilt the scales; he actually was happy about his derring-do.

Hardly secured in his vows, Nadal felt the stirrings of another insistent demand: to divest himself immediately of his benefices and the patrimony due him in Majorca. Again he could not restrain himself; he needed instant action. He sought Ignatius' counsel. Ignatius, inclined toward a delay, tried to restrain him. Nadal demurred. He made a veiled threat: Ignatius would bear responsibility for any spiritual harm that continued possession of his properties might inflict. Ignatius yielded a bit and directed Nadal to seek advice of two priests skilled in canonical procedures, Fr. Gasparo de Dotti and Fr. Cristóbal de Madrid. The two experts suggested that Nadal delegate a few persons in Majorca to administer the renunciation of his property according to two norms: the administrators were to make sure, first of all, that Nadal's sisters and other relatives who might be in need received an adequate share, and secondly, that the rest of the estate be earmarked for the poor. Ignatius and Nadal agreed with Dotti and Madrid. In Majorca the surrogates fulfilled their commission. When they had taken care of Nadal's relatives, they sent him what was left, one hundred gold pieces, for distribution to the poor.[8]

About four months after Nadal became a novice, Ignatius one day facetiously remarked that he considered appointing him minister of the community. As minister he would assume responsibility for material care of the house and observance of external discipline. Ignatius knew that this responsibility placed a man at the center, where his traits, unpleasant as well as pleasant, were visible to all. It made for a fine schooling in humiliation. A few years later he thought of making service as minister one of the "testings" (*experimenta*) of the tertians, Jesuits in the final year of spiritual formation, but he never implemented that idea. Usually he put a novice through that test.

Elaborating on his teasing suggestion that he might appoint Nadal minister, Ignatius drolly observed that that post would be a fine training ground in the art of governing. And still more, he went on, he might put under Nadal a man who deserved to be dismissed from the Society because of disobedience (*hecharle un hechardizo*). That would indeed be a supreme test of a superior's wisdom, tact, and mettle.[9†]

Not long after this episode, probably in April, the banter stopped and Ignatius designated Nadal minister of the residence. In his new post, unseen layers of his character peeled away. With sober zeal and fussy legalism he went about his task. He was bossy. He was abrasive. He addressed others brusquely. Ignatius inflamed an unpleasant situation by delegating him to impose penances on members of the community while remaining the anonymous instigator of the penances. The choler of the community rose against Nadal. Quite abruptly, Ignatius then dropped his erstwhile mild and gentle manner toward the hapless minister. He chided him for the least defect in the house. He gave him some extremely severe reprehensions (*buonissimi capelli*). At times Nadal trembled in Ignatius' presence, yet he

---

†9 *Mon Nad*, I:24, n 2 on 74–75. Here Ignatius was playing on words in an old idiom, *hecharle un hechardizo*. Basically it means to toss to him someone useless or worthy of rejection. In the context of the incident it means to toss to Nadal (or match him up with, or fix him with) someone who deserves dismissal from the Society because of disobedience. Two Jesuits have helped me unearth the meaning of this sixteenth-century phrase, Fr. José Sanchez and Fr. Fernando Picó. *Mon Nad*, V:75.

claimed that even amid those shivers of fear his heart remained at peace. He did not always receive those scoldings with gentle grace, however. On occasion he made it clear that he thought Ignatius had gone too far. Yet Ignatius held his purpose: he wanted Nadal to see clearly the intimate and essential tie between holiness and humility.

One day Nadal heard Ignatius affirm in a very explicit way the essential character of that tie. The two men were walking a corridor of the Professed House. Nadal asked Ignatius for a maxim that would help him make progress in the life of the spirit. Ignatius replied that that was really not necessary. What Nadal knew was enough. "Just do that," advised Ignatius. That answer did not satisfy Nadal. He persisted. "I turned to him," he related, "and implored him for the love of Our Savior to give me some idea that would help me." With utmost gravity and direct-ness Ignatius addressed his spiritual Hotspur: "Master Nadal, desire insults, failure, injuries, reproaches. Desire to be seen as a dunce, to be universally despised, to have everything of yours stamped with the Cross, and all for the love of Christ Our Lord. Desire to be garbed in his dress. This is the way to perfection, to spiritual vigor, joy, and consolation." Nadal recalled that "with these words, or words like them, he [Ignatius] manifested an abundance of devotion."[11]

Ignatius' stress on humility as core of the Jesuit vocation aroused the intellectual curiosity of the theologian within Nadal, and he sought its inner meaning in the tradition of the Church. Through Holy Scripture, the Church Fathers, and other ecclesi-astical writers he ranged, combing their works and jotting down their views. His long list of citations fills twenty-two pages of the *Monumenta Historica Societatis Iesu,* a theologian's quest for the in-telligibility of a virtue that Ignatius wove into the substance of Jesuit life.[12]

Ignatius used another means to lead Nadal to understand the Society's spirit and structure: he enlisted Nadal's help in handling the general's vast correspondence with Jesuits and others about the world. On June 2, 1546, in Ignatius' name, Nadal wrote to Peter Canisius and the other Jesuits at Cologne. He gave a summary of the Society in Europe and the Indies: the colleges in Padua, Valencia, Gandía, Coimbra, Alcalá, and Valladolid were demanding considerable attention; the plan-ning for other colleges in Bologna, Trent, Paris, and Toledo was consuming much time; the Jesuits in Barcelona, at the court of Charles V, and in the Indies—ten scholastics had just been sent there—had to be cared for. Ignatius' concerns led Nadal's mind through Europe and beyond. They revealed two things about Ignatius: first, the regnant position he gave the general in the structure of the Society and the care he lavished on jots and tittles.[13]

In December of 1546, Nadal wrote to King Ferdinand of the Romans. Ferdinand had announced that he wished Fr. Claude Jay, then at the Council of Trent as representative of Otto Cardinal Truchsess von Waldburg of Augsburg, to be the new bishop of Trieste. According to their Constitutions, Jesuits vowed not to accept ecclesiastical honors save under orders from the pope, and already five of them (Simão Rodrigues. Pierre Favre, Diego Laínez, Nicolás Bobadilla, Paschase Broët) had declined offers of episcopal appointment. Ignatius protested to Ferdinand personally. He asked others to do the same. Nadal was one of those he enlisted.

Nadal explained to Ferdinand that it was the Jesuit spirit of poverty that accounted for the Society's notable achievements: "Our men know no other spirit." A change, even though imposed for a noble reason, could only alter the Society's pristine spirit and dissipate the momentum of its lofty impulse. Nadal argued secondly that Jay as a bishop would be confined in his spiritual ministry to the territory of his diocese, but as a Jesuit he was free to preach and teach throughout any number of dioceses. The more general good should prevail over the less general. Nadal presented a third argument: Ferdinand's designation of Jay would establish a bad precedent that could lead to the extinction of the Society. Other Christian princes would want Jesuit bishops; soon the Society would disappear into the ranks of the hierarchy.

Nadal's final argument portrayed Ferdinand's action as an opening of the door to ambition. Catholics knew that the "way of simplicity" was the Jesuit way. A Jesuit who accepted an episcopal appointment would expose the Society to the charge of hypocrisy. Men currently attracted to the Jesuit "way of simplicity" would recoil from entering the novitiate; others, motivated by ambition, would seek admission as an avenue to high ecclesiastical distinction. "We feel," wrote Nadal, "that if one of our men becomes a bishop, it will spell the complete destruction of the Society." He pleaded: "We turn to your Majesty to protect us and free us from this danger. Do not force your most devoted servants to do what they judge would be the wrecking of their vocation and the ruin of the spirit that God Our Lord in his divine goodness has given them."[14] Nadal echoed Ignatius' own letter to Ferdinand.[15]

For all its energy, Ignatius' campaign hit a stone wall. Pope Paul backed King Ferdinand, and he made this clear to Ignatius. Ignatius widened his drive. At least twice he spoke to the pope personally; he canvassed the cardinals in Rome; he enlisted the aid of Duchess Leonor de Osorio, wife of the Spanish ambassador. At Trent, Laínez and Salmerón enlisted several bishops to protest Jay's appointment. Even the Society's "protector," Rodolfo Cardinal de Carpi, sent his objections to Ferdinand. Pope Paul, however, remained firm in his decision.

Ignatius fell back on an especially powerful resource. Margaret of Austria, young wife of Ottavio Farnese, the pope's grandson, was one of Ignatius' penitents. He asked this strong-minded woman to plead his cause with her papal grandfather-in-law. She did. She asked Paul to defer Jay's appointment until she could personally appeal to King Ferdinand. The pope yielded and so did Ferdinand. Ignatius had won what Nadal called "the row about the episcopal appointment" (*tribulatio episcopatus*). By having a part, even a minor one, in that heated episode, Nadal learned in a most intimate and explicit way Ignatius' understanding of the Society's role in service to the Church. He had had one of the most instructive of his novitiate experiences.[16]

In another unpleasant episode Ignatius enlisted Nadal's help. When he settled in the Professed House in Rome in late November of 1545, Nadal learned that Ignatius was in a bind. A Catalan woman wanted to become a Jesuit. Isabel Roser, a pious, aging widow of Barcelona who had been very kind to Ignatius during his years as a student and beggar in Barcelona, had come to Rome in the spring of 1543 against Ignatius' advice. She had been in Rome a little over two years when Nadal entered the novitiate. Soon after Isabel's arrival, the Jesuits discovered that they had an unexpected difficulty. Br. Esteban de Eguía spent two years in her service as butler, janitor, and escort. Ignatius found relief from her insistent tokens of affection and her pleas to become a Jesuit by assigning her to assist wayward women seeking spiritual and social renewal at Casa Santa Martha.[17]

Isabel's objective, however, was acceptance into the Society of Jesus. For two years Ignatius kept her at a distance. She finally took her pious desires personally to Pope Paul. He not only granted her wish but also ordered Ignatius to accept her under his charge. On Christmas Day of 1545, in the presence of Ignatius, Isabel and two of her friends pronounced their vows in the Church of Santa Maria della Strada.

To Nadal's irritation, Isabel, while keeping her residence at Santa Martha, hovered more and more about the Professed House. He bridled at the sight of Jesuits preparing meals for the three women. He chafed at her forwardness in assuming the duties of nurse for Ignatius when he was ill. He boiled at her demands for more and more of Ignatius' attention to her worries and scruples. By April of 1546, Ignatius, surfeited with Isabel's molehills, appealed to Pope Paul for relief. Paul heard Ignatius through, and agreed that Ignatius could cut Isabel and her friends loose from the Society.[18]

Ignatius commissioned Nadal to carry out the delicate mission of officially notifying Isabel of the pope's decision. On or near October 1, 1546, Nadal went to Casa Santa Martha with Ignatius' letter, read it four times aloud in the presence of witnesses, and handed it to her. With gentle delicacy Ignatius explained to Isabel that his duties as general of the Society and his unabated illness made it "not fitting for this little Society to have special charge of women bound to us by vows of obedience." With the pope's approval he saw it was to God's greater glory "that I should withdraw and separate myself from this care of having you as a spiritual daughter under obedience but have you rather as a good and pious mother." Because Ignatius envisioned his Society as an order of priests, there was no role for an unordained woman. The acceptance of Isabel posed tremendous problems for the life and work of the early Jesuits. Isabel's temperament did not make the situation any easier. She was a rich and independent woman who preferred to adapt religious life to her style rather than to modify her life to conform to religious regulations. Isabel died a Franciscan, however, and there seems to have been no prolonged bitterness between Loyola and Roser. The experience with Isabel did, however, ratify Ignatius' reluctance to expand his order to include a branch for women.

This vivid lesson Nadal passed to other Jesuits. "We conclude from this—and this was always the mind of Fr. Ignatius—that it is foreign to our Institute to have the special care of women." His reasons rose from the frustrations Isabel had inflicted on Ignatius: a work of this nature is full of vexation and fuss; it occasions talk; it even has pitfalls fraught with danger.[19]

In what Ignatius was rather than in what Ignatius did Nadal found an even more trenchant teacher. From Laínez he learned much about the history of Ignatius' personal life. Laínez assured him that at that moment Ignatius was a highly special divine choice for the gift of an intense and profound familiarity with God (*Est Deo familiarissimus selectissime*). In years past Ignatius had visions of Christ and of the Blessed Virgin Mary, present to him in the form of images. As time went on, the corporeal character of those visions yielded to purely intellectual and abstract insights within God's unity.

Nadal learned even more from Ignatius himself as he lifted the veil from his past life. Inspired by St. Paul's recitation of what happened in his life (so Nadal thought), Ignatius recounted his vexations, his imprisonments, his sicknesses, his sins. He told of his easy converse with the divine Persons of the Trinity and the various graces he received from them. The greater gifts came during converse with the Holy Spirit. Ignatius revealed that as often as he prayed he found the divine Essence in itself, and that in prayer he followed no particular order but found God in various kinds of meditation. In the transforming power of prayer he rooted the efficacy of apostolic work. What God gives in prayer, Ignatius told Nadal, is what animates word and deed. "Your words are sterile unless you transmit to them those personal secrets that God opened to you in your prayer."[20]

Ignatius' life verified this. His intense contemplative prayer gave his speech a special power. Over all that he did, the Holy Spirit held sway. It struck Nadal that Ignatius' activity had an inner meaning: the showing forth of God at work in him through divine grace. Ignatius' words, therefore, carried the fire and power of God given him in prayer. And still another effect of his fidelity to God's grace Nadal learned from Ignatius. At the beginning of his personal turning to God after the battle of Pamplona, Ignatius sought people of holy repute to talk with about the life of the spirit. But those conversations, he thought, fell flat. Something was lacking. Eventually this early impulse dissolved, and he sought another guide in the advance to holiness. The guide he found was converse with God alone.[21]

Nadal therefore grew in his knowledge of Ignatius, but his recollections, ample though they are, could never catch all those eddies of feeling and thought that moved between and about the two men. From those conversations, however, Nadal forged a firm conviction: the young Society needed a written life of Ignatius. "May Ignatius write his life," he noted. "At this time he could do nothing more worthwhile for us and the Society."[22] In Ignatius Nadal saw the Society's most potent advocate before God. "The utterly pure spirit of Fr. Ignatius, raised to God and united with him, is what enables the Society to carry on and earns God's favor."[23] Nadal prayed: "Lord, grant that I may have the spirit of Fr. Ignatius."[24] He also asked God for Ignatius' virtues, his height of contemplation, his victory over the world, the flesh, and the devil. Here was born an insight that Nadal expanded through the years: Ignatius was the most perfect exponent of that special grace peculiar to the Society of Jesus. This became one of the crown jewels of Nadal's ascetical and mystical theology.

Among the Jesuits in Rome Nadal began a quiet campaign to urge Ignatius to write his autobiography. It was a story that the Society of Jesus could not afford to lose. He found Ignatius reluctant. But Nadal persisted and, as shall be seen, he won. For him Ignatius had become the measure of all things Jesuit.

Nadal had other teachers besides Ignatius, however. They came to Rome from faraway places and reported on the Jesuit enterprises in Cologne, Naples, Louvain, Trent, Augsburg. Nadal met those men and heard them report varied ways the Society was serving the Church. They stretched his imagination beyond the walls of the Roman house, mentors helping Ignatius in the formation of his novices.

One of those Jesuits who came from afar was Pierre Favre, whom Nadal had known years before at Paris. Favre arrived in Rome from Spain on July 17, 1546, summoned by Ignatius to join Laínez and Salmerón as theologians at the Council of Trent. Now forty years old, he had worked since June of 1539 in Germany, the Netherlands, Portugal, and Spain. During those seven years, this gentle, intelligent Savoyard showed a peculiar power that made him, in Ignatius' mind, the master of the Spiritual Exercises among the first Jesuits. Princes, bishops, theologians felt that force that made Johann Cochlaeus exclaim: "I am delighted that at last we have discovered a master of the affective life."[25]

Favre had many things to tell Ignatius and the others, but his time was short. A week after his arrival he developed a fever and on August 1 he died. Nadal vividly remembered Favre's gentle persuasive power, his ability "to draw water from a rock." Some of Favre's reflections on his pastoral work impressed Nadal: his insistence on a priest's ardent love for the other person and the avoidance of the least sign of annoyance or harshness; his refusal to use a frontal attack on a person set in the way of sin (one, for example, living in concubinage); his preference to reach the other's heart by conversation on the passion of Christ, the example of the saints, the import of heaven and hell; his objective to move a person to shame by picturing the beauty of holiness that goes beyond obedience to the commandments.[26]

A year after Favre's death, a twenty-six-year-old Dutch Jesuit came to Rome, summoned there from Florence by Ignatius. Peter Canisius had been a student at the University of Cologne when he met Pierre Favre at Mainz in the spring of 1543, made the Spiritual Exercises under his guidance through a month, and on his twenty-second birthday, May 8, decided to enter the Society of Jesus. Favre was charmed by the new novice. He wrote to his friend Gerard Kalckbrenner, prior of the Cologne Charterhouse, "I have grown in my love for our Cologne, which found within itself to rear such a pure soul."[27]

Peter brought to Rome accounts of his experiences during the uncertain combat between Catholics and Protestants for the see of Cologne, and of his participation for three months in the Council of Trent as representative of Otto Cardinal Truchsess von Waldburg of Augsburg. For the first time Nadal met the man who would be his mainstay during his future labors in Central Europe.[28] About a month later, probably in October 1547, two Belgians came to Rome, summoned by Ignatius: Fr. Cornelius Wischaven, a former secular priest and native of Mechlin, and Peter Vinck, a young scholastic and native of Brabant, each with his personal history of meeting the Society of Jesus at that vibrant crossroads of German, Flemish, and

French civilization, the University of Louvain. Wischaven and Vinck would be companions of Nadal in Jesuit projects in different parts of Europe.[29]

Jesuits were, however, not only arriving in Rome. They were leaving also. Nadal remembered especially the departure of Diego Laínez and Alfonso Salmerón for the Council of Trent early in 1546. They had been particularly kind to him, making him feel at ease as they chatted with him about their preparations for the work ahead in the council.[30] Memories of this kind molded his conviction that it was the Society's vocation to serve the Church in the apostolate of the mind. Trent's demands on Laínez and Salmerón played a subtle part in Nadal's formation as a Jesuit.

Of the community that had gathered about Ignatius—they numbered usually between thirty and thirty-eight during the years 1545 to 1548—several were transients. They were what a general congregation 430 years later called a *"communitas ad dispersionem* . . . a community of men ready to go wherever they are sent."[31] That was the scenario Nadal saw played before his eyes: Jesuits of diverse provenance heading for countries not their own. At this guildhall of Jesuit life, he greeted and said farewell to his fellow religious on the move. Nadal began to learn that a highway, rather than a house, was the better symbol of the Society. Here was the planting of an idea that blossomed very soon into one of Nadal's classic phrases: "The ultimate and even the most preferable of the Society's dwellings are not the professed houses but the highways. . . . We identify the Society's finest and ultimate dwelling of the professed fathers with a journey. (*In domibus professis non est ultima vel etiam potissima habitatio Societatis, sed in peregrinationibus. . . . Ultimam ac perfectissimam Societatis habitationem dicimus peregrinationem professorum.*)"[32]

In contrast to those Jesuits of the highway, another Jesuit who indirectly helped Nadal to understand the Society's way was a homebody. Juan de Polanco came to Rome in March 1547, called there from Florence by Ignatius. This thirty-year-old member of a wealthy family from Burgos had entered the Society as a secular priest six years earlier, after making the Spiritual Exercises under the direction of Diego Laínez. Ignatius, who had been making slow headway in his heavy responsibility of writing constitutions for the Society because of the mass of routine correspondence, appointed Polanco his secretary. By talent and temperament Polanco fitted smoothly into the routine of that post. He helped Ignatius put together the primitive text of the Constitutions, the one scholars identify as Text a; he composed two documents, *Siguense 12 Industrias con que se ha de ayudar la Compañía para que mejor proceda para su fin* and *Constituciónes que en los colegios de la Compañía de Jesús se deben observar para el bien proceder dellos a honor y gloria divina* as aids for Ignatius in his planning; he gathered materials from his study of the constitutions of other religious orders. He did most of the actual writing of Text a.[33]

Nadal watched the interplay between Ignatius and Polanco at firsthand. There is nothing to suggest that they worked alone in a tightly guarded security room. In the closeness of the community, Nadal must have heard ideas that moved back and forth in the flow of daily conversation. This was the beginning of his exegetical training in the Constitutions. Years later, when he would be called upon to explain phrases on the printed pages, he moved from a firm base in his memory of Ignatius and Polanco honing, refining, clarifying their ideas. He knew the cost exacted by the document whose interpretation would become the main responsibility of his life.

4

Groping for a Theology of the Jesuit Spirit

*The spirit of the Society is a certain brightness that fills
one and gives him guidance.*

Nadal in his *Orationis observationes*, 1546–1547

One day in 1546 Nadal had a visit from an old friend. Antonio
Castañeda, the hermit in Majorca to whom he had gone to
learn the way to prayer, arrived in Rome. Antonio came at the
suggestion of Fr. Nicolás Montañans, who wanted him to take
care of the Church of the Most Holy Trinity at Miramar.
Montañans urged him to seek approval for ordination to the
priesthood and the necessary dispensation from the canonical
irregularity he had incurred by service in the army. Antonio
called at the Professed House to see Nadal. Ignatius was not
happy at this reunion. Wary of a man who had twice withdrawn
from a Franciscan novitiate, he received the news of Antonio's
arrival with a distinctly chilly reserve. Nadal was angered.[1]

Undeterred by the pique he caused Nadal, Ignatius pressed
his reserve harder. Someone had introduced Antonio to the
Duchess Leonor de Osorio, wife of the Spanish ambassador.
One day Ignatius had an appointment with Leonor at her home
to receive some relics she wanted to give him. He sent Nadal
instead, and with a two-edged message for the duchess: beware
of trusting too readily a man you hardly know. Nadal saw through
Ignatius' strategy: the message was meant for him as well as for

the duchess. Upset, he felt impelled to protest to Ignatius on the spot in defense of his friend's integrity. However, in what he called an act of self-conquest, he did what Ignatius told him to do. In his *Chronicon Natalis iam indo a principio vocationis suae* ("Chronicle") he made a curt entry: "Dealing with the hermit did me no harm."

Nadal then tried to bring Ignatius to think kindly of Antonio. He told him that Antonio had high esteem for Ignatius' holiness. Ignatius bridled. He predicted: "This man will not last three years in the way of life he has undertaken." He proved correct. Antonio received permission to receive Holy Orders and, in Palma de Majorca on April 25, 1547, was ordained priest by the Carmelite bishop Rafael Linas. Invested with the benefice and care of the Church of the Most Holy Trinity in Miramar, as Fr. Nicolás Montañans planned, he practically ended his penitential life in his hermitage. Nadal heard this and recognized the fulfillment of Ignatius' prediction. "I hear," he wrote, "that the hermit is now taking on a far freer style of life."[2]

The incident of hermit Antonio meshed with an attitude of Ignatius that Nadal was discovering. He noted Ignatius' reserve and caution about "professionals" in prayer; he usually did not make much of what people told him about their spiritual relish during prayer. Ignatius looked for soundness of judgment. This was essential; sweetness and delight were not. Some seven years later a Portuguese Jesuit, Luis Gonçalves da Câmara, then the minister of the Professed House, recorded a frequent saying of Ignatius': out of a hundred people who give themselves glowingly to prayer, ninety are victims of illusion. Then Câmara hesitated. Was he reporting Ignatius' remark accurately? He thought that perhaps Ignatius had said ninety-nine out of a hundred were deluded.[3]

Ignatius' reserve tempered but did not quench Nadal's ardent desire to give prayer a lively place in his life. He brought from Majorca a basic burning desire for union with God, fed by the teaching of hermit Antonio and by his reading the Pseudo-Dionysius. He entered the Spiritual Exercises with an expectation of receiving a vision or a revelation. These strong impulses continued through his life. Many he recorded.

In the archives of the Society of Jesus there is a document of 561 pages composed by Nadal with the notation on page 1,

Orationis observationes. It contains 1005 reflections on prayer and the interior life within the Society of Jesus. Many of the reflections are deeply personal, though sometimes expressed in the third person. Most are terse, even abrupt, of only one to six lines. Sometimes the verb is missing; sometimes a single word appears on a line. Some smack of the style of Kempis. Snippets have appeared in various volumes of the *Monumenta Historica Societatis Iesu,* but only in 1964 did the entire *Orationis observationes* appear in print.

Through the three years Nadal was in Rome at Ignatius' side, he made about 184 entries in his manuscript, possibly as many as 216. A few excerpts from a page picked at random should give an idea of his style (p. 66):

Divine Power. All ecclesiastical objects, images, altars, churches, sacramentals, feasts, ceremonies, all these carry the imprint of the divine power.

A certain person asked Christ to deem him worthy of the Cross. This certain person realized, however, that he was wrong in seeking the Cross at the very moment he was trying to rid himself of the Cross he was then actually bearing in the form of his distress from bad health and depression of spirit.

Sensible consolation is not to be sought. There was a certain person whose prayer seemed pointed toward his consolation and joy in the service of God. It became clear to him, however, that what he should be feeling was distress because of his sins. Toward this objective should his prayer be directed. For the future, therefore, let this person pray not for sensible consolation but for the realization that he deserves every kind of desolation and suffering. If indeed he will seek consolation, may his understanding be that consolation will advance God's greater glory and will be entirely according to God's will.

The Incarnation. In the Incarnation there is a brightness coming from heaven into the world and enveloping it. It is the divine power inserted into man; it is the glory of the world, of the angels, and of the just fathers. It is the terror of demons, the renewal of a creature in the experience of the spiritual.

The Nativity. The Nativity of Christ is the going of grace to work in the world. So is it with prayer in the Society. It is a stretching to embrace works of service.[4]

These excerpts show the *Orationis observationes* to be a series of disparate and unconnected reflections. They lie on a page like a heap of burning coals on a brazier, each aglow and each independent. Together on a page they throw a spiritual light and warmth without an internal literary unity. Each retains its own dimensions, its own contours.

Nadal's style was distinctly theological. In language and concept he wrote as one versed in theology. Usually curt and technical, often awkward, Nadal's language shunned literary grace. And his concepts, scriptural and scholastic, reflected the tradition of theological literature through several centuries. Yet the literary provenance of the individual reflections is often extremely difficult, even impossible, to determine. Nadal had indeed made a complete commitment to the Jesuit way of life, but he brought to that commitment the intellectual and spiritual impress made over more than thirty years in Majorca, Alcalá, Paris, and Avignon. At age thirty-eight, he could not shed that impress. A study of the text of the *Orationis observationes* is like an examination of an old piece of cloth spun from the flax of diverse regions: only the closest scrutiny can trace the origin of any section of the cloth. Only minute attention to language, concepts, turns of phrases could discern the presence of a Pauline, a Dionysian, possibly even a Scotist influence in the thought and feeling of a man who desired to be fully Ignatian. Such a study would take years of patient textual analysis.

What follows is simply a précis of some of the main insights that Nadal jotted down during his early years in Rome with Ignatius.

God's Presence in the World

The intelligibility of the world rests in God. The meaning of being and action in the world must be traced to God. "Do not tarry in any creature. Move from it, to pierce your way to God." God's presence in the world includes, of course, his presence within humankind. "God is in us. We exist. God exists. Our being is from God and is in God. With reflection on our being we perceive God within us. And we adore him." Sin alone is what human beings can claim as their own within themselves. The truth within them comes from God. "May you ever find God within you, never yourself." "As you act in God and from

God, free yourself of self-seeking. Find God in himself. Simply rest in him. Also seek him in all things."[5]

God's Activity in the World

The initiative is ever with God. The world exists because God is giving. To honor the saints is to affirm this truth. It is a recognition that the magnificent gift of God's grace is at work in them. The saints, open in their reception of God's gift and unreserved in their cooperation with it, grow into objects most beautiful. "If you see something good, hear something good, conceive something good, refer it to God's glory. . . . God is molding it. God is investing a creature with his own glory." God's continuing action in the world, Nadal realized, touched his own person. Each morning on awakening he tried to greet the new day as if it were the first morning of his own creation and redemption. God at that moment was continuing to give existence. Christ at that moment was continuing to pour out his redemptive graces. This realization of God's action in the world Nadal endeavored to deepen. He wanted to feel it deeply, since creatures then became a gateway to "the understanding, the contemplation, the love, the adoration of God. This is the way God wants it to be." A luminous understanding of this ever-flowing power of God instructs man on his utter dependence on God. It leads to "the extinction of those impudent flashes of pride that shoot through the mind."[6]

Life in God and in Christ

The epistles of St. Paul permeated Nadal's theology. In them he found material for contemplative prayer. He pronounced what he called "a practical principle": humankind acting through Christ Jesus, in God and for God. The quest for Christ was an imperative that Nadal identified with Paul's "having the mind of Christ." This touched every point of life, alerting one to ask what would be the attitude and conduct of Christ if he were present at this moment. "It is like sensing that Christ is dwelling within us." "When you approach the time of your prayer, always dispose yourself by the inner understanding of St. Paul's words: 'The Spirit helps us in our weakness. For we do not know how to pray the way we should. But the Spirit himself prays for us with

sighs too deep for words.' And also with the inner understanding of St. Paul's other words: 'We have received the spirit of
sons, in which spirit we cry out "Abba, Father." The Spirit
himself bears witness to our spirit that we are children of God.'
This teaching of Paul, if felt intensely within yourself at the
opening of your prayer, will have a penetrating influence. It,
first of all, gives a sense of lowliness and a sense of the Spirit
working within us. It then inspires us to hope, it unites us to
Christ, it endows us with familiar converse with the Father."[7]

The Role of the Heart in the Spiritual Life

In his quest for Christ Nadal placed his heart at the head of the
column. The heart was where Christ made his home. There, in
the heart, was where Christ was to be discovered, at one time
dying on the Cross, at another rising from the dead and teaching his disciples, at still another ascending into heaven. In his
heart Nadal sought to relive the mysteries of Christ. This disposition opened his heart for the entry of the Holy Spirit. "God the
Spirit vivifies. The sense of the Spirit charges the heart with
life." Nadal conceived the will as at once the most sensitive, the
most tender, the paramount faculty of humankind. He identified
the seat of this precious faculty with the heart. On his own heart
Nadal sought to imprint the wounds of Christ. And it was to his
heart he turned in his search for Christ: "Ask your heart to show
God and Christ to you. Grace makes this possible." In the ascent
to God the heart's relish for spiritual things is a starting point.
"The mounting to God in virtue rises out of wisdom and the
heart's taste of love."[8]

Action and Contemplation in the Life of a Jesuit

Ignatius told Nadal a story. A certain king had two sons. One
son the king sent off on a twofold mission: to carry out highly
sensitive negotiations, and to wage some acutely challenging
wars. The other son he kept at home to share his table. For the
first son he reserved the greater reward. Ignatius applied his
story to the active and contemplative lives. The finer need is
reserved for the one immersed in charitable activity rather than
for the one wrapped in contemplation. Nadal, recalling that
Ignatius recited his story with deep conviction, gave a straight-

forward interpretation: "Here I understand [Ignatius to mean] that the active life—about which I shall speak in another place—is superior to others" (*sed hoc loco intelligo activam* [*de qua alias*] *superiorem aliis esse*).[9]

"The active life is superior to others." This statement opened a chest full of ascetical terms that took varying meanings through the history of ascetical literature. Nadal adopted one honored schema that made a threefold division: the active life, the contemplative life, the higher active life. According to his adaptation of it to the Society, a Jesuit entered the active life by examination of conscience, penance, meditation on sin, the conquest of evil habits, mortification, the development of virtue; he entered the contemplative life by moving his prayer into contemplation of the mysteries of Christ's life; and finally the higher active life by assuming the responsibilities of an apostolate and remaining constant in his combat against his sins and in his contemplation of Christ's life. When he interpreted Ignatius' story, Nadal had his ascetical terminology in place, a prelude to his many efforts to explain the meaning of work and prayer in the Society of Jesus. The active life that Ignatius in his story found superior to all other lives Nadal identified with what he called the higher active life.[10†]

The Apostolic Dimension of Jesuit Prayer

Nadal learned early that he had reason to learn, as indeed did every Jesuit, about the interlocking of prayer and work in the

---

†10 The roots of the terminology Nadal adopted go back into medieval Franciscan tradition. Nadal chose this terminology rather than the one associated with St. Thomas Aquinas, who made a threefold division of the active life, the contemplative life, and the mixed life. Despite the difference of nomenclature, the two schemas were not very far apart. St. Thomas did not always identify the active life with business and mere external action; sometimes he put under that heading "the ordering of the soul's passions" and the development of the moral virtues. At other times St. Thomas divided the active life into two classes: the one that consists totally in external occupations, such as showing hospitality and giving alms; the other that flows from contemplation into preaching, teaching (*contemplata aliis tradere*). Nadal's terminology never became widespread in the Society. See Miguel Nicolau, S.J., *Jerónimo Nadal: Obras y Doctrinas Espirituales* (Madrid, 1949), 327–38. Other quotations of Nadal in this section are in *Mon Nad*, IV:646.

Society. Practice could not wait for finely spun theories. On Ignatius' orders he joined other Jesuits on their preaching expeditions into the piazzas of Rome. He was also assigned to lecture on theology to the diocesan clergy of the city.[11] He soon had a good dose of the kind of apostolic demands made of a Jesuit. He saw young scholastics, who had heavy schedules of class and study, trying to meet their obligation to pray. Weighing the demands of each, he favored the labor of study. "Prayer in the Society should be so arranged and practiced that it does not distract from those labors that are proper to us. It is, therefore, incumbent on us to apply ourselves to this problem until we have received from Christ the ability to make the right accommodation."[12]

Nadal therefore recognized that he had a problem to solve. From that point on, he strove to reach a formula that would capture the correct rapprochement between prayer and work in Jesuit life. On one early venture at Rome he discovered that his prayer should have a dimension that embraced his fellows and their needs. He knew that the Holy Spirit was poured out into his heart. But the breadth of the Holy Spirit's mission extended beyond the measure of his own heart. It embraced his neighbors. With the coming of the Holy Spirit came an apostolic task. "As often as you pray, you should stretch your prayer to cover your neighbors." In his prayer at Rome, therefore, Nadal detected an inherent characteristic that drew him out of himself toward others: the universal mission of the Holy Spirit poured into the hearts of all. This was a theological starting point for his protracted effort to comprehend the interpenetration of a Jesuit's prayer and work.

The Spirit of the Society of Jesus

Nadal had a need for definition. His training in scholastic theology impelled him to express in precise language the essential nature of the Society. At Rome he tried to do so in terms of light. "The spirit of the Society is a certain brightness that fills one and gives him guidance."[14] To him it seemed that this had been Ignatius' experience. A bright light inundated his spirit and pointed the way he should go. This was the earliest of Nadal's attempts to define the Jesuit spirit. Through the years he would put together quite a collection of definitions.

The Way of Liturgy

Nadal had a keen awareness of the Church. Personal holiness he desired, but withdrawal "into our own thoughts" he reproved. A failure of hope in the ways of the Church to holiness he abhorred. "More complete is the personal perception of the Spirit where the Church as a whole opens itself to that same Spirit."[15] And the Church does this in its liturgical calendar. Nadal judged that his sharing in the action of the Holy Spirit would be richer if he lived in tune with the worship of the Church. At the end of his life he would design his finest theological writing according to the liturgical calendar of the Church.

As Nadal's personal story traced these various themes, it attested to the intensity, the animation, the impatience, the excitability, the unsteady moods that his contemporaries noted in him. An old drift of soul persisted beyond his Majorcan days: the driving, demanding urge for mystical contemplation. Early in the Society he even formulated the goal of life in terms of contemplation. Painters, he noted, draw their first lines awkwardly; but they persist. They start anew. They carry on until they produce a polished work. "So must you do in the life of the spirit. . . . Such must be your program as long as you live: to go forward in the way of the spirit toward the contemplation of eternal things."[16] Mystical desires guided his pen even as he tried to give an intellectual articulation to his life's purpose.

Impatience for prompt satisfaction intensified his desire. But he was learning a hard lesson. Experience and reflection in Rome taught him to tame his yearnings for instant gratification. Through the Spiritual Exercises and converse with Ignatius he learned the basic asceticism of purification of the heart. Mortification was essential. Christ's way to glory through the Cross set the style, "so that he who wants to travel the way of the spirit should first be moved to a desire for mortification."[17] Further he noted that "to move along the authentic road of contemplation, there must be an interior sense of repentance, at least in a generic way. Repentance, not only for sins of the past but also sins of the present—including those that are forgotten—should abide in you. Shame and humility meet before the face of God. From this meeting springs confidence in God. Here is the basic groundwork for contemplation. It is pride to approach prayer without first cleansing the spirit."[18]

Nadal learned still another restraint: to place the service of God before his desire to enjoy the light of higher prayer. He came to see that he had been asking God for a reward before he had done his work. He admonished himself to focus on the task of the moment. "God will give you what he wants to give. As for you, serve him in simplicity and purity of heart because of what he is in himself."[19] A thirst for sensible consolation at times tinted his yearning for contemplation. He prayed that joy and consolation would permeate his service of God, but this desire he checked with the memory of his sins; he replaced his thirst for consolation with the desire to feel the punishment and desolation he deserved.[20]

Good resolutions, Nadal discovered, were not enough. Still, his yearning for consolation continued to simmer beneath the surface. On December 6, 1547, the feast of St. Nicholas, he sensed the holiness of St. Nicholas "in a certain gentle brightness." Yet a tinge of regret and compunction touched him. He judged himself shameless "in seeking consolation and contemplation more than sorrow." In lament for his sins should be his repose.[21]

At times Nadal soared. His urgent spiritual thirst was gratified; he was confident that he had tasted the force of mystical prayer. For two years he prayed for what he called "a mystical understanding" of the Our Father. He asked God for "spiritual alms." And for two years he was denied. Then came a day when he received "a light that illumined the meaning of the phrase, 'who art in heaven.'" He felt his mind "taken up to heavenly things, perceiving the Father as creator and donor of sonship to men through adoption." On another occasion he rejoiced in a sweet familiarity with God in prayer that he found beyond his power to describe. He knew that this exalted experience was completely grounded in the goodness and mercy of God. Between himself and God coursed a marvelous and sweet conversation as between friend and friend. "In short, it is within you to experience what David meant when he said, 'He fulfills the desire of all who fear him.'"[22]

At times Nadal languished in gloom. On his departure from Majorca for Rome he did not jettison the melancholy that had so tyrannized his life there. It often recurred; it ruled like a conquering army. As has been seen, Ignatius detected this strain early and felt anxiety about his new novice. During one period of temptation Nadal meditated on the temptations of Christ in the desert and found strength in the words of the Lord: "Not on bread alone does man live but in every word that comes from the mouth of God." He learned a lesson: "the life of the spirit is not built on consolation but on the word of God, even when heavy desolation weighs on everything."[23]

Bad health aggravated his depression. Amid his chafing, he recognized one day that his sufferings forced him to face reality. He had been directing his inner thirst to the passion of Christ and asking that he be worthy of the Cross. Then he was struck by the chasm between this lofty desire and his impatience with the suffering his depression and bad health inflicted. "This cross is so easy, and you do not carry it. What if a heavier one were given you? Do not desire to taste the heights. Take to yourself the lowly things."[24] Nadal swung, therefore, between ardent dash and dragging dole. The mountain and the valley remained dominant contours of his spirit. They presaged the pathos of his closing years.

Two diverse doctrinal magnets pulled Nadal's ardent desire for union with God and tugged him off a steady and resolute course. The power of those two magnets came from two of his teachers, Ignatius Loyola and the Pseudo-Dionysius. From Ignatius he learned the lesson of seeking God in the objects and happenings of this world. In language that reflected Ignatius' "Contemplation to Attain the Love of God" in the *Spiritual Exercises,* Nadal recalled: "In created things God's power is to be felt. It is the creature, therefore, that God wants to be the jumping-off point of our understanding, our contemplation, our love, our adoration of him."[25] God invests all things with his wisdom. A feature of his power that enables all things to continue in existence is his giving a person the capacity to discern in creation the truths of his divine wisdom. "That is the common way of contemplation."[26] This teaching expanded Nadal's awareness of the physical, the individual, the specific beings of the world about him. He learned to recognize God actually molding the things he looked upon, investing them with his divine glory. With emotional intensity he sought a keen realization of this presence of God's power in creatures, since such a realization is the gateway "to the understanding, the contemplation, the love, the adoration of God. That is the way God wants it."[27]

Yet even as Nadal was learning these lessons from Ignatius in Rome, murmurings from his studies in Majorca insisted on being heard. The Pseudo-Dionysius lived on as a lively teacher. From him Nadal learned to reject images and concepts, and to enter into that spiritual interior darkness wherein shines God's mystical brightness. Very early in his novitiate he resolved: "At all times I should turn my mind on God by the way of humble and devout abstraction. This way, advancing as it does by a progressive setting aside [of the play of the imagination and the stir of the intellect], ends in a simple and humble desire, which does not empty a soul of joy but moves it toward that darkness in which God is found in spirit and in truth."[28] The Pseudo-Dionysius, therefore, cut a distinctive channel for Nadal's desire of God, a channel of abstraction and negation, quite diverse from the Ignatian channel shaped by the singular, the specific, the here-and-now.

The two styles could hardly work comfortably side by side within Nadal's spirit. Yet at least once during his Roman days he put them in juxtaposition in his *Orationis observationes*. In one entry he identified the way to contemplation with abstraction and negation; in the next he identified it with the perception of God manifesting his power in the molding of creation.[29] From his earliest days as a Jesuit, an irksome tautness entered his soul. One day he reached beyond the world to find God; on another he sought to find him in the world. One day he was a spiritualist; another day a "materialist." He never did solve this practical problem. All his life, impulse continued to carry him one way, then another.

The previous few pages show how secure a place the *Orationis observationes* has in any history of Nadal's life. The *Chronicon Natalis,* on the other hand, tells the story of the first epiphany of his inner spirit, unfolding as it does the stresses, the woes, the aspirations he felt in his earlier life, especially in Majorca, and later in Rome during his Long Retreat of Election and the two years that followed. The *Orationis observationes* is an even more fulgent epiphany, more detailed, more ample, more reflective; it intensifies the bright light cast by the *Chronicon Natalis.*

Nadal began his *Orationis observationes* after he entered the novitiate in late 1545. Even in its earliest segment, it does more than tell the story of the ebb and flow of his first three years as a Jesuit. It also suggests much about earlier happenings in his life, on which the *Chronicon Natalis* is severely reserved, even silent. As has been seen, the *Chronicon Natalis* tells nothing about the teachers under whom Nadal studied or the courses he pursued. The *Orationis observationes* breaks that silence, not indeed by bold and loud assertion but by soft, gentle, and suggestive whispers. In it Nadal professed, for example, his preference for a theology of the heart rather than a theology of the mind; this suggests the influence of the Franciscan Francisco de Osuna when that question was much in the air at Alcalá during Nadal's studies there. He saluted the will as a spiritual faculty superior in dignity to the intellect, an allusion probably to study in the Scotist school of thought at Paris, where Pierre Tateret, who died ten years before Nadal arrived, had been the most celebrated of Scotist thinkers whose influence perdured. That Nadal chose to use the category "the higher active life" in his schema of the interplay between the contemplative and active lives hints at contact with Franciscan literature, particularly that of St. Bonaventure who popularized the precise schema that Nadal adopted.[30]

These are whispers indeed; not so explicit as the *Chronicon Natalis*'s recording of Nadal's Dionysian reading in Majorca and his study of Hebrew at Avignon. But those subtle allusions in the *Orationis observationes* to Franciscan and Scotist thought fill more than just a bit of the wide spaces left empty by the *Chronicon Natalis*. Nadal therefore evoked his past as he penned the account of his present, and implicitly acknowledged the lasting impact of earlier spiritual impressions. This Jesuit carried within him the wellsprings of Dionysian, Franciscan, and Scotist attitudes. By the end of his stay in Rome he had limned a bold and sure portrait of his intellectual and spiritual character. The earlier and fainter etchings became surer and stronger. In mid-March of 1548 his development as a Jesuit under the immediate tutelage of Ignatius came to an end. Ignatius put him on the road.

5

Light and Shadow in Sicily

For a time I was of a mind to quit Messina and free
the Society from its heavy hand.

Nadal to Ignatius Loyola, December 1551

On March 13, 1548, Pope Paul III received Nadal and nine other Jesuits in audience. They came to the pontiff to ask his blessing on an apostolic mission they were about to start. Peter Canisius, in "a graceful and pleasing Latin speech," explained that the group were on their way to open a college in the city of Messina in Sicily. Paul blessed them, urged them to combat Lutheran doctrine and to raise confidence in the Church's general council assembled at Trent. On March 18 Nadal and his companions mounted their horses and rode south from Rome. By appointment of Ignatius, Nadal was the superior.[1]

Ultimately what led to this educational venture in Messina were the reports that had circulated through the Spanish domains in the Mediterranean about the success of the first Jesuit school opened by Ignatius—in Gandía in November 1545, at the request of Gandía's duke, Francis Borgia (Francisco de Borja). The civil authorities of Messina decided they needed a like institution. By that time, too, Ignatius' friends Juan de Vega and his wife Leonor de Osorio had been moved by the emperor to Sicily, where they were promoted to the positions of viceroy and vicereine of the island. Vega endorsed the hopes of the Messinans. On December 6, 1547, Fr. Jerónimo Doménech alerted Ignatius to expect a joint proposal from the city senate of Messina and the viceroy of Sicily that the Society establish a college for lay students. Doménech also warned him that the government of Messina had in mind the eventual foundation of a university. That same month the senate framed its final request. They asked Ignatius for five professors to teach grammar, rhetoric, philosophy, and theology. They also asked for five scholastics who, as they pursued their own studies, would "give assistance in works of Christian zeal." Ignatius, already committed to other works and fearing overextension of the Society, declined. At this juncture, Vega personally asked Ignatius to open a college. Vega insisted and finally prevailed. In March of 1548, Ignatius wrote Doménech that he was sending some of his best men to Messina.[2]

Ignatius chose ten men, of whom four were priests: Nadal, Peter Canisius, Frenchman André des Freux, and Belgian Cornelius Wischaven. They made the first leg of their trip, to Naples, on horseback. It took five days. Along the way they debated with various fellow travelers who challenged the worth of vows and sacred images; they argued with a Moor about the Holy Trinity. Wischaven almost broke his neck when his horse went over a precipice. Each evening Nadal groomed and fed the horses. The second leg of their trip, from Naples to Messina, they made by ship. It took twelve hectic days. The captain inched his way along the coast through heavy seas and under thundering skies. Several times they had to find haven in small coastal villages, where they tarried a day or more. At least twice, unable to reach their ship by its rowboat from a village because of the choppy waves, they had to walk some miles along the shore until they reached a spot where the sea was calm. Wischaven seems to have been the only one not prostrated by seasickness. Canisius and the scholastic Isidoro Bellini suffered most. The last stage of the journey, the sixty miles from the Calabrian town of Tropea to Messina, they made in the early morning of Sunday, April 8.[3]

At the wharfside awaiting them were Fr. Jerónimo Doménech and a physician, Dr. Iñigo López. Doménech promptly led them to meet Vicereine Leonor de Osorio. Three days later, in the Church of San Nicolò, which had been assigned to the Society, they introduced themselves formally to Messina. Five of them delivered Latin orations before the viceroy, the municipal magistrates, and the aristocracy of the city. Peter Canisius spoke on the study of eloquence. Despite this fancy introduction, the Jesuits discovered that their living quarters were not yet ready—nor was the school. They were given temporary accommodations in a house near the archbishop's curial headquarters, where, on April 26, they opened classes in Latin, grammar, rhetoric, dialectics, Greek, and Hebrew. Nadal gave lectures in scholastic moral theology.[4]

That makeshift program, however, came to a quick halt. The summer heat came early, which gave the city's officials four months of grace to complete their construction of the residence and school. It also gave the Jesuits time to prepare a circular on what their school was about. By October they had printed and distributed throughout Sicily a prospectus of their educational program. This, the first program of studies ever published by a Jesuit college, carried an unmistakable stamp: a preference for the system of the University of Paris. Ignatius admired the structure within which he had studied at Paris. So did Nadal. The Sicilian advertisement explicitly stated that the Jesuits would follow "the method and the order that is used at Paris," the best possible for attaining a perfect and smooth mastery of the Latin tongue.[5]

This French import was the finest gift the Jesuits made to Italian education. The "method and order of Paris" brought to Messina what the Italians lacked in their schools, "method and order." In Italy professors followed no schedule; they lectured sporadically. Students wandered freely from one subject to another; young men who had not mastered grammar attended lectures on Cicero and Vergil. Those still trying to master literary subjects frequented classes in philosophy and law. The "method and order of Paris" challenged that sloppy regimen. Classes were regular; students advanced step by step according to their mastery of the prescribed material; they were kept constantly active with repetitions, examinations, written exercises, disputations. In place of chaos, the Jesuits installed a tightly disciplined institution. Nadal and his fellow Jesuits planted an outpost of order on a wild educational frontier. Ignatius had called Paris "the mother of our first fathers." Paris was also the mother of this first Jesuit college designed primarily for the laity.[6]

Nadal opened the formal school year in October of 1548, and he did it with a flourish. Viceroy Juan de Vega and the Sicilian nobility attended the solemn ritual. Peter Canisius and Benedetto Palmio delivered Latin orations. Poems written by Jesuits adorned the walls of the school. This exuberant display set the style of Nadal's leadership in Messina. He kept the school in the public eye. In May of 1549, for example, he engaged the Dominicans in public theological disputations. Through an eight-day period the Dominicans presented four such debates, which they threw open to the public. Nadal led a Jesuit delegation to the Dominican church, where he, Canisius, Freux, and Isidoro Bellini entered the debates. Nadal assured Ignatius that God's providential hand guided the Jesuits, "giving us such zest and acuity in argument that the reputation of our college has grown splendidly throughout this entire island."[7] Nadal in turn played host to the public at theological disputations at the Jesuit college, some of which went through two days. He also opened to the city's citizens his regular classes on moral issues. Those were especially popular. He periodically ran academic spectaculars. On the feast of San Nicolò in 1550, priests and scholastics, encouraged by the facile pen of Fr. Annibal Coudret, displayed some 1140 Greek and Latin verses they had written.[8]

Religious celebrations gave Nadal other opportunities to advertise the school. He chose the second Sunday of Easter, May 5, 1549, for the solemn installation in the Church of San Nicolò of some relics of the virgins of Cologne. Peter Canisius, when a young student at the University of Cologne, developed a lasting devotion to the 11,000 virgins, who, as the legend went, gave their lives for the faith under the assault of Maximilian. During the trip from Rome to Messina, Peter had written to Fr. Leonard Kessel, rector of the Jesuit community in Cologne, requesting two of the virgins' skulls. When the relics reached Messina, Nadal planned to introduce them to the faithful in the grand manner. He organized a colorful procession in which students, the vicar general of the diocese, judges, nobility, leading citizens, a concourse of people, all dressed in their festal best, carried torches and marched in song to the call of trumpets. In a richly decorated coffin they bore the relics. At the church Nadal offered Mass. Because the time for lunch was pressing, however, Nadal deferred his sermon until after the midday repast. In the afternoon a large number of the people returned to hear him and to venerate the relics.[9]

Nadal used this sermon to educate the people about the Society of Jesus, explaining in particular a point of the Jesuit practice of poverty. The people were startled, he wrote Ignatius, "when I stressed that we were not looking for financial recompense for any of our services, be it for the public veneration of relics or any other spiritual ministry. I told them that this was the Society's way of doing things. I insisted that our entire purpose was to help souls to the full extent of our abilities." The people marveled, not knowing what to make of this novel approach to priestly ministry.[10]

What Nadal did at Messina was but one instance of how the Jesuits, during this age of popular esteem of relics, took the remains of the saints on long voyages of relocation, especially from countries in the north to Spain, Portugal, and their domains in Europe and overseas. Pierre Favre had brought seven heads of the Cologne virgins to Portugal five years earlier. A "devotional system" met an educational system at Messina and made a striking alliance.[11]

The touch the Jesuits gave the spiritual ministries at San Nicolò speedily attracted many in Messina. Sacred lectures, that peculiarly Jesuit device by which the scriptures were explained in a popular way on a regular basis, drew large audiences. During the summer of 1550, for example, the Jesuits gave a series of scriptural lectures every Friday morning and every feastday on the life of Christ as presented in the gospels. More at ease as a scriptural lecturer than as a popular preacher, Nadal found the lecture format congenial to his talents. The stellar preachers were Peter Canisius, André des Freux, and Isidoro Bellini. Crowds packed the church. At times many could not get in. "At San Nicolò, every Sunday is Easter Sunday" was a remark that went about town.[12] Growth in knowledge of the faith stimulated a lively sacramental life among the people. Within six months after their arrival in Messina, the priests were overwhelmed with confessions. "We cannot handle them all," wrote Nadal to Ignatius, "even when we do nothing else from morning to night."[13] The numbers who received Holy Communion also mounted. Nature also stimulated popular devotion at times. One day in August of 1549 a severe earthquake struck Messina. Terror gripped the people. Several died. The rest rushed in droves to San Nicolò to make their confessions.[14]

Gradually Nadal and his community moved from San Nicolò into other parts of the city and into suburbs. In mid-1550, on Sundays after Vespers, they conducted lectures on St. Paul in the town's cathedral. They responded to many requests from monks to preach in monastic churches. But they simply could not honor every request. As Nadal wrote Ignatius: "We cannot accept all the invitations we would like to, so busy are we."[15] To one special request for help Nadal gave a definitive No. And he directed it to a friend. Bartolomeo Sebastiano de Aragón was bishop of the nearby diocese of Patti and Inquisitor of Sicily. He made the Spiritual Exercises under Fr. André des Freux and resolved, among other things, to relieve the financial plight of priests who were so poor that they had to steal time from their spiritual ministries to earn a living by manual work. He also asked Nadal to have the Society assume some duties of the Inquisition. Nadal refused. Involvement in criminal proceedings, said he, went contrary to the Jesuit way of doing things. Bishop Sebastiano de Aragón, somewhat nonplused, wondered why a group so dedicated to the Church would not want to stamp out heresy. His disappointment, however, did not turn him against the Society; he continued to seek Jesuit help.[16]

On Sundays and holy days, after preaching and lecturing at San Nicolò and at the cathedral, Nadal and his community took to the streets. "Some of our men," wrote Nadal to Ignatius in December of 1551 "go out in bands of two to fish—so the saying goes—for souls in the neighborhood; some visit the hospitals and the prisons. One remains on duty at our church to talk to people who come seeking information."[17] Even amid all these mounting pastoral concerns, the lot of the poor especially troubled Nadal. Early in September of 1550 he enlisted the town fathers of Messina in a citywide drive to collect alms. They divided the city into twelve districts; in each district they designated a noble and a commoner to collect the money. "We hope to turn this into a massive drive," commented Nadal.[18]

An institution that became associated with the Society early on was the sodality, or pious confraternity.[19] In many towns of sixteenth-century Italy, groups of men and women entered pious alliances under the patronage of the Blessed Virgin Mary or of another saint. It was an age of organized quest for holiness. This religious impulse moved into Messina and soon enveloped the Jesuit community. As early as the summer of 1549, some sixty men of the city asked the Jesuits to compose for them a constitution as their guide to greater holiness. They particularly desired to help the aged and the prisoners as a part of their program. Women too wanted to set up a sodality. Nadal and other Jesuits agreed to help and ultimately drew up a program of prayer and practical apostolic charity. Among the obligations assumed by the sodalists were confession and reception of Holy Communion at least once a month and presence at an exhortation on Sundays and feastdays. A year and a half later, Nadal made a happy report to Ignatius: the sodality was in full swing. Once a month the sodalists distributed to the poor and to prisoners the alms they had collected; he had every hope that this work would grow into "an enterprise of wide service to the Lord."[20]

The fame of the Jesuits in Messina was increased by strange happenings that began to occur at San Nicolò. Fr. Cornelius Wischaven was at the center of those oddities. For years this pious Belgian felt strongly attracted to the care of victims of diabolical possession. Peter Canisius had been impressed by Wischaven's work with the possessed in Flanders years before. Pierre Favre was not, and he told Canisius that Wischaven had already burned his fingers in that dubious and fitful area of ministry. But Favre's caution did not stop Wischaven, and he now turned San Nicolò into a center for exorcisms. A little over a year after the Jesuits arrived there, a young woman, judged to be in the grip of the devil, was carried to San Nicolò. For three months various remedies had been tried, including lodging her in an area outside the city reserved for the possessed. Someone then suggested moving her to the Jesuit church. They carried her, bound with cords, into San Nicolò during Mass, and started to pray for her. At that moment Fr. Wischaven entered and spoke to the disturbed victim. She calmed down, regained her reason, and promised to go to confession. Wischaven conducted an exorcism that lasted an hour. The devil raised a loud rumpus, begged not to be cast into the fires of hell, and left the girl seemingly dead. Attendants loosed her bonds. She revived, went to confession, and returned home giving glory to Christ. In vivid detail Nadal described this moving scene for Ignatius. Impressed by what he saw, he did not share Favre's doubts about Wischaven's powers.[21]

This feat gave the Jesuit church an even wider popularity. Two and a half years later, Nadal informed Ignatius that it had become ordinary to bring the possessed of Messina to San Nicolò. "During the past four days," he wrote in December of 1551, "three or four people have been liberated from the devil. Today we are busy with two more. May the Lord give them freedom."[22]

In late December of 1551, Nadal wrote Ignatius that many people in Messina publicly proclaimed their feeling about the Jesuits in words such as these: "Blessed be the Lord, who has sent us the Society of Jesus, the forger of many holy achievements."[23] A few days later he again wrote to Ignatius, this time saying that he found the people of Messina an obstinate lot. "For a time I was of a mind to quit Messina and free the Society from its heavy hand."[24] Seemingly something had gone awry overnight.

In reality, Nadal was describing in those reports two diverse developments: in the first, the warmth with which the general populace received the Jesuits' pastoral and sacramental care, and in the second, the stiff legal resistance of the city's senate to control of the school by a group of foreigners. Those two distinct themes ran parallel through Nadal's stay in Messina.

Nine months after the Jesuits arrived in Messina, Pope Paul III, in his bull *Copiosus in misericordia,* of November 16, 1548, issued his official approval of the founding of a university in Messina, an honor the city had been seeking since at least the previous century. The terms were important. To the Society he granted government of the university; to the Jesuit general he gave power to appoint the rector; to the senate of Messina he granted management of the nonacademic features of the institution.[25] At long last Messina had the academic status it sought.

Within six months, the whole project was in jeopardy. In May of 1549 a new body of senators took office. Breaking with their predecessors, they found *Copiosus* unacceptable, especially the Society's control of the faculties of law and medicine. Insisting that those faculties be under their jurisdiction, they demanded that *Copiosus* be revised. Nadal discussed the matter privately with the senators. He learned a great deal and found that the Messinans had a deep sense of local rights and local autonomy. They wanted to hold control of an institution of such public import as a university. The outsider they regarded with a passionate suspicion. Nadal quickly detected their determination to control what the Jesuits were trying to establish. Nonplused by what he encountered, he wrote to Ignatius on July 1, 1549: "I am amazed by how hotheaded and suspicious these people are, how bent they are on freedom from foreign restraint. They reject any semblance of control of the university by an outsider."[26]

Ignatius repulsed a suggestion that he seek a revision of *Copiosus*. He knew that in the papal court were men who distrusted the Society as an organization bent on worldwide power. He did not wish to fuel their fires by asking the pope to amend a papal bull already formally published. Ignatius' stand put Nadal in a bind. Caught between the senate's demand for revision of *Copiosus* and Ignatius' refusal to seek revision, he tried to reach a compromise with the senators. They showed little interest. Despite this impasse and the legal uncertainty it created, Nadal determined to keep the Jesuit project alive at least on a modest scale. In October of 1549 he issued a bulletin for the new academic year that listed classes in the humanities only. The higher classes in philosophy and theology he suspended. The cutbacks were serious and humiliating. The high spirits that charged the academic ceremonies of the year before had evanesced. An outcry, however, arose from a surprising quarter. The students of philosophy and theology, left in the lurch, took their loud and angry protests to the viceroy and the senate. They prevailed, and within a few days the Jesuits resumed their classes in those disciplines. The university—what Polanco called a college with the façade of a university—limped along.[27]

In that same October of 1549, Nadal made a serious political mistake. Exasperated by what he considered the obduracy of the senate, he called upon Vega to force it to accept the bull *Copiosus* as it came from the pope. To Ignatius he made the observation: "These people are moved more by fear than anything else." Vega, initially reluctant to take issue with a people with whom he already had his hands full, finally agreed to use force, and jailed some of the leading citizens. Nadal did not have the political acumen to see the implications of his alliance with Vega. To the Sicilians, Vega and the Spaniards were intruders. Friendship with them could only exacerbate his relations with the senate. Vega, for all his apparent wisdom and kindness as a governor—he built roads and bridges, opened public hospitals, attended to the complaints of the poor—was better known for his cruelty. For light offenses he had persons, nobility and ordinary citizens alike, whipped or stretched on the rack. Those guilty of moderate violence underwent the piercing of a hand with a spike; those who used foul language had their tongues perforated. But Vega's greatest affront was his Spanishness. He was a foreign intruder. And for all in Messina to see, he stood at Nadal's side as a sponsor and friend. The Jesuits paid a heavy price for that. Through the sixteenth century they never received full acceptance by an important part of the Sicilian people. They remained strangers.[28]

Sometime during that unpleasant academic year of 1549–50, Nadal and the senate, spurred possibly by the presence of the viceroy, made another try at negotiations. They worked quietly and without fanfare. By April of 1550 they reached a compromise. The senators agreed to drop their insistence that the bull *Copiosus* be revised by the pope; Nadal agreed that the Society, although technically in control of all faculties in the university, would in practice hold aloof from the faculties of law and medicine; both sides concurred in allowing the students to name the rector, subject however to the approval of the rector of the Jesuit college within the university. On April 14, 1550, Vega ratified the agreement. Nadal was elated. On May 5 he informed Ignatius that the Society had at long last taken possession of the university. "We hope that the whole operation will work out so smoothly that the city will remain completely satisfied."[29]

The city, however, did not remain completely satisfied. New senators were elected in May, and they came into office breathing fire. They denounced the agreement their predecessors had recently made; they demanded that the pope amend *Copiosus* in favor of local control; they cut the financial allotment to the Society from 2000 scudi a year to 1500; they demanded that the finances of the school be managed by two appointees of the city; they insisted that the prefect of studies be designated by the archbishop of Messina. His early enthusiasm again deflated, Nadal wrote to Ignatius about the inevitable cutbacks he would have to make in the coming October: "At the opening of the new school year we shall not be able to give the lectures peculiar to a university."[30]

And so it happened. In October, Nadal opened the school's third year with its program pared to the bone. He kept its classes in humanities and dialectics; higher studies were dropped; the philosophy and theology students from Calabria and Sicily were sent home. Jesuit scholastics who had been sent to Messina to pursue the higher disciplines had to be transferred to Padua. At first Ignatius refused to accept this development; he instructed Nadal to insist on the rights of the Society as enunciated in *Copiosus*. Nadal by now knew the futility of that stern approach. Anxious not to lose the hard-won beachhead the Society had made in Sicily, he persuaded Ignatius to accept this humiliating setback and allow five Jesuit teachers of the lower grades to remain and weather the hardships of the financial pinch.[31]

Juan de Vega again intervened to coerce the new senators to moderate their intransigent line. He dispatched the syndic of the realm, Giovanni Battista Seminaria, to force a change. The syndic failed. Vega gave up. Worn out by the resistance, he winced at the prospect of further battle and another humiliating defeat. He urged Nadal to silence his demands for the Society's control of the university and to settle for simply a college with five teachers to handle grammar, humanities, rhetoric, Greek, and Hebrew. Juan de Osorio, a friend of Nadal, helped him in the new round of negotiations. On January 4, 1552, Nadal and the city of Messina signed a compact about the university. Neither side had won. The Society, shorn of its hopes, could not carry on the university. Neither could the city, devoid as it was of intellectual resources. Nadal relished the coil the senate had wound about itself. "If they want even only a few more classes, they will have to talk with us. And should they want to push on toward a full-scale university, they could not carry it off without us."[32]

The pent-up contempt for the Spanish regime in Messina poured out in 1557, the year Vega left Sicily on reassignment. Nadal, who had been summoned to Rome by Ignatius five years earlier, was not present to witness what Fr. Francesco Stefano, a teacher at the college, reported. "What held the Messinan's hatred in restraint was the lash of Juan de Vega. Now they have vomited their locked up venom against the viceroy and our college." And eleven years later, in 1568, Fr. Melchior Gallegos asked Fr. General Francis Borgia to be changed from Messina. "Our least Society is not too well loved in this city." The Spanish stamp on the school, Gallegos said, was a major burden.[33]

Of Messina's social and political realities Nadal had a blinkered understanding. A Spaniard, he showed no appreciation of Sicilian resentment of Spanish dominion. The Messinans' natural desire of freedom to control their own institutions he did not comprehend; he confessed that this desire "amazed" him. Nor did he appreciate the significance of his close relationship to a viceroy who was seen in the popular eye as a hated outsider. To dismiss Messina's senators as "hotheads" hardly evidenced a delicately nuanced judgment on a sensitive issue. Difficult and intransigent they indeed were. Their view of the Jesuit role in the university was obtuse. But Nadal never asked why. If he had, the wrinkles might have been ironed out.

During those vexations Nadal and his staff gradually gave a structure to the new institution, especially the classes of Latin and Greek, which survived all the strictures imposed by the senate. Faced with the need for a specific program for the day-to-day running of the school, Nadal asked Ignatius for guidance. Ignatius returned the problem to Nadal, and told him to draw up a body of directives and send them to Rome for his examination.[34]

Behind the scenes, withdrawn from the rush of public life in Messina, Nadal composed what he called the *Constitutiones Collegii Messanensis* (*Constitutions of the College of Messina*). He divided the document into two parts. Part I, in which he treated the piety and the good conduct that should pervade the school, had twenty points. Those points called for daily Mass, catechism, monthly confession, monthly Holy Communion (depending on the advice given in the confessional), exhortations to make a daily examination of conscience and daily mental and vocal prayer. They forbade swearing and playing forbidden games; they urged continuing prayer for good and holy thoughts and for the strength to shun idleness and useless activity.

Part II of the *Constitutiones,* in which Nadal treated the academic program, had twenty-six points. He outlined a curriculum that advanced from Latin grammar to rhetoric, to philosophy, and then to theology. In the literary stages he set as the goal a mastery of expression in finely chiseled Latin poetry and prose. In the higher studies he stipulated the exposition of Aristotle's *Ethics* as well as the study of Euclid, of the French mathematician and astronomer Orontius Fine (d.1555), of the German astronomer Johann Stoeffler (d.1531), and of the Austrian astronomer and mathematician Georg von Peurbach (d.1461). Nadal stipulated Hebrew grammar and readings, explanation of the Pauline epistles, and exposition of moral theology through the device of cases of conscience. Through the texture of the two parts he wove directives for repetitions, exercises, contests, and disputations, all designed to keep the intellectual wheels of the students spinning.[35]

Nadal the educator worked rapidly. He was practical. To elaborate a metaphysics of education did not enter his ken; realistic organization was imperative. To fit together the hundreds of small fragments of textbooks, schedules, and methods into a compact unity evoked from the greenhorn rector some rather notable organizing skills. Nadal's *Constitutiones Collegii Messanensis* became one of the seminal documents in the development of Jesuit education, but only a whit of what was to flow from his pen on that subject.

Three years later, before Nadal quit Messina, Ignatius asked him for further ideas on the running of a college. By the end of 1551, Ignatius had opened six colleges besides those at Gandía and Messina; among the six was the Roman College, which he inaugurated on February 3, 1551. Pressed by the need for detailed instructions for a batch of new teachers and administrators, Ignatius wrote Nadal on June 27, 1551, asking him to detail the curriculum, the sequence of classes, and the methods of teaching used in the Messina College. Nadal, fully occupied with other obligations, delegated Annibal Coudret to answer Ignatius. Coudret finished the task in three weeks and had his document in the post to Rome by mid-July. He organized his *De Ratione Studiorum Collegii Messanensis* (*Plan of Studies for the Messina College*) into nineteen sections. Practical, like Nadal's work of 1548, Coudret's *Ratione* gave a thorough, detailed, and precise outline of the length of classes, the identity of texts and authors, the kinds of exercises, the maintenance of discipline. He concentrated chiefly on the Latin classes through rhetoric. A few sections he devoted to Greek, one to Hebrew, and one to dialectics.[36]

Ignatius applied Coudret's *Ratione* to the Roman College, the darling of his enterprise in education, the institution he wanted to be the exemplar of all other Jesuit colleges, whose regime he envisaged as the one common to all the Society's schools. By way of Rome, therefore, Nadal's Messina gave guidance to the Jesuit teachers in the new colleges opening in Germany, France, Portugal, Spain, the Netherlands, Austria, Bohemia, and Poland.

Besides the structural "order and method of Paris," the Jesuits at Messina adopted a cultural ideal that was the fashion of that age. Since the late fifteenth century the Brethren of the Common Life in the Netherlands and in the lower Rhineland had educated youth in Catholic devotion and Latin eloquence, two objectives they welded into a unity that has been called Devotional Humanism (*pietas litterata*). That same ideal of *pietas litterata* was spread by Philip Melancthon, Johann Sturm, and Mathurin Cordier among the Protestants. The Jesuits at Messina, dressing their fledgling school in the latest of fashions, insisted on Catholic religious practice even as they called on the ancients of Greece and Rome to be the models in attaining *ars dicendi*. The Jesuits, like the Protestants, expurgated their classical texts (Ignatius insisted on this) lest the students be touched by pagan ways of thought and conduct. "The traits which had most clearly characterized the Humanism of the Renaissance were the ones most vigorously excluded from the ambit of the *pietas litterata*. The Cordiers and the Nadals had no wish to see a revival of the Roman past."[37]

At Messina under Nadal's leadership, therefore, was begun the Jesuit adaptation of the classical education of the Renaissance humanists to the religious ideals of the Society's Constitutions, as earlier "the Benedictines had based their teaching on an adaptation of the classical education of the later Roman Empire to Christian aims."[38]

The college and the church symbolized the public side of Jesuit life. There was also a private side. As rector, Nadal was responsible for the religious spirit and discipline of the community. His reports to Ignatius about the men in his charge were generally optimistic. At this early date, indeed, he formulated a norm of religious fervor that he kept through the years: blind obedience and total abnegation. According to this norm he gave his community a high rating, describing its members as obedient and selfless men "walking in the pure spirit of the Society." He cited examples of their mortification: in a special room, individuals, with his permission, took the discipline; there, too, hair shirts were stored, as well as two or three sackcloth garments that were worn by those assigned to serve table and wash the dishes.[39]

On occasion the community performed penances in the dining room. They chose, for example, the Carnival Days of 1550. Nadal reported to Ignatius: "During the Carnival, when everybody was caught in the madness of the masquerade, the

Lord inspired our men each evening to take in the dining room various kinds of mortification such as self-flagellation. All wanted to do these penances in the streets. The city's authorities, however, forbade them. The reason for the ban: the upset and commotion caused last summer by two of our community who did penances in public. The town's officials judged that those mortifications achieved no positive good. But we are hoping they will change their minds." Three years after their arrival in Messina, Nadal reported that the Jesuits continued to keep their fervor at a high pitch. In literary and spiritual exercises they maintained a single-minded sense of purpose "to grow steadily in the Lord." This fervor spilled into the town and touched people. Christian family life and the spirit of forgiveness were burnished by the ardor that radiated from the Jesuit residence.[40]

Despite Nadal's idyllic portraits, squalls occasionally descended on the community and ruffled its harmony. A few Jesuits had trouble with Nadal. They found him overbearing, impetuous, and rude. Fr. Cornelius Wischaven had some especially barbed words. Two scholastics, Stefano Baroëllo and Isidoro Bellini, had problems with obedience under Nadal, and spoke of leaving the Society. Baroëllo found his superior proud, stern, unfeeling. Nadal learned of Baroëllo's criticism and told Ignatius that he wholly agreed with the charges. "I am indeed proud, stern, unfeeling. And even more. What he [Baroëllo] did not mention is that I am impetuous, indiscreet, negligent. . . . But what I had in mind when I dealt with him the way I did was to give him a schooling in obedience, since, good fellow though he be, he was not grasping the meaning of that virtue. . . . Now that he seems chastened, I no longer have to keep my stern mien and manner."[41]

Ignatius sent Nadal a word of encouragement. He did not treat the situation very solemnly but reminded Nadal of an incident in his own novitiate. One day Ignatius teased Nadal about making him minister of the community and putting under him—*echarle un echadizo*—a man who was disobedient and deserved dismissal from the Society on that score. Torment of that kind would polish him in the art of governance in the Society. That time, Ignatius gently reminded him, was at hand. Nadal had not been unforewarned.[42]

Nadal therefore had his Jesuit critics in Messina. But he also had his admirers. Fr. Benedetto Palmio wrote to Ignatius in

September of 1551 what he thought Nadal meant to the Jesuits in Messina. He wrote of a man "by whose spirit all of us are fed and nourished. How much he means to us is made clear by how deeply we miss him when he is absent. For who is there more industrious than he, who more ardent? How does he get any rest? What labors are there from which he spares himself? When is he not on the *qui vive* in his quest for God's glory and the salvation of his neighbors?"[43]

Now and then the monotony of common life was broken by strange happenings. During the early period of Wischaven's exorcisms in the church, sorrowful nocturnal cries sounded within the residence. Night after night the wails went on. Some Jesuits thought a soul in Purgatory might be crying for help. Mass was offered for the distressed soul. The cries ceased.[44]

The community probably found its greatest encouragement in the young men who asked to be received into the Society. In September of 1549, Nadal admitted two, a talented twenty-two-year-old Frenchman and a nineteen-year-old Messina noble-man, a student of Peter Canisius, strongly grounded in Latin and Greek literature, of sound judgment and social grace. Months before these two became novices, though, Nadal had pondered the function of the novitiate in Jesuit life and in July of 1549 had proposed to Ignatius a novel plan. Up to that time, Jesuit novices had resided within one of the established colleges under the supervision of a priest. Nadal recommended that the novices be lodged in a house of their own, distinct from the college community.

Ignatius answered through Juan de Polanco. He liked Nadal's proposal; for some time he had been thinking likewise. As early as 1547 he had written to Fr. Simão Rodrigues in Portugal about the advantages of separate houses for the novices. In the imple-mentation of the plan in Messina, he recommended that Fr. André des Freux reside with the novices and that Nadal continue to live with the college community. At first Nadal had trouble finding a house not far from the college, but he finally negoti-ated a sale and, on February 19, 1550, Ash Wednesday, the novices, now some thirteen, moved in. Their novice master was Fr. Cornelius Wischaven. They were a fervent lot, and Nadal had to rein them in from excess in use of the discipline and the hairshirt. Their novitiate was the first set up as a separate entity in the Society.[45]

Parents sometimes opposed their sons' decision to enter the novitiate. One night the mother of a novice appeared outside the house with a crowd of people who supported her in her maternal anger. She made an uproar. The young man finally came out to speak with her. She caressed him; she threatened him; she made promises. But she lost. Her son turned and went back into the novitiate. At other times novices turned the tables on their protesting parents, exhorting them to confession and better lives. One novice persuaded his father to leave his concubine. Then there was excess on the other side of the scale. Some novices soon experienced what so many in religious life before and since have known: they can become the darlings of certain people. Isabel, the viceroy's daughter, doted on them. They had to respond with Greek and Latin verses, and at her bidding they had to give practice sermons in her presence.[46]

In February of 1551, Nadal had to make a trip of one hundred and eighty miles from Messina to Trapani, a city on Sicily's northwest coast. Juan de Polanco used a pungent phrase when recording the incident in his *Chronicon Natalis*; he wrote that Nadal did so "under constraint of the viceroy" (*coactus a viceregente*). Amid angry protests of his students, Nadal was forced to cancel his classes. Having appointed Anton Vinck as acting rector, he left for Trapani on February 16.[47]

Nadal had sought the viceroy's support in his hassle with the senate of Messina; now he had to pay a price: conformity to the viceroy's wishes. In this he became the prototype of many Jesuit rectors over the centuries. The success of the colleges depended on the benevolence of monarchs, princes, nobles. Those rulers often expected the Society to take its measure from their policies. Polanco's phrase anticipated large cuts of Jesuit history, during which many a rector was *coactus a viceregente*.

In a way, it was glowing reports about the Jesuit college in Messina that triggered Nadal's enforced trip to Trapani. In Palermo, a city fifty miles east of Trapani on the island's north coast, the senate, inspired by what they heard of the Jesuit institution at the other end of Sicily, petitioned Ignatius to open a college in their city. Ignatius commissioned Diego Laínez and Jerónimo Doménech to develop the practical details, and on September 8, 1549, he dispatched from Rome eleven Jesuits of five nationalities. In his concern for this new project in his jurisdiction, Juan de Vega banked on the advice of Laínez and

Doménech, but through 1550–1551 he lost both consultants. Ignatius summoned Laínez to Rome and dispatched Doménech to Spain to untangle some legal questions about his family inheritance. Shorn of his advisors, Vega summoned Nadal to Trapani, where he was then holding his viceregal court.[48]

At Trapani Nadal did more than consult with Vega. With the help of Vega's daughter Isabel he opened a house for the rehabilitation of prostitutes. Backed by Vega and his son Suero, he launched throughout the island an appeal for funds to relieve the poor. Vega wrote to political leaders in all quarters of Sicily to ask their support of the drive; Nadal netted some 1000 gold pieces. He also organized a religious confraternity of gentlemen, like one he guided in Messina. On one occasion he assisted a gentleman of the city who was condemned to the gallows. This gentleman, as Nadal explained it, "had given himself completely to the devils," and attempted suicide. Nadal counseled him, changed his attitude, heard his confession, and accompanied him to the scaffold.[49]

After six or seven weeks with Vega in Trapani, Nadal obtained leave from him to visit Palermo, where he arrived in early April. His first impression of this lovely city was flat; he found several Jesuits ill and concluded that Palermo was an unhealthy town. Yet he took measures to see that the continued existence of this college of some three hundred young men would be guaranteed. Working from the temporary contract made by Laínez and Doménech, whereby the city promised five hundred gold scudi a year for a two-year period, he obtained assurance from the town fathers that the sum was pledged *in perpetuum.* He then saw the contract through the process of obtaining approval from Ignatius, from the viceroy, and from the emperor.[50] Not money alone gave promise of continued Jesuit presence in Palermo. Nadal met some young men who wanted to join the Society. He quickly procured a house proximate to but separate from the college, and there four youths under Fr. Pietro Venusto started their novitiate. Soon four or five others joined them. In early June, after two months in Palermo, Nadal returned to Messina.[51]

6

Dismay at the Moslem World

May the Lord in his goodness help me and bear me up in my pitiable state amid such barbarous infidelity.

Their law, a bestial thing, attained its supremacy by force of arms. The Mohammedans have always established themselves by force of arms. I know this to be the case here. They have no reason to listen to us. May the Lord give such resolve to his faithful ones that they will once and for all confound all infidels and convert them to the Catholic faith.

Nadal to Ignatius Loyola from Africa,
August and October 1551

Hardly back in Messina, Nadal wrote to Ignatius about an ominous shadow of fear that hung over the city. Danger was lurking beyond the horizon of the Mediterranean. On June 19, 1551, he reported: "Two or three times daily we preach in the monastery churches of the city, exhorting the people to prayer during this current crisis. Fear of the Turkish fleet pervades the town. . . . All are deeply impressed by the actions taken by His Excellency [Juan de Vega], not just his military preparations to meet the enemy but also, and mainly, his pious and Christian endeavor to solicit prayer and pious works to move the merciful and powerful Lord against all the enemies of his holy Catholic faith."[1] Eight days later Nadal boarded a trireme of the Spanish fleet. Almost overnight he was caught up in the great naval contest

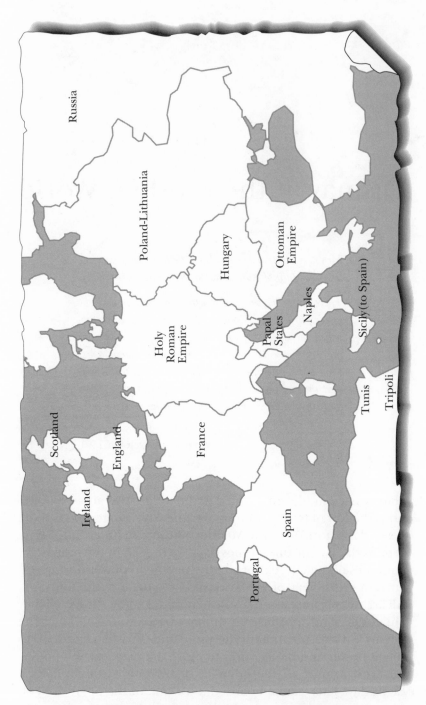

Europe and Northern Africa at the time of Nadal

between Turks and Catholics that lasted through most of the sixteenth century. For six months he was away from his community and his college.

The "shadow of fear" over Messina that Nadal reported to Ignatius was caused by an audacious Moslem sea captain named Dragut. In the spring and summer of 1550, Dragut, spreading terror through the coastal towns of the Habsburg domains on the Mediterranean, set up bases at Monastir and El Mehedia, southeast of Tunis. His blue crescent implanted on a flag of red and white became all too familiar to the Habsburgs. Under Hernando de Vega, the eldest son of Sicily's viceroy, the Spaniards fought back, took Monastir, and on September 10, 1550, after a rough siege, captured the Moslem garrison at El Mehedia. There, in the settlement's mosque, Fr. Diego Laínez, the first Jesuit military chaplain, preached a stirring victory sermon.[2]

In the next year, 1551, Dragut launched a counterattack. On August 16, he won a stirring victory when he took Tripoli, where the Knights of St. John of Jerusalem had been established since 1528. Even earlier, rumors were spreading that he was advancing on El Mehedia, where undisciplined Spanish troops were showing signs of mutiny. Juan de Vega prepared a second expedition under command of his son Ferdinando—Hernando had died suddenly only a short time before—to strengthen the shaky garrison at El Mehedia.

This was the campaign Nadal wanted to join. He hesitated, however, since he wondered whether Ignatius would approve so long an absence from his community. He finally reasoned his way to an affirmative answer. Ignatius, he knew, had an active interest in the Spanish campaigns in Africa, and in the previous July had obtained from Pope Julius III an indulgence for those who engaged in "the war for the glory of Christ and the spread of the Holy Faith." He also recalled that Ignatius, in a rather formal gesture, had directed him to write a document that contained this broad command: "carry out in the service of God Our Savior the good pleasure of the viceroy." "I noted the viceroy's concern for Africa," reasoned Nadal. "I offered to go along with him. He accepted. May the Lord ever guide me." On June 27 he joined the fleet.[3]

Nadal took a Jesuit companion, one of his troublemakers, Isidoro Bellini. Bellini, professor of philosophy at the Messina College and still a scholastic, was to preach to the troops. In

this high adventure he found the beginning of a spiritual renewal. He made a general confession. To his fellow Jesuits he
announced: "The next time you see me you will behold one
who has become through and through a man of the spirit."
There was no next time, for he did not come back. He was
drowned at sea.

Bellini and Nadal sailed aboard the flagship *Praetoria*, Antonio Doria commanding. On July 4, disaster struck the fleet. A
severe storm swept down the Mediterranean as they were off the
island of Lampedusa, halfway between Malta and the African
coastline. Eight of fifteen triremes went under. Some 1000 men
were lost. The *Praetoria* was driven onto the rocks of Lampedusa.
Bellini tried to jump from the ship to a rock. He missed, fell into
the sea, and was caught between the wreckage and the rock.
One of his arms was severed. For a half-hour he wallowed in the
water before the crew hauled him back to the damaged ship,
which by then was rapidly breaking up. There he lay until he
went under with the shattered vessel. Witnesses recalled that he
met this calamity with fortitude.

Nadal was more fortunate. Among the last on deck, he grabbed
a rope that had been thrown from the rock. Garbed only in his
underwear, and somehow holding on to some relics, he was
dragged to the rock. He knelt to say a prayer of thanksgiving.
Another trireme took him aboard. Someone gave him Turkish
clothes. Garbed as a son of Mohammed, he finally landed in
Africa.[4]

The remnants of the expedition camped at El Mehedia.
Hearing reports that the Turks were on the march from Tripoli,
they dug in to await the assault. During those few weeks, Nadal
assumed a heavy pastoral program among the troops. He
preached, taught catechism, and gave scriptural lectures. He
visited the base hospital; he investigated reports about a
Franciscan friar who allegedly was in Africa without permission;
he heard confessions. Some of the Spaniards played a spiritual
waiting game, telling Nadal they would confess if the Turks
actually showed. Among the soldiers who confessed were some
priests and religious who had apostatized and enlisted in the
army.

Ferdinando de Vega tried to arrange a theological debate
between Nadal and a leading Moslem in the area. "I was planning," Nadal wrote Fr. Anton Vinck, "to give some time to

learning the Moorish language but I was not able to do it."⁵
Through those busy days, Nadal had his community constantly
in mind. He wrote, begging for prayers for himself, El Mehedia,
and the enveloping Mohammedan world; he exhorted them to
fidelity to the Society of Jesus. In a few intense sentences he
opened his heart to them. "Take hold of and taste that clear
spirit of the Society, which is now your guide and will ever be so.
Place a guard about that peace that rests within the innermost
part of your soul. Admit not a single note of sadness. The Lord
gives me abundant consolation whenever I think of you, because all of you are inscribed in Christ and in the spirit of his
Society at the very center of my heart. And this in a way that is
beyond my power to express."⁶

Nadal wondered whether it would be feasible to establish a
Jesuit house in El Mehedia. This in turn forced him to modify
his attitudes toward the Moslems. The vast stretches of North
Africa and the omnipresence of the Mohammedan faith dismayed and frightened him. He felt ill at ease. He sensed hostility on all sides. To Ignatius he wrote: "May the Lord in his
goodness help me and bear me up in my pitiable state amid
such barbarous infidelity. For me it is a staggeringly large sorrow
to look over a land as extensive as Barbary and see it filled with
stubborn hostility."⁷ He saw little hope of bringing the Catholic
faith to the people of that countryside. Lines of communication
were meager. Transportation did not exist. Any Catholic penetration of the interior would have to look to Spanish arms.

He observed to Ignatius that the Moslems' confidence in
their religious law had to be broken. Spanish conquest alone
could do that. "Their law, a bestial thing, attained its supremacy
by force of arms. The Mohammedans have always established
themselves by force of arms. I know this to be the case here.
They have no reason to listen to us. May the Lord give such
resolve to his faithful ones that they will once and for all confound
all infidels and convert them to the Catholic faith."⁸ Nadal, as
usual, had found a simple formula: confound and convert. For the
moment, he advised Ignatius, the need for Jesuits in Africa was
limited to two men to work among the Spanish troops. The
Moslems were impenetrable. The foundation of a Jesuit community would have to wait on a Spanish conquest of the area.

By late August, Nadal was getting restless. He had been in
Africa two months, and the Spanish and Turkish armies had not

clashed. He had anticipated an early battle, but signs of it were nowhere evident. Feeling that his reason for being there had evaporated, he wrote Ignatius that he wanted to get back to Messina. Then he became not just restless but anxious. The lack of news from Europe troubled him. For six weeks no Spanish galleys from Messina appeared. In late October he wrote to Ignatius that he had received no mail, either from him or from the Jesuits in Sicily.

His absence from the opening of classes at Messina intensified his anxiety and pricked his conscience. He wondered whether he had acted correctly in leaving Sicily. Fearing that he might have crossed Ignatius' will, he wrote him a worrisome letter to justify his actions and appealed to Ignatius' formal directives at the start of the Messina venture that he carry out the good pleasure of the viceroy.[9] The disquiet he felt in Africa was an aftershock of the "trembling" he sometimes experienced in Ignatius' presence. Nadal's reverence for Ignatius ran deep, but fear of the master still stirred uneasiness. This incident may have been an inkling of the scrupulosity that would torment his last years.

Finally, in late October or early November, ships from Sicily arrived, carrying a new commander of the garrison, Sancho de Leiva. Nadal promptly made plans to return to Sicily with the retiring commander, Ferdinando de Vega. Leiva, however, refused to let him go. Nadal schemed to stow away in the hold of one of the ships. A sense of etiquette, however, prompted him to make what had the appearance of a routine courtesy call on Leiva before he resorted to his ruse. He tried to be jocular, suggesting that he really could not take leave of Africa, since, if he did, the troops would rise in mutiny. Leiva saw through the trickery and ordered his soldiers to abduct Nadal and hide him where Vega might not find him. Nadal, however, eluded the would-be kidnappers and was aboard Ferdinando de Vega's trireme when the fleet weighed anchor on November 11, 1551.[10]

Vega soon reached Palermo and Nadal spent a few days there, then sailed with the fleet to Messina. He had been a tiny part of an expedition that wrote no glamorous page in the annals of naval warfare, overshadowed by two memorable battles that were etched into the history of the Mediterranean: the disastrous campaign of Emperor Charles V against Algiers ten years earlier (1541), when in a violent storm he lost about one hundred and fifty ships and 12,000 men, and the Catholic victory at Lepanto in 1571, when the Catholic fleets under Don John of Austria crippled the Turkish armada.

On November 24, just before Nadal reached Messina, the college's acting rector, Anton Vinck, wrote to Fr. Juan de Polanco about the spiritual regime of the scholastics in the community. "The entire program," he reported, "is not so hidebound that change is ruled out. In fact, at any given moment it can be altered, adding something here, dropping something there, according to what seems better. Fr. Nadal has followed this approach and does not tie the scholastics to observance of a precisely set program but looks to the Constitutions to straighten all this. Since he realizes that everything in this area of Jesuit life is tentative and undetermined, he has not used his authority to impose a definite program on the scholastics. . . . Ordinarily in our residence we have an hour of prayer beyond Mass and the general examination of conscience."[11] Vinck left much unsaid. He did not indicate whether the prayer was vocal or mental, whether it was continuous, whether it was done in common or at a particular time of day. Perhaps he could not have been more precise than he was. At any rate, Ignatius himself was changing his mind and nuancing his statements on prayer in the Society's early years.

During that fluid period, Nadal gave an instruction on prayer to the Jesuits at Messina—*Instructio 'de oratione.'* The text, devoid of literary grace, is basically a list of headings he expanded in his talk. The oldest of Nadal's instructions on prayer, it reflects the same ambiguity that Vinck's letter manifested. He said nothing, for example, about the time for mental prayer. He focused rather on some broad guidelines—each Jesuit should, according to his ability, do some mental prayer each day; a Jesuit who found meditation difficult should ask his superior to let him turn to the life of Christ for material of prayer; rectors and novice masters must care for the prayer of those in their charge.

Despite the generally practical tone of his instruction, Nadal, even at this early date, tersely presented a key principle on Jesuit prayer he would develop in a theological way in the years ahead. He taught Jesuits to look beyond themselves to others in their prayer: the quest for peace in Europe, the needs of the Church, the campaigns against the Turks, and Ignatius and the other Jesuits in Rome. He urged them to keep in mind the two Jesuit colleges in Sicily, the city of Messina and its government, and the Society's benefactors. The personal grace he suggested they ask for themselves was an increase in their hearts of the spirit of Christ and of the Society of Jesus.[12]

In this instruction and in his *Orationis observationes,* Nadal gave early intimations he was moving toward a doctrine that would have Jesuits' prayer resonate with apostolic work and action. To the Jesuits of the Messina College he suggested the contours of a Jesuit at work. "Let each of us hold that pure disposition of love by which, with singleminded simplicity, we make our quest in all things the glory of God. That disposition of love should color and form all our virtues. There should follow from this a definite result: even as we live these virtues, the disposition of love will reign sweetly and strongly [*suaviter et fortiter*] within us." He summarized his thought with a thud: Meditation and contemplation in Jesuits' lives, unless they live "in action and the doing of God's will," are destined to die.[13] Here was an early hint of his capacity for judgments curt and flinty.

In mid-December Nadal learned that his assignment to Sicily was ending. He heard from Ignatius that he was to move to Trent in secret to replace Diego Laínez at the Council of Trent. Laínez was seriously ill and recommended Nadal as his replacement. Ignatius sent that order on November 29. Within a few weeks, on December 19 , he changed it. Nadal was to report to Rome, not Trent. Salmerón had warned Ignatius from Trent that a sick Laínez was of more value to the council than any two or three others who might be sent to cover for him. Ignatius informed Nadal that he wanted him in Rome for a month.[14]

Nadal acted rapidly on Ignatius' order. On January 6, 1552, he left Messina for Catania, sixty miles to the south, where Juan de Vega then was, to clear his departure with the viceroy. Vega did not give him immediate release but held him for three weeks to put into order some local projects: establishing control over a fund of 1000 gold crowns for the building of an orphanage; opening a hospital for persons with incurable diseases; collection of a fund for renovation of a Capuchin friary; distribution of 100 gold pieces to the poor. In the name of the Society, Nadal began negotiations for a college in Caltagirone. At the end of January Vega at last gave him leave to go to Rome. He asked Nadal to carry some letters to the Holy See and to present two requests to Ignatius: for his help as advocate with the pope on certain points of business and for his assurance that Nadal would be returned to Sicily. Nadal delayed his departure a bit so that he could celebrate in Catania the feastday on February 5 of the city's patron, St. Agatha. The next day he left for Rome.[15]

Nadal arrived in Rome on March 1, 1552. Ignatius put in his hands a copy of the Society's General Examen and Constitutions. This document was the culmination of almost three years of study and discussion by Ignatius and Polanco. By late 1550 they had revised and polished the primitive text (a) and composed what became known as Text A. Ignatius invited several Jesuits, including the Society's "cofounders," to a conference in Rome to review and criticize that text. A number, including Claude Jay and Francis Xavier, could not free themselves for the trip to Rome. About ten actually attended. Step by step, through January 1551 they perused the text with Ignatius and Polanco. Salmerón took the lead in suggesting changes, most of which Ignatius accepted. By the beginning of February 1551, the General Examen and the ten parts of the Constitutions were basically in place.[16]

Ten months later, however, a large gap suddenly appeared in that document. In December of 1551, after three years of experimentation, Ignatius made his broad and definite commitment of the Society to the formal education of laypeople, and thereby marked out a distinctive field of work about which the Constitutions said nothing. Faced with the need to make extensive additions to the Society's law, he turned to Nadal, as well as to others, for help in framing the new legislation.

Nadal stayed in Rome only two months. During that sojourn occurred a high point in his Jesuit life. On March 25, the feast of the Annunciation, he knelt before Ignatius and pronounced his final vows as a professed father of the Society of Jesus. While he was still in Sicily he had received approval from Ignatius to make his solemn profession, but he delayed this event until his return to Rome so that he could do so in the presence of Ignatius. Back in Rome, he made an unusual request. He had read in the Constitutions that only the professed fathers are members of the Society of Jesus in "the most precise meaning of this name." Feeling unfit to be accepted into that singular group, he asked Ignatius that he be excused from pronouncing the solemn vows of a professed father and be allowed rather to make the simple vows of a spiritual coadjutor. Ignatius declined. On March 25, therefore, Nadal became a member of the Society of Jesus "in the most precise meaning of this name."[17]

During his study of the Constitutions, Nadal heard the first whisperings of a vocation-within-a-vocation. As he studied that document, he felt the pull of a desire to give himself thoroughly to the understanding, under the tutelage of the Holy Spirit, of the Sacred Scriptures, those Constitutions, and the Society's Rules. He felt drawn to complete obedience to the Jesuit Institute. He called it a special kind of guidance, and he hoped to see it shine in his own person as a Jesuit doing Jesuit works. Those attracting forces persisted. One day he visited the chapel of Saint Sebastian in the Catacombs. As he prayed he felt distinctly called to be an exegete of the Institute of the Society of Jesus. Amid surges of assurance that this vocation, undertaken with the support of St. Peter and St. Paul, would help the Church, he wrote: "A certain person perceived that he could not possibly do anything more worthwhile than edit with utmost exactness the Constitutions and the Rules, and, with scholia, elucidate the Constitutions as well. A full-dress presentation of the Institute in its entirety, that is the objective."[18]

Nadal did not mention in his journals whether he told Ignatius of the strong stirrings within his heart. In mid-May, however, Ignatius gave him three directives that fitted into his vocation-within-a-vocation: return to Sicily and explain the Constitutions to the Jesuits there; write his own reflections on the Constitutions and send them to Rome; compose legislation for Jesuit colleges and universities designed for the education of the laity. To that threefold directive Ignatius added another, a touchy one Nadal was to execute in Naples on his way to Sicily.[19]

Six months earlier, Ignatius had dispatched ten scholastics of five nationalities to open a college in Naples. He appointed Fr. Andrés de Oviedo rector and Fr. Nicolás Bobadilla supervisor. Within weeks the venture was a mess. Oviedo and Bobadilla wrangled about the boundaries of their jurisdiction. In letter after letter, Ignatius tried to get the two men to work together. He sent long and detailed lists of practical instructions. Nevertheless, he failed to bring harmony between them. Things worsened as Bobadilla accused Oviedo of teaching Protestant doctrine. The Neapolitan people spread nasty rumors about the "ugly things" (*cose brutte*) that were happening at the Jesuit college. The duke of Monteleone, Ettore Pignatelli, informed Ignatius that Bobadilla "rubs his listeners the wrong way."[20] This was the tangle that Ignatius asked Nadal to undo. Nadal left Rome on May 18 or 19. At Naples he found the college and the residence in disarray. Few rules were observed. Bobadilla's characteristic freewheeling methods kept the enterprise off balance. Rebuff for his flamboyant *pronunciamentos* in Germany, even by Emperor Charles V, had not curbed the high spirits of this zealous, erratic, and intellectually limited Castilian. Reports circulated that he was showing an easy disdain for the authority of the Fathers of the Church, downgrading their teachings and proposing his own views. Nadal spoke candidly to Bobadilla. He appealed to the recently composed Constitutions, in which Ignatius had written: "Novel doctrines ought not to be admitted." A Jesuit who wants to hold an unusual doctrinal opinion, Nadal continued, should submit to whatever the Society determines in this area. Nadal counseled Bobadilla to stay with commonly accepted interpretations of scripture and theological tradition, and to stop advancing his personal opinions.

Polanco thought Nadal quite heroic: "Not without danger did Nadal fulfill [Ignatius' mandate]." Nadal failed, however, to bring harmony between Oviedo and Bobadilla, and about June 1 he left Naples for Messina. Easement came a few months later, when Ignatius appointed Alfonso Salmerón superior in Naples and directed Bobadilla to move into the wider area of the Neapolitan Kingdom as a free-lance preacher.[21] Relations between Nadal and Bobadilla, though, were seriously strained. Never again did they become friendly and at ease with each other. And some nasty incidents lay ahead.

Nadal arrived in Messina on June 10. Juan de Vega gave him an especially warm welcome, since Vega was seeking help for his daughter Isabel who was seriously depressed. Nadal knew this, because Ignatius had alerted him to Isabel's state, given him a letter to deliver to her, and instructed him to help the disconsolate young woman. Isabel's problem: she did not want to marry the man her father had picked for her. Vega, anxious to tighten his ties to Sicily, wanted Isabel to marry a Sicilian nobleman. He gave her a choice: the marquis of Gerace or the count of Luna; he himself preferred the latter. Isabel wanted neither. She became seriously ill. She spoke of entering a convent.

Nadal did two things. First he asked Fr. Cornelius Wischaven, who had guided so many students of Louvain to the religious life and the priesthood, to test the worth of Isabel's talk about becoming a nun. If his plan was to shake Isabel from that objective, he chose the right agent. Wischaven called on Isabel. Exuberantly he depicted the beauty of religious life. So exaggerated was his praise of nuns and their life that she laughed outright at his descriptions. She was apparently so repelled by his sugary words that she abandoned all talk of entering religious life and eventually dismissed the possibility with scorn. And second, Nadal delivered Ignatius' letter to Isabel.

In this letter Ignatius repeated what he had written several times with affection but with firmness: obey your father. Isabel yielded—for a time. Then she swung to gloomy indecision and again wrote to Ignatius. This time Ignatius did not answer her directly, but sent her a laconic message through Nadal. "It strikes me," he told Nadal, "that I would be acting improperly toward her father, if I should again write directly to Doña Isabel." Nadal delivered this curt rebuff. She finally did what Ignatius told her to do: she obeyed her father and married the Count of Luna. The marriage was a happy one.[22]

Nadal remained in Sicily eight months. At Messina and Palermo he gave conferences to the Jesuit communities on the Society's Constitutions. He presented Ignatius' statements on the Society's purpose, its way of life, its juridical structure, its ministries, its characteristic virtues, its stress on union of mind and heart among Jesuits. The practical operations of college and residence he brought into accord with the Constitutions. That document was to be their norm of policy. As he went about his task, he jotted his reflections on the throes of practical implementation and sent them to Ignatius.[23]

The most tangible literary memorial of Nadal's second visit to Sicily is thirty pages of the *Monumenta paedagogica Societatis Iesu.* It was his response to Ignatius' request for suggested legislation on the Society's colleges and universities to be inserted into the Constitutions. In this work, which he called *De studii generalis dispositione et ordine* ("A University or a Studium Generale"), he divided classes, outlined subject matter, scheduled disputations and repetitions, dictated literary pieces to be memorized, composed programs in Greek, Latin, Hebrew, and Near Eastern languages, set down syllabi for mathematics and astronomy, philosophy and theology, scripture and moral questions. In a separate section he drew an especially detailed study of the office of rector. He described the rector's responsibilities, his mode of governance, his guidance of teachers and students, his supervision of examinations. In another section he described the degrees that would be granted by a Jesuit university.

This was the document Ignatius was especially eager to have. From it and others, such as the one composed by Fr. Martín de Olave, prefect of studies at the Roman College, he extracted the material for eight additional chapters he inserted into Part IV of the Constitutions. Chapter 17, "The Officials or Ministers of the University," bore an especially strong nadalian imprint. This chapter opened with a general statement on the post of rector and closed with the distinctive insignia to be worn by the rector, the chancellor, and the beadle.[24]

Nadal's return to Sicily could not be kept secret. Although Ignatius sent him to work primarily with the two Jesuit colleges, other persons, including the viceroy, bishops, and paupers sought his help. Through his correspondence from that period streams a torrent of details about his labor among the people of the island. In Messina he enlisted aid for a credit bank (*mons pietatis*); in Trapani he found a better endowment for the home for prostitutes he had opened a year earlier; in Palermo he begged and bought the freedom of people in jail for unpaid debts, more than fifty at Christmas in 1552. Also in Palermo he arranged that some families take under their care about twenty paupers, and he obtained daily nursing care for a dozen grievously sick and poor persons; in Catania and Caltagirone he set up two orphanages and arranged for their funding.[25]

The success of the colleges at Messina and Palermo whetted the desires of many Sicilians for more Jesuit institutes. Glowing stories about the college founded by Ignatius in Rome for the education of young Germans for the diocesan clergy[26] moved some to approach Nadal with the suggestion that he open colleges for the education of secular clergy in Palermo and Messina. He resisted all their invitations with the explanation that there was a dearth of human resources in the Society and that the two colleges in Sicily must sink their roots more deeply before there could be expansion.[27]

As during his first visit to Sicily, Nadal's correspondence makes repeated mention of Juan de Vega. The influence of the

Spanish civil power continued to permeate the Jesuit enterprise. Nadal knew well that any opposition from the viceroy could hamper the Society's ministries. To Ignatius he wrote: "I shall put my mind to the task of adjusting rectors' styles of governance in our [Sicilian] colleges to the Constitutions if the viceroy does not give me too much to do at court."[28]

Yet Nadal did more than simply strive to maintain the viceroy's goodwill: he actively sought Vega's assistance even in internal problems of the Society. In Messina, Nadal wanted the novices to wear long habits, but he feared a loud outcry from their fathers, repelled by the sight of their sons in clerical garb so blatant. He therefore withheld the order until Vega visited Messina. Nadal banked on the viceregal presence as a restraint on parental anger. The strategy worked. Only one gentleman, the father of Carlo Faraone, gave a howl. Nadal wrote Ignatius: "However, I spoke with him. He's content."[29] One wonders what role Vega played in the quelling.

The arrival of Jerónimo Doménech from Spain toward the end of 1552 adumbrated Nadal's approaching departure. After a brief visit to Rome for consultation with Ignatius, Doménech was appointed provincial of the newly created province of Sicily. Nadal suggested to Ignatius that Doménech's return to Sicily would, with the good grace of the viceroy, free Nadal for another assignment. If this were the wish of Ignatius, Nadal suggested that he act quickly, since it was anticipated that the Turks would move against the island within a few months. On January 21, 1553, Ignatius dispatched an order for Nadal to return to Rome.[30] In early March Nadal left Sicily, never to return to this proving ground of his abilities as a superior, teacher, organizer, educator, army chaplain, and exegete of the Society's Constitutions.

So ended Nadal's first extra-Roman assignment, save for the first months of 1552. It showed Nadal that Jesuit life could be untidy. Taking an enterprise with little or no special preparation was to be expected: opening a university, writing curricula and academic programs, serving as military chaplain, organizing a fund-raising drive. From those unexpected quarters came invitations to action. Nadal and his community received on-the-spot training in the practical implications of Jesuit vocation. A Jesuit had to be ready; his life was not going to be comfortable or quiet.

Nadal drew a more ample and extended self-portrait as a man of action and enterprise, a man of organizing powers and mastery of details, a juggler of many things. In Sicily he sketched in very broad lines his thoughts on prayer in the Society, a quite unspectacular beginning of an impressive achievement. Even then he had one of his key ideas: Jesuit prayer stretched to include others and their needs. His apostolic instinct was there from the beginning.

In educational ventures, Nadal left a number of loose ends. A vexing question was left over the Jesuit presence in Sicily: the extent to which Jesuits became dependent on the political structure of the island, and the extent to which the political powers of the island took the Society for granted as an instrument of their authority. Nadal was leaving a laboratory cluttered with tools, matériel, and designs; for Messina had been a testing area, where the Society had its first school designed primarily for lay students. There were regulations, religious and academic, first designed by Nadal and then amplified by Coudret. There was collision with the local independence of Messina's senators and disillusion brought on by bargaining with them; there was a reliance on Spanish authority so resented in Sicily; there was a spiritual dynamism that radiated from the college community through the city; there was a prospect of the college's becoming fertile soil for vocations to the Society.

During that period of experimentation, Nadal, for all his budding managerial skills, had a narrow view of the political realities with which he had to deal. A Spaniard, he did not appreciate the Sicilians' resentment of Spanish dominion. He was even naive enough to wonder at the anti-Spanish feeling. He consistently sided with Vega despite Vega's obtuse cruelty. He did not stand back from the "laboratory" to make a searching critique of the experiment. He did not provide a penetrating analysis of the implications of the Society's alliance with political power, be it a city council or an aristocracy or a monarchy. Jesuit dedication to the ideal of educating youth free of charge forced the Society into a dependence on those who could carry the inevitable expenses.

There were at least two inherent dangers for the Society as a whole that Nadal did not perceive. The first danger was the loss of freedom. The Jesuit ideal as embodied in a college needed legal protection. But legal protection carried the potential for legal tyranny; the ghost of secular interference lurked in the wings. Ahead lay many legal battles by the Society to retain its freedom. They would be wearing, and often the secular authority won the last round. Because Nadal was, in this case, unable to rise above the particular to the general, he did not foresee the broad implications of his procedure for the Society as a whole.

The second danger was identification of the Society with the rulers and the powerful of Europe. Nadal never did catch the full damaging implications of his close association with Juan de Vega. Despite his acceptance by many people in Messina, in the eyes of others, Nadal stood shoulder to shoulder with the highest—and must abhorred—power in Sicily. This image foreshadowed similar images in the Society's future. Often the legal wrangling between the Society and a powerful benefactor could be annoying, but the colleges stood before the populace as the symbol (and often the reality) of close ties between the Society and a powerful layperson. This peril Nadal did not foresee; for him, it was a necessary pact with the social texture of the century. Here again Nadal did not recognize the under-vibrations of his own special experience in Messina.

7

Dispelling the Darkness
of Ignorance

*In short order everything in Portugal seems to have
been put back into the normal channels. The entire
affair has been more of a wholesome purge than a
damaging blow. So it strikes me. Glory to God.*

Nadal in his *Ephemerides*, 1554

Nadal arrived in Rome on April 3. On April 10, Ignatius gave
him a document naming him general's delegate (*commissarius*)
of the Society in Portugal and Spain, and investing him with all
the authority the pope had given Ignatius as general superior.
Ignatius further advised Nadal that he enjoyed full power to
make changes "according to our mind, which you know." The
Jesuits of the Iberian peninsula, he insisted, were to obey Nadal
as they would obey himself. The next day Nadal was traveling
north to Genoa, where he would await a ship to Spain.[1]

Fr. Juan de Polanco prepared for Nadal's coming. He wrote
ahead to tell Fr. Diego Mirón, the provincial of Portugal, to
expect a man of acute speculative and practical judgment, of
courage in starting major enterprises, of intense vitality in getting
things done. "He knows our Fr. Ignatius very well, since he has
had extensive dealings with him. I think that he has grasped and
penetrated the Society's Institute better than any other I know
in the Society." Polanco explained to Mirón that Nadal's mis-

sion had a twofold objective: first, to organize the schools, and second, to promulgate the Society's Constitutions. Under each heading, continued Polanco, Nadal had special qualifications: his experience in organizing the two colleges in Sicily, the best-run in the entire Society; his sound understanding of Ignatius' aim for the Society of Jesus.[2]

Ignatius sent Nadal with this marked urgency because the Portuguese province was in distress. He wanted to go there himself, but sickness made this impossible. Fr. Miguel de Torres, whom Ignatius had dispatched to Portugal the year before as visitor, diagnosed the province's problem: each man was mapping out his own route, was fostering his own pet enterprise. Too few were faithful to the Jesuit way of life.[3]

For seven years the central figure amid the disarray of the province was Fr. Simão Rodrigues, one of Ignatius' first companions in the founding of the Society of Jesus. In 1546 Ignatius appointed him the first superior of the new province of Portugal. In that fast-growing province, ninety-five scholastics were then studying at the University of Coimbra. Pierre Favre, one of the first to detect something awry in Rodrigues's style of governance, noted his failure to give firm guidance and instruction to young men in the Society: he allowed them, for example, to perform exotic forms of penance. This freedom spread into all areas of the province's life: scholastics sassed superiors, sought invitations to stylish dinners, insinuated themselves into nooks of the nobility, acquired knickknacks that promoted delicate living. Rodrigues set the style by hobnobbing with the nobility and by absorption in the goings-on at the court.[4]

Ignatius, made aware of this state of affairs, removed Rodrigues from office, replaced him with Fr. Diego Mirón, and sent Fr. Miguel de Torres as a visitor to help Mirón set the province aright. To ease Rodrigues's embarrassment, Ignatius appointed him provincial of the recently established province of Aragon. Rodrigues refused to go. He spread stories about Ignatius—that he used the wealth of Francis Borgia to enrich the Loyolas, sent the dregs of the Society to Portugal, skimmed off the cream of Portuguese talent for use in other nations. Ignatius, calling on the solemnity of Rodrigues's vow of obedience, ordered him to Aragon. Rodrigues obeyed.

After some months, however, he left his post without permission, returned to Lisbon, and took up his residence at the home of the duke of Aveiro. Fr. de Torres ordered him to return to

Aragon. He refused to go. On July 24, 1553, Ignatius wrote to Fr. Diego Mirón about Rodrigues's refusal to obey Ignatius' command to go to Rome: "Tell Master Simão that you have the authority, if he remains obdurate in his disobedience, to dismiss him from the Society. Tell him that he is being dismissed as an obdurately and incurably disobedient man who is inflicting hurt on the entire Society."[5] Fr. Mirón, his successor in the post of Portuguese provincial, ordered Rodrigues to talk with Ignatius. Rodrigues finally yielded, and on June 26, a few weeks before Nadal arrived in Lisbon, left for Rome.[6]

During those exchanges between Rodrigues, Mirón, and Torres, members of the province took sides. Some backed Rodrigues; others approved Ignatius' decision to move him. During late 1552 and early 1553, Torres interviewed each of the province's 135 men. He gave each a choice: attest his loyalty to Ignatius or leave the Society. Thirty-three either were dismissed or left of their own accord. Several who remained were confused and troubled in spirit. Too many had been bruised in this nasty tangle for peace to descend on the province immediately. That was the crisis that awaited Nadal.[7]

On April 18, seven days after he left Rome, Nadal boarded a ship at Genoa and sailed with a fleet for Barcelona. Storms forced them to seek haven at Nice for two days. Nadal suffered seasickness. On May 5, seventeen days out of Genoa, the fleet reached Barcelona. From that city Nadal wrote to Ignatius: "I have stopped here eleven days, four or five more than I intended." That short sentence summarized the story of his trip across Spain to Portugal: delay after delay as he was asked by Spanish Jesuits to unravel their difficulties.

In Barcelona, for example, he met six Jesuits, four priests who were doing pastoral work and two scholastics who were studying at the university. They were snarled in a legal tangle with the local parish of Santa Maria del Pi because they wanted to build a small church. The parish objected, resting its case on a royal decree, granted in 1300 by King Pedro of Aragon, which forbade the building of a new church or monastery within either the old or new walls of Barcelona. The governor of Catalonia, Dom Pedro de Cardona, who worshiped at Santa Maria del Pi, backed the parish. Nadal, with the support of the bishop, Jaime de Cazador, founded the Society's case on a recent rescript from the Holy See granting it permission to build a church. Lawyers were invited to the discussions. The

Cities in Spain and Portugal visited by Nadal

break came when the governor recognized in this instance the higher authority of the Holy See. Through it all Nadal counseled his fellow Jesuits to maintain courtesy and restraint. He set an example and received an invitation to preach at Santa Maria del Pi. His sermon did not impress his hearers. "Very learned," they said, "but hardly elegant."

With that bit of litigation behind him, Nadal started the journey across Spain. Through May, June, and early July he made his way by fits and starts through Valencia, Cuenca, Alcalá, and Madrid. On July 7 he arrived in Lisbon.[8] Gratifying news awaited him there. Less than two weeks earlier, on June 26, Rodrigues, prodded by Fr. Mirón, had finally left Lisbon for Rome. With him traveled Fr. Melchior Carneiro, whom Mirón appointed to be not only his companion but his superior as well. Nadal had avoided the embarrassment of a confrontation with Rodrigues.

His gratification, though, did not last long. Word came from Rodrigues's brother that Rodrigues was returning to Lisbon. And so he was. Somewhere on the road he heard that Nadal had come to Portugal, and Rodrigues promptly decided to return and present his side of the story. Nadal acted just as promptly to send word that under no circumstances was he to come back, since Nadal had no intention of becoming involved in Rodrigues's personal problems. He also wrote to Carneiro: "You are to give him the letter I have addressed to him. If he does not yield and continue to Rome, but insists on coming back here, you are to order him for me, in virtue of his vow of holy obedience, to continue to Rome." Again, Rodrigues obeyed in virtue of his vow.[9]

Nadal opened his visitation at the college of São Antoão in Lisbon, where a dozen Jesuits were teaching about three hundred and thirty youths. His tools were an abridged copy of the Society's Constitutions—two months later he received a complete copy by mail from Rome—and a list of fifty-one rules known as Common Rules, which guided such details of Jesuit life as demeanor at table and conduct outside the house, all based more or less on the discipline at the Roman College. He organized a procedure of several steps: each day for an hour he gave a conference on the Constitutions and the Common Rules; he heard the general confession of each man; in confidence he sought from each information about defects of others; he admonished each about the defects that others noted in him.[10]

Fr. Miguel de Torres was impressed. He admired not only Nadal's conceptual grasp of the Constitutions but also the warm affection he had for the spirit that animated them. "All of us are consoled by what we are learning about the Constitutions, especially as it comes from the living voice of Fr. Nadal. . . . Just to call attention to the Society's spirit is not enough. It has to be done by one who himself has imbibed that spirit and can tell others about it with authority." Torres thought the tide was beginning to turn. Ignorance of the Jesuit way of life was lifting, a void was being filled, the ideal of the Jesuit vocation was being purified. He called Nadal's talks "a crying need here." He asked Ignatius that Nadal be left there for years to come.[11]

Nadal was in Lisbon only a week when he sensed a change. Elated by the warm and friendly welcome that greeted him, he perceived a strong desire to know more about the Society. What the community seemed to enjoy most were the tidbits of news and the stories he related about Ignatius and other Jesuits in Rome, and about the Society's expansion. He was their living contact with the Society's founder and his designs. "So intense has been the joy, delight, and devotion of the Jesuits in Lisbon in hearing my exposition of the Constitutions that I feel the Society in Portugal has entered a renewal of spirit."[12]

More than the interior spirit of the Jesuit staff of São Antoão concerned Nadal. He had the solidity of the financial foundation of the college to worry about, and he spoke to King João about that. The monarch advised him to appear before the municipal government and present his needs. He did that on July 22, 1553, describing the Jesuit colleges in Sicily and offering to staff a college in Lisbon of three classes in grammar, one in humanities, and one in rhetoric, as well as classes in Greek, Hebrew, and moral theology, provided the city would guarantee an adequate endowment. The city did so. King João gave assurance of his personal support, as did several wealthy Lisboans.[13]

After little more than a month in Lisbon, Nadal left on August 16 for Évora, where a college was aborning. A few years earlier, the king's younger brother Henry, cardinal archbishop of Évora, had asked Simão Rodrigues to accept the new college he was planning to build at Évora. Nadal arrived as the structure was nearing completion. He found a building "very large and lavish in its marble work. There is a notably big fountain with fresh water; there is ample property for growing a kitchen garden, four times as large, I think, as the one we have in Rome." In Ignatius' name he accepted the college. With the cardinal he arranged for a modest beginning of three classes in humane letters and one in moral theology, taught by four Jesuits. Guided by his experience in Sicily, he put on the college "the Italian stamp (*al modo de Italia*)." On August 28 he attended the formal opening of classes, at which Fr. Pedro Jean Perpinyà gave a stirring address. Within the community he explained the Constitutions and Common Rules, interviewed each, and heard their general confessions. On September 4, after sixteen days at Évora, he returned to Lisbon.[14]

The Society's college at the University of Coimbra, its largest in Portugal, remained to be visited. For a full month, however, Nadal delayed the long trip to the north because an event of unusual importance held him in Lisbon. On October 1 he formally opened a professed house at the Jesuit church of São Roque, separate from the College of São Antoão. To add to the pomp of the splendid ceremony, he had at hand one of the ecclesiastical wonders of the day, a former Spanish grandee in the habit of a Jesuit. King João had earlier written Fr. Francis Borgia, former duke of Gandía and viceroy of Catalonia, inviting him to visit the Portuguese court. Borgia, who was then in Spain preaching and explaining the nature of the Society of Jesus to the nobility and aristocracy, accepted the invitation and arrived in Lisbon on August 31 while Nadal was still at Évora. King João and his court gave Borgia a warm welcome, delivering each day at the college of São Antoão cakes and delicacies for the celebrated guest. When Borgia bumped his head on a lintel, the court's finest doctors were promptly dispatched to care for him.[15]

Nadal gave Borgia a prominent place in the ceremony of October 1 at São Roque. King João was present, as were the archbishop and the leading courtiers. Nadal celebrated the Mass, and Borgia delivered an ardent sermon. At the Communion of the Mass, Nadal received the solemn vows of three professed fathers, the final simple vows of two priests and three brothers, the first vows of two novices, and he invested two postulants with the religious habit. During this part of the ceremony, Borgia knelt near the king and in a low voice explained the meaning of the vows in the Society of Jesus. Exultation was high. Jesuits wept. Noblemen wept. The event turned into a lucid lesson to the laity on what the Society of Jesus was about, as well as a clear call to the Jesuits themselves to understand afresh their vocation. Thus did Nadal intend it to be.[16†]

More quietly and without fanfare, Nadal followed still another tack in trying to heal the wounds of the province. He approached the men who, in their loyalty to Simão Rodrigues, had left the Society. He spoke kindly, yet candidly, trying to show them the justice of their dismissal by Fr. de Torres but refusing to rehash their old grievances. "I told them," he wrote Ignatius, "that I did not want to hear their special pleadings. I simply said that, if they wanted to return to the Society, I would pursue the matter further with them." He offered to send them to Rome if they were willing to adjust to the Jesuit way of life. None accepted. In his report to Ignatius, he recounted his special solicitude for the four who had been the ringleaders of the pro-Rodrigues movement, Antonio Brandón, Melchior Luis, Alfonso Télez, and Miguel Gomes. He told them "that the Society will treat them as God treats all men, overlooking their faults and failures, and remembering all the good things they had achieved." They showed little interest, and in fact moved their own program a step further. Under Brandón they planned a new and separate Society of Jesus. Brandón even went to Rome. There he became lost in the maze of Roman history and disappeared; with him dissolved the idea of a new Society of Jesus.[17]

On October 5 Borgia left for Andalusia in Spain. Nadal went north to Coimbra, where he met a community of about seventy men in the Jesuit college, situated in a hilly and lovely section of the city called da Ribela. Eleven years earlier, Francis Xavier, during his year's wait in Portugal before a fleet sailed for the Indies, had become convinced that the University of Coimbra would make an excellent center for the intellectual training of Jesuit scholastics. To obtain financial security for a college at the university, Xavier won the assurance of King João that the project had his support. Now, eleven months after Xavier's death in the Far East, Nadal arrived to visit his legacy. He found a community badly bruised by the conflicts that had centered on Simão Rodrigues. Numbers had dropped fifty percent in

---

†16 Astráin, *Historia*, 1:634–35. Nadal recalled one negative aspect of the highly charged occasion. Yielding to the importunate requests of the Jesuits present, he gave a sermon. He said it fell flat and was roundly criticized. This was an early indication of a theme that would recur: Nadal's lack of talent as a pulpit orator. *Mon Nad*, II:18.

seven years. A mere handful of young men entered the novitiate. In 1552 there were only four novices. The next year there
were ten. That same year, amid the shambles of Xavier's hopes,
there arrived Ignatius' strong letter of March 26, 1553, on the
virtue of obedience and its role in Jesuit life. Nadal followed the
letter by about six months. As the visitation proceeded, he
noted a sense of contentment and unity settling on the community. Apart from the community he set up a house as the
novitiate. The next year eighteen novices entered.[18]

Before Nadal finished his task in Coimbra, other business
called him elsewhere. In late October he took on what would
prove to be a wild-goose chase, a futile round trip of almost
four hundred miles to Santiago de Compostela, the city of
Spain's greatest shrine, in northwest León. A wealthy gentleman, recently deceased, had provided in his will for the foundation of a college there. The Dominican archbishop of
Santiago, Juan Álvarez de Toledo, asked Ignatius to accept
responsibility for it. An influential member of the local aristocracy, Alonso de Acevedo y Zúñiga, count of Monterrey, backed
the plan to bring the Society of Jesus to Santiago. Nadal arrived
in Santiago on November 2 at a most inopportune time, since
neither the archbishop nor the count was at home. He therefore
had to deal with the city government alone. The town fathers
assured him they would gladly welcome the Jesuits to teach in
the university they hoped to open—but on their terms. They
insisted that the city retain control of the institution, and they
spelled out explicitly what this meant in practice: the Jesuits
would hold their posts or be dismissed at the pleasure of the
city. The canons of the cathedral chapter supported the city.
Prodded perhaps by memories of Messina's senators, Nadal
rejected the city's offer, left Santiago after only a day and a
half, and turned back to Coimbra.[19]

There, Nadal spent eight days in conferences on Jesuit life,
receiving the vows of scholastics in a ceremony of religious
renewal, and answering questions presented by the community.
When he left Coimbra, he intended to move quickly by way of
Lisbon to Spain, in order to open his visitation there. For twenty
unpleasant days, however, he was held captive in Lisbon; the
one who tied him there was a nobleman but also a Jesuit and
somewhat of a brat.[20]

Teotonio da Braganza was a brother of the duke of Braganza,
head of Portugal's most prestigious house after the royal family.

When a student, aged nineteen, at the University of Coimbra, Teotonio left his college, climbed the wall, and found refuge in the Jesuit house. He wanted to be a Jesuit. Despite royal commands and emotional pleadings to return home, Teotonio held out. For three years he was a fervent and mortified Jesuit. At Salamanca and Alcalá he pursued his university studies. Then he began to identify with the faction that backed Simão Rodrigues. Ignatius, anxious to save his vocation, summoned him to Rome. On his way, Teotonio received at least one letter from Rodrigues, venting his anger against Torres and Mirón. At Barcelona he wondered whether he should return to Portugal to continue the fight for Rodrigues. Teotonio then became ill, and doctors advised him to return home.

When Teotonio arrived in Portugal he was indeed very sick and had to be carried by a stretcher to the home of his mother and his elder brother in Vila Viçosa, twenty miles from Évora. He wrote Nadal, asking that he be allowed to recuperate there. Nadal agreed and sent a Jesuit to be a companion. By late October or early November—Nadal was in Coimbra—Teotonio felt well enough to travel to Lisbon. Three days or more he spent with Fr. Antonio Brandón, Fr. Melchior Luis, and others of the dismissed group. Ignoring his doctor's orders, he took residence in a Dominican convent at Benfica, a league outside Lisbon.[21]

When Nadal arrived in Lisbon from Coimbra in December, he persuaded Teotonio to move to the Jesuit college. There, Teotonio spoke straightforwardly to Nadal, the rector, and other priests of São Antoão: he charged that Simão Rodrigues had been treated badly; he asserted that he had no obligation to concur in the attitudes of the Society; he announced that his obligations to the Society stopped with his doing what he was told to do. For three weeks Nadal tried to bring him to a better frame of mind. He failed. The local superiors gave Nadal some hard advice: Teotonio had no place in a Jesuit community.[22]

The story of this confrontation did not remain behind Jesuit walls. Not only did the Braganza brothers and sisters put forward their solutions, so did the king, and, ultimately, it was the regal plan that was followed. Teotonio was told to go to Vila Viçosa and reside with his mother and his elder brother. Should he feel disposed to study, he would have at hand Fr. Mauricio Serpe, whom Nadal had assigned to be his tutor. On December 13 Nadal wrote to Ignatius, "Tomorrow, without fail, we shall, with the Lord's help, leave. Staying in Lisbon these twenty days has been a great hardship—and all because of Don Teotonio." In a report to Ignatius on the Portuguese province, which fills nineteen pages of the *Monumenta Historica Societatis Iesu,* Nadal gave seven to the twenty-three-year-old Teotonio. In the next two years, the "tragedy of Don Teotonio," to use Nadal's descriptive phrase, broke all bounds and made Nadal's limited experience with the man seem tame.[23]

Teotonio finally reached Rome on October 14, 1554, after stopping at Venice to see Simão Rodrigues, who was then planning, in his restless way, a pilgrimage to Jerusalem. This meeting was the last thing Ignatius wanted, and it took three letters from the general to get Teotonio away from Rodrigues and on to Rome. Once in Rome, Teotonio complained about the difficulty of studies, occupied two rooms in the infirmary, demanded permission to get away from Rome for two weeks at a time, required organ music to settle his nerves, left the house whenever he chose, and once, in a rage, hit one servant in the Jesuit house and bloodied the eye of another. Ignatius finally abandoned hope of changing Teotonio and concluded that he must be dismissed from the Society. But Ignatius, ever the diplomat, left the final decision to dismiss or not dismiss Teotonio to King João. "For your Highness is not only King and Lord, but the Father of this lowly company." King João agreed with Ignatius that Teotonio should go. On September 9, 1555, Loyola wrote to Fr. Diego Mirón that God had relieved the Society of a great burden with the dismissal of this troublemaker. Ignatius later discovered more information about Teotonio's Roman days that confirmed the dismissal: the aristocrat had a bank account and kept two servants to take care of his mail! Although several members of the Braganza family harbored resentment toward the Society because of Teotonio's dismissal, he himself did not suffer. Years later he became archbishop of Évora.[24]

When he left Lisbon for Spain on December 14, Nadal carried much more than the dismal memory of Teotonio's tantrums. With pleasure he recalled explicitly the cordial reception that the other hundred Jesuits gave his conferences as they put the past behind them and lived in the present. "Little by little things are falling into place," he told Ignatius. In his diary he wrote: "In short order everything in Portugal seems to have been put back into normal channels. The entire affair has been more of a wholesome purge than a damaging blow. So it strikes me. Glory to God." The rector of the Lisbon college, Fr. Inácio de Azevedo, remarked on the intimate grasp Nadal had of the Society's Institute, a grasp embedded deeply in his own spirit. He admired the clarity, the energy, the prudence with which Nadal arranged affairs in the communities. He told Ignatius, "He [Nadal] seems to me to have been handpicked by Our Savior to achieve what you sent him to do."[25]

The Portuguese story taught two powerful lessons. The first was that the Spiritual Exercises alone do not the Jesuit make. Another ingredient was essential: a sure understanding of the Society's Constitutions. Some one hundred and thirty Jesuits in Portugal had made the Spiritual Exercises but did not know the Constitutions, and, as Fr. Miguel de Torres observed, each was mapping his own route. This ignorance was what Nadal wiped out, and he gave the province a sense of its corporate identity to replace the incoherent individualism that had been in possession of the province. The second lesson taught by the events in Portugal concerned aristocratic restraint on the Society's freedom.

Because of his breeding, Ignatius had a basic esteem, even preference, for the highest class of society, a common prejudice in sixteenth-century Europe. This partiality even colored the Constitutions. In his legislation regarding the qualifications needed for admission into the Society, Ignatius listed "the extrinsic gifts of nobility, wealth, and reputation" as making an otherwise worthy applicant even more fit "to the extent that they aid toward edification." Ignatius continued: "The more an applicant is distinguished for those qualifications, the more suitable will he be for this Society unto the glory of God our Lord, and the less he is distinguished by them, the less suitable."[26] Later in the Constitutions, in his description of the qualities that should mark the superior general, Ignatius again showed his leaning toward the nobility. Even though he identified nobility, reputation, and a background of wealth as extrinsic endowments, he legislated that "other things being equal, these are worthy of some consideration."[27] His deference toward King João and the Braganzas showed this deep respect. Neither Ignatius nor Nadal, however, apparently realized the danger inherent in their yielding to the king the decision about Teotonio. They gave up a decision that rightly belonged in their hands alone: the erratic Teotonio deserved prompt dismissal from the Society. Hovering over the prince, however, were aristocratic benefactors whose wishes could not be ignored. By permitting the nobles a say in the internal affairs of the Society, Nadal and Ignatius tied cords about their freedom.

After ten days of travel, Nadal arrived in Córdoba on Christmas Eve of 1553. During a month's stay there, two influential people in southern Spain forced him to define his thinking on one of the most troubling social and religious problems of the day. Catalina Fernández de Córdoba, marchioness of Priego and countess of Feria, a generous benefactor of the Society, a relative of Fr. Francis Borgia, and one of the most powerful women in the Spanish aristocracy, asked the Jesuits in Córdoba to refuse to accept into their ranks men of Jewish and Moorish ancestry. On the other hand, Fr. Juan de Ávila, a secular priest known throughout Andalusia for his zeal and devotion, and today a blessed on the Church's calendar, upbraided the Society for excluding men of Jewish and Moorish descent. These conflicting attitudes tossed Nadal into the turbulent crosscurrents of the national controversy on *limpieza de sangre* (purity of blood).

Through the second half of the fifteenth century, as the number grew of Jews in Spain who were baptized, often under pressure, the feeling mounted that the New Christians were somehow tainted. In 1449, a statute that restricted the social life of Jewish converts became the first of many such statutes. A century later, in 1547, the archbishop of Toledo enacted a series of legal measures that excluded descendants of Jews and Moors from offices in the Church. The next year, Pope Paul III ratified that legislation, and in 1555 Pope Paul IV did the same. King Philip II gave his confirmation in the following year. Official church policy had step by step been firmly established against the New Christians, a term meant to designate Catholics of Jewish and Moorish blood. It in fact affected Christian Jews more than Christian Moors, since Jews were usually an urban, mercantile, and educated people, while Moors were generally rural, agricultural, and less educated.[28]

Most religious orders followed suit. In 1491 the Hieronymites forbade acceptance of New Christians into their order; in 1496 the Dominicans in Ávila did the same, followed in 1531 by their fellow Dominicans in Toledo. The Franciscan Conventuals joined the trend in 1525. Because of insistent requests by the marchioness of Priego that the Jesuits in Córdoba adopt the same policy, Nadal had to decide: would he buck the tide in the Spanish church and deny the marchioness her requests?[29]

When he arrived in Córdoba, Nadal found Francis Borgia— still on his free-lance assignment to explain the Society of Jesus to the Spanish aristocracy—organizing with a few other Jesuits a college situated in a handsome residence, the gift of Don Juan de Córdoba, a wealthy priest attached to the city's cathedral. An early decision Nadal had to make was the choice of a rector of the new community. After he had discussed the matter with Borgia, he picked Antonio de Córdoba, a secular priest who was a novice and the son of the marchioness of Priego.[30]† A canon of the cathedral of Córdoba at twelve and, at the age of twenty-five, appointed a cardinal *in petto* by Pope Julius III, Antonio abandoned a promising ecclesiastical career for the Society. As Nadal explained to Ignatius, in his decision he considered the special circumstances that attended the college's opening as well as the business details to be ironed out. Nadal was aware of the presence of Don Antonio's mother, but he made it clear to Ignatius that she had not sought to have her son appointed rector; nor had the main donor of the college. Besides, according to Nadal, the novice grasped the meaning of the Jesuit way of life. Before Nadal left Córdoba, he received the first vows of the rector.[31]†

---

†30 Promising as Antonio was, his appointment brought Nadal face to face with a vexing problem that he would deal with many times in Spain: the shallow reservoir of experienced Jesuits. Not all the inexperienced rectors had the admirable characteristics of Antonio, and their tenure often ended unhappily. Francisco de Rojas was rector of Zaragoza. A Castilian, Rojas knew Ignatius and his companions as early as 1538 in Rome. He seems to have joined the Society around 1540. He was ordained in 1544 with little or no theology. In 1547 Ignatius appointed him rector of the new college in Zaragoza. During his visitation, Nadal noted Rojas's instability. He found him shaky in his vocation and flawed by "a streak of Spanish moodiness and pride." Rojas left the Society in 1556, two years after Nadal's visitation and diagnosis, because Ignatius refused to grant him the ardently desired solemn profession of four vows unless he devoted four years to theological study. See Georg Schurhammer, S.J., *Francis Xavier, His Life, His Times*, vol. 1, trans. M. Joseph Costelloe, S.J. (Rome, 1973), 447; *Mon Nad*, I:238; *Pol Chron*, III:347–48, 367.

†31 *Mon Nad*, I:223–24; Rahner, *Ignatius Letters*, 382–90. Antonio's brothers attained distinction. An older brother, Gómez Suárez de Figueroa, count (later duke) of Feria, became celebrated in the service of King Philip II as Spanish ambassador to the courts of Queens Mary and Elizabeth of England.

Even before Antonio became a Jesuit novice, however, the marchioness had made her mind clear on the issue of *limpieza de sangre:* the Jesuits in Córdoba must be free of tainted blood; the college must be socially acceptable to the Spanish aristocracy; the staff of the college must be as racially pure as the Viscayans in the faraway land of the Basques. She therefore insisted that no New Christians be admitted into the Society at Córdoba.[32†]

Nadal, however, was not lost on an uncharted sea. Ignatius had drawn a course for him to steer when certain Spanish Jesuits provoked him by opinions on the New Christians that matched those of the marchioness. Fr. Antonio Araoz,[33†] a favorite at the Spanish court, which he knew well, reflected the court's attitude in his emphatic opposition to the acceptance of New Christians into the Society. Fr. Diego Mirón, provincial of

---

A younger brother, Don Lorenzo Suárez de Figueroa, became a Dominican bishop of Sigüenza (Rahner, *Ignatius Letters*, 382–83).

†32 Rahner, *Ignatius Letters*, 382–90; *Pol Chron*, V:527. This emotional issue, aggravated by gossip, lingered long in Córdoba. On September 1, 1572, Fr. Juan Ramírez wrote to Fr. General Borgia, "More than 600 students attend our college in Córdoba. Among them are the sons of the noblemen of Córdoba, gentlemen of the utmost purity of blood. Many of them feel attracted to the religious life and to our Society, but, because of our sins [the acceptance of the New Christians], not one of them comes to us. All join the Dominicans at their convent of Saint Paul. The reason is this: the story among the nobility is that only Jews enter the Society. These are their words. San Paulo is the place for noblemen. This opinion is as strong as if it were built of lime and stone (*cal y canto*). So strong is this sentiment that if someone has the misfortune of entering the Society, he is regarded as having been garbed in a sanbenito" (Astráin, *Historia*, 3:591).

†33 Araoz, a native of Vergara and a nephew of Ignatius, was the first Jesuit to enter Spain after the Society was approved. He entered the Society in 1540 and pronounced his final vows on February 19, 1542, scarcely two years after his admission. From the beginning, Araoz received wide freedom from Ignatius to preach throughout Spain, a task that showed his gifts as a preacher. When he was not even seven years in the Society, and much of that time spent as a free-lance preacher, he was appointed the first provincial of Spain. Araoz became the darling of the Spanish court, and in his cultivation of those connections he neglected the government of the province. Despite Araoz's grave defects, Ignatius kept him in authority. Ignatius drew back from a possible offense to the Spanish court in the hope that Araoz would be a good connection at the center of the Spanish government. As we shall see, Araoz was another example of aristocratic connections leading to the corrosion of Jesuit ideals.

Portugal, echoed Araoz. Ignatius, however, instructed Araoz that the Society rejected *limpieza de sangre* as a norm to determine a man's qualification to be a Jesuit: he was not convinced "that the rejection of New Christians was to the service of God." Yet he moved carefully and pragmatically, recommending caution in the application of openness to the New Christians. Knowing the need of prudence among a people easily incensed and angered by any dissent from *limpieza de sangre,* he outlined for Araoz a moderate policy. "If [in Spain], because of the feelings of the court and the king, it seems unwise to admit New Christians there, send them here [to Rome]." Not disposed to launch an all-out crusade for his principle of non-discrimination, he advised prudence (*circumspección*), lest feelings of Spain's powerful be riled. No good could come from stirring a storm.[34]

In Córdoba Nadal followed a like course. He decided that any qualified New Christian who applied at Córdoba for acceptance into the Society was to be sent to Francis Borgia, wherever he might happen to be in Spain at the time, to determine the place of a novitiate. By this stratagem Nadal hoped to avoid offense to the marchioness and yet keep the door open to those local New Christians who desired to be Jesuits. Ignatius modified Nadal's plan a bit. He directed that not all New Christians of Córdoba who desired to enter the Society need be sent to Borgia. A few could be admitted at Córdoba, even if it irked the marchioness of Priego. He was willing to take that risk. Yet he did not wish to go too far. He cautioned Nadal to adapt the plan in a moderate and circumspect way in consideration of the marchioness's sensibilities. Ignatius was not interested in some uncompromising crusade for "pure" policy; he was seeking a practical adaptation to a sensitive situation. This decision eased entry into the community at Córdoba of some especially gifted New Christians, of whom Fr. Francisco Gómez, a distinguished preacher and professor of theology, was one.[35]

Even as he skirmished with the marchioness of Priego, Nadal came under fire about the New Christians from another quarter. The marchioness chided Nadal because the Society received New Christians; Fr. Juan de Ávila, the most influential spiritual leader in Andalusia, scolded him because the Society did *not* receive them. A secular priest of attractive personality and persuasive eloquence, Juan, during his growth in spiritual maturity, quietly drew about himself several other secular priests, to whom he imparted his aspiration to achieve in the sacerdotal life a harmony of work and prayer. Throughout Andalusia he opened fifteen schools, some of which developed into colleges. When he met the Jesuits, he recognized in them a mirror of his own ideals, and he became the best recruiter of Jesuit vocations in southern Spain.[36]

Nadal, struck by the likeness between Ávila's ideals and those of the Society, freely expressed his admiration of him. Ávila spoke to Nadal of the hope he had to form an association of priests whose way of life would resemble the Society's save for the vow of obedience and certain other obligations. This, however, he had not realized. He told Nadal, "I have been like a child who tries his utmost to push a stone up an incline and fails every time. Then along comes a man who with ease pushes the stone to the top. Fr. Ignatius is that man." Ávila had wished to enter the Society, but bad health and his need for specially prepared dishes ruled that out. Instead he turned his disciples to the Society. One of the best was Fr. Gaspar de Loarte, who became the most prolific of Jesuit writers on spiritual subjects in Italy in the last half of the sixteenth century. Loarte was a converted Jew.[37]

Ávila took a special interest in the New Christians, since he was one himself and had been harassed by the Inquisition. Apparently unaware of the position taken by Nadal at Córdoba, he charged the Society with a policy of excluding New Christians from its ranks. As evidence he offered certain statements of Antonio Araoz and Diego Mirón. He rebuked Nadal to his face. Nadal, never supine, straightforwardly told Ávila that he was in error. A lively exchange followed.

Nadal first attacked the position taken by Araoz and Mirón and denied that it represented Jesuit policy. "I told him," he wrote to Ignatius, "that his charge was groundless and that we are happy to receive men of Jewish ancestry." Ávila remained unconvinced and returned to his charge. Nettled, Nadal intimated to Ávila that he was cantankerous and stubborn in the face of the facts, a man led indeed to the truth but refusing to give his assent. In the face of such obstinacy, Nadal could only throw up his hands in helplessness. Then, he challenged Ávila: present a man of Jewish origins and qualified for the religious

life, and he would be accepted into the Society. Ávila presented
Luis de Santander. In his diary Nadal crisply noted: "I accepted
him and took him with me to Alcalá."[38]

Ávila's tiff with Nadal did not dampen his desire to see the
Society grow. He remained on the lookout for "outstanding
men" to direct to its ranks. "He has made our concerns his
own," observed Nadal. Ávila lived fifteen years more, an ever
staunch friend and critic of the Society. Fearing that it was
diluting its quality and setting its sights too low, he took its
superiors to task for admitting "a mob."[39]

Through January of 1554, Nadal explained the Constitutions
to the growing Córdoban community. He received the first vows
of Antonio de Córdoba, son of the marchioness of Priego, and
some others who had completed their novitiate. And after his
deep plunge into one of Spain's most tormenting social and
religious problems, Nadal left for Toledo, where he arrived on
February 4 or 5.[40]

Since the Jesuit college in Alcalá lay within the archdiocese of
Toledo, Nadal paid a courtesy call on the archbishop and primate
of Spain, Juan Martínez Guijeño. The two met in the tense
atmosphere of an uneasy truce between the archbishop and the
Society after a rough-and-tumble legal battle of five years. In the
late 1540s Martínez had begun to send signals of hostility to the
Society: he showed suspicion of the Spiritual Exercises; he made
a false charge that the majority of the Jesuits in Alcalá were New
Christians; he chafed at the exemption from local hierarchies
that the Society received from the pope. In 1551 he had taken
the offensive in two edicts: first he revoked the faculties of
priests who made the Spiritual Exercises; then he forbade Jesuits to preach, hear confessions, administer the Holy Eucharist,
or offer Mass in the archdiocese, and he ordered his priests,
under pain of excommunication and a fine of 5000 maravedis,
not to allow Jesuits to offer Mass in parish churches. Before
long, Ignatius, Papal Nuncio Giovanni Poggio, and Pope Julius
III formed a chorus insisting that Martínez rescind those decrees. He yielded only when Poggio warned him that, should he
remain obstinate, he would be picked up, put under arrest, and
shipped to Rome.[41]

This recent history troubled the atmosphere in which Nadal
first met the archbishop. In a gesture that first seemed most
cordial on the surface, the prelate told Nadal he would welcome

a Jesuit settlement in the city of Toledo. It only repeated, however, an offer he had made earlier to Ignatius: he would build a Jesuit college in Toledo if the Society would close its ranks to New Christians. Ignatius refused. And now Martínez exclaimed to Nadal, "Come to Toledo if you care to. Come to me. But with this understanding: you will be served a ban on any New Christians in the group that comes." Nadal declined the invitation. "I told him the condition was out of the question. I did this with utmost simplicity, to avoid offending him. This good archbishop had unfriendly feelings for the Society."[42]

One day in Toledo was enough to assess the Society's uneasy relationship with Spain's primate. On February 6, Nadal arrived in Alcalá, where he found a community of thirty-five men, for the most part scholastics studying at the university, the largest Jesuit community in Spain but hardly a showcase of the Jesuit way of life. At the center of this misguided group was the rector, Fr. Francisco de Villanueva, a forty-five-year-old Estramaduran whom Pedro de Ribadeneira years before had described as "a destitute rustic, a runt of swarthy complexion, utterly unlettered, foul and contemptible in the eyes of men." For ten years he had been rector at Alcalá, since 1544, when, still a scholastic and a student of grammar, he had only two other scholastics in his care. During that decade his community reached thirty-five.[43] To his credit, Villanueva had tried to give form to his community before the Constitutions were issued and when directives from Rome were inadequate. Acting in the dark, he arranged a daily order in the house that Nadal found incompatible with the Constitutions.

What Nadal discovered included the following: each morning the community spent an hour of prayer together in the chapel; each evening they did the same; after dinner and supper they spent fifteen minutes before the Blessed Sacrament; on Fridays and Saturdays they fasted; they slept six hours—10:30 P.M. to 4:30 A.M. in winter, and 9:30 P.M. to 3:30 A.M. in summer. Nadal quickly made changes. He abolished the two days of fast, added an hour of sleep, shortened the visits to the Blessed Sacrament. But he met stiff opposition when he tried to reduce the schedule of the scholastics' prayer.[44]

Ignatius himself, to guide Jesuit priests who had pronounced final vows, excluded in general any set legislation on the time of prayer beyond the two daily examinations of conscience—Mass and the divine office he presupposed. The Jesuit at the end of his formation, as Ignatius envisaged him, was a man athirst for prayer who, with his confessor or superior, would draw a program of prayer that took into account his health, work, talents, and graces. For the scholastics, Ignatius prescribed, beyond Mass and the two examinations of conscience, a half-hour of prayer, mental or vocal.[45]

Nadal canceled the evening hour of prayer in Villanueva's schedule and met little dissent. When he tried to reduce the scholastics' hour of morning prayer to a half-hour, though, he raised a mighty storm. Several priests, most likely Antonio Araoz and Francis Borgia, argued against this adjustment to Ignatius' legislation. They had two principal reasons: first, Jesuits without more prayer than that laid down by Ignatius could not be sustained in the religious spirit; second, it was embarrassing to hear the Society's critics deplore the little time Jesuits devoted to prayer. So Nadal temporarily condoned the full hour of morning prayer for scholastics but recommended that they move gradually (*poco a poco*) toward Ignatius' legislation.[46]

Prayer, therefore, was a primary concern during that stay in Alcalá. Nadal tried to meet that concern by writing a small work called *Orden de oración* ("An Instruction on Prayer"). In eighteen observations or commentaries, all lapidary in style, he listed the ideas on prayer he thought a Jesuit should know: the Spiritual Exercises as the Society's special guide on prayer; the link between a Jesuit's prayer and his apostolic purpose; the bond of a Jesuit's prayer and practice of virtue, especially obedience; a Jesuit's set purpose to find God in all things; a Jesuit's quest to stir devotion in all he does; the role of a Jesuit's thoughts that arise during morning prayer in coloring the action of his day; a Jesuit's need for alertness against distraction from his apostolic style of life by sweetness and ease in prayer.

Those ideas were strong, positive, and sound. But Nadal made one mistake, a juridical one. The discontent with Ignatius' legislation on prayer voiced by Araoz and Borgia pushed him into a bad blunder. In his "fifth observation" he yielded to their complaints and condoned an extra half-hour of compulsory prayer for scholastics above what Ignatius required in the Constitutions.[47] He put it clearly in the record that he saw fit to alter Ignatius' design. He was to discover that he had touched the untouchable. He had tampered with the Constitutions in an especially sensitive area. In a withering rebuke, Ignatius told him he had no business doing that.

Together, the Messina *Instructio 'de oratione'* and the Alcalá *Orden de oración* suggested a significant stage in Nadal's intellectual development. A little earlier in Rome he sensed that he had received a special vocation within his Jesuit vocation: a call to give himself to expounding the Society's Constitutions and Rules. Now *Instructio* and *Orden* signaled the first inklings of a vocation within his Jesuit vocation: to search for the meaning of Jesuit prayer. Jesuit prayer more and more captured his intellectual roamings. Jesuit prayer became his "specialty."

Villanueva did nothing to ease Nadal's work at Alcalá. A stubborn man accustomed to ruling and directing others, he received Nadal's correction with bad grace. Nadal informed Ignatius of this. "Fr. Villanueva is a good fellow. I have, nevertheless, found him obstinate in clinging to his own opinion. He has little obedience of judgment. I am not surprised at this, since he has not lived under a superior and therefore has not learned what it means to obey."[48]

In a way, Villanueva was untouchable. Residing in the Jesuit residence was Fr. Alfonso Ramírez de Vergara, a secular priest, doctor of theology, generous benefactor of the college, and friend and confidant of Villanueva. Subtly and effectively he intruded into the administration of the college. Before long he had it on a leash; he demanded a voice in all major decisions and authority to veto changes in the Jesuit staff. Glumly Nadal reported to Ignatius. "He [Vergara] claims control of the college. He threatens to stop his gifts if we transfer Villanueva or any other Jesuit of equal stature from Alcalá."[49] Vergara's intrusion meant that his friend Villanueva enjoyed a power over policy that Ignatius never envisaged in a Jesuit rector. Nadal clearly saw the implications of the Vergara-Villanueva alliance. In Alcalá the Society had lost control to the rector. "The Society enjoys no freedom of action in that college save when it meshes with the policy of Villanueva."[50]

Nadal tried to break Vergara's hold on the college without offending him. Adopting a stategy of distraction, he thanked him for his gifts to the Alcalá institution and at the same time listed several other budding Jesuit colleges in Spain that needed financial aid. He hoped Vergara's generous instincts would draw him away from Alcalá to another city. Vergara did not budge. Instead, his intrusion into Jesuit affairs in Alcalá mounted through the years. Seventeen years later, in 1561, Nadal would find the doctor still in residence and attended by a Jesuit brother who acted as his personal valet. He did not dare expel the guest. The college needed his donations. In this frustrating episode, Nadal learned how, in the crunch, money talks.

More boisterous but more tractable was the case of Don Jerónimo de Vivero, a relative of Francis Borgia. In a magnanimous gesture, which proved to be a mistake, Ignatius had offered Vivero the hospitality of the Alcalá college, cautioning him however that he should not expect quarters to be provided for his entourage. That condition Vivero ignored, and when Nadal arrived he found not only Vivero but his seven valets settled in the Jesuit living quarters. Nadal sent a blunt report to Ignatius. "I found him [Vivero] and his seven valets in the entrails of the college (*in visceribus collegii*). We have the world inside the house. Although Master Jerónimo is a decent chap and his valets are good fellows, he has not, as far as I can see, been touched with the spirit of a religious house."[51] With the aid of Francis Borgia he finally eased the unwanted visitor and his valets out of the college.

Vivero, Vergara, Teotonio, Brandón—all played the millstone around Nadal's neck. But they could not balk his task as lamplighter. By his illuminating instructions on the Society's Constitutions and Common Rules in Lisbon, Évora, Coimbra, and Córdoba, he dispelled the darkness of ignorance that enveloped many Jesuits. At Alcalá he lit an especially bright lamp.

8

The Alcalá Conferences

In short, the Society grounds its prayer in all things
and finds in all things God and his devotion, for it
does not set its prayer in the mold of the hermit.
Rather, it embraces action and joins its prayer to
action. In this way the Society's vocation is fulfilled;
in this way is obedience carried out.

Nadal at Alcalá, 1554

The heart of Nadal's visitation in Alcalá was his daily conferences on Jesuit life. There, for the first time in Nadal's travels,
ample notes were taken of what he said, notes far more illuminating than the skimpy outline of his talks in Messina and the
scattered splinters of information in his correspondence from
Lisbon, Évora, Coimbra, and Córdoba. A twenty-six-year-old
Portuguese scholastic, Manuel Sá, who had then been in the
Society nine years and was a student at the University of Alcalá,
jotted Nadal's instructions down in a rather full form that fills
sixty-eighty pages in the *Monumenta Historica Societatis Iesu*.[1] These
Alcalá conferences show that Nadal had, early on, many key
ideas, which he would stress through the ensuing years. Some of
them follow.

To God Alone Does the Society Owe Its Origin

God alone put the Society in the world. At each stage in Christian
history, God, concerned to build up his church, places in the

world persons like St. Francis and St. Dominic to meet special needs. In that distinguished company of holy men, God placed Ignatius (a rather bold suggestion for Nadal to make while Ignatius was still living). At a time when esteem for religious life reached an ebb, God brought forth Ignatius and his Society of Jesus. The Society's divine origin was recognized by Pope Paul III when he said "The finger of God is here."[2]

The Society of Jesus as God's handiwork remained a favorite theme of Nadal through his life. He grasped it early. With it he opened his talks to the Jesuits in Alcalá. And still more: on God's wisdom and goodness alone, he insisted, the Society's increase depended. The Society growing was God working; the Society expanding was God loving: "On this truth alone does our hope rest."[3]

To the Society God Gives a Particular Character

God molds the Society according to a special pattern by a distinctive grace. In the first sentences of these conferences, Nadal told his fellow Jesuits that it would be worth their while "to take note of what is proper to our religious order." Through the Church's history, God desires diverse forms of reverence and worship. To achieve this diversity, God at times shapes a religious order into a distinctive mold. He placed Ignatius in the world, and from him wanted a different form of honor and worship. To him therefore he gave a distinctive grace. From God through Ignatius this distinctive grace is passed to the Society. It molds the Jesuit's practice of virtue; it is the grace "by which we live and are guided."[4] A Jesuit must keep in mind that his spiritual development—his way of, say, prayer and obedience—takes a unique form that is delineated by the Society's special vocation. Virtue in the Society should take a distinctive shape. Nadal called this the "particularization" of virtue. God, through a singular grace, "particularizes" a Jesuit's virtue. "We must therefore, under the impact of this distinctive cast of mind and singular flow of grace, live the virtues according to our Jesuit way of understanding them."[5]

Nadal communicated to the scholastics a strong sense of identity, a conviction that Jesuits were different and gave the Church a kind of service different from all others. With the drive of immediacy, he urged that they were the unique choice of God to meet special needs of the Church in that turbulent age. Even though at that point the Society numbered scarcely eight hundred members, he put before those young men the daring proposition that they, then and there, were taking a place in the Church's history fully as important as that taken in the thirteenth century by the Dominicans and the Franciscans. A heady drink! At this early date, perhaps, were sown the seeds of that pride and self-sufficiency of which a renowned Jesuit historian of the eighteenth century, Fr. Guilio Cordara, accused the Society of his own day.[6]

Nadal became a coiner of phrases, who beat an idea into a precise formula. This theme of the Society's special grace was one such idea. At this early stage, however, he had not yet hit on a unique formula, for in his conferences at Alcalá he at one time linked the Society's special grace to obedience, at another to apostolic service, at still another to God's greater glory. He was starting to resolve a problem that remained constant: the best articulation of the Society's special grace.

The Prime Exemplar of Fidelity
to the Society's Distinctive Grace Is Ignatius of Loyola

Nadal gathered as many details of Ignatius' life as he could. In them he found the first tangible example of being true to that special grace God was then sending into the world. In the steps of Ignatius' life he recognized God, forming the future Society of Jesus. Nadal therefore urged his fellow Jesuits to study that life in order to discover what their vocation meant. He called Ignatius God's instrument for communicating this distinctive Jesuit grace to the Society's members. "God raised Fr. Ignatius, gave him a distinctive grace, and through him gives this grace to our men (*y mediante el a nosotros*)."[7]

As at Manresa, Ignatius forged, under God's guidance, the Spiritual Exercises and discovered in the meditations on the Kingdom of Christ and the Two Standards the essence and the purport, the range and sweep of his vocation, so the Jesuit, by making those Exercises and those key meditations, has before him the meaning and the tenor, the compass and the thrust of his own call. As in his pilgrimage to the Holy Land Ignatius sought a deep knowledge of Christ the Lord, so the Jesuit makes his spiritual pilgrimage through meditation on the life of Christ, "in which we are immersed without cease." As at Paris, Ignatius denied his taste for prolonged solitary prayer in order to master his studies, so the Jesuit does not allow the pull toward prayer to deflect him from the obligation of the lecture hall and the reading desk.[8]

In these conferences at Alcalá, Nadal appealed in only a limited and restrained way to the events of Ignatius' life as the epiphany of Jesuit vocation. In later years his biographical study of Ignatius would expand notably. At Alcalá it was one of his favorite themes, and in future talks he swung expansively in his development of that subject. At this time he kept it all in a nutshell.[9]

The Quest of the Society of Jesus: The Greater Service and Honor of Almighty God in All Things

A frequent expression on Ignatius' lips was: *A major gloria divina,* which identifies a penchant that "our men" must somehow make their own, "in no lackluster way but with energy in every area of life (*summe, cum maximo augmento in omnibus*)." This penchant Nadal attributed to a special power given by God to the Society. [10] Again, this is but a terse presentation of a rich idea Nadal would later amplify.

The Jesuit's Ideal: To Be a Companion of Jesus

This ideal, said Nadal, the Society urges each member to attain. He grounded his argument in an incident in Ignatius' own life. In October of 1537, Ignatius, Pierre Favre, and Diego Laínez were traveling to Rome from Vicenza in Italy. Nine miles from Rome, at La Storta, the crossroads of the old Cassian and Claudian ways, the three entered a chapel. There Ignatius received a vision of God the Father and of Christ with his cross. The Father was placing Ignatius close to Christ to be Christ's servant, and was saying "I shall be with you." Nadal interpreted Ignatius' vision as a clear indication that God had chosen him to be close to Christ, to be his companion.[11]

Nadal expanded on the implications of this closeness to Christ. Christ founded the Church amid tribulation; Ignatius founded the Society amid affliction. Christ suffered assault; Ignatius endured attack. Ignatius, reported Nadal, interpreted these sufferings as the molding of his person into likeness to

Christ. Still further, the primitive Church suffered dissension within and persecutions without. The young Society had recently been tormented in Portugal by discord within; at the moment it was under Dominican attack from without. Likeness to Christ, likeness to the Church—there was the Society's ideal, the Jesuit's ideal.[12]

The Society's Constitutions Are God's Message to Jesuits through Ignatius

Nadal saw a resemblance between the composing of the New Testament and the composing of the Society's Constitutions. Before the appearance of the New Testament, Christ's apostles and disciples lived according to tradition. Peter said to the other apostles: you know our manner and order of life. Go forth and live it. Before he wrote the Constitutions, Ignatius said the same to the first Jesuits who had gathered about him. As the early Church expanded, however, lines of communication became strained and oral accounts, in peril of thinning, were recorded. So with the Society: as it expanded, the traditions from Ignatius had to be captured on paper. Ignatius' experience, Nadal recalled, taught him much about the different qualities of men who became Jesuits. Unless the Society's way of life were put in print, correct and sure guidance of those men of diverse character would be impossible. The tradition would weaken. The primitive spirit would be lost.[13]

As Ignatius wrote, reflected Nadal, God at his side was inspiring him. This inspiration gave to the Constitutions a special authority that no future additions and elaborations would enjoy. Within the Constitutions, therefore, rested a peculiar power to draw Jesuits of that early age to the highest spiritual peaks. Under God's guidance, Ignatius offered a guide to what a Jesuit should aspire to be. On each Jesuit, therefore, fell the duty of making the Constitutions live in his heart. Nadal congratulated the men at Alcalá that they were contemporaries to the production of a document so precious.[14]

The External Life of the Society Is Ordinary; Its Interior Life Is Extraordinary

Nadal made this distinction basic in his instruction to fellow Jesuits. Their food and clothing were common. Their prayer and devotion were uncommon. A Jesuit, he told them, was a man of the spirit who walked in the spirit. A Jesuit's unremarkable trappings helped him to be adaptable (*accommodatissimus*) in dealing with the laity, to set them at ease. These close and facile contacts, however, exact a price: a remarkable interior life of union with Christ in prayer. Lacking the safeguards of other religious orders, a Jesuit secures his position only by strong moorings to an intense interior spirit.[15]

The Core of Jesuit Prayer Is in the Finding of God in All Things

Of all subjects in his Alcalá conferences, Nadal gave most time to prayer. Sá's notes on that topic fill ten pages of the *Monumenta Historica Societatis Iesu*. Nadal noted that the Constitutions do not cover prayer in any extended way because Ignatius presupposed the Spiritual Exercises had been made. Nadal thought that more had to be said, and he therefore developed a number of points specifically on Jesuit prayer.[16]

1. A Jesuit's prayer is oriented toward the practical service of the divine majesty. It engenders action far beyond the Carthusian vocation. Nadal called this thrust toward practical service the "breadth of love" (*amplitudo caritatis*), which meshes neatly with the Society's urge to bring souls to greater service and devotion, all to the greater glory of God.[17]

2. A Jesuit's prayer does not reach perfection in the intelligence alone. To "taste" what is understood is necessary. Nadal recalled Ignatius' dictum that prayer does not consist in abundance of ideas but in relishing what is contemplated. A word that Nadal used more and more in his conferences and his *Orationis observationes* was "taste" (*gustus*).[18]

3. A Jesuit's prayer carries into his work. Here Nadal coined one of his special phrases: the residue of ideas (*reliquiae cogitationum*). There is a "residue of ideas" that arises in prayer and lingers in a Jesuit's busy life. A Jesuit leaves his formal morning prayer with certain convictions, attitudes, and ideas that remain in his memory and inform the action of the day. These fruits of prayer (*reliquiae cogitationum, ex oratione remanentes*) penetrate his interior and help him to labor with fervor.[19]

4. To illustrate the relationship between a Jesuit's prayer and action, Nadal selected the image of the circle. Like the line of a circle, a

Jesuit's prayer flows into his work and his work into his prayer. The flow is continuous: there is no interruption. The image of the circle remained one of Nadal's favorites.[20]

5. To find God in all things is the best expression of Jesuit prayer. "We should," said Nadal, "make finding God in all things our main preoccupation. This is the advice Fr. Ignatius gives us. In this is our supreme tranquility and consolation."[21] "Finding God in all things" describes the flow and direction of a Jesuit's prayer. From this distinctive form of prayer, which is easy to practice, arises a Jesuit's devotion. And cooperation with the Holy Spirit gives a Jesuit a distinctive facility in finding God in all things.[22]

Nadal was especially concerned that scholastics recognize the link between this form of prayer and their arduous hours of study. In the novitiate they acquire a taste for prayer and learn its strong attraction, but, as did Ignatius at Paris, they must dominate this appeal in order to become learned men. He tried to help them understand the Constitutions' restrictive legislation on their prayer: their studies to equip them for the Society's purpose are the will of God; their practice of awareness of God in the material they study is prayer; their obedience is a prayer and a sacrifice pleasing to God; their daily examinations of conscience, attendance at Mass, and attention to sermons, spiritual reading, and spiritual conversation all spell a continuous prayer. Still more, "When the time given to study is completely guided by the Spirit, that time must be regarded as time spent in prayer. . . . In short, the Society grounds its prayer in all things and finds in all things God and his devotion, for it does not set its prayer in the mold of the hermit. Rather, it embraces action and joins its prayer to action. In this way the Society's vocation is fulfilled; in this way is obedience carried out."[23]

Jesuit Prayer Presupposes a Profound Self-Denial

Even as he prays and practices virtue, a Jesuit severely mortifies his flesh. His penance is unceasing, and he finds his supreme self-denial in obedience. He gives himself without reserve to his superior. In the Spiritual Exercises he enters with determination upon a resolute program of ridding himself of all impediments to perfection. A cutting purgation assails his venial sins and drives him toward conquest of his inclinations to evil. Nadal echoed Ignatius' preference for a mortified man who surrenders his self-will to God over one who seeks absorption in prayer.[24]

The Jesuit Seeks a Harmony of Learning and Holiness in His Life

The Society of Jesus keeps before its men the ideal of forming within their lives a union of the spirit of learning (*letras*) and the quest for holiness (*spiritu*). Each Jesuit should aim to be a learned man of devotion. In this harmony placed at the service of the Church Nadal saw the work of God's providence. He dreaded the stupid holy person (*personas idiotas y devotas*). A Jesuit is expected to articulate theology with accuracy. Faulty expression and consequent doctrinal error he must eschew. To meet these obligations he must master scholastic theology, that instrument of precise and clear expression.[25]

In the chronology of Nadal's life, the Alcalá conferences suddenly appear as an unexpected gift of a tray of diamonds, a rare display of ideas he had been threshing in his mind for eight years and was now passing to other Jesuits. Without doubt he presented them earlier in Portugal, but it was at Alcalá that they were first recorded in detail. For those interested in how the Constitutions were introduced to hundreds of young Jesuits, Manuel Sá did a valuable service. Aside from what Nadal wrote in his *Orationis observationes,* Sá was the first to sketch the features of Nadal the theologian in quest of a definition of the Jesuit.

Nadal left Alcalá on March 5. During the next four weeks he gave no indication that he adverted to the irony of his defending something he had roundly condemned twenty years before. During his studies at the University of Paris he had rejected Ignatius' invitation to make the Spiritual Exercises, suspicious as he was that Ignatius was tainted by the doctrines of the *alumbrados* of Spain. Now, at Valladolid and Salamanca, he spent a month exonerating the *Spiritual Exercises* of the charge of illuminism.[26]

Nadal was not upset by this charge. Four months earlier, when he arrived in Córdoba from Portugal, he received a letter from Fr. Antonio Araoz, who repeated a story he had heard from a friend of the Society, Don Bernadino Pimental, marquis of Tavara: a holy war was being launched against the *Spiritual Exercises.* "Bishop [Melchior] Cano found the *Exercises* intolerable and felt compelled to shout in the streets that these *Exercises* contained statements that smacked of the doctrines of the *alumbrados*. This charge Cano was ready to prove."[27] Pimental asked anxiously whether the Jesuits were aware of any expression in the *Exercises* that failed to convey its precise meaning with utmost clarity.

Nadal took the challenge very seriously, however. He clearly recognized the danger of identifying the *Spiritual Exercises* with the divisive spiritual force of the *alumbrados,* and in Melchior Cano he saw one of the most incisive and capable critics of that movement. To Araoz he proposed that the Society mount a counterattack. He began to make notes as he pondered the issue during his travel from one community to another. Those casual notes extended over two years.[28]

Early in his university formation, Nadal identified as an enemy of orthodoxy that mystical movement that condemned external religious practice, rejected authority, and insisted on individual freedom to follow the guidance of the Holy Spirit. Some in that movement, known as *recogidos*, stressed recollection, withdrawal from all created things, even from the humanity of Christ, so that they might be completely open to divine movements within them. Others, known as *dejados,* stressed self-abandonment, the stripping of themselves of all knowledge so that they might reach a state of utter quiet before God. Nadal shared the hostility of the Inquisition to those spiritual tenets.[29] So did the brilliant forty-five-year-old Dominican friar, Melchior Cano.

By his intellectual and spiritual formation, Cano was well tuned to challenge the *alumbrados*. At Salamanca he had received a disciplined and rigorous intellectual formation. A high respect for the mind tilted him against any teaching redolent of individualism and mysticism and made him wary of any doctrine proclaimed to have come from promptings of the Holy Spirit. The appearance of new writings on the warmth of the heart's response to grace, the richness of the affective life, or the interior character of devotion spread unease among the disciplined disciples of the mind. Cano's spiritual formation underlined ascetical practice and apostolic activity, inspired in large measure by the austerity and the energy of the Italian Dominican Girolamo Savonarola, whose life had a wide influence among Spanish Dominicans. Men of that school looked askance at the doctrine of passive openness to the penetration of God's grace. They turned their fire on the *alumbrados*.[30]

Cano also had a painful experience that made him wary of new books on spiritual subjects. He had burned his fingers by writing a prologue to a Castilian translation of *La victoria di si mismo* (*Victory over Self*), a work by the Italian Giovanni Battista Carioni de Crema. In 1552 the Holy Office condemned *Victory over Self*. Embarrassed that his name had been tied to a condemned book, Cano thereafter channeled his loyalties to the Church into unmasking spiritual teachers who, in his judgment, were not adequately grounded in the living tradition of the Church. He became a watchdog. So indeed he described himself, and he barked along a wide front. Not at all the mere anti-Jesuit crank some Jesuits tended to depict him, he battled fellow Dominicans as well, including such notables as Luis de Granada and Archbishop Bartolomé de Carranza, when he thought that they were soiled with erroneous doctrine.[31]

Cano read the *Spiritual Exercises* and found expressions he thought resonated with the teaching of the *alumbrados*. He made annotations on his copy of the *Exercises* and sent it to Archbishop Juan Martínez Guijeño of Toledo (whose aversion to the *Exercises* was noted in the last chapter). At one place where Ignatius wrote about indifference he noted: "This comes from the *alumbrados*." On the margin of a copy of the papal bull approving the *Exercises* he wrote: "Astonishing, this approval." The extent of the impact made by Cano's critique eludes measure, but among a small and important circle that included Toledo's archbishop, Cano had an influential voice. In 1553 the archbishop renewed his attack on the *Exercises* and appointed a commission headed by another Dominican, Fr. Tomás de Pedroche, a professor of theology at the Colegio de San Pedro in Toledo, to examine the book.[32]

Pedroche shared Cano's chary view of talk about interior devotion and inspiration. He questioned Ignatius' intellectual competence to write on spiritual subjects, since one incapable of composing in Latin was open to serious questioning. He charged that Ignatius drew his doctrine more from "the interior experience of sin and the unction of the Holy Spirit than from books." He branded much of Ignatius' knowledge as rooted in the *dejados* and the *alumbrados*, "who have put aside revelation transmitted in books, and instead transmit what the Spirit tells them." Those people, Pedroche pointed out, hold it infallible that the Spirit of God unceasingly talks to them.[33]

Annotation no. 15 of the *Spiritual Exercises* Pedroche found unacceptable. In that Annotation Ignatius insists that the director of the Exercises "ought not to urge the exercitant more to poverty or any promise than to the contrary, nor to one state of life or way of living more than to another. Outside the Exercises, it is true, we may lawfully and meritoriously urge all who probably have the required fitness to choose continence, virginity, the religious life, and every form of religious perfection. But while one is engaged in the Spiritual Exercises, it is more suitable and much better that the Creator and Lord in person communicate Himself to the devout soul in quest of the divine will, that He inflame it with love of Himself, and dispose it for the way in which it could better serve God in the future. Therefore, the director of the Exercises, as a balance at equilibrium, without leaning to one side or the other, should permit the Creator to deal directly with the creature, and the creature directly with his Creator and Lord."[34] This troubled Pedroche. He asked: if outside the Spiritual Exercises it is acceptable for an adviser to urge a person to make one choice rather than another, why is this excluded during such an extended period as the usual thirty days devoted to the Exercises? He continued: "This clearly is a doctrine of the *dejados* and the *alumbrados,* since they put aside all teaching by sound and knowledgeable masters and dispose themselves to hear the Spirit and God speaking within their souls."[35] He filed his complaints with the Inquisition.

Nadal reached Valladolid by March 13 and there decided to respond to Pedroche's charges. He did not take the issue to the public by sermon or lecture but brought it privately to the attention of a man of authority whom he knew personally. Dr. Diego de Córdoba had been syndic in Sicily when Nadal was there, and now, in Valladolid, Córdoba was on the council of the Inquisition. He sympathized with Nadal and offered to help him, but the tack he took disconcerted Nadal. He suggested that Nadal give him a copy of the *Spiritual Exercises,* which he would submit to the Inquisition for examination. His reasoning was simple: clearance by that august body would dispel the mists of disquiet about the Jesuits that hovered over some pulpits, chanceries, and universities of Spain.

Nadal, however, recoiled. He observed that his fellow Jesuits were "deeply upset by the suggestion" of bringing the Inquisition into the dispute. He concurred with that feeling and gave

Córdoba's friendly advice a brusque dismissal. He refused to yield a copy of the *Exercises;* he brushed aside the idea of filing a petition of approval with the Inquisition. And he based his argument on legal grounds: a book confirmed by the Holy See—as the *Exercises* had been—should be submitted to no other tribunal anywhere. In a scrappy mood, Nadal threw the gauntlet before Córdoba: a move by the Inquisition would mean a fight. The Society would ask the backing of the pope. But then, in the midst of that tense drama, he had to leave Valladolid and move to Salamanca to visit the Jesuits there.[36]

A major light in the eminent Dominican theology faculty of Salamanca for years had been Melchior Cano. Nadal had now reached the very platform from which this sharp critic of the Society and the *Spiritual Exercises* thundered his warnings. But he did not meet him. Since the close of the second period of the Council of Trent (1551–1552), the friar had been nominated and consecrated bishop of the Canary Islands. Within a short time, however, he resigned both his see and his professorship at Salamanca and became entangled in disputes of one kind or another until his death in 1560.[37] Nadal, for his part, issued no public challenge to the Dominicans, but within the Jesuit community he presented several critiques of Cano's position on the *Exercises*. Those critiques he supplemented with exhortations on the Society's Constitutions and Rules, with personal interviews, and with hearing confessions. Fr. Juan Suárez sent an elated report to Ignatius, in which he described the joy Nadal brought to the Jesuits there, "hungering as we were for the bread he came to distribute to us, a food so essential for our sustenance."[38] Spanish Jesuits responded in the same joyous way as the Portuguese had to hearing this authoritative exposition of their Institute and of its meaning for their lives. And this, more than concern for the reputation of the *Spiritual Exercises,* was Nadal's main obligation. With the eight Jesuits in Valladolid he spent a week, from March 13 to 20, and with the seventeen in Salamanca he stayed about ten days. The next stop on his schedule was Medina del Campo.

For months Nadal had been planning an unusual event to take place at Medina del Campo. He wrote to Fr. Antonio Araoz (provincial of Castile), Fr. Francis Borgia (peripatetic preacher), Fr. Francisco Estrada (another roving preacher), Fr. Miguel de Torres (visitor in Portugal), and Fr. Diego Mirón (provincial of

Portugal), directing them to meet him at Medina del Campo in early April. He himself arrived there on the fourth.

To the assembled group he announced some major decisions Ignatius had made. For several months he and Ignatius had had extensive correspondence about Ignatius' wish to multiply and rearrange the provinces in Spain. In hand he had the approved design. He informed them that Ignatius was cutting southern Spain from the province of Castile and making it the new province of Andalusia. Fr. Miguel de Torres was to move from Portugal and become superior of the new province. Fr. Antonio Araoz was to continue as provincial of the now considerably trimmed province of Castile. To fill the vacancy left in the province of Aragon by Simão Rodrigues's desertion, Ignatius designated Fr. Francisco Estrada. Fr. Diego Mirón was to continue in the post of provincial of Portugal. For Borgia, Ignatius reserved a special distinction—that of delegate of the general (*commissarius*) in Spain.[39]

The meeting was not a smooth and genial one. Araoz stayed one night only and left in a huff. He resented the trimming of his province's territory and the appointment of Borgia as his superior. Nadal remembered the event well. "The next day he said he had serious business that called him away. It strikes me he took the division of his province in a rather churlish way."[40] This show of petulance confirmed Nadal's misgivings about the continuance in office of a man who neglected his duties as provincial and who openly opposed Ignatius on two sensitive issues: the admission of New Christians into the Society and the Society's refusal to undertake regular spiritual direction of women. Ignatius knew those serious gaps in Araoz's measure as a Jesuit but thought his presence at court would have a value that outweighed them. He wrote Nadal, "On the basis of information I have received, I believe that by being at court he will accomplish much for the divine service."[41] Nadal was not so sanguine and intimated this to Ignatius. "I hope he will give more attention to his duties as provincial than he has given. This hope I rest in the Lord. I hope also that he will drop the secular business in which he has been so heavily involved."[42]

Estrada received his appointment with much moaning and groaning. In a drastic turn for a man who for years had been on the move, he had recently set his heart on a life of solitude and theological study; he wanted no part of the day-to-day business

of a provincial. The spring within this dynamic man of the
highway and the pulpit had gone slack. Nadal tried to make an
adjustment that would placate the withdrawn provincial by giving him two assistants, one to administer the province and the
other to assist him in his theological studies.[43] This was the first
and probably last time that an adjustment of this kind was made
to accommodate a Jesuit provincial.

Borgia's appointment as the general's delegate also gave
Nadal misgivings. He detected in the former duke a tendency to
take command and to move on his own. The previous January,
in Córdoba, Nadal had received the first vows of Fr. Bartolomé
de Bustamente at the close of his novitiate. Now, only three
months later, he discovered that Borgia, without a word to him
but with Ignatius' approval, had admitted Bustamente to his
final profession. Nadal was miffed, not because Ignatius did
what he had a right to do but because Borgia kept him in the
dark. Borgia, he suspected, had gone behind his back because
he was afraid Nadal would block the final vows of a priest hardly
out of the novitiate. Not long after this episode, Borgia again
moved without taking Nadal into his confidence. In Simancas
the Jesuits were negotiating purchase of a house; Borgia entered
the talks and closed the deal. Even though Borgia had the
authority of the general's delegate, Nadal felt aggrieved and
lamented, "He did this without consulting me."[44]

Something more fundamental than those incidents, however, troubled Nadal about Borgia. He told Ignatius he feared
Borgia had not securely grasped the Society's style of action.
Borgia's good will, his work for the Society's expansion in
Spain, and his study of the Constitutions Nadal praised, but his
hold on the Society's distinctive ways he doubted.[45] Nadal's
concerns were grounded on Borgia's personal history. In October of 1546 Ignatius received the recently widowed duke of
Gandía into the Society.[46†] Five years, however, were to pass

---

†46 In light of Borgia's subsequent legislation on prayer and his continual
attraction to excessive prayer, and of Nadal's fears that Borgia was not sufficiently familiar with the Society's ways of proceeding, it is important to note
that at Borgia's profession of vows in February of 1548 was the controversial
Fray Juan Texeda. He and the Jesuits Andrés de Oviedo and Francisco Onfroy,
influenced by the reformist prophetism that Texeda espoused, threatened
the spiritual orientation of the newly founded order. See Manuel Ruiz Jurado,
S.J., "Un Caso de Profetismo Reformista en la Compañía de Jesús: Gandía
1547–1549," *AHSI* 43 (1974): 217–66.

Francis Borgia

before Borgia actually renounced his estates and donned the Jesuit's habit in Rome. For those five years, he continued to live to all appearances as the duke of Gandía. Almost immediately after he made his startling appearance in Rome, Ignatius sent him to Spain to contact the aristocracy and seek their support of Jesuit colleges. Throughout Spain, Borgia traveled at will. An intimate knowledge of the Society's life, especially in the practice of obedience under a local superior, he had hardly acquired at all.

Nadal was especially concerned about this deficiency in Borgia's formation as a Jesuit.[47†] Anxious that he might not have grasped the central importance of obedience in Jesuit life, Nadal gave him special instructions to insist on obedience to the Society's Constitutions and Rules by all, superiors and subjects alike. He toyed with giving him a seasoned and knowledgeable Jesuit as companion and counselor, but no such Jesuit was available.[48]

Nadal's failure to find a practiced Jesuit when he needed one made vivid how small was the reservoir of men fit to assume the post of superior in the new Society. Scholastics were entering the order in large numbers; colleges were multiplying rapidly. Such growth quickly overtook the few tried and true men who had the talent and stamina to govern and lead. Ignatius, for example, appointed Fr. Diego Mirón, aged twenty-six, rector of the Coimbra college when he was but one year in the Society. And Fr. Miguel de Torres he designated rector of the Salamanca college when he was two years in the Society. The rector of the Medina college and host of Nadal's conference, Pedro de Sevillano, was still a scholastic. Nadal told Pedro he should advance to his priestly ordination, and then advised Ignatius, "Although he has only little grasp of grammar, I think he has enough."[49] And the rector Nadal himself appointed at Córdoba, Antonio de Córdoba, was (as we have seen) still a novice.

The Medina meeting lasted about three weeks. In its juridical decisions it recorded the story of the Society's expansion in Spain. It also exposed the nub of a serious internal weakness:

---

†47 A few months later Nadal's misgivings were confirmed. In Murcia, the rector, Juan Bautista Barma, showed Nadal the hermitage, in a secluded spot, that he prepared for Borgia (*Mon Nad*, II:30). Within two years, Borgia's strong leaning to the contemplative life led to a confrontation with Nadal.

too many men with too little formation had been placed in positions of leadership. The Constitutions had not yet been sent to the communities outside Rome. Any direction from Ignatius was therefore piecemeal and mainly by correspondence. Although Nadal's visits began to remedy the problem, many, if not most, were ignorant of the nature of the Society and did not know the impact of obedience within the daily life of a Jesuit community. Intelligent and cultivated as they were—Torres was the brightest, Borgia the most urbane—they lacked a fullness of formation in Jesuit life.

Through the next five months, from early May to late September, Nadal visited eight colleges: Valladolid (a repeat), Burgos, Oñate, Zaragoza, Cuenca, Valencia, Gandía, and Barcelona. He followed the now familiar routine of interviewing the Jesuits, hearing their confessions, delivering conferences on the Society's Constitutions and Rules. The communities were small, some but a year old. Burgos numbered five men, Oñate six, Valladolid eight. Some were involved with odd problems. At Oñate, for example, the widow of the recently deceased donor of the house continued to live there after the Jesuits moved in. To assure "a respectable ambience," Nadal convinced the widow she should move out. But the location of the house also disturbed him; only a hedge separated the Jesuits' garden from their nearest neighbors; but this he could do nothing about. Inside the house he likewise noted objects that displeased him: benefactors had given gifts that jarred the spirit of simplicity, including several precious glass decanters of old Cantabrian artisanship. These he wanted to sell, but he held back. "The truth is that I did not dare sell them. News of that would likely reach the ears of the donors."[50]

In the community at Valladolid, Nadal met a practice that he felt affronted frugal and austere living. The Jesuits there kept a stock of sweets. This cookie-closet he closed and then gave orders, as he had done earlier in Portugal, that no Jesuit was to accept such goodies or any delicately prepared food save what might be necessary for the sick.[51] Picayune defects these were, surely, and not nearly so damaging to Jesuit life as the tenure of several raw, odd, and even wayward superiors.

Despite those handicaps under which many Spanish Jesuits lived, they were still able to light a spark of religious idealism in the spirits of many young men who asked to be received into the

Society. In the first four months of 1554, nine entered at Alcalá, ten at Valencia. At Salamanca, Nadal approved the acceptance of eleven, but directed that they enter at intervals and not at one time in order to assure that each would receive a careful and sound introduction to religious life. Following the design of separate novitiate communities he had set up in Messina and Palermo, he opened novitiates in Coimbra, Córdoba, and Simancas.[52]

The most memorable of the young men Nadal accepted into the Society was probably Pedro Martínez, a free-wheeling, unfettered twenty year old. When Nadal was in Valencia in January 1553, in the earliest stage of his visitation, four university students visited him and asked to be admitted into the Society. With them came Martínez. Nadal explained that the cramped quarters of the Jesuit house forced him to delay accepting them. He sent them away and exhorted them to persevere in their aspirations and to continue their studies. Martínez was not put off so easily. He went to his lodgings, tied his belongings into a bundle, returned to the Jesuit residence, and demanded immediate acceptance into the Society. Nadal explained that only the pantry was empty. Martínez responded that he had not come to sleep. Nadal accepted him and somehow squeezed him into a corner of the house. Thirteen years later, this impetuous young man was killed by the spears of Native Americans on the coast of Florida as he landed to preach the gospel, the first Jesuit to die for the faith in the New World.[53]

During much of his last five months in Spain, Nadal carried a heavy worry, which at times pushed him near to panic. At the close of the meeting of superiors at Medina del Campo, Francis Borgia went to Tordesillas to visit the emperor's demented mother, Juana "La Loca," whose ramblings he had the capacity to calm. Within a few days after Borgia's departure, Nadal heard rumors that Prince Philip, on the eve of sailing for England to marry Mary Tudor, had said he intended to obtain for Borgia membership in the College of Cardinals. Nadal flinched at the thought of Borgia in crimson. For Francis to accept the red hat would surely invite disaster on a religious order that explicitly repudiated ecclesiastical honors.[54]

What Nadal now heard was but the latest episode in a story that had been unfolding for three years. Soon after Borgia had arrived in Rome in 1551 and announced his membership in the

Society of Jesus, Pope Julius III considered making him a cardinal. With Ignatius' leave, Borgia fled Rome for the Jesuit college in Oñate, where he was ordained priest on May 23. In 1552 Pope Julius again mentioned bringing Borgia into the College of Cardinals. The news troubled Ignatius profoundly and threw him into a state of doubt. He began to see reasons why Borgia should accept the honor; he also had his reasons why Borgia should continue to decline the dignity. Finally, Ignatius asked the members of his community to join him in three days of special prayer. Those three days he found painful, anxious, upsetting, but on the third day he came to a clear, quiet, peaceful decision: God's greater glory called for the refusal of the red hat. Ignatius spoke personally with Pope Julius and four cardinals of the curia, persuading them that Borgia could serve the Church better as an unhonored Jesuit outside the College of Cardinals. Ignatius' initiative blocked the appointment.[55]

And now, two years later, as Prince Philip reopened the prospect of a crimson-garbed Borgia, Nadal raced to Tordesillas. There he received a shock: he found Borgia waffling. Troubled in conscience by repeated evasion of the pope's wishes, Borgia lost his assurance that refusal of the red hat was correct. He declined to assure Nadal that he would stand firm against the honor. Nadal spoke bluntly. "Three times I warned him as he sat there on his sofa: if he received the red hat I would lose all trust in a man who, even as he presented himself to the public as one learned in the law of Christ, had set his heart on honors."[56] Borgia remained ambiguous and left Nadal on tenterhooks.

A month later, as Nadal was visiting the college in Zaragoza, he received a letter from Pedro de Ribadeneira. Rumors, wrote Pedro, persisted about Borgia and his impending reception of the red hat. Nadal, sounding like a man dismayed, dispatched a letter to Borgia. To depart from the Jesuit way of poverty and simplicity for the way of ecclesiastical honors, he charged, would reveal what Borgia thought of the Society. The impression could not be avoided that Francis regarded the Society as a petty, ha'penny organization, nothing more than a feather on the scale when weighed against the robes of a prince of the Church. It would be a "frightening paradox and a monumental calamity" (*un paradoxo terrible y miseria extraordinaria*) to find Francis, who had chosen to be humble, poor, and lowly, addressed as "Most Reverend Monsignor." The figure of Cardinal

Borgia would open the gate of ambition to other Jesuits, especially those of the gentle class who had the right connections for
securing churchly distinction. "This would be the undoing of
the Society before it had even been put together."[57]

Nadal continued on a high emotional pitch. "In my mind's
eye I see the entire Society prostrate at the feet of Fr. Francis,
begging him in the Lord not to accept the red hat, or at least
not until he has first submitted the whole matter to Fr. Master
Ignatius." He pressed Borgia: the pope and the emperor know
that a Jesuit may not accept an ecclesiastical honor without his
superior's consent. "When the pope and the emperor probe
your attitude toward churchly honors, they are doing nothing
less than trying to induce you to do what your religious commitment forbids." He again urged Borgia to write promptly to
Ignatius.[58]

About the same time, Nadal heard also from Fr. Juan de
Polanco, who wrote in the name of Ignatius. Polanco sounded
even more panicky than Nadal as he recounted rumors then
floating through Rome about a red hat marked for Borgia. "It
is the common opinion of Jesuits here, from top to bottom,
that if he [Francis] fails to resist to the utmost, he will not only
commit a mortal sin but will also do widespread damage. He
will tear down as much as he has built up by his abdication of
high social status, by his sermons, by his example before the
entire world. . . . I am planning to write to him instantly. I shall
in no way hedge but tell him bluntly what everyone here
thinks."[59]

Once again Ignatius blocked the red hat. With Polanco's
letter he sent special instructions for Borgia: he was to pronounce immediately the five additional vows the Constitutions
require of all professed fathers as safeguards against inroads of
ambition and wealth. Of the five, the one that had immediate
pertinence was this: "The professed should similarly promise to
God our Lord not to seek any prelacy or dignity outside the
Society, and, as far as in them lies, not to consent to being
chosen for a similar charge unless they are compelled by an
order from him who can command them under pain of sin."[60]

Borgia made no fuss about Ignatius' instructions. During a
stay at the Spanish court, he pronounced the additional vows.
On August 22, 1554, he sent a copy to Ignatius. He also took
action to scotch Prince Philip's plans to obtain for him the red

hat. Since Philip had sailed for England and since Emperor Charles was then in Germany, Princess Juana was the regent of Spain—and Borgia was her spiritual director. He asked her to send requests to her father and her brother to drop any design to put him in the College of Cardinals. Juana did so. In Rome, Ignatius once more asked Pope Julius III not to make the appointment. Borgia remained an unbedecked Jesuit.[61]

In that same summer, in the midst of the Borgian anxieties, Ignatius received a major disappointment for which Nadal blamed Araoz. Ignatius, having heard of Prince Philip's plans to sail to England and marry Mary Tudor, saw an opportunity to establish a Jesuit mission in England. He wrote to Araoz to try to find places for some Jesuits in Philip's entourage. Araoz spoke to the prince. Philip said that he did not want to bring Jesuits until he had spoken to Queen Mary. Knowing Araoz's close friendship with Rui Gómez, Philip's closest confidant, Nadal could not but feel that Araoz had tried only halfheartedly. When Philip's fleet weighed anchor and pointed toward England with several secular priests and two or three friars aboard—but no Jesuits—he judged it a black day for the Society. Borgia thought the same.[62]

As his Spanish visitation drew to a close, the memory that possibly pained Nadal most was of something he saw during a short stay at Loyola. Drawn by reverence for Ignatius, he made a side trip to Loyola from Oñate. He enjoyed the visit save for one thing that upset him. "It was a sheer delight," he recalled, "to visit the birthplace and home of Fr. Ignatius. . . . There I saw the room in which Fr. Ignatius was born. It has been turned into a kitchen. I think this is disgraceful."[63]

In late September Nadal was in Barcelona, awaiting a ship to Genoa. With him were Fr. Gaspar de Loarte and Fr. Diego Guzmán, two priests of Jewish descent who had requested admission into the Society, and the Portuguese scholastic who had taken notes on his conferences at Alcalá, Manuel Sá. On September 29, their fleet weighed anchor. Nadal's usual ill fortune at sea persisted. Past Marseilles a storm hit the fleet and dispersed it. On one of the first days in October, Nadal's ship finally sailed into the port of Genoa.

The Portuguese-Spanish experience drenched Nadal in a perennial human struggle: to give to an ideal "a local habitation." In the copies of the Society's Constitutions and Common

Rules, he carried with him the printed articulation of an ideal—all tidy, neat, and compact. To give that ideal a human form constituted the essence of his visitations. He enjoyed mixed success. In Portugal he transformed a restless, confused, even mutinous province into a tranquil, single-minded, enthused group of men. In Spain he left a leadership in which the ideal attained but a stunted bloom; some key Jesuits there would win no blue ribbons at a garden show. This was a chastening experience. In both countries, he encountered many instances of secular interference in the internal affairs of the Society. The realities of his experiences could not but temper any unrealistic expectations he might have had about complete success in putting into human shape the ideal he voiced in word.

9

A New Perspective of Jesuit Purpose

I believe that God Our Lord raised the Society and gave it to the Church to down these heretics and infidels. . . . This conviction grips me: in no part of the world is the Society, supported of course by God's grace, more needed; in no part of the world would the Society be more helpful. . . . I think that the task of helping Germany in its religious life is reserved to the Society.

Nadal to Ignatius, from Germany in 1555

Nadal feared Ignatius. As a novice he had at times trembled in his presence. This early fear surfaced as he made his way to Rome. Ignatius had directed him to proceed promptly to Rome once he arrived in Italy. Ashore at Genoa, Nadal felt a desire to make a little detour to visit the shrine of the Blessed Virgin Mary at Loreto. Remembering Ignatius' order, he denied that desire. "I didn't dare go," he wrote in his diary.[1]

On October 18, after almost two weeks on the road from Genoa, Nadal reached Rome. Even before he arrived, Ignatius marked him for a new and wider responsibility. Through 1554, Ignatius was grievously ill several times. In April, Polanco suggested to him that he appoint a deliberative body composed of Fr. Martín de Olave, Fr. André des Freux, Fr. Luis Gonçalves da

Câmara, and the Society's secretary (Polanco) to handle the most serious problems during the periods of his sickness. Through June, July, and August Ignatius could hardly work, so ill was he. The deliberative body urged Ignatius to appoint Nadal as vicar general on his return from Spain.[2]

Ignatius adopted the suggestion, but he did not do it by direct appointment. He asked the priests, scholastics, and brothers in Rome to choose his aide. On November 1, 1554, the priests convened. The scholastics and brothers delegated four of the priests to file their ballots. Ignatius did not stand aloof from the meeting in quiet detachment; he gave it a decided direction. He appointed Nicolás Bobadilla to preside, but did not want him elected vicar. He even had a mind to make him ineligible for the post. His personal preference was Nadal. In his short account of the meeting, Nadal made an arresting statement. "Whether Fr. Ignatius," he wrote, "let the members of this session know his wish I do not know." Why did he make that comment? He may have been intimating that such a story was abroad at the time, but he could not say for sure whether it was true. For three days, the priests discussed the choice they had to make. Fr. Cornelius Wischaven spoke bluntly about Nadal, with whom he had lived in Messina. He recalled his rector as an irascible man. This charge Nadal publicly admitted; before all present he deplored his short temper. In the vote, Nadal received thirty-two of the thirty-four ballots cast.[3]

Immediately a minor disagreement arose about the correct title for the post Nadal now held. Ignatius directed Nadal, Bobadilla, Polanco, and a few others to consult on this question. Some suggested vicar general; others favored general's delegate (*commissarius*). Nadal himself preferred no title, declaring he wanted nothing that would even seem to weaken the general's authority. "Nothing is more essential for the Society than the authority of the general." In the end he was designated vicar general.[4]

Nadal soon received a sharp taste of the authority he so firmly upheld. On November 22 he reviewed with Ignatius one of the problems he had met during his recent Iberian visitation. He recalled the urgent request the Jesuits at Alcalá had made for an increase in the amount of prayer prescribed in the Society, and he told how he allowed the community to add a half-hour to what the Constitutions prescribed for the scholastics. He emphasized that he personally backed and defended the Spanish request. He pressed vigorously for Ignatius to concur. Insistently he tried to change Ignatius' mind and bring him to his own way of looking at the issue. Ignatius lay sick in bed and heard him out. He said nothing.

The next morning, however, Nadal faced an irate Ignatius. In the presence of Fr. Luis Gonçalves da Câmara and others, Ignatius, flushed with anger, turned on Nadal. With barbed words he rebuked him for his failure to insist that the Spaniards adhere to the Society's legislation on prayer. Câmara recalled Ignatius saying that "the truly mortified man needs only a quarter of an hour to achieve unity with God in prayer." Nadal took the tongue-lashing in silence. For all his speculating about the nature of Jesuit prayer, he had not quite plumbed the depths of the convictions Ignatius had expressed in the Constitutions. Câmara, standing on the sidelines, was startled by Ignatius' outburst. He wondered at Nadal's humble acceptance of this humiliation.[5]

Ignatius concluded his dressing-down by giving Nadal an instruction on the way a Jesuit should deal with his superior. "I surmise," remarked Nadal, "that he [Fr. Ignatius] did this because of the brash and importunate way I spoke to him." Yet, despite his strong displeasure, Ignatius kept Nadal close by and listened to his counsel with respect. It showed in little ways. Since his return from Spain, Nadal had made suggestions for better management of the Roman residence. Ignatius "followed my advice and shifted a number of things in the running of the house."[6]

This episode is instructive in that it illumines one of the most elusive subjects in the early history of the Society: the Jesuit way of prayer. Many Jesuits did not grasp Ignatius' teaching. Although Nadal was described by Polanco as the man who best understood Ignatius' mind and purpose, and although Nadal did more than any other to develop a theology of prayer in the Society, he still seriously muffed the practical implementation of Ignatius' teaching. He failed to respond correctly to a challenge to the Constitutions' directions.

Nadal's reverence for Ignatius did not lessen because of the recent humiliation. For some time he had been convinced that in Ignatius' life rested the most precious deposit of the Society's spirit, a conviction he expressed in his conferences to other

Jesuits. To unearth that deposit, he and other Jesuits often asked Ignatius to reveal the story of his inner life. Ignatius hesitated. By April 1553, when Nadal left Rome for Portugal and Spain, he had done nothing. Eighteen months later, Nadal returned to Rome and was delighted with what he was told. In August 1553, Ignatius had confided to Fr. Câmara that God had made it clear to him that he had an obligation to open the door on his interior history and that he had made up his mind to do so. In September he began to dictate his account to Câmara. Interruptions were many, but the start was made. In his pleasure Nadal assured Câmara that Ignatius could do nothing greater for the Society than to tell his story. Now at last Ignatius was really founding the Society. He urged Câmara not to relent in keeping "the Father" to his dictation, and he himself often urged Ignatius to push on.[7]

Nadal's urgency in obtaining Ignatius' story rested in a long theological tradition that reached as far back as the age of the Merovingians. Through the centuries, monks developed a "theology of the special mediator." Christ is the universal mediator for the eternal saving of the entire human race. For each state of life, however, God chooses a special mediator to guide those in that state to a closer imitation of Christ. For monks, God designated St. Benedict. Benedict's power came from God's initiative in choosing him to be the model and master of the Christian life for those entering upon the monastic way.

St. Benedict exercised his special ministry in several ways: by his life, by his Rule, by his intercession. In his life he showed his monks what God wanted to see realized in their lives. He was their model. In his Rule he showed how, practically, monks could adopt his likeness and could mirror, as he had done, the life of the Son of God. He was their lawgiver. By his intercession in heaven, he still wins continuing graces for the monks to put on Christ in their special style. He is their spiritual father and intercessor. All those ideas Nadal gathered somewhere in his reading and study, but he gave no hint of precisely where. What monks had been attributing to St. Benedict for centuries, he attributed to Ignatius—for Ignatius was as much the model, the lawgiver, the living intercessor for Jesuits as St. Benedict was for St. Bernard and a host of other monastic theologians.[8]

In early March 1555, Ignatius resumed the dictation of his story, but Nadal was not there to applaud. He was in northern

Italy on his way to Germany. This excursion across the Alps had its origin in high places. The Emperor Charles V, crestfallen as a result of the military setbacks he suffered in late 1552 and early 1553, decided to quit Germany for good and turn over the German affairs of the Empire to his brother Ferdinand, king of the Romans. Even though he was leaving with the sad recollection that he had failed to restore religious unity to Germany, he nevertheless summoned another imperial diet to meet in Augsburg at which Ferdinand would preside. The diet opened on February 5, 1555.[9] To head the papal representation at Augsburg, Pope Julius III appointed Giovanni Cardinal Morone, knowledgeable veteran in German affairs. Julius and Morone asked Ignatius for two Jesuit theologians to assist the papal delegation. The two most obvious choices were Diego Laínez and Alfonso Salmerón, the duo who had worked together at Trent and Bologna during the first and second phases of the church council. Ignatius, however, passed over Salmerón—and with reason. In 1541 Salmerón and Morone, then bishop of Modena, had a heated argument about justification and the value of good works. Although the quarrel had been patched up, Ignatius feared—or so Nadal guessed—that Salmerón's presence at Augsburg might offend Morone. Ignatius chose Nadal.

The choice made sense. The Constitutions had yet to be promulgated in the college in Vienna and in several colleges of northern Italy. Augsburg would be a convenient starting place for a visit to Vienna, as well as to the colleges in Venice, Piedmont, and Lombardy. Ignatius therefore invested Nadal with the power of general's delegate to explain the Constitutions in the Jesuit communities in those areas. He also instructed him to solicit funds, recruit young men for the German College, expand the Vienna college, and assess the prospects for new colleges for the training of Jesuits in Augsburg, Ingolstadt, Prague, and Hungary.[10]

Ignatius' plan for Nadal was clear enough, but putting him and Laínez in the same harness at Augsburg involved a risk. The two men were frequently at odds. When Nadal was a novice, Laínez had been especially kind in his efforts to make him feel at ease amid his new surroundings. That Nadal recalled with gratitude. But now, ten years later, his recollections were different. Laínez and he, he wrote, rarely saw eye to eye. Ignatius knew about the tensions between the two, but he threw them together in the hope that a common assignment would drain their mutual hostility.

Putting them together, however, raised a touchy issue: in which of the two should the authority of superior be invested? Ignatius handled this question gingerly and ambiguously. Each man was to have the same authority; neither was to be subordinate to the other. When together, their concurrence would be necessary to implement a decision about Jesuit business. When separated, each would enjoy the authority of general's delegate and speak in the name of the general. And in their roles as theological advisers at Augsburg, they were to follow the directions of Cardinal Morone.[11]

Nadal left Rome on February 16, 1555. He did so with an anxious heart. Since serious sickness continued to prostrate Ignatius for long periods, Nadal urged Câmara to nurse the general carefully and advised him that the Jesuits at the Rome residence "could do nothing more beneficial for the Society than to care for Fr. Ignatius' health in order to enable him to remain at the helm of the Society for a very long time to come."[12]

Nadal took with him a mentally disturbed Bavarian scholastic named Jonas Adler. At Florence, Laínez joined them. They made their way through Bologna, Trent, and Brixen (now Bressanone). Somewhere along the way the two Spaniards of equal authority and strong feelings had a nasty spat. "I threw a punch at him," recalled Nadal.[13] On March 24 they arrived in Augsburg.

During his first week in that meeting place of Catholics and Protestants, despite a warm welcome by King Ferdinand and Otto Cardinal Truchsess von Waldburg of Augsburg, Nadal was edgy. Irritable and truculent, he again flared up at Laínez. "Clearly I was sick in spirit," he confessed abjectly. At dinner at Cardinal Morone's residence, he spoke bitingly about the Protestants. Apparently the cardinal and Laínez admonished him that he was going too far.[14]

In the evening of March 29, only five days after Nadal arrived in Augsburg, dismaying news broke upon the town: Pope Julius III had died. Two days later still, in early morning, Morone and Truchsess left for Rome and the conclave. Two days later still, Laínez, on Truchsess' orders, left with Bishop Luigi Beccadelli for Florence. Nadal found himself the only Jesuit at an imperial diet that offered him no official work.

A yearning for peace and a conviction that a political compromise had to be made permeated the congress. Yet considerations of compromise in dogma and liturgy had evaporated; each confession stood undaunted. So the delegates set a more limited goal: peace among the imperial estates despite their differences in religious profession. They were acknowledging the impracticality of trying to find, at that moment, any accord in a religious credo. The destiny of the diet fell, therefore, into the hands of the princes, the jurists, and the civil servants. Nadal recognized the import of this development: discussion of theology was ruled out. He so informed Ignatius. He planned to remain in Augsburg only a short time longer.[15]

During the unsettling events of his first week in Augsburg, Nadal learned much about the religious situation in Germany; he received his initial lessons from some experienced hands. Bishop Urban Weber of Laibach (now Ljubljana, Slovenia), who had helped Fr. Claude Jay openhandedly in founding the college in Vienna, he found easy to talk to and deal with. He liked Dominican Fr. Pedro de Soto, confessor of Emperor Charles V and a man "of wide humanity, charming and gracious in his opinion of us." In King Ferdinand, who ambitioned the opening of a Jesuit college in Prague, he perceived a man whose "goodness and high idealism are so outstanding that he has become an instrument for God's great glory." In the papal nuncio in Germany, Zaccaria Delfino, he found a ready and friendly learner about the Society and its institute.[16]

What Nadal derived from these men and from his personal observation in Augsburg shocked him. All he knew about the Lutheran religion he had learned from books. In Augsburg he met it face to face in men vibrantly dedicated to the Lutheran heritage. It appalled him. In distress he wrote to Ignatius about a nation clearly under the domination of the devil, a diet that was doing nothing, a daily growth in the number of Lutheran believers, a widespread and scornful trampling on "evangelical truth by everyone." It changed his thinking about the mission of the Society of Jesus.

Germany rapidly became Nadal's primary apostolic preoccupation. He could not reflect on that country without "many tears and unbounded pity." He saw little hope for the "great and noble nation," crippled by "extreme need and the deepest misery." He felt drawn to stay there. Delfino and Weber strongly urged him to do so. He revealed this desire to Ignatius, but in carefully chosen words. Ignatius, he could never forget, frowned on a Jesuit who tried to pressure his superior with importunate speech. Even as he made clear to Ignatius that an assignment to Germany would delight him, he assured the general that he remained at his beck and call. "You know," he wrote, "that the good Lord has planted in me a certain feeling for religious obedience in regard to the will of my superior. I have no recollection of giving preference to one thing or another without first discovering my superior's will. If you should decide that I ought to stay in Germany, I would accept your order with intense joy and the resolve to carry out your wish." Germany had moved into Nadal's ken with a great glow. That glow lasted and never dimmed.[17]

Within his first weeks in Augsburg, Nadal also learned a couple of things that were sure to disappoint Ignatius. Cardinal Morone warned him that there was little hope of collecting money for the German College in Rome. For hard-pressed German Catholics, that college was very far away. Nadal nevertheless made inroads on their generosity. If they did not promise funds, they did promise him young men. He persuaded King Ferdinand and some bishops to send forty-eight youths to the German College with their expenses paid. This happy agreement, however, cracked under a dispute between Ferdinand and the bishops about the share each should bear of the financial burden.[18]

Cardinal Truchsess and Fr. Pedro de Soto also dampened Ignatius' hope of enlisting benefactors to found colleges in Germany for the training of Jesuit scholastics. They told Nadal that German bishops and laity wanted seminarians trained for German parishes and some to be German bishops. They were therefore reluctant to contribute to the training of young men who, by force of the Jesuit Constitutions, might not accept parochial duties, would refuse episcopal ordination (unless ordered by the pope to accept), and might never serve as priests in Germany. They wanted the fruit of their money to stay in Germany, in German parishes and German dioceses.[19]

Nadal knew Ignatius would be hurt by this rebuff. He therefore tried to mitigate the setback on other grounds. Conceding the force of arguments put forth by Truchsess and Soto, he supported their stand with a reason of his own, a reason no

German could receive with mirth: Germans did not have the makings of good Jesuits. He saw little hope of attracting German youth to the Society. "Germans by nature do not adapt easily to a life of austerity such as we live . . . especially at the present time when all Germans either feel outright hostility toward religious life or at least experience little attraction for it."[20] He suggested that Ignatius modify his hopes, drop his plan for founding colleges for Jesuit scholastics, and establish regular colleges for the laity at which boarding facilities would be provided for young men who had no desire to be Jesuits but who would possibly develop a vocation to the diocesan clergy. Nadal would, however, retain the ordinary obligation of founders to provide for the upkeep of a certain number of Jesuit scholastics in studies in proportion to the number of Jesuits on the teaching staff. He reminded Ignatius that this plan meshed with the Society's Constitutions.[21]

The core of Nadal's suggestion was not original. In one form or another, the idea had been on the minds of Jesuits since Claude Jay visited Germany and Austria ten years earlier. Only two years before Nadal arrived in Germany, Jesuits in Vienna discussed opening a college for "youths of noble blood" designed like the German College in Rome. Central to that concept was provision of boarding facilities. Several Jesuits urged this dimension of the Society's educational venture because they could not compete with the erosion of faith and morals the boys suffered by going home each day and mingling with their old friends and sometimes even members of their own families.

There lurked in this plan, too, a hope that from boarders some vocations to the Society might emerge. These Jesuits thought the discipline experienced in a boarding school might ease the painful transition from lay life to religious life. Nadal was not so sanguine. Among German and Austrian young men he saw only the none-too-robust possibility of a few vocations to the secular priesthood, because of the influence of Protestantism. Modest as was his hope, he nevertheless presented the suggestion with apprehension. Knowing the danger of arguing for an idea too forcefully, he wrote to Ignatius, "I hope you will pardon me if I have gone too far in pushing my viewpoint."[22]

In mid-April Nadal left Augsburg. He postponed his initial plan to go promptly to Vienna, since Cardinal Truchsess had asked him to go first to Dillingen and to evaluate the university there, an institution very dear to the cardinal. Truchsess wanted a report he could send to the pope. From the rector and professors, Nadal received a cordial welcome. For four days he examined the program of studies, the academic exercises, the quality of the students. He listened to lectures, participated in disputations. Despite several fine features of the university, he noted several lacunae. The university needed two professors of theology, one of philosophy, and four of Greek and Hebrew. To Ignatius he promptly sent a suggestion: "I would like to see the Society provide this help."[23]

Germany evoked from him what would be the cry of his lifetime: "In the suffering of today's world, the most heartrending and unbearable is to look upon the distress and the ruin of a nation so great, so powerful, so noble. Hope is high that with God's grace she can be helped. I am convinced that God wants to provide that help through the Society, backed with the authority of the Apostolic See." Those first few weeks in Augsburg and Dillingen implanted in Nadal's mind a fresh view of the purpose of the Society of Jesus. "I believe," he confided to Ignatius, "that God Our Lord raised the Society and gave it to the Church to down these heretics and infidels."[24] Lutherans became the whetstone on which Nadal sharpened his thoughts about the Society's presence in the world. Given this purpose, logic demanded that the Society channel into Germany its finest resources of talented and learned men. Nadal held this new conviction through the years.

On April 23 he and Jonas Adler left Dillingen for Vienna. Three days overland brought them to Regensburg. After five days on the Danube they reached Vienna. During the trip on the river, some Protestant passengers fanned the fire of Nadal's polemical spirit by debating whether they should hang "these papists [Nadal and Adler]." At Passau the boat made a stop. Nadal and Adler paid a visit to the bishop, Wolfgang von Klosen, who gave them a magnanimous welcome and saved them from the contemplated hanging by putting at their disposal a skiff fully provided with food and drink for the rest of the ride.[25]

On May 1, Nadal and Adler reached Vienna. Three years earlier Fr. Claude Jay, gentle and attractive founder of the city's Jesuit college, had died and left a community of Jesuits that included Frenchmen, Belgians, Spaniards, Italians, Germans,

Austrians, Hungarians, and Dutchmen. When Nadal arrived, the community, now thirty-eight, operated a school for three hundred boys. There he met two men who had given Jay sterling support in guiding the school through its first difficulties: the stolid and dutiful Belgian, Fr. Nicolas Lanoy, and the intelligent and reliable Dutchman who had been at his side in the founding of the college in Messina seven years earlier, Fr. Peter Canisius.

Within the community Nadal followed the routine he had used in Portugal and Spain: he gave conferences on the Constitutions, spoke with each Jesuit personally, clarified domestic rules, and officiated at the renewal of religious vows. He did something special for the Vienna community, too: he gave some directives "against the heretics." What those directives were Nadal did not mention. In the renewal of vows he sensed a burst of spiritual elation.[26]

In the college's church, however, he found two practices that yawed from the Constitutions: the chanting of the divine office and the singing of the Mass. To correct this, Nadal moved cautiously between two opposing demands: his responsibility to correct violations of the Constitutions and his worry about the wishes of King Ferdinand and Bishop Weber, who wanted neither the chanting nor the singing to be dropped. He managed a compromise. He arranged that those students of the college who were members of the choir would chant the office only at Vespers on solemn feast days and that a secular priest would be retained to sing the Mass.[27]

In the structure of the college he introduced an innovation: he opened an elementary school. He placed it under Jonas Adler, the scholastic who had come with him from Rome and who later left the Society because of psychological problems. The Society regarded the teaching of basic reading and writing as a work worthy of the Society but rarely undertaken because of lack of men. Nadal explained to Ignatius why he took this unusual step in Vienna. "I found it unsufferable, Father, to have tots of so tender an age under guidance of heretics or of men suspected of heresy. Practically every teacher in this Catholic country comes under either of those two headings. With no prior fanfare about the opening of this school, up to eighty youngsters registered. Jonas Adler is intensely happy to be in charge of the school. I myself am thoroughly overjoyed to see these little angels snatched from the hand of the devil precisely by means of this school." The Habsburg government undertook to construct a new building for "these little angels."[28]†

Then, in the college, Nadal unleashed a storm. He tried to confiscate the books and catechisms written by Protestants. Parents and even the boys themselves raised their hackles; in the purchase of those books they had invested a lot of money. Many students refused to surrender their volumes. Parents who had bought the books for their sons glowered with anger at the intruder from Rome. Nadal had a rebellion on his hands. Realizing he had to make amends for the property he had snatched, he promised to give the poorer students similar books written by Catholic authors. King Ferdinand bore the expense.[29]

Books became an obsession with Nadal. The Lutherans dominated the publishing fields. A spate of books came from their busy pens. Catholic authors seemed mute, so little did they produce; Catholic readers complained that the only works they could find were by Lutherans. Nadal spoke to the Austrian chancellor, Johann Albrecht Widmanstadt, and with his help established a Catholic printer whose publications would bear the mark of Habsburg approval in their contest "with this Lutheran pestilence." Into Peter Canisius' busy schedule Nadal interjected a crush of publishing projects: an enchiridion of the decrees of the Council of Trent and the Sunday gospels and epistles annotated with the Catholic interpretation, a compendium of Christian doctrine, a Latin translation of letters from Jesuit missionaries in the Indies, digests of works of Georg Witzel (a German apologist against the Protestants), various versions of the divine office including that of the Blessed Virgin Mary, a prayer book, a catechism for children (*la carta abcedaria per li putti*). Dutch Jesuit Nicholaes Goudanus, who had composed an index of questions taken from St. Thomas as an aid to the study of theology, was to help Canisius.[30]

---

†28 *Mon Nad,* I:311; *Cons,* no. 451. Adler's mental suffering overwhelmed him. He went from Vienna to Prague. There he left the Society. He then traveled to Rome and was readmitted. Sent to Trier, he again left the Society. He became a court preacher for the elector of Trier. Again he went to Rome and asked to be received into the Society. This time superiors refused. Twice he attempted suicide (*Mon Nad,* II:35 and n 5).

Nadal enlisted help outside the Society. He sought a directive from King Ferdinand that the royal official historian draw a chronological chart showing the succession of events in the Church's history, its councils, and heretics and their heresies. The purpose of this project was to show the continuity of the Catholic Church's authority, faith, and doctrine in Germany; to demonstrate the unbroken duration of Germany's obedience to the Catholic Church; "to offer in a terse way everything that can refute the heretics of Germany and can bolster the Catholics."[31] He told Ignatius that Germany needed Diego Laínez's theological and literary skills. "Over and beyond what his publications would achieve, Laínez by his presence and preaching would make a fine impact in this city and at this imperial court, on which depends, humanly speaking, the fate of so many peoples." Two months later Nadal again made this point with Ignatius.[32]

This burst of projects shows the measure of Nadal's worry about the Church in Germany, a worry that intensified as he moved from city to city. From Vienna he wrote to Ignatius on May 8, 1555: "The truth is this: ever since I arrived in Germany, I have been charged with a dream so aglow and a hope so fervid in the Society's ability to succor these peoples that the thought of staying here gives a lift to my spirit. No question, this conviction grips me: in no part of the world is the Society, supported of course by God's grace, more needed; in no part of the world would the Society be more helpful. It is more than a matter of opposing, with God's grace, the heretics. There is the very grave danger that if the remnant of Catholics here are not helped, in two years there will be not one in Germany. Everybody says this, even the Catholic leaders. What stirs me most is the awareness that practically everyone has lost hope that Germany can be salvaged. . . . I think that the task of helping Germany in its religious life is reserved to the Society."[33]

Nadal made clear to Ignatius where his heart lay. But he knew Ignatius' insistence on religious indifference. "Nothing, by God's grace, moves me so powerfully as the principle of submitting my will and judgment [to my superior] in obedience and religious indifference." He hastened to assure Ignatius that he ranked his yearnings for Germany behind the primacy of obedience to his superior. By mid-June he completed his visit to the college and the community. On June 20 he left Vienna for Italy. With him he took two scholastics who were assigned to continue their studies in Rome. As they passed through Villach, one of the scholastics was assured by some Protestants that the Jesuits would be, as were the Knights Templar, wiped out one day.[34]

Germany and Austria severely jolted Nadal. They struck him with the force of a new continent arising from the sea before the eyes of an explorer. As a Catholic and a Jesuit, no longer could he think as before. Rubbing shoulders with vital and hard-driving Lutherans shocked him. Encountering unnerved and ignorant Catholics appalled him. His stay north of the Alps did what his expedition into Africa had done six years earlier: it brought out the soldier in him. The challenge of the Lutheran replaced the challenge of the Moslem. The enemies of the Catholic Church were at the gates. He smelled the smoke of battle. This was where he belonged; this was where the Society of Jesus belonged. Still more, this was why God put the Society of Jesus in the world. Years later, toward the close of his life, one of his ambitions remained: "to write against the heretics." As soon as he entered Augsburg in 1555, he put a chip on his shoulder. He never took it off.

On July 4 he arrived in Venice. A long list of colleges awaited his visitation: Venice, Verona, Padua, Argenta, Ferrara, Modena, Bologna, Genoa, and Florence. In Portugal he had learned how one erratic Jesuit could throw his schedule into disarray. Teotonio da Braganza had chewed up precious days by his adolescent tantrums and spells of moodiness. In North Italy Nadal had had a like experience. Now, twice during this tour, he interrupted his work and traveled to visit a moody and recalcitrant Jesuit in Bassano. It was Fr. Simão Rodrigues, living in a hermitage there.

This unstable member of the first ten Jesuits continued to worry Ignatius, who granted him the judicial trial he requested on charges of malfeasance in Portugal. Rodrigues was found guilty. Ignatius lifted most of the penances imposed by the judges. But Rodrigues did not settle down. A restless spirit drove him from fancy to fancy. He wanted to be a hermit independent of Jesuit superiors; then he set his heart on a pilgrimage to Jerusalem; then he turned back to his desire to be a hermit. In that summer of 1555, he had settled in a hermitage in Bassano. His umbrage toward Ignatius persisted. He even turned a phrase of the *Spiritual Exercises* against the general, admonishing him that "love is proved by deeds."

Cities in Italy visited by Nadal

Nadal first interrupted his schedule in mid-July. After visiting the colleges at Venice and Padua, on his own initiative (*mea sponte*) he went to Bassano. Knowing the strained relations between Rodrigues and Ignatius, he hoped to effect a reconciliation. Through two days, the conversation between the two men swung between friendly chitchat and serious debate. Until noon of the first day together, they did not get beyond ordinary pleasantries. Then Nadal challenged Rodrigues: why was he living as a hermit when the Society needed workers? Rodrigues defended his unusual status: he was in Bassano by religious obedience. (Ignatius had indeed allowed him to gratify his desire to live as a hermit.) Nadal remonstrated that the tone of some of his letters to Ignatius was deplorable. Rodrigues countered that, since he was a founder of the Society, he was entitled to great liberty in his mode of expression. Nadal admonished him that, as a founder, he was expected to show great humility. They got nowhere. On the next day, July 22, the Feast of St. Mary Magdalen, each offered Mass for the other. But concord eluded them. For a good part of the day they meandered through their memories of past events, yet each statement seemed only to be an invitation to make a distinction.[35]

On the next day Nadal left Bassano. The separation was cordial enough, for Rodrigues accompanied his visitor a bit down the road from the hermitage. Nadal reported to Ignatius that Rodrigues was well and amply stocked with provisions. He offered him a small amount of money, but Rodrigues declined. "I suspect," Nadal wrote, "that he has money and no expenses. He's doing well." Nadal warned Ignatius that, should Rodrigues return to the regular life of the Society, he would not be disposed to do any work. "He would want to do nothing save while away his time amid nicely cushioned circumstances. He told me clearly that his working days are over."[36]

About eight weeks later, Nadal returned to Bassano. Ignatius instructed him to speak once more with Rodrigues and assured Nadal that he had complete authority to resolve this unhappy situation. On this visit Nadal had a measure of success. He brought Rodrigues to what he called "something of a middle ground" (*aliquam mediocritatem*), and he left the disgruntled man in an effusive mood. With warm words for his visitor, Rodrigues wrote Ignatius that Nadal was at that moment with him in Bassano "and cheers me mightily by his being here and chatting with me. I am sorry for the worry that I caused him. I am also sorry for my letters that, he tells me, upset you." He asked Ignatius to send him a blessing so large that it would stretch right to the Bassano mountains.[37]

Nadal interleaved the visits to Rodrigues between his visits to the eight colleges in northern Italy. Those colleges composed what could be called a Jesuit Triangle. One line went from Venice and Padua through Ferrara and Modena to Genoa, another line from Genoa to Florence, and the third from Florence through Bologna and Argenta to Venice and Padua. The eight colleges within that triangle were mere saplings, with the average number of Jesuits in each about ten. Argenta had four; Genoa, Ferrara, and Venice had twelve. The average number of students was about one hundred. Modena, the weakest, sometimes dropped to twenty boys; Genoa, the strongest, enrolled about two hundred. In those colleges Nadal followed the routine he had developed in Portugal and Spain: conferences on the Constitutions and the Common Rules, interviews with each Jesuit and the hearing of their general confessions, adjustment of local twists and turns to the pattern of the Roman College. The amount of time given to formal prayer by scholastics he brought into accord with the Constitutions. Ignatius' rebuke on the length of prayer had left its impress.[38]

Physical facilities differed from city to city. In Ferrara the Jesuit quarters were clean and the school was adequate. In Genoa the bustle of a bakery beneath their rooms ruffled the Jesuits. In Modena they tried in vain to leave their cramped quarters in an unhealthy part of the city, where three had died in three years. Nadal thought of closing the school. In Venice they settled in a section of the Priory of Santa Trinità offered them by their Benedictine friend, Prior Andrea Lippomani, but they lost a good measure of privacy. Between the prior's quarters and the Jesuit section ran an open passage through which lay persons, including women who laundered the prior's linens, went to and fro. Nadal found this intolerable, and obtained Lippomani's kind consent to close the passage. In Padua he ousted the gardener, who had his residence in a corner of the school's garden.

Benefactors often made the difference between a school's success or failure. The archbishop of Genoa, Girolamo Sauli, assured Nadal of a greater income to remedy that college's financial plight, but Nadal was unable to set the precise details before he left for Rome. During the negotiations, moreover, Sauli put Nadal in an awkward position. He suggested that the Jesuits and the Barnabites unite. Ignatius had earlier encountered a similar proposal from Fr. Francisco de Medde, a member of the Minors of the Observance, that the Jesuits unite with the Theatines and the Somaschi. Loyola rejected all these proposals with the same answer: the service of God would be better achieved with each order pursuing its own character, purpose, and spirit.

Andrea Lippomani's generosity outstripped his resources. He had assured the Jesuits in the Venice college of bed and board, but at supper for the twelve of them the table held only a melon and six pieces of bread. Nadal gave the rector, Fr. Caesare Helmio, permission to beg, but secretly lest he hurt the feelings of Prior Lippomani.

The college in Modena moved steadily toward the brink of ruin. The bishop of the city and the duke of Ferrara promised financial help but kept their purse strings tightly tied. Increasing hostility isolated the Jesuits even more: the city council disliked their work; the diocesan clergy held excommunication over the heads of those who sought counsel of the Jesuits; the Dominicans voiced outright disapproval.

In Ferrara, on the other hand, the Jesuits had their Lady Bountiful—but she exacted a price. The pious wife of the city's governor, Maria Frassoni del Gesso, insisted that French Jesuit Jean Pelletier be left in Ferrara. The Society was not to move him.

The quirks of some Jesuits also demanded attention. In Venice Nadal met two scholastics who vexed him. Arnold Conchus flaunted his disobedient spirit; for a penance Nadal sent him on a pilgrimage to Rome. Another scholastic listed in the Society's records simply as "Pietro" had an odd view of his vocation. He planned to stay in the Society two years: adequate time, he thought, to study enough to make his way in life as a layperson. Nadal dismissed him.

The rector of the college in Genoa likewise irked Nadal. Gaspar de Loarte, one of the two New Christians he had brought from Spain a year earlier, wanted to open his preaching apostolate in Genoa in the grand manner, in the pulpit of the city's largest church. Nadal urged him not to try for a big splash lest he then be asked to drop to a smaller church.

Loarte ignored Nadal's caution. In his diary Nadal noted, "I yielded to his wish. And what I thought would happen happened."

An old European curse thwarted Nadal's schedule at least twice. The plague was abroad in northern Italy during that summer and fall of 1555. Florence and Bologna closed their city gates for a week lest strangers import the disease. In Padua, Nadal, anxious to keep the school and the church open during the epidemic, ordered the Jesuits to avoid hearing confessions of people confined to their homes lest they become infected and bring a quarantine on the school and the church. More than plague endangered Nadal's life. Even far from the Mediterranean, an old bugbear—travel over water—hounded him. On one trip across the Po, the boat, loaded with horses, almost went under.[39]

Hastings Rashdall once wrote: "Ideals pass into great historic forces by embodying themselves in institutions."[40] He was writing of the university as one achievement of the medieval genius embodying its ideal of life in a concrete form. During the three months Nadal spent in the northern Italian Jesuit colleges, he demonstrated his capacity for taking Ignatius' ideals and embodying them within the structures of colleges. This talent had first revealed itself at Messina in Sicily, then in Portugal and Spain. Austria and northern Italy honed his practical skills more finely. With his power to articulate Ignatius' ideals in conferences he meshed his power to articulate those ideals in colleges. In him, the thinker and the builder met. All the colleges he had visited were, save Messina, started by others. But with his strong practical sense, his grasp of details, and his experience of the limitations imposed by local history, he gave them a visible coherence, a structural wholeness, and a recognizable character. More than any other Jesuit, he invested Ignatius' idea of a school with the capacity to become a historical force.

During this tour north and south of the Alps, Nadal thought much about Ignatius and his plans for the Society. His letters to Rome show this. Perhaps the most vivid story he heard about Ignatius during this period reached him in July. In Bologna, he and Fr. Alfonso Salmerón crossed paths as Salmerón was on his way with a papal mission to Germany and Poland. Salmerón told Nadal that in one day Ignatius had dismissed from the Society ten Jesuits attached to the German College. "And on that day Fr. Ignatius appeared to be far more content than he usually is."[41]

Nadal reached Rome again, on October 5 or 6. The first Jesuit he met there was Laínez, who greeted him with the news that Ignatius intended to send him to Spain very soon. A little later he met Ignatius. Ignatius became irked when he discovered that Laínez had scooped him about Nadal's next assignment. He also let Nadal know that he was displeased Laínez and Nadal had not worked smoothly together on their trip to Germany eight months earlier.[42]

The busy circuit through Bavaria, Austria, and northern Italy hid a mystery about Nadal. His correspondence teems with hundreds of details about contracts, schedules, travels, housing, food, books, and benefactors. Save for the conventional closings of his letters—"May the Lord ever strengthen us in his grace" and "May the Lord give us the grace to sense his holy will and do it fully"—Nadal uttered nary a peep about his surging, driving life of prayer. But, even as he wrote his letters, he scratched away at his *Orationis observationes*. Neither set of documents, however, intimates the existence of the other. A reader of the correspondence would never guess at the existence of the *Orationis observationes*; nor would a reader of the *Orationis observationes* guess, save for one or two fragments, at the corpus of business letters.

The memory of Ignatius made Nadal wistful. The recollection of Ignatius' mystical graces especially set him musing. On this pensive note he opened his private notes of this period. Devoutly he recalled Ignatius' close union with God and the wisdom and holiness that emanated from that high union. And in the well of his soul, this recollection churned again the deep waters of his desire for mystical prayer. An old heartache of the Majorcan days reawakened. Gentle though this aching was, it demanded gratification. It was urgent. "I must in all gentleness take hold of his [Ignatius'] elevation of soul and practice of high virtue."[43]

Through his notes of 1555, Nadal's persistent search for the higher gifts appeared time and again. He reflected, for example, on the meeting of Christ and the Samaritan woman at Jacob's well. "Christ sits at the well of grace and talks to the Samaritan woman to teach us a lesson: when in our need we ask Christ for something tangible, let us lift up our spirit a bit and listen to Christ speaking within us and inviting us to ask him for things that are spiritual." He reflected on the Holy Eucharist. "Through the sacrament of the Eucharist we put on Christ. In it we grasp something that gives us the capacity to experience God." Feeling God, perceiving God, experiencing God—these themes cut deep through Nadal's notes of 1555.[44]

These themes he interleaved with jottings on that special topic in mystical theology called "the spiritual senses." Here he followed St. Bonaventure and other classical authors in their speculation about mystical prayer. Nadal's language on the spiritual senses, however, often lacked precision. At times he wrote of the faculty of perceiving spiritual objects (*sentido espiritual*); at other times he wrote of the act of perceiving, of feeling spiritual objects (*sentimiento espiritual*). On occasion he slipped from one to the other in mid-paragraph and lost thereby a single consistent meaning.[45]

For these spiritual faculties, wellsprings of the graces of higher prayer, he had high esteem. He drew the classical distinction between two kinds of "senses of the spirit": first, those that correspond to the external senses of hearing, seeing, touching, tasting, and smelling. These he located at the level of the corporeal and the imaginative. Second were those that correspond to the interior senses of the soul at the level of the higher faculties of mind and will. The latter especially absorbed Nadal's study and speculation. A person who tastes interiorly the sweetness of divine gifts is impelled to cry out: "My heart and my flesh rejoice in the living God" and "My soul thirsts for thee; my flesh pines for thee."[46]

In *De la oración, especialmente para los de la Compañía* ("On Prayer: Especially for Those of the Society"), a work written nearly a decade later, Nadal expressed more clearly his understanding of the spiritual senses. He wrote of the principal spiritual senses as "extensions of the three theological virtues. From the conviction of faith comes the power to hear; from insight into faith comes the power to see; from hope comes the power to smell; from the union of love comes the power to touch; from the joy of love comes the power to taste. These spiritual senses are aids that dispose the soul for the higher graces Jesus Christ Our Lord gives to those who ask for them. He who possesses these graces recognizes them for what they are."[47]

Within the fine and noble faculties of these spiritual senses Nadal recognized an essential dependence. Their efficacy heightened or weakened in the measure of purification of the external senses. On this premise Nadal hammered without cease. For himself he prayed that his external senses be untouched by sensations that carried spiritual corruption, and that this purity of the species grasped by the external senses, as well as the unalloyed delight of the external senses, permeate his interior corporeal senses and his interior spiritual senses. Fidelity to the basic purity of the sensations, he knew, reaps for the spiritual senses a harvest of delight. Still more, God refreshes a soul with gifts of understanding, ardor, and joy. Nadal flew his kite high, but he kept it tied to the bulwark of purification.[48]

Purification implies penance. This implication Nadal evoked many times through 1555: penance must be at the base of all aspiration to higher prayer. He mastered this lesson during his novitiate in Rome, when he learned from Ignatius that spiritual growth depends on the radical surrender of self-will. That lesson endured. He reminded himself that beginners must grasp this lesson thoroughly and must resolve to do penance throughout their lives. So intense must this resolve be that, even if future directors counsel a concentration on other spiritual exercises, "the genuine sense of penance and mortification will nevertheless live on." Nadal could not have been more adamant. Other paths, he wrote, end in superficiality. Neglect of mortifying moral blemishes ends in squandering God's graces. This loss must be "strenuously" (*vehementer*) avoided.[49]

Penance therefore is essential, but for more than making satisfaction for sin. The intense grasp of spiritual truths demands penance, for through penance the external senses are purified. Time and again in 1555 Nadal returned to this theme. "Penance must ever be the option." "To the cross must preference ever be given." "Penance breaks down, sin rules." "To tribulation and suffering must precedence be given, since in them the power of Christ glows more truly."[50]

The theology of purification, for all its vigor, was, in Nadal's mind, sprung from a wider theological truth: God's action in the soul. Through that action coursed God's power, animating the soul and drawing it to higher gifts of prayer. Into purification coursed a divine power that gave the soul audacity for purifying conquests of mortification. The spirit of purification lived with the life of God present in the soul.[51] Reflections of this kind excited Nadal's yearning of decades: to experience God's action within his soul. "Faith lifts you up and over to hope. Faith and hope lift you up and over to charity, to the Divine Power, to the Holy Spirit dwelling and working within you. All this opens the spiritual understanding of what it means to love God above all things and so to fulfill the first and highest law. To one who experiences the love of God poured into our hearts through the Holy Spirit . . . all this is clear."[52]

Nadal sought to move beyond the perception of God's power and the dwelling of the Holy Spirit within him. He aspired to that delicate fidelity to the graces that drew him into a close identification with Christ. "The Holy Spirit has given you the gift of union with Christ Jesus and his Might. Use this gift assiduously, so that you may come to the spiritual insight that you are really understanding with his mind, choosing with his will, remembering with his memory, living and acting completely in Christ and not in yourself. To attain this perception in this life is to reach the highest perfection. It is really Divine Power at work. It brings an awesome sweetness."[53]

Nadal's spiritual notes of 1555 are a tangle of personal experiences and snippets from technical theology of the mystical life. They record his effort to give a theological interpretation of his efforts in purification and in intimate perception of God. He did not, however, forge a synthesis. He did not put into a neat package his disjointed pieces of mystical theory and personal interior experience. Nor did he offer a harmonious melding of his interior yearnings and his exterior undertakings. As he ranged from meeting Protestants in Augsburg to opening a printing house in Vienna, from feeding hungry Jesuits in Venice to stiffening a wobbly college in Modena, he gave no hint to others of the busy beaver burrowing through the soil beneath his exterior life, striving to reach the light of a day illumined by the sun of mystical union with God.

10

A Garbled Assignment

Fr. Ignatius had directed me to help Master Francis.
He wanted us to work together on the more serious
problems. When, however, I detected that Fr. Francis
resented my association with his governance, I held
myself in check. After two or three setbacks in offering
my advice, I stopped.

Nadal about Borgia, 1556

Only fifteen days after Nadal arrived in Rome from Germany
and northern Italy,[1†] Ignatius sent him to Spain to conduct a
visitation there. It was a painful and hobbling experience.
Ignatius made it so, perhaps unwittingly. On October 21, 1555,
he signed three documents. In one, to Nadal, he listed detailed
instructions for the visitation. In the second, to Francis Borgia,
the general's deputy in Spain, he gave a briefing about the
mission Nadal had there. In the third, to Fr. Antonio Araoz,
provincial of Castile, he outlined Nadal's duties in Spain.

---

†1 During this brief stay, Nadal aided Ignatius with some administrative
business and participated in a meeting of several priests that reached conclusions about the Society's Constitutions. The stay may have been brief, but it
was long enough for Nadal's impetuous tongue to get him in trouble again.
Ignatius mentioned that he wanted a document written on obedience and
that he intended to give this commission to Fr. Cristóbal de Madrid, a Spanish
secular priest who was still a novice. Nadal blurted out: "What novice could
carry that assignment off?" Ignatius nevertheless commissioned Madrid (*Mon
Nad*, II:38–39).

Between the document to Nadal and the document to Borgia, Ignatius left a serious discrepancy. He foresaw that the presence in Spain of two men invested with the powers of general could lead only to confrontation. He therefore made an accommodation. Following his practice of never putting Borgia under the jurisdiction of another, he tilted his accommodation in favor of the former duke. He instructed Nadal that his powers as vicar general were to be suspended in Spain but would remain in place throughout the rest of the Society. He told Borgia the same thing. He also informed Nadal that in Spain, although without the power of vicar general, he was nevertheless not to be subject to any superior. This he did *not* tell Borgia. Borgia readily and understandably concluded that he would be Nadal's superior in Spain. By this lapse Ignatius so set the two main Jesuit cogs in Spain that they did not mesh. The entire visitation was distressed by the grinding and whining of wheels out of gear.[2]

In certain areas of his instructions, Ignatius seemed to be trying to perform a juggling act. In admitting priests to solemn vows, Nadal and Borgia were to share authority; in giving directives to provincials and rectors about the Constitutions and Common Rules, Nadal was to do nothing without first conferring with Borgia and receiving his approval; in making contact with potential benefactors of the Roman College, Nadal was to enjoy almost unlimited authority; in changing Jesuits from one place to another, Nadal could act freely, save for Borgia and Fr. Antonio de Córdoba; in choosing companions on his begging tours, Nadal was to have complete freedom. This body of distinctions only made more clumsy the relationship between two men who already had different understandings of their roles in the coming visitation.[3]

Ignatius let it be known that in the visitation he had a double purpose: Nadal was to assist Borgia in promulgation of the Constitutions and in governance of the Society in Spain; Nadal was to join Borgia in a quest for funds for the seriously straitened Roman College. Ignatius may also have had an unwritten reason. Only a few months earlier, Ignatius openly acknowledged that some Spanish Jesuits were pressing him to send Nadal back to Spain as general's deputy. Behind their insistent requests lurked the implication that they would like to see Borgia replaced. Ignatius never spelled out that implication publicly; in any event, he left Borgia in Spain.[4]

On October 23, Nadal left Rome for Genoa. With him went Fr. Luis Gonçalves da Câmara, the Portuguese priest who had received the dictation of Ignatius' autobiography, and Fr. Pedro de Ribadeneira, who had business to conduct for Ignatius in the Netherlands. At Florence, Ribadeneira left the other two and proceeded to Flanders. At Genoa the trip came to a halt.

Uncertain sailings and bad weather through November and most of December kept Nadal and Câmara in Genoa. During this long wait, thirteen scholastics assigned to Portugal for studies joined them. Nicolò Sauli, brother of Genoa's archbishop, received the entire party into his home at nearby Carignano. On December 5, Nadal wrote to Ignatius that the seas and winds were still uncertain. Bad experiences at sea in the past churned his apprehensions. "May the Lord get us to Spain in good time and with only a tiny dose of seasickness," he wrote to Ignatius. A week later the baggage was stored aboard a ship but bad weather continued to hold them in port. Nadal's last letter from Genoa, on December 13, reported that they were still waiting for a break in the weather. At last it came and, on December 21, they sailed out to sea, two months after they left Rome.[5]

Ten days later they opened the New Year by landing at Alicante on January 1. Shortly thereafter Nadal visited the marquesa de Elche, sister of the troublesome Teotonio da Braganza, who received him kindly despite her anger with Ignatius and the Society over the dismissal of her brother. A few days later they went to Murcia. There the bishop outfitted them all with new clothes. Nadal gave final instructions and dispatched Câmara and the scholastics to Portugal. He moved to Valencia to begin ten months of begging for the Roman College and spot-checking the religious spirit of the Jesuit colleges.[6]

During those ten months, Nadal and Borgia frequently conferred. They soon locked horns. Nadal discovered that Borgia had been violating the Constitutions in his organization of some new colleges. Borgia had drawn up some contracts between the Society and benefactors in which, for the pledge of a certain financial foundation that assured bed and board to the Jesuits, the Society guaranteed a certain number of teachers in, say, Latin, Greek, and philosophy. Those terms were correct. But Borgia went further. With the count of Monterrey and the bishop of Plasencia he made contracts in which, for a guarantee of physical sustenance of the Jesuits, the Society pledged a preacher, a confessor, and a professor of theology. Since

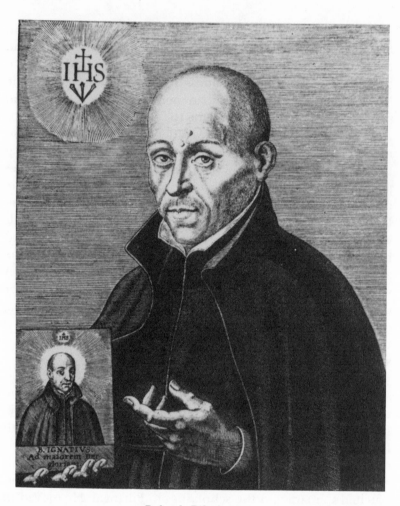

Pedro de Ribadeneira

preaching, hearing confessions, and teaching theology were spiritual ministries—as teaching Latin, Greek, and philosophy were not—and since the Constitutions prohibited the acceptance of temporal remuneration for spiritual ministries, Borgia's contracts were out of order.

Nadal called Borgia's attention to these violations of the Society's law, and he cautioned him that Ignatius would not approve his contracts. Borgia bridled and made no effort to hide his huff. Nadal caught the signal: his presence in Spain rankled Borgia. And he was correct in predicting Ignatius' response. The general refused to endorse Borgia's irregular contracts.[7] Some twelve years later, Nadal and Borgia would change roles on the issue of college contracts. In Germany, Nadal would plead for a mitigation of the Constitutions' ban on contracting for the Society's spiritual ministries. In Rome Fr. General Borgia would reject Nadal's arguments and hold him to strict interpretation of the Society's law. And once more sparks would fly between the two men.

On the issue of college contracts, Borgia was not alone in incurring the disapproval of Ignatius. Nadal, too, ran afoul of the general. Ignatius had devised a way of supporting the scholastics who were engaged in the academic part of their formation. He asked founders of colleges, in exchange for the Jesuit teachers, to carry the living expenses of some of those young Jesuit students. In 1553 he drew up a formula, which did not, however, specify any definite number of scholastics as he would do a little later. Nadal, however, anticipated Ignatius. He *did* specify, by stipulating in the contracts that for each teacher the Society provided to a college the founder would sustain two Jesuit students. His precision brought a rebuke from Ignatius. He had no business outrunning the general in exactitude. This reproof angered him. In a tiff he scrawled a sizzling reply to Ignatius. But calm soon returned. He destroyed his fiery message and penned another in words humble and cordial.[8]

Undismayed by Borgia's umbrage, Nadal continued to express his reserve about the general's deputy's way of doing things. At one college, Borgia allowed a certain Master Montesa to live in the Jesuit quarters. Nadal told Borgia that he disapproved. Borgia took into a Jesuit residence a man wounded in a brawl; Nadal demurred. Borgia reserved a section of a Jesuit house for visitors; Nadal frowned. Borgia had his fill of all this.

One day at Simancas when he, Nadal, Fr. Juan Bautista Barma, and Fr. Antonio Araoz were together, he openly chided Nadal for his "troublesome" visit. "I pretended," Nadal recalled, "that I did not notice his outburst. After all, I knew full well that I was not his subject."[9]

Borgia, however, thought otherwise. Nadal *was* his subject. The gremlin of Ignatius' imprecise instructions was at work and in Valladolid brought the two men into a painful confrontation. Fr. Barma was preparing to pronounce his final vows as a professed father. Borgia arranged an elaborate feast, to which he invited such distinguished guests as Prince Philip's son Don Carlos, the papal nuncio, several nobles, and superiors of other religious orders. Nadal disapproved of this grand display. During the feast, out of the blue, Borgia turned to Nadal and ordered him to go to the pulpit in the dining room and explain in Latin to the guests the Institute of the Society of Jesus. Nadal was angered. Knowing that Borgia had no authority to give that order, he resented being taken off guard and unprepared for that kind of talk. A spasm of indignation instinctively crossed his face. He could not check it. But he did what Borgia ordered, and for an hour elucidated the Jesuit way of life to the guests. His own reflection on the episode: "It did not turn out too badly." Fr. Pedro de Tablares, who was there, thought Nadal did well. And the members of other religious orders found it instructive.[10]

The array of celebrities at Barma's feast reflected the honored position Borgia still enjoyed among the socially elite of Spain. He remained a confidant of Emperor Charles; he had ready access to the imperial court. This piqued Nadal's curiosity a little. He wanted a glimpse of what went on in the high places of Spain, and asked Borgia to take him along on one of his visits to Prince Carlos. Borgia did so. What Nadal saw did not impress him; he thought he had been privy to quite a batch of blather. In his diary he entered the observation: "Only once did I go to see Prince Carlos. Twaddle, twaddle . . . "[11]

Borgia's resentment of the visitation made it especially difficult for Nadal to deliver to him a special message from Ignatius. Ignatius had directed Nadal to convey to Borgia a reprimand because of his severe penances. He was to moderate them. Nadal recalled the tense moment: "On a certain occasion, the

two of us were in a small library together. I ventured to tell him
that Fr. Ignatius wanted him to stop torturing himself with
disciplines and other penances. In ire he exploded, 'Between
the two of you, you will drive me to the Carthusians.'"[12]

Two other Spanish superiors added to Nadal's discomfort.
Antonio Araoz, provincial of Castile, lashed him with a biting
criticism of the law on prayer in the Constitutions. He wanted the
imposition of longer prayer. Nettled by Ignatius' restraining
rules, he vented his anger on Nadal. Nadal answered in kind. The
encounter turned into a heated shouting match (*vehemens
concertatio*). Araoz did not reserve his venom for Nadal alone. He
resented Borgia, who he thought was intruding on his turf. "Fr.
Araoz," notes Nadal, "is not on good terms with Fr. Francis. He
has washed his hands of governing his province, since Fr. Francis
has taken practically the entire operation into his own hands."[13]

Fr. Francisco Estrada, provincial of Aragon, gave Nadal a
severe reproof for a favor Nadal had done him. Two years
earlier, when Nadal informed Estrada that Ignatius had appointed him superior of the Aragon province, Estrada, thirsting
for contemplation and study in theology, balked at taking the
post. Nadal pampered him by arranging that Estrada have two
assistants, one to handle the routine governance of the province,
the other to assist him in his theological studies. Now, in 1556,
Estrada turned on Nadal. Disgruntled by the accommodations
Nadal had arranged for him, he released a torrent of abuse on
Nadal. Nadal had his fill. "I retorted words that cut even more
deeply than the words he loosed at me. That shut him up. He
stopped badgering me."[14]

Sickness salted Nadal's wounds. At one point, for several days
he drank water charged with sarsaparilla. It helped. He took
larger draughts. Then the sarsaparilla excited his catarrh. He
stopped taking the potion. At another time during this illness
the strength of his right hand drained away. His thumb became
so limp that only with difficulty was he able to write.[15]

Nadal took stock of the tangled mess of his relations with
Borgia. He decided to retreat before Borgia's resentment. "Fr.
Ignatius had directed me to help Master Francis. He wanted us
to work together on the more serious problems. When, however, I detected that Fr. Francis resented my association with
his governance, I held myself in check. After two or three

setbacks in offering my advice, I stopped." He left Borgia a free hand. "As far as governance was concerned, I became a man of leisure."

This surrender to Borgia was nothing less than evasion of duty. Nadal was doing no better than Araoz, the frequent butt of his criticism.[16] Clarification of the chain of command was essential. The time had long come to correct misunderstandings planted by Ignatius' imprecise instructions, but Nadal let that time slip, threw up his hands, and accepted the humiliating stings of Borgia's lordliness. His guiding principle was not clear. If personal growth in humility motivated him, he had no business putting his personal spiritual perfection before the task Ignatius had given him. In any event, he faltered when he should have stood firm.

During this period of self-imposed leisure he began to collect his reflections on the Society's Constitutions. This work fills twenty-two pages of the *MHSI* and is called *Annotationes in Constitutiones* ("Remarks on the Constitutions").[17] The opening paragraph was a loud, thundering one of high emotional intensity and Nadal kept this high pitch through many parts of the *Annotationes*. As he wrote, he imagined himself addressing fellow Jesuits. "As I set about making some brief observations on the Society's Constitutions and Rules with Christ Jesus as my guide—by God was he made our Wisdom—it occurred to me that I should first ask: what is a religious order? I beg you, my dear fathers and brothers in Christ, bear with me, a foolish and prosaic nonentity. Pray for me. If I write something that throws light on our Institute, recognize that it is from the Father of lights and inspirations in answer to your sacrifices and prayers in Christ Jesus. If, however, you judge what I say to be foolishness, oppose it, denounce it, obliterate it. Then give me a penance for my rash and haughty words."[18]

Nadal returned to several ideas he expounded in his conferences of 1554: God's presence and action in the successive ages of the Church; the Society of Jesus as a gift of God's grace to the current age of the Church. Some of these he amplified: Jesuits are more than men of community, they are pilgrims; Jesuit life resembles the life of the apostles.[19]

Some peculiar twists of the *Annotationes* and some comments on them follow:

In the course of history, God is at work in each age. "If we study the ages of the Church, never was grace more plentiful than when trials were more acute. Was there ever greater distress in the Church than when Christ was killed on the Cross? That age was the most grace-filled of all, the age by far most sublime." And so through the centuries of the martyrs, the monks, the friars that followed, to this moment in the sixteenth century. The latest in that long line of graces given the Church is "this least congregation."[20]

The coming of the Society of Jesus is the streaming of God's power into the current world, a judgment that throbbed with audacity. To compare a group of nine hundred men with the great religious orders of the past smacked of knight-errantry. Yet Nadal pierced the veil of the future correctly.

Again, Nadal developed an idea he proposed two years earlier in Spain, and one to which he would return later: the Society's inner life and purpose are designed according to those of the apostles. He pushed that idea further. The apostles were initially called to learn about Christ; Jesuits, in their first probation, are invited to learn about the Society's Institute and its grace of vocation. The apostles' call then broadened into an invitation to follow Christ, to listen to his teaching, to order their lives according to that teaching, in short to equip themselves for apostolic responsibility. During their second probation, the Jesuits' call widens into an invitation to a formation in virtue and letters to ready them to take the apostolic duties of a professed father. The apostles were sent to preach the gospel to every creature, to administer the sacraments, to care for the spiritual needs of all. Jesuits have the same vocation: to preach, to lecture on scripture, to teach catechism, to counsel, to give the Spiritual Exercises, to administer the sacraments: in short, to engage in every ministry of the word.[21]

Nadal pushed his comparisons a bit too far, to some rather farfetched, even silly, conclusions. The apostles avoided tasks that distracted them from prayer and ministry of the word; Jesuits have spiritual and temporal coadjutors who take tasks that would otherwise constrain the free movement of the professed fathers in preaching the Word. The apostles were sent, by Peter undoubtedly, to every land; Jesuits are dispatched by the successor of Peter to every people. The apostles did not wear the garb of monks; Jesuits wear the clothes common to clerics of Rome, a dress not unlike the garb of the apostles. The apostles did not take the duty of singing psalms and hymns; Jesuits do not chant the divine office in choir.[22]

In this lengthy section of the *Annotationes,* Nadal honed more finely his perception of Jesuit mobility. The apostles had no houses where they lived together; they were always out winning people to Christ. "Jesuits have this special purpose: not only to live as brothers in houses but also to be on the road fishing for men, especially in places where we see no other fishermen."[23] The image of the Jesuit as a man of the road fascinated Nadal. The more it absorbed him, the more he blurred the picture of the Jesuit living fraternally in a dwelling with other Jesuits. The early balance he set between the Jesuit "in a house" and the Jesuit "on the road" he gradually tilted in favor of the Jesuit "on the road." The tilt toward the road gave a true picture of Nadal's Jesuit.[24]

The Jesuit took the road to labor for others. This concept seeped through Nadal's thinking on the Society. So convinced was he that labor for others was a distinctive grace of the Society that he wrote: "A task that ordinarily strikes one as hard and perilous is for us sweet and easy because of the illuminations of divine light that are given us. Emphatically, therefore, we take measure of our spiritual progress according to the intensity with which we take work for the salvation and perfection of our neighbor."[25] Nadal directed Jesuits to avoid false modesty about this distinctive vocation. "This vocation is a copy and a showing of the apostolic way of life. We should not be embarrassed because of this divine grace given us and the Church. God did not want this grace hidden under a bed but placed on a lampstand to throw its light."[26]

On September 17 or 18, while meeting with Borgia and the three Spanish provincials in Valladolid, Nadal heard news that brought his visitation to an abrupt halt. A letter from Pedro de Ribadeneira, then in Flanders, to Borgia announced that Ignatius had died in Rome on July 31. "At first I was filled with sadness," he wrote. "Then a certain strength and joy of spirit prevailed." But he faced a serious personal problem: was he still vicar general, invested with authority to convene a general congregation to elect the new general? He judged that he was. Borgia and the provincials agreed. But then Nadal began to doubt. Did his power as vicar general in fact continue after Ignatius' death? Despite his doubts he decided to alert all the provinces to prepare to elect delegates to the general congregation. Events in Italy made him anxious to leave for Rome as soon as possible. A lull in the war between the Holy See and Spain opened the highways. Lest resumed hostilities close the roads, he wished to start immediately.[27]

Borgia could not join him, since his doctors judged the trip would jeopardize his life. Araoz, Estrada, and Bustamante either refused outright to go or showed little inclination to do so. Nadal asked what they thought of his going to Rome alone. He recalled the sequel. "They consulted. Through Bustamente they communicated their judgment: I should not go to Rome; I should stay in the province of Aragon until the time was set to convene a general congregation. This opinion troubled me. I do not know how many suspicious thoughts ran through my head that they were not dealing with the issue honestly. Later it occurred to me that they were hoping to run the election away from Rome. (This they tried to do in the next year, and they tried with great gusto.) I therefore hid nothing of my disgust for their opinion. I rejected it openly: I made no pretense of doing anything else. I told them that I wanted to leave for Rome the next day, and that is precisely what I did. I arrived at Torquemada later the same day."[28]

Frankness and forthrightness did nothing to sweeten short tempers. "Because of my free tongue," continued Nadal, "Fr. Francis and all the others became angry with me. So far was I from a mood to temper my remarks that I reached the point of blasting Fr. Francis, who kept nagging me." He advised Francis that what respect he had for him was based not on his erstwhile title of duke but on his current identity as a Jesuit. His message to Borgia was blunt: get off your high horse and stop playing the duke.[29]

Separation from Borgia and the provincials did not lessen Nadal's bad temper. With ill grace he received the kindness of others. Looking for a horse, he was edgy lest he acquire a nag. Master Montesa graciously offered him a fine horse. "With little show of gratitude I accepted his offer. For my brusque manner I was truly sorry." He covered thirty miles to Torquemada by nightfall. At Torquemada a fever hit him. The next day, grumpy and tightfisted, he haggled with a merchant over the price of a partridge. These slivers of irritation stuck in his memory. He thought them worthy of inclusion in his *Ephemerides* ("Diary").[30]

Somewhere, perhaps at Burgos, he received news from Polanco that the professed fathers in and about Rome, Martín de Olave, André des Freux, Diego Laínez, Nicolás Bobadilla, Ponce de Cogordan, and Juan de Polanco, had elected Diego Laínez vicar general and that the general congregation was to convene in spring of 1557. This surprising news had the makings of a confrontation between himself and Laínez, especially since relations between the two men had not been easy. Nadal, however, quickly extracted the fuse; he declined to press his own title to the post and openly backed Laínez. "This news did not upset me," he wrote.[31]

The election of Laínez as vicar general was a complex story. At his death, Ignatius left a maze of doubts about who held the highest authority in the Society. He had not revoked Nadal's authority as vicar general, but Nadal was thousands of miles away from Rome. Grievously sick and only days before his death, Ignatius placed the governance of the Society into the hands of Polanco and Fr. Cristóbal de Madrid. In that foggy situation, Polanco, preoccupied with assuring the legitimacy of the new vicar general, thought an election would establish the desired legitimacy. He did, therefore, what the Constitutions prescribed in the event a general died without designating a vicar general: he summoned the professed fathers in and about Rome to elect a vicar general. On August 4, six votes were cast; Laínez received the majority.

Polanco had acted quickly, perhaps compulsively, but illegitimately, since he had no authority to convene the professed fathers in and about Rome. According to the Constitutions, the one invested with that authority is the rector of the house in which the general dies. On July 31, the rector of the Roman Professed House, where Ignatius died, was Fr. de Madrid.[32]

On September 20, Nadal left Burgos for Barcelona amid a barrage of sniping, bad temper, and suspicion. The dismal results of his work with Borgia were matched by the meagre returns of his fund-raising for the Roman College. Although he collected 3000 ducats, half came from Borgia's inheritance and the other half from assets of Fr. Antonio de Córdoba. In 1556 money was hard to get in Spain. The Roman College, far away in Italy, had little appeal to the Spanish aristocracy at a period when the Holy See under an anti-Spanish pope and their own nation were on the brink of war with each other. Besides, the ongoing struggle with the Moslems in North Africa drained large sums off from the Spanish Treasury.[33]

About mid-November, Nadal sailed from Barcelona for Genoa by way of Nice. After passing through several Jesuit colleges in Italy, he arrived in Rome on December 10.

Nadal finished his second visitation of Spain in bad health and in bad humor. Some of this he invited. His failure to inform Borgia that Borgia was not his superior muddied their relationship. His passive acceptance of humiliation affected his mission: his personal preference for mortification took precedence over the common good. Ignatius' outline for Borgia of Nadal's mission was inadequate. It did not make clear that Nadal was not subject to any Spanish superiors. The harvest of bickering naturally grew. Nadal's failure to correct the problem left unstemmed a tide of minor bickering. Nadal's judgment erred, and as a result he endured unnecessary mental suffering.

But this was merely the first problem that unfolded from Nadal's 1556 visitation. As a result of his visitation, he appreciated even more the need of men with aptitude and talent for governing. The rapid growth of the Society ran ahead of its ability to supply a multitude of superiors needed in the many new houses. Estrada, Araoz, and Bustamente—even Borgia—had traits of temperament and character that impeded sound, sensible, loving, and sensitive government. Moodiness, haughtiness, and prickliness vitiated government in Spain.

11

A House Divided

*Come now, Reverend Bobadilla, face reality. Admit
that you deserve the pummeling you are getting from
us. . . . All the fathers and brothers of the Society
repudiate you, reject you, disavow you.*

Nadal to Bobadilla in August 1557

Nadal reached Rome during a truce in the three-month war
between the Holy See and Spain. The troops of the Carafa
pope, an ardent Neapolitan patriot who detested the Spanish
"barbarians" then occupying the Kingdom of Naples, failed to
halt the steady march northward of 12,000 disciplined troops
under command of Fernando Álvarez de Toledo, duke of Alba.
With the Spaniards skirmishing at the walls of Rome, Antonio
Cardinal Carafa, the pope's nephew and secretary, seized the
armistice offered by Alba. During that lull in the fighting, Nadal
made his way into Rome.[1]

Under normal circumstances the Society would have elected
a new general superior early in 1557. But circumstances in Italy
were not normal, and the Jesuit election was one of the casual-
ties of the Papal-Spanish war. Not until July 2, 1558, only four
weeks short of the second anniversary of the death of Ignatius of
Loyola, would the new general superior be chosen. For two
years, Jesuit plans swung like buckets in the well of Pope Paul's
war. Not until Paul and King Philip made peace could the
superior be elected.

Despite ominous signals raised by the rallying of Alba's troops in late August of 1556 in Naples, Laínez hoped to convene the general congregation in late October or early November. Sometime in September, just after Alba started from Naples for Rome, Laínez visited Pope Paul to ask his blessing on the approaching congregation. Paul chatted amiably. Then, "changing his voice," he warned Laínez: the Society's way of life and the congregation's decisions completely depended for their validity on the approval of the present Holy Father; Laínez should not count on the approbations given by previous popes, since what one pope did another pope could undo. Laínez spoke to Polanco about that meeting. They agreed it might be advisable to convene the congregation somewhere out of reach of the pope.[2]

In his correspondence with the provinces, Laínez wrote about "the troubles of the times" and the possibility of assembling at either Bologna or Loreto or Genoa. A cardinal, however, warned that he would be risking the displeasure of Pope Paul should he take the congregation outside Rome, so Laínez settled for Rome. Then Alba's quick advance—he took Tivoli on September 26 and Ostia on November 18—forced him to push back the date of the congregation to April 1557. He sent official notices to the provinces: the delegates were to assemble in Rome in April.[3]

When Nadal arrived in Rome on December 10, he was quickly incorporated by Laínez into the top-level consultations on preparations for the congregation. Nadal and Polanco became the vicar's closest confidants. Another Jesuit looked on with simmering anger. Nicolás Bobadilla regarded Polanco and Nadal as men of the second hour; neither had been, as indeed he was, one of Ignatius' first companions. He felt left out. He saw himself excluded from the inner circle, especially when for days they went off by themselves. He felt sorry for Laínez and exonerated him of all blame. He considered him a dupe of the other two. "Master Laínez is a good person, but he is letting those two sons of his do the actual ruling. They have led him into so many blunders."[4] Months later Bobadilla's resentments would break out to fashion an internal crisis among the Jesuits in Rome.[5]

Early in 1557, Laínez's plans for the congregation to gather in April were shifted by papal diplomacy. During the truce with Alba, Cardinal Carafa quietly lined up France as an ally. With the prospect of French troops marching on Rome, Paul IV became cocky. On January 19, the official word from the Holy See went through Italy: the pope had again taken arms against Spain. On February 12, Paul named a tribunal to try Emperor Charles V and King Philip on charges of treason and rebellion against the rights of the Holy See.

Philip became enraged. He retaliated with a decree that no Spaniard was to take up residence in Rome and Spaniards then in Rome were to leave within three months under pain of loss of their possessions. This decree fell heavily on Spanish Jesuits and on the plans of Borgia and the Iberian provincials to leave for Rome. Even after Philip's decree, Borgia sought to leave Spain on a free-pass. Unable to get one, Borgia consulted Papal Nuncio Leonardo Marini, who advised him against trying to leave the country. Unwilling to abandon hope, Borgia then suggested that the council be held outside Rome and offered a few possible sites: Barcelona, Avignon, Narbonne, and Perpignan.[6]

During February, as the pope launched his ecclesiastical bolts against the Spanish leaders, Nadal almost choked to death during an attack of catarrh. This sudden brush with eternity frightened him. It jolted him into resolve to keep himself disposed to meet death gracefully, his hope grounded in Christ Jesus.[7]

The post-armistice phase lasted eight months, until the combatants signed the Peace of Cave on September 7, 1557. At least four times during those months Laínez sought an audience with Pope Paul. The main question almost always was: since King Philip forbade the departure from Spain for Rome of Borgia and the Spanish delegates, would the pope permit the convening of the congregation in Spain? Paul's reply varied with the reports from his generals and his diplomats. In late April or May, as the non-Spanish delegates to the general congregation were arriving in Rome, Laínez met Paul and raised the question of transferring the congregation to Spain. News from the battlefield at that time was bad. Paul turned on Laínez. "What do you intend to do in Spain?" he asked, "Join Philip's schism and heresy?" Seemingly bemused by the question, Laínez replied simply. "No, that is not what we have in mind."[8]

A month later, about June 10, Laínez again presented his request to Paul. By this time the pope could not fail to see that his Franco-Papal alliance was coming apart, largely because of squabbles about tactics and strategy among field commanders. Alba's troops were unstoppable. On June 3, Piero Strozzi, a *condottiere*, brought Paul a message from King Henry II of France: French troops located between Rome and Naples were needed on other fronts; they were to be withdrawn from the papal war. Paul realized his defeat was in the offing. Soon he must sue for peace. Calculating that the Jesuits, especially Borgia, could help him in dealing with the Spanish monarch, he received Laínez affably and quietly listened to his request to allow the congregation to be held in Spain. Gently and quietly he asked Laínez to give him time to consider the matter, and then to return for a definite answer. Laínez left in high spirits. He hoped that at last the Society could begin choosing its general superior. Almost a year had passed since Ignatius died.[9]

Only a few days later Laínez's hopes lay in ruins. He returned to the pope, but Paul refused to see him. Several times Laínez spent hours in the antechambers. Paul still refused to see him. On June 18, as Laínez waited in a corridor of the Vatican, Paul and his entourage approached. Laínez bowed in courtesy. Without a word Paul passed by. Laínez, surprised and troubled, nevertheless waited, expecting to be summoned at any moment to the pope's presence. No summons came. Two cardinals, Bernardino Scotti and Johannes Reuman, then came to see the pope. Laínez asked them to remind Paul that he was awaiting an answer to the question whether the Society might hold its general congregation in Spain. Scotti returned with three directives for Laínez from the pope: the vicar was to hand over, within three days, the Constitutions, and all bulls and papal rescripts that dealt with the Society; he was to present a list of all Jesuits residing in Rome; he was not to allow any Jesuit to leave Rome.[10]

Laínez was stunned. The next day he convened the priests of the Roman College and told them what had happened. To avert a calamity to the Society, he instructed them to recite litanies every day, to take the discipline each week, to fast often. He directed the scholastics and brothers to receive Holy Communion twice a week. The priests he asked to pray daily for the Society in their Masses, and three days a week to make the Society's welfare the prime intention of their Masses. The community responded generously.[11]

Laínez's message set Roman Jesuits abuzz with speculation. Puzzling over what had caused Paul's latest spell of anger with the Society, they sifted a host of memories of Giovanni Pietro Carafa (Paul IV) blowing hot and cold in his attitude toward Ignatius and his group: his tiff with Ignatius in Venice twenty years before; his reminder to the Jesuits on Ignatius' death that they should not trust in their Constitutions and papal bulls, since he intended to review them; his failure to complete this project. Their speculations yielded nothing sure. Most Jesuits attributed Paul's recent rebuff of Laínez to "holy zeal."[12]

During that flurry of rumors, Nadal made entries in his *Orationis observationes*. Here he changed his usual style. In Germany and northern Italy, save for a few fragments here and there, he kept records of his exterior life and his interior life in separate columns, neither reflecting any impact by the other. Now he welded the two. Interior and exterior made one experience. Pope Paul's request for the Society's documents, for example, stirred him deeply. On June 18, the day Paul asked for the Society's Constitutions and papal approbations, and the next two days Nadal felt a keen perception of the Society's peculiar character. So intense was his joy that he could not adequately express it; he could say only that he was caught in intense feeling. On the eighteenth he thought of offering his Mass for the Society in its current state of peril. He could not. Putting aside all anxiety about damage to the Society, he offered his Mass simply to the glory of God. Through two days his freedom from fear and anxiety continued. Even an effort to concentrate on the pope's curt message evoked no apprehension. Rather, a certain sweet and beautiful light touched his mind.[13]

In that "sweet and beautiful" light, Nadal experienced several spiritual insights. He received clearer understanding of God's action in the world; he was endowed with a purer perception of the Holy Eucharist as the food of the soul and as the force of union among the faithful; he attained a clearer sense of his sins and the sweet consolation of doing penance for them. "In short, a powerful and sweeping light in all things."[14]

In the midst of that shower of consolation, Nadal nevertheless experienced mixed feelings toward Pope Paul. He felt drawn to give obedience to Paul in all things. He also felt compassion for the pontiff placing himself in opposition to the Society. In Mass and in prayer, he asked the Lord to take Paul to himself and to temper the divine judgment should it spell doom for the pope. Nadal then caught himself. He changed the formulation of his prayer. He asked God to let Paul live long so that he might render help to the Church.[15]

The three days of interior joy then came to a sudden end. The following day brought gloom. At his morning prayer, feelings of inferiority inundated his soul. He saw in himself but a pittance of worth. Tears flowed in abundance. These emotions awakened memories of a like feeling of years before, when, summoned by Ignatius to pronounce the solemn vows of a professed father, he was overwhelmed by the thought of his paltry gifts and by persistent desire to hide in the shade of his indigence and give his service to the professed fathers as a spiritual coadjutor. But his current feelings cut much sharper. He felt impelled to look upon each of the Society's professed fathers as his superior. In none was he inclined to see any blemish. Those feelings of abasement and abjection, he said, gave him a freedom of spirit: a confusing day indeed![16]

More confusing days followed, as Nadal lurched from one emotional extreme to another. His early nonchalant attitude toward the pope's request for the Society's documents deserted him, and he began to worry. He wished to show deference to the pope; yet he feared that Paul might make changes in the Constitutions that would alter the essential character of the Society. This fear yielded to a surge of confidence. In August he felt sure the Society would weather Paul's scrutiny. Again he was not so sure. During this suspense, he felt impelled to think kindly of whatever Paul would decide and to accept it with a devout spirit. Yet even these pious resolves did not dampen his fighting spirit. He did not intend to sit passively awaiting papal judgments. "With singleminded intent we must take every step within our power to make sure the pope gets a correct understanding of what our Institute is."[17] Somehow or other Pope Paul must be briefed.

Through these months the flame of Nadal's interior life was hardly a steady, serene, quiet one. It flickered, it threw fitful light, it cast tremulous shadows. Gloom and joy curvetted in that unstable flame. Nadal's notes fluttered as eerily. They swung between elation and depression, confidence and self-contempt. They were not the gentle rises and falls of an undulating countryside; they were the sharp and frightening drops from high peaks to deep canyons. Behind Nadal's fluctuations lurked a disconcerting spur of compulsion. Ignatius had noted this constraint and stress and had worried about it. That it continued to hold Nadal in thrall did not bode well for the future.

Some time during those days of seesawing emotions, Nadal discovered, as did other Jesuits in Rome, why Pope Paul had suddenly closed the door to Laínez. A French Jesuit, Fr. Ponce de Cogordan, had sent a message informing the pope that Laínez's request to assemble the general congregation in Spain was inspired by desire to escape papal influence. Fr. Nicolás Bobadilla made the same charge in a message to Rodolfo Cardinal di Carpi.[18] This allegation alarmed Paul. It kindled the latent suspicions he always harbored against Ignatius and the Society. As war between the Holy See and Spain was winding down, a nasty internal fight was gathering momentum within the Society.

Bobadilla was at the core of this strife. His anger at being frozen out of the Society's central planning for the congregation inspired revenge against Nadal and Polanco, and to a lesser degree against Laínez.[19] He molded his resentment in a legal argument that challenged the validity of the office of vicar general, which Laínez then held. His reasoning ran as follows: the Constitutions did not yet have the force of law; that required the approbation by a general congregation; they had been issued by Ignatius with a view to changes and additions in light of experience; they were therefore still being framed and ratified and thus were not final. The office of vicar general, based on constitutions that lacked the force of law, had no validity. Laínez's authority was therefore null.

Bobadilla's legal argument continued. With Ignatius' death, the Society, lacking legally approved constitutions, returned to its state in the papal bulls of confirmation. Those bulls made no mention of a vicar general. The government of the Society rested, therefore, with survivors of the original members enumerated in *Regimini militantis Ecclesiae*. Bobadilla circulated his ideas among the delegates who were assembling in Rome for the general congregation in the spring of 1557. He won over four: Fr. Simão Rodrigues, Fr. Paschase Broët, Fr. Giovanni Battista Viola, and Fr. Adrian Adriaenssens.[20]

At this point Nadal rose as the most articulate spokesperson in defense of Laínez, his office, and his authority. He came out of his corner swinging hard. He wasted no time on genteel introductions. He called Bobadilla's legal arguments with contempt, "Bobadillan sedition." With the back of his hand he brushed aside Bobadilla's four allies in a series of *ad hominem* arguments. Rodrigues, he recalled, had a history of disobedience, restlessness, hostility for Ignatius, and close association with the Portuguese aristocracy. Viola, a free-wheeling spirit, had spent several casual and easy-living years in France. Adriaenssens' way of life demonstrated his almost complete ignorance of the Constitutions. For Broët, Nadal felt pity; he saw the Frenchman as guileless, innocent, and not well-versed in the Constitutions, an easy prey for the Bobadillan trap. And all this was only the first salvo.[21]

Bobadilla widened his target. Advancing beyond his charge that the Constitutions and the office of vicar general lacked validity, he pummeled the structure of the Constitutions themselves. He criticized Ignatius' body of legislation as a maze of obscurities, a labyrinth of tangled riddles. In this broadened campaign he suffered an immediate setback; he lost the allegiance of his allies, Rodrigues, Broët, Viola, and Adriaenssens. He had gone too far even for them. Only Ponce de Cogordan, his original companion in complaint, stayed at his side.[22]

Despite his losses, Bobadilla heightened his search for allies and took his grievances to influential clergy and laypeople. One such clergy member was Fr. Gasparo de Dotti, governor of Loreto, whom Ignatius admitted into the Society and instructed to retain his governor's post. In August, Bobadilla outlined for him his legal arguments against the validity of the post of vicar general.[23] But he went beyond legal subtleties. Turning on Laínez, Nadal, and Polanco, he released a withering assault on their persons and policies. He scorched the program of prayer and penance Laínez had asked of the Roman Jesuits after Pope Paul requested the Society's official documents. Behind that program he saw the machinations of two villians, Nadal and Polanco, who were riding high and leading Laínez up dead-end alleys. All three he accused of acting "as silly children" (*pueriliter et stulte*).

That was his refrain throughout the document: they acted as silly children. Ten of his charges, in fact, opened with the words *pueriliter et stulte*. Point 8 for example, read: "As silly children did they carry on when they ordered self-flagellations and litanies.

Nicolás Bobadilla

You would think they had fallen into the hands of a tyrant."
Other points followed in the same vein. Point 10 read: "As silly
children did they deport themselves when in our meeting they
denied a hearing to some, and in gesture and in word showed
their contempt for those who disagreed with them." Point 11
read: "As silly children did they conduct themselves when they
slyly tried to make Laínez vicar and invest him with the authority of general superior." Point 12 read: "As silly children did they
act when they failed to call the first founding fathers, as indeed
justice, charity, and seniority demanded." The worst offense
Bobadilla attributed to Laínez, Polanco, and Nadal, however,
was an effort to blame the mismanagement of the Society, for
which they were at fault, on those who disagreed with them.[24†]

Throughout August Bobadilla persevered. He sent two memorials to Pope Paul. The first he called "A Very Short Updating
on the Society of Jesus for His Holiness." It had seven points. He
repeated his earlier charges, but especially elaborated two: first,
the Constitutions were a baffling labyrinth of legislation, riddled
with conundrums and irrelevancies, beyond the comprehension of superiors and subjects; second, a reverence for Ignatius
had so grown among some Jesuits that they regarded every deed
and word of his as a revelation of the Holy Spirit. "A discreet
man Ignatius certainly was, but, as Your Holiness knows, still a
man who held his own opinions with the grip of a bulldog. Let
us select what is good from his legacy. But in order to rid
ourselves of the current reign of falsehood over truth, let us not
stubbornly defend what is bad in that legacy. This is my hope in
Christ and in Your Holiness."[25]

The second memorandum Bobadilla sent Pope Paul was
called "A Very Short Scheme to Help His Holiness Achieve the
Reformation of the Society of Jesus." This too had seven points.
The main thrust was a pressing need to have the Society's
Constitutions and other documents thoroughly examined and
revised by the Holy See. He even had a title for Paul's renovation
of the Society: "The Reformation of All Apostolic Bulls of the
Society of Jesus by Paul IV, Supreme Pontiff." He was confident
this program would save the Society; he confided to Paul that it

---

†24 *Mon Nad,* IV:121–23. Bobadilla forgot that he himself had voted in the
election of the vicar general, placing his notes in the hands of Juan de
Polanco.

would "suffice to restore us, with God's grace, to our spiritual purpose. Personally I now feel comforted that I have unburdened my conscience to Your Holiness. May Your Holiness carry on with supreme felicity."[26]

Bobadilla and Cogordan included several laypeople among their contacts, so Laínez had a fairly clear picture of what they plotted. Practically all their writings reached him. He assigned brothers as companions on their excursions from the house, who reported the people whom Bobadilla and Cogordan visited. At times on the streets of Rome they dropped papers, which the brothers retrieved. At other times, when they left their rooms, someone snatched papers left in the open. Often the recipients of complaints from Bobadilla and Cogordan were out of sympathy with the two and relayed the messages to Laínez, who therefore had a fairly full briefing on the tactics of his two critics. He instructed some experienced Jesuits to speak with them. He asked Nadal and others to write refutations of their charges.[27]

Nadal worked rapidly. He composed at least three documents, all most likely in August of 1557. He did not write without bias, but virtually condemned Bobadilla. In his diary he piled charge upon charge against him. He recalled, first of all, Bobadilla's unusual conduct after Ignatius' election as general superior in April 1541. All Ignatius' first companions who were in Italy at the time, save Bobadilla, promptly made their solemn profession as Jesuits. Bobadilla declined. Three doctors of theology were asked to present an opinion on Bobadilla's refusal. They judged that he was obliged to pronounce his solemn profession. He did so in early September of 1541, five months after the others.

Nadal followed with a crisp litany of Bobadilla's frailties: Bobadilla had ever been at odds with Ignatius; he was ignorant of the Society's Institute; he looked down on his companions; in apostolic ministry he let his pride run free by preaching about himself; he was accustomed to tag the Church Fathers with unseemly epithets; he was given to calling the Society's coadjutors his servants; in Germany he drank to excess, a failing that gave rise to the expression "Bobadillan wine"; he was impatient at games; he portrayed himself as a person of influence with the princes of Germany even though they looked on him as a fool; he was given to calling one person a child, another a jackass; he made a public spectacle of himself by getting into an angry argument with laypeople (and this in the home of a man who was living in concubinage). Small wonder that he called Ignatius a malicious sophist, an adulation-lapping Basque. With a head so cluttered with acrid memories, Nadal could hardly be disposed to write with judicial calm and fairness.[28]

Nadal probably intended his first memorandum for Cardinal di Carpi. He contested several of Bobadilla's statements about the meetings of delegates Laínez had convened in the previous spring. He reserved his sharpest criticism, however, for Bobadilla's juridical arguments. Bobadilla claimed, as has been seen, that the Constitutions, not yet approved by a general congregation, were still in the state of ratification; therefore they lacked the force of law; therefore the office of vicar general created by the Constitutions was invalid. Bobadilla raised a central issue: did the Constitutions at that moment have a definitive and final authority? He thought not. Indeed, Ignatius had declared that the full legal force of the Constitutions depended on approval by a general congregation. Pope Julius III had stipulated that a general congregation must be convened "to establish or change the Constitutions."[29]

Bobadilla carried his argument further. Since the Constitutions, still without the sanction of a general congregation, lacked full legal force, the Society had to fall back on the papal bulls that gave it the right to exist as a religious order. Bobadilla based his argument on those papal bulls. In *Regimini militantis Ecclesiae* (1540) and in *Exposcit debitum* (1550), Pope Paul III and Pope Julius III, having listed all ten of the first Jesuits by name, approved, confirmed, and blessed *their* Institute, gave *them* permission to establish Constitutions with a view to preserving the Society. The popes spoke of all the first ten Jesuits in equal terms. The new order was their common project. Bobadilla concluded that at that point the highest authority in the Society was invested in those of the first ten Jesuits who still lived. He was one of them.[30]

Nadal rejected Bobadilla's reasoning. He admitted that Ignatius had not closed the Constitutions as a completed work, that he wanted to keep them open so that both he and a general congregation could make changes in the light of experience. He therefore agreed with Bobadilla that the Constitutions were in the state of ratification, and thus open to modification and amplification. But he disagreed on their current authority. As did Bobadilla, he found support for his contention in the papal bulls. He argued that Pope Paul III and Pope Julius III had given the general authority to compose, with the advice of his associates, Constitutions. The legislation Ignatius had composed, therefore, was invested with papal authority.

Nadal corroborated this argument with his personal experience. He recalled that Ignatius had sent him to Sicily, Spain, Portugal, Germany, and northern Italy precisely to promulgate the Constitutions and to see that they were honored by the Jesuits in those areas. Ignatius' desire to keep the Constitutions open to modification did not, he argued, erode their papal authority. "We have indeed admitted that the Constitutions have not yet received their capstone. But nothing more than that. For, in the current state of affairs, the Constitutions in the form they have been set forth are not wanting in authority."[31]

Both men argued well. Both were right to an extent. Both found support in the papal bulls of approbation of the Society. An area ripe for legal disagreement lay in two phrases in *Exposcit debitum* of Pope Julius III: the phrase that gave the superior general "with the advice of his associates" authority "to set constitutions in place," and another phrase that said that a general congregation "must necessarily be convoked to set constitutions in place or to alter them." From a collocation of the two phrases arose the serious legal question: what authority did the Constitutions have between the time the general superior "set constitutions in place" and the time the general congregation, convoked to "to set constitutions in place," gave its approval of what the general had composed? *Exposcit debitum* did not answer that issue in clear, definitive language. That was a soft spot in the bull.

Bobadilla and Nadal took opposite ends of that soft spot. Bobadilla started from the phrase: "The council [general congregation], which must necessarily be convoked to set constitutions in place or to alter them. . . . " Nadal started from the phrase: "This superior general, with the advice of his associates, shall possess the authority to set constitutions in place." They moved toward each other through a heavy legal mist. Misunderstanding was easy.[32]

Logically, from his base, Bobadilla could have raised his argument from the moment Ignatius started to promulgate the

Constitutions through the visitations of Nadal to Sicily, Portugal, Spain, and Germany. At that moment, and at any moment through the five years up to Ignatius' death, the Constitutions lacked the necessary "putting in place" by a general congregation. Logically, Bobadilla could have charged that Ignatius was acting improperly, since he was promulgating a document that lacked the *imprimatur* of a general congregation as required by *Exposcit debitum.* Did he deliberately withhold this challenge until Ignatius died? Did this challenge occur to him only after Ignatius' death?

Most likely the thought of a challenge never crossed Bobadilla's mind until months after Ignatius died. At the time of Ignatius' death he certainly did not raise the issue. Indeed, by casting a vote for the vicar general, he showed his acceptance of the authority of the Constitutions, by virtue of which the election was held. Only when Nadal and Polanco excluded him from discussions about the Society's affairs did pique and frustration drive him to challenge what they were doing.

Probably, too, the argument he formulated was not his own. He had taken his case to a number of lawyers in Rome, and the arguments he presented had all the marks of the sharp, incisive reasoning of minds accustomed to interpreting documents with precision. What Bobadilla presented was most likely the brief of one or more lawyers. This excursion into legal intricacies probably would not have happened if Laínez, Nadal, and Polanco had showed Bobadilla the courtesy of bringing him into the inner councils of the Society during that important phase in its early history.

Nadal started from the other side, from the phrase that read that the "superior general, with the advice of his associates, shall possess the authority to put constitutions in place." That power was a papal power; it perdured. Nadal summoned the testimony of history. Ignatius not only composed the Constitutions; he also promulgated them and wanted them observed. So did Ignatius understand his power as superior general. And so did he exercise it, without demur, through five years. His death did not terminate the authority of the Constitutions, according to which the Society already lived through five years.

Legally and technically, Bobadilla had the edge on Nadal. Practically and realistically, Nadal made more sense. Legal refinement produced a logical but odd conclusion. Argued with sharp logic, Bobadilla's contention left the Society hanging in midair between Ignatius' completion of the Constitutions and approbation of those Constitutions by a general congregation. Bobadilla's charge, if pushed to its ultimate, could have been relieved only by prompt assembling of a general congregation at the moment Ignatius finished his draft of the text. Neither Ignatius nor any other Jesuit ever envisaged that lawyers would detect a legal chink in the papal bull and open a ruckus that would embarrass the Society.

Nadal's first critique of Bobadilla's position was therefore a legal one. But he did not stop there. He added a personal slur on Bobadilla. Bobadilla had told Ignatius that he found the Constitutions a confusing welter of legislation hard to grasp. Nadal scoffed at Bobadilla's assessment. "The fact that some points of the Constitutions are difficult for Nicolás to grasp is cut from an old cloth. Everything is bound to be difficult for a man who from the Society's origin was spiritually alienated from both the Institute and the general superior, who almost never lived in the Society according to the principles of obedience, and who now, for the first time after a freewheeling and lax way of life, has put on the righteous facade of a supremely obedient religious."[33]

That brief blast was a herald of greater noise to come. Nadal directed his second memorial to Bobadilla personally. Relentlessly, acridly, harshly, and unfairly, he jabbed at Bobadilla.

> Before I take up with justice and charity—your habitual phrase—the ideas you are promoting, I would like you to answer this question: why is it that in all you write—your many sermons, letters, memorials—in support of an aristocratic form of government in the Society, your tone is so utterly worldly and profane? You say: 'In justice I should be a superior. Therefore I want to be a superior.' I confine myself to this precise point, the one you are incessantly harping on: 'In justice I should be a superior.' I pass over your other assertions, all filled with the spirit of the world. . . .
>
> If we would allow this spirit to infiltrate the ranks of religious orders, Fr. Bo, the institution of religious life would one day be put into its grave. Wrangling for a position of dignity, like your line of reasoning, has no place in true religious life. Quite the contrary: in true religious life, each one, humble in self-knowledge and self-contempt, strives to prove that he should *not* be made a superior, so

inept, so evil, so worthless is he. Each aims to show that neither justice nor equity, nor even right reason gives him any claim to be a superior. Yet you are pushing hard, and in the name of justice, to become a superior. What is it, I ask, that makes you want, in the name of justice, to be a superior save your personal belief that you are worthy of that position and others are not, that you possess religious wisdom and others do not, that you know the Institute of the Society of Jesus and others do not, that you are a good and upright man and others do not approach you in those qualities?

These are your claims. Not only do you proclaim them, you enlist lawyers, public servants, to invest them with a legal foundation. Does not this conduct reflect the world and ooze with vanity? Does it not clearly carry, not only into the Society but into all religious families as well, a contagious disease? Should not this spirit be thoroughly castigated by indictment, by censure, by admonition? Look, Father, at the limits to which your importunate—I shall not add other adjectives—self-esteem is pushing you.

You, however, will bellow that justice and charity back your cause. You will shout that we are putting your conduct in a false light and therefore are distorting your thought. Loud will be your claim that you take your stand on the authority of papal bulls and from them you deduce your arguments. Come now, Reverend Bobadilla, face reality. Admit that you deserve the pummeling you are getting from us. First of all, the papal bulls did not invest the first companions of Fr. Ignatius with the authority to govern the Society. This I will make clear as I elaborate my position. But suppose that the bulls do indeed give this authority—which they do not—they would not give it to you. Indeed they could not. They could not invest authority in a man who had lived the way you have in the Society, a man who alone of the Society's pioneers has gone into battle to win the position of superior general, a man who alone was so driven by his restless and seditious spirit that he gave support and encouragement to Ponce [de Cogordan] when he delated the Society to that Supreme Pontiff who, as you and Ponce have admitted by spoken and written word, will, if he can, bring down the Society in ruins.

With all this said, suppose that what I have written is not true. Suppose that all the papal bulls designate you alone or, if you wish, proclaim that in justice you alone are the superior general. Suppose still further, Fr. Bobadilla, that all the rest of us in the Society beg and entreat you to acquiesce and be our superior. Suppose all that. You still would be acting wickedly by letting your greedy hands seize the superior's post, by failing to refuse it, by not giving preference to others over yourself. . . . The only way you can stand uncondemned is to admit that you are not worthy of the post and that you are ignorant of the Society's Institute. . . . In short, all of us would take offense unless you issued a firm statement that you would not accept so serious a responsibility except it were forced on you.

But, as a matter of fact, what is your strategy? With all your might you are pushing a crackling campaign to prove that in justice you should be the superior. You have splashed this affair throughout the entire city by taking it to lawyers, public pleaders, and judges. You have violated civil law. You have condemned the bulls given us by popes. All the fathers and brothers of the Society repudiate you, reject you, disavow you. You have flown in the face of all this. Does not your conduct smack of the work of a viper? Does it not invite every kind of contempt? If not stopped dead, will it not end with the Society in desolate ruin? And yet you pout. You say that we are snowing you under with words. It is not our words that are overwhelming you. Your own antics are doing that. At this point, however, I am going to subside. I am afraid that what I could say might disedify someone in the city who may have missed the earlier news about you and your capers.[34]

Nadal's argument then took a strange and illogical turn. He asserted his authority as a superior over Bobadilla. Relying on his election and confirmation by Ignatius as vicar general three years earlier, he argued that if Laínez were indeed not the vicar general, then Nadal held that post. He was simply speaking with the candor of a superior addressing a subject. This argument had the flash of a rapier. But it missed the mark by failing to note that Bobadilla's contention went beyond the mere identity of the vicar general. Bobadilla denied the very existence, then and there, of that office in the Society.[35]

Nadal had made a graceless show of bloated rhetoric. He used an unproven assumption: that Bobadilla was acting from personal ambition. Bobadilla presented an arguable legal issue. Correctly Nadal tried to respond in legal form to that issue. But in pinning the label of personal ambition on Bobadilla he went beyond the evidence. Bobadilla had in fact declined an offer by King Ferdinand of the Romans of a place in the hierarchy as bishop of Trieste. Nadal's excitable and impulsive nature pushed him into a biased harangue.

Nadal's third document of August 1557 was the longest. In essence it developed the legally reasoned document he had already addressed to Cardinal di Carpi. He stressed Bobadilla's basic contentions: the first ten Jesuits were cofounders of the Society of Jesus; the Constitutions, unfinished and in the state of ratification, lacked authority; the office of vicar was invalid; Laínez therefore held a nonexistent post. Those contentions Nadal had already addressed. Now he expanded his refutation.

His chief arguments ran as follows:

1. Ignatius alone was the founder of the Society of Jesus. The papal bull of confirmation of the Society recognized the first ten members of the Society as the roster of the Society at that moment, nothing more. Ignatius, however, enjoyed a spiritual ascendancy. Through the Spiritual Exercises and by personal example, he drew to the religious life the nine men who joined him in the petition to the Holy See for approval of the Society. After Pope Paul III issued *Regimini militantis Ecclesiae,* Ignatius' companions elected him their general superior, the one to whom obedience was due in law. "One father only, one founder only have we always known." Bobadilla could not, therefore, justly be regarded as a cofounder of the Society.[36]

2. The Constitutions were sufficiently completed to be invested with authority. Ignatius himself had judged that they had attained the point of refinement that fitted them for promulgation. Ignatius wished them to be observed. This he had told several Jesuits, including Laínez, Polanco, Doménech, Madrid, Câmara, and Nadal.[37]

3. The office of vicar general was a validly constituted office. Though not explicitly mentioned in *Regimini militantis Ecclesiae,* the office was implicitly embedded in that document. The Constitutions, which were issued by virtue of *Regimini militantis Ecclesiae,* explicitly declared that a vicar should be elected to govern the Society until a general congregation convened, if the deceased general had not designated one. Therefore it was correct to say that the office of vicar general was implicit in *Regimini militantis Ecclesiae.*[38]

4. The majority of the Society's professed fathers had approved the Constitutions as early as 1551. By 1550 Ignatius had finished that document, save the section on colleges and universities for lay students, and had called the available professed fathers to Rome to study the text together and to voice their criticism. Francis

Borgia, Antonio Araoz, Andrés de Oviedo, André des Freux, Diego Laínez, Alfonso Salmerón, all experienced men, attended. They spoke freely. Salmerón was the most vocal in his critique. The fathers worked through January of 1551 and then approved the corrected text. Nadal looked on this assembly as a milestone in the Society's history; he likened it to a general congregation. Against Bobadilla's opinion he threw the weight of this "congregation" of 1551.[39†]

5. Diego Laínez had genuine authority to govern the Society. Even if it were granted that the authority to head the Society devolved on the five surviving pioneers (as Bobadilla contended), the fact was that all save Bobadilla recognized Laínez as the legitimate holder of that authority. Still more: when the professed fathers in and about Rome voted, after Ignatius' death, to make Laínez vicar general, Bobadilla joined in that election and cast a vote. (Bobadilla, in Tivoli at the time, did not go to Rome because he was sick, but he sent word that he cast his ballot for Polanco's choice.) Therefore Laínez was chosen in an election condoned by, consented to, participated in by Bobadilla. Nadal knew that he had pierced Bobadilla in a soft spot. He had the blade between the ribs. He twisted it. "This you cannot deny, Bo. Your own hand, your own signature, pin you down and refute you."[40]

Nadal did not silence his adversary. Bobadilla continued his campaign and clucked with satisfaction when Nadal conceded that the Constitutions needed the capstone of approval by a general congregation. "Although Nadal and his associates had

---

†39 *Mon Nad,* IV:137–38. Nicolás Bobadilla was invited to come from Tivoli. He excused himself. Later Ignatius gave him the text for review. Bobadilla read but a little, saying that he found the document difficult to comprehend. Eventually Nadal recognized that Bobadilla had a strong point in his contention that *Exposcit debitum* called for approbation of the Constitutions by a general congregation. He tried to fill that gap with the meeting of the professed fathers called by Ignatius in January 1551. He spoke of that meeting as "like a general congregation." But of course it was not a general congregation in the real sense of the words. Ignatius had not convened the meeting as a general congregation. The procedures for the convocation of a general congregation were not followed. Its likeness to a general congregation did not make it a general congregation. Jozef de Roeck, S.J., "La Genèse de la Congrégation Générale dans la Compagnie de Jésus," *AHSI* 36 (1967): 283. For Salmerón's role at this gathering, see William V. Bangert, S.J., *Claude Jay and Alfonso Salmerón* (Chicago, 1985), 204–7.

magnified the import of the Constitutions and their authority in extended detail, they now admit that the Constitutions are in the state of ratification."[41] And in the background lurked other points Nadal himself had made a few months earlier.

Bobadilla intimated that there was a push for Spanish preponderance in the Society. Himself a Spaniard, he made an effort to appreciate the lot of the German, French, and Italian delegates to the general congregation during an era of intense strain between Spain and France and the Holy See. With mettle he argued against the convening of a general congregation in Spain. For the French, Germans, and Italians a trip to Spain during war and international tension would be perilous; entry into Spain might mean a berth in a Spanish jail rather than at a general congregation. Yet it would be intolerable for the Spaniards to hold a congregation without the other nations.

Bobadilla had other arguments: in the event of a protracted war, a general elected in Spain might never get to Rome; the departure of Jesuits for Spain for the congregation would upset the people of Rome, then under siege by Spaniards; Pope Paul IV would certainly disapprove, because of a natural fear that the Jesuits from Rome might take the role of spies and give inside information about Rome to Philip II; to other nations, watching the spectacle of the Spanish Jesuits, who were in the majority, carrying the congregation to their own country, the Society would become despicable. "Italy is the Society's central ground. It is not fitting that the head should go to the feet."[42] He possessed a stronger sense of the Society's international character than other Jesuits of his own country. Meanwhile, less dramatic features of the Society's life absorbed Nadal's time and talents.

12

The Workshop
of the Holy Spirit

With the door of your heart opened to Christ, receive,
in the sweetness of your soul, the Holy Spirit and bond
with him in his divine handicraft.

Nadal in his *Orationis observationes,* 1557

During the crisis that engulfed his office of vicar general, Laínez gave Nadal an administrative post: he named him superintendent of the Roman College. On June 25, a week after Pope Paul IV rebuffed Laínez, Nadal moved into the Roman College on Via Minerva. He was not entering the unknown: at the beginning of that year (1557) he had gone there to deliver a number of exhortations to the Jesuit community. A copyist recorded two of them, the one he gave on January 2, the other on January 4. Neither was novel in its ideas; both repeated key thoughts Nadal had developed in his conferences at Alcalá a year earlier.

In quick succession he recounted major phases of Ignatius' life. In each phase he indicated the formation of Ignatius that was taking place under certain special divine graces: one that molded Ignatius in the way of conversion and penance, another in the way of apostolic desire to help others, another in the way of study of the sacred sciences. In imitation of Ignatius through those stages, each Jesuit is formed in "the true spirit of our Society." Nadal extended this quest of resemblance to Ignatius beyond the individual Jesuit to the Society as a body. "Indeed," said he, "the successive stages of the Society occurred in the way our father's life advanced."[1]

From that early date, the relationship between Jesuit prayer and Jesuit apostolic engagement absorbed Nadal profoundly. He told the Roman College community, "The Society gives itself to prayer and the taste of spiritual things: but in such a way that it is lured into helping its neighbors. If it were otherwise, and if the Society lacked apostolic desire, that devotion, even though in itself good, would imperil our Society." The Roman scholastics were hearing what the Alcalá scholastics had heard. Scholastics of other countries would soon be hearing the same themes.

Nadal moved into the Roman College in June, but not with the highest zest. He saw an administrative structure he did not like. The rector, Fr. Sebastiano Romeo, was rector in name only. Three other men shared governing power: Laínez (vicar general), Polanco (secretary), and Madrid (rector of the Professed House). This odd arrangement had been in place almost a year when Nadal moved in. On August 19 of the previous year— Ignatius had died three weeks before that—Polanco gave an exhortation at the college and informed the community that they should see in Laínez, Madrid, Romeo, and himself their superiors, their true fathers of body and soul. Nadal did not intend to be a fifth wheel. But he held his peace and decided on a policy of "hands off" the governance of the college.[2]

His strange predicament impeded his spirit of prayer. The first day at the college brought him acute desolation. He could not make even a beginning in prayer. Deliberately he expressed a preference: in order to have a living experience of the third degree of humility, he chose to suffer desolation rather than enjoy consolation. The next day he faced with dread. He feared another dose of sterility. But God's grace swept him into a profound prayer experience. He turned to contemplation of the mystery of Christ's Nativity. "So moved was he in the perception of this mystery and so intensely illumined was he that he was led, with a strong flow of tears, to the thirst of contemplating Christ Crucified. It was as though this light and this elevation of mind brought him to understand that contemplation of Christ Crucified was where he belonged."[3] This consolation lasted for some time. He found that it helped him during the current anxieties in the Society, what he called the give-and-take of the

Fathers (*colloquia patrum*). From Christ's words to the thief, "To-day you shall be with me in paradise," Nadal understood that in "the today" of his contemplation of the passion, he would find his paradise. Part of "the today" of his suffering was the odd structure of governance he found at the Roman College.[4]

Early in August, the logjam about the office of vicar general began to break. Cardinal di Carpi, fearing that the protracted dispute was damaging the Society's reputation, intimated that he was planning to take direct action. Laínez informed the cardinal he would cooperate. Carpi summoned Bobadilla; Bobadilla refused to appear. Repeatedly Carpi sent his request. Bobadilla continued to decline, pleading that he was extremely busy and that he was not disposed to argue his case without a lawyer at his side. On August 9, Carpi, unable to get Bobadilla to come to him, went to the Professed House, assembled all the priests including Bobadilla, and interviewed each one. Bobadilla warned Carpi: if he passed a negative judgment against him, Bobadilla would appeal to Pope Paul. This did not faze Carpi. He made a clean-cut decision: the governance of the Society was in Laínez's hands, but Laínez should not decide major issues without consulting the professed fathers in Rome. All save Bobadilla and Cogordan concurred in Carpi's decision.[5]

In the days that followed Carpi's visit, Bobadilla fell silent. This silence seemed ominous. It worried the other Jesuits in Rome, who feared Bobadilla would execute his threat and take his grievance to Pope Paul. Laínez consulted some of them and decided to go to the pope first. He requested an audience with Paul. This, his fourth visit to the pope since the spring, continued the story of Paul's roller-coaster moods in his relations with the Society of Jesus. Laínez came to know the highs and lows of those moods intimately. Chided by Paul in April for flirting with treason, warmly greeted in May, rejected in June, he entered the lion's den again in late August. The lion oozed grace and sympathy and offered his help to resolve the Jesuits' internal strife.

Recent events in his war made it clearer than ever that the pope would soon have to sue for peace with Spain. On August 13, Alba's troops sacked Segni. In France on August 10, under the walls of Saint-Quentin, Spain's troops routed the force of Constable de Montmorency. Two weeks later, on the twenty-seventh, Saint-Quentin fell. Cardinal Carafa read the handwrit-

Diego Laínez

ing on the wall. He interpreted it for François, duke of Guise: "This is the ruin of Italy." Guise received orders to quit Italy; he was needed in his beleaguered France.[6]

Amid the rubble of his grand strategy, Paul thought the Spanish Jesuits could aid his necessary and humiliating request for peace with King Philip. To help the Jesuits heal their internal wounds, he asked Laínez to suggest the name of a cardinal who would be assigned to adjudicate the dispute. Laínez declined. He told Paul he preferred that the pope designate the cardinal. Paul chose the Dominican Michele Ghislieri, Cardinal of Alessandrino, the future Pope Pius V and canonized saint. Ghislieri's assignment gave Bobadilla new hope. He wrote more memorials. He sounded Jesuits who he thought favored his position: how did they intend to answer the questions Ghislieri could be expected to ask? Ghislieri went to the Professed House. He showed utmost kindness. He spoke with each of the priests. On September 7, Bobadilla had his turn. Ghislieri reviewed a long series of questions with him. Bobadilla proposed his basic arguments. He insisted that his friend Cogordan justly resented a penance given him for sending a memorial to the pope without consulting Laínez.[7]

During the inquiry, Bobadilla suddenly left Rome. A friend, Guido Cardinal Sforza di Santafiora, wanted Bobadilla in Foligno to help spiritual renewal of a monastery of Silvestrines. Nadal recalled in his diary: "And so, within a few days, destitute of hope for his cause, he left Rome." Bobadilla's departure left Cogordan isolated. When Cogordan met Cardinal Ghislieri, he intended to stress four points, but he did not get beyond Point One. In Point One he told the cardinal of his distress because Laínez had given him a penance for sending a message to the pope. Ghislieri became annoyed. He knew that a penance had indeed been imposed on Cogordan, but he also knew that it was not for communicating with the pope. It was for misrepresenting the motives of those who voted to hold the general congregation in Spain and for accusing them of trying to evade papal supervision. Ghislieri asked, "What was the penance imposed on you?" "One Hail Mary," answered Cogordan. Ghislieri flared in anger. He told Cogordan he wanted to hear no more.[8]

The cardinal pronounced no formal sentence. That was not his responsibility but the pope's. But he gave his assessment of the sad affair. He believed that Bobadilla and Cogordan had acted in a crafty, self-seeking, worldly manner. What Nadal called "the Bobadillan and Pontian disruption" (*e turbine bobadillano et pontiano*) therefore moved to the pope. Paul read Ghislieri's report with dismay. He could hardly believe the shenanigans Ghislieri recounted. As he turned the pages, he made the sign of the cross as though to fortify himself against the spiritual blindness that can take hold of men. He promptly lifted his ban against Jesuits leaving Rome.[9]

Despite this friendly gesture, unease still oppressed the Roman Jesuits. Pope Paul had not returned the Society's bulls and Constitutions he had demanded two months earlier. He had given them to Cardinal Scotti and Cardinal Reuman for examination. The cardinals, doubtful about some features of Jesuit life, asked Laínez for a Jesuit who could answer their doubts. Laínez appointed Nadal. Eventually Pope Paul returned the documents to Laínez, condemning nothing. He merely noted that Cardinal Scotti had reservations about the absence of choir in the Society, and suggested that this issue might be raised later.[10]

And so peace came to the Jesuit ranks. Ponce de Cogordan received an assignment to Assisi. Bobadilla, in Foligno, reported his work for the spiritual renewal of the Silvestrine monks there. "Instruct Polanco to tell me how the Society fares, and to have my valise forwarded to me. It is at the home of Master Romolo, the presiding judge of the Cardinal Camerlengo. Master Romolo will send it. I need it very much, since here in Foligno they are pressing me to lecture and preach. As usual, I am in bad health. For the rest, I shall keep you posted on my activities." He made no mention of the grave issues he had raised.[11]

Peace descended also on the Papal-Neopolitan border. On September 7, Spain and the Holy See ratified the Peace of Cave and ended hostilities. King Philip's ban on Spanish Jesuits traveling to Rome was lifted. Laínez wished to convene promptly a general congregation in Rome, but the approach of winter prevented him. By the time his summons could reach the provinces and the delegates prepared to travel, the sea lanes and highways would be treacherous. He was forced to postpone the meeting for eight months, until May. Practically all the delegates who had come in the previous spring returned to their provinces.[12]

Nadal reviewed briefly the recent episodes in which he had had so prominent a part. Nothing more serious than defeat of their cause had been done to Bobadilla and Cogordan. Among Jesuits he noted a general disposition that kindness and charity should prevail, that members of the Society should be guided not by a spirit of spite but by one of magnanimity.[13] The welcome peace Nadal described could not, however, absorb the acrimony spilt during the debate. Neither Bobadilla nor Nadal left that dispute untarnished. Bobadilla let pique and resentment lead him into wayward and wanton actions. He took his grievances to the laity; he pronounced wild and silly charges against Nadal and Polanco. Nadal built such a reservoir of animosity for Bobadilla that he could no longer approach the dispute with a cool and detached judgment. His invective and abuse twisted the scales of justice. He poured scorn even on the reasonable parts of Bobadilla's legal arguments. For neither man was it his finest hour.

Amid all the bombast of the Spanish-Papal conflict and the Bobadillan-Nadalian contest, Nadal continued his entries in his *Orationis observationes.* He saw February 5, 1557, the feast of St. Agatha, as a memorable date in his life. He knew that his fellow Jesuits found him prickly, gruff, harsh, and intransigent. Earnestly he asked St. Agatha to obtain for him the grace of transformation. A wave of spiritual sweetness flooded his soul. The hawk became a dove. "With this grace, a complete change occurred in the thrust of this person's interior inclinations, a change from a churlish manner to a winning comity. This person felt a delightful freedom of spirit."[14]

A test of his transformation came during the debates in the spring of 1557 among the fourteen Jesuits who had been able to assemble in Rome for a general congregation. Laínez sought their counsel on this grave issue: should the congregation assemble in Spain or in Rome? In the initial ballot, Nadal stood alone in favor of moving to Spain. He admonished himself to maintain humility and simplicity of heart, to refrain from pushing his opinion ahead of others, to yield the place of honor to what others thought. He commended to God the views opposed to his. He felt confident that his prejudices would dissipate with his superior's decision.[15]

Despite his preoccupation with those demanding debates and the uncertain meanderings of the Papal-Spanish war, Nadal still felt the loss of Ignatius deeply. Yet with all his grief he had a keen sense of Ignatius living in glory. The figure of Ignatius remained a watermark in his memory. He recalled Ignatius as the man with his mind ever in heaven (*elevatio perpetua*). Ten years earlier, as a novice he had formed this image of Ignatius. He could not forget it; it remained untarnished. And this was the form he wanted to give his own life. He longed to imitate Ignatius, the man with his mind ever in heaven.[16]

Nadal reflected on this aspiration to be another Ignatius. Reflection forced him to nuance his quest. He detected a danger in seeking to imitate the saints in the unusual graces given them by God. He used a corrective: imitate the saints in the ascetical means they used in disposing themselves for God's higher gifts. This corrective he applied to himself "when he had desires to imitate Father Ignatius' contemplation and perception of spiritual things."[17]

The first anniversary of Ignatius' death occurred during the heat of the brawl with Bobadilla. Nadal did not connect his devotion to Ignatius with the nasty episode in which he was immersed. He prepared for the anniversary "with a general confession made out of devotion for Fr. Ignatius and with a resolve to renew his spiritual life." On the anniversary itself, he experienced "a renewal of spirit. It was as though I were now being received into the Society for the first time. I felt a deep awareness of my vocation, of the Society's Institute, of the life of Fr. Ignatius in each of its details. Nothing in that life did I find that cannot provide us with a forceful and holy model for our imitation."[18] After the anniversary Nadal kept aspiring (*orabat*) to assume the likeness not only of Ignatius but of two other deceased Jesuits. At the Communion of his Mass, he prayed to Christ that he "be given the grace of resembling Fr. Ignatius, Fr. Favre, and Fr. Xavier. Within, I seemed to hear Christ telling me that he was giving me this grace." Later that year, probably in November, Nadal made a terse entry in his notebook: "What Fr. Ignatius esteemed, that I must esteem and cherish."[19]

After Ignatius' death Nadal often reflected on the Society's purpose. He set a general principle: the Society has its peculiar charge, which is care of those souls to whom no one else is attending and care of those who indeed are receiving pastoral heed but in a sloppy way. "This is the Society's reason for existing; this is the Society's peculiar power, its honor in the Church."[20]

At his death, Ignatius was corresponding with Jesuits in places as distant as Goa and Bahia, Yamaguchi and São Paulo. Two areas especially preoccupied him because of the Church's endangered position: Germany and the Indies. Nadal inherited these concerns. Germany he came to know by living there, the Indies by reading the ample correspondence from Jesuits who were laboring in the Far East. In 1555, for the first time, he linked Germany and the Indies in a peculiar image, which he repeated in years ahead. He pictured the body of the Society carried forward on two wings: the two parts of the Society that operated where spiritual needs were most acute, Germany and the Indies. The force for the Society's thrust came from Jesuit labor in the two most spiritually indigent areas of the world.[21]

This image shaped Nadal's practical tactics in Germany. To help the German church, he commissioned Peter Canisius to publish Latin translations of letters received from Jesuits in the Far East. In the years ahead, the Indian letters remained an important instrument with which to explain to the German people the international scope of the Society's labor for the universal Church. Nadal never went to the Indies, but his letters to Ignatius from Augsburg and Vienna echoed his love for the German-speaking peoples. His notes resonated with the fervor that fired his words to Ignatius. "A certain person was taken completely with the desire to go to the help of Germany. He offered his Mass for that intention. . . . With intense feeling he desired to achieve God's glory—an unsullied glory—in Germany. This glory he felt compelled to seek, driven as he was by a desire that was bathed in a certain bright and luminous sweetness. It was a glory that he thought would expel every tinge of heresy. This would be achieved in Christ Jesus, to whom be infinite and eternal glory. Amen."[22]

Nadal's love for Germany, brisk, busy, astir, and apostolic as it was, did not sidetrack his mystical bent. If anything, his desire to penetrate the mysteries of God and of his church grew more insistent. The early imprint of the Pseudo-Dionysius remained: what the mind is able to grasp is not God; intellectual perceptions must be bypassed; a firm stand must be made in faith. In this way, Nadal judged, he would encounter the darkness that throws light (*caligo illustrans*). At Pentecost (June 6, 1557) Nadal recalled the coming of the Paraclete in strength and power. "A certain person experienced on this feast the wonderfully sweet and strong action of the Spirit. . . . Prayer for this driving power of the Spirit must be unceasing, humble, and confident."[23]

Nadal felt that contemplation finds its fulfillment when with grace it touches the divine light. During the uncertain months after Ignatius' death, Nadal's urge for mystical knowledge intensified. It gave a sharp bite to his criticism of the theology of his day. Arid intellectualism, he thought, had enveloped theological studies. In the wake of a theology parched and sere followed prayer dry and stale because intellectual activity held dominance. This trend, Nadal determined, must be stopped.[24]

A new star rose higher and higher in Nadal's spiritual firmament: it was the heart. It guided him away from the ascendency of the mind. He experienced God leading him to a shift of loyalty, from the intellect to the affections. "A certain person longed to contemplate the truth. It was given him to recognize that God is love itself, to be perceived and grasped in the heart."[25] Continuing prayer fortified Nadal's shift from mind to heart. He kept asking God for an understanding of "pure truth." Two scriptural passages especially impressed him: "Lord, I am not worthy to have you come under my roof" (Luke 7:6) and "For this people's heart has grown dull . . . lest they understand with their heart" (Mt. 13:15). These texts showed him that "pure truth" was comprehended only in deep humility before the power of God. They showed him that the intensity of his desire for God, not the labor of his intellect, was what settled "pure truth" within the crypt that was his heart.[26]

Nadal therefore opposed the intellectual stress of the theology of his day. That theology underlined the conceptual grasp of God in faith. But God was grasped in faith only in part. It was in the heart that God was attained in love, "the love that unites God perfectly to us and clearly shows him in the Holy Spirit." It was in "the sweetness and light of his heart" that Nadal called on his Guardian Angel. It was on that heart that he would imprint the humility of Fr. Ignatius. The heart was the workshop where every enterprise was forged, since it was in the heart that the power of the Holy Spirit did its most perfect work. In the heart every grace and every supernatural understanding had their beginnings. "With the door of your heart opened to Christ, receive, in the sweetness of your soul, the Holy Spirit and bond with him in his divine handicraft."[27]

In entry after entry, Nadal wrote about the achievements of the Holy Spirit in his heart. It was in his heart that he grasped the thrust of the Jesuit vocation toward souls destitute of all aid.

It was in his heart that he perceived the authenticity of that vocation. It was about his heart that a great light shone, tied to his faith and hope.[28] He therefore defined his heart as the atelier of the Holy Spirit. It was in that atelier that he found another heart, the heart of Christ. He became enamored of Christ showing forth his love through his heart. He felt assured that Christ would send his heart to Nadal's poor heart.

But then he doubted: he feared illusion. Against this fear, he felt a trust that Christ was indeed conferring many gifts on him, "not only his carnal heart, created love, but also his uncreated and infinite heart. This person could not focus on that thought without experiencing in his heart intense emotion. He felt a certain power that overcame the weakness of his heart."[29] At Christmas of 1556, the newborn Christ sucked in (*sugit*) Nadal's heart, drew it, and united it to himself. With this unusual Christmas grace, Nadal's heart expanded. He wrote further: "Mary gave her milk to the Infant Christ. Christ himself gives our heart his milk. Indeed, by this milk is nourished his own divine presence within us."[30]

Aside from these passages in which he wrote of the heart as the workshop of Divine Labor, Nadal often used words that gave his *Orationis observationes* a notably mystical tint. *Light, sweetness, brilliance, clarity,* and *gentleness* were nouns that he rooted in his soul. *To feel, to experience, to sense, to perceive, to grasp,* and *to penetrate* were verbs that told of interior movements of his soul.

Light and delight attended his awareness of the Holy Trinity embracing his soul. With clarity and sweetness he sensed the Holy Trinity present in all things. Grace and light rose from his heart to chase shadows of temptation at a period when, sick in body, desolate in spirit, harassed by temptation, he fled to Christ in prayer. Light was a definition of the Jesuit vocation, a triad of lights. It gave a clearer perception of the earlier light of Christ's invitation to "faith, grace, and truth."[31] It pointed to another light: the interior feelings of the heart, the divine power giving strength to continue a work undertaken for God's glory. A certain "light in God" penetrated him and opened his eyes to realize that God in his divine power was at work in him, as he prayed the Holy Trinity to put its seal on the Cross in his life. Light rose within his soul as he found strength in the example of the Blessed Virgin's faith during the stress of temptations against his faith. From cleanness of heart arose "a light in which truth shimmers." Over the Society's special grace to strive firmly and gently for all virtues a light glowed.[32]

On Pentecost of 1557, Nadal found himself helpless to explain the radiant, gentle, sweet light with which God in his kindness raised his mind to prayer. A week later, on the vigil of Trinity Sunday, he visited the Basilica of Saint John Lateran. (This was just before Pope Paul IV asked for the documents of approval the Society had received from earlier popes.) "With tears this person felt a great devotion, especially when he focused on the life of Christ as he recited the Rosary. He then stopped the Rosary and gave his attention to the relics housed in the basilica. He touched, among other things, Christ's handkerchief soaked with blood. After viewing the relics, even as his devotion continued, he gave himself to prayer. He found it impossible to pray for himself. He prayed for the works of the Society: bringing succor to heretics and infidels and assisting in the renewal of the Church. This prayer was not so much a prayer of petition as a certain gentle and calm contemplation of those [Jesuit] works, bathed in a light that made them present before him.

"When he turned his prayer toward less worthy objects, he felt a certain magnanimous and gentle pull toward the enterprises of the Society. When, for example, he got wrapped in himself or prayed for himself, he heard a voice [in Catalan]: 'Do not worry. God will be with you.' Doubts troubled him that the expression 'Do not worry' might mean putting a value on slackness of spirit. He then heard a voice that gave the correct interpretation: 'Do not worry means: be tranquil.' When he lowered his attention to things other than the concerns of the Society, he saw clearly that nearly all his actions were sinful, performed not exclusively for God. He came to a thorough understanding, in the brightness of a higher light, that he had to begin a new life—a peaceful, radiant, sweet life realized in Christ through the action of God at the deepest point of his heart. He also felt hope for the recovery of his health to the extent that it would be helpful. May the Lord, One and Three, be blessed through the ages. These experiences occurred on the vigil of the Feast of the Holy Trinity."[33]

To the end of the year, Nadal's experiences of light were buoys that marked the stream of his interior life. On the feast of St. Catherine, November 25, he found that his interior light and grasp of truth intensified in the measure that he deepened his humility. A little later he defined humility as a light from heaven that shone forth the glory of God. At Mass on the feast of St. Thomas the Apostle, December 21, he prayed for an increase of faith. A strong and sure light arrived where earlier a darkness had enveloped his belief.[34]

That was the last of Nadal's entries in his *Orationis observationes* of 1557. Light shone within him as he closed the door on that year. Through all of 1557 he had muted a familiar theme of earlier years: the need for continuing penance and self denial. Caution about mystical experiences lessened. His heart, the luminous workshop of the Holy Spirit, had become during that year the hub of his interior universe.

As Nadal made those jottings through 1557, he was composing a work about Ignatius. This project, sixty-eight pages in the *MHSI,* reflected a political cast of events in Paris during the last two years of Ignatius' life. In January of 1551, King Henry II had approved the presence of the Society in France, granted it the *droit de naturalisation,* and approved the foundation of a college. Two years later he affirmed these grants. Two powerful authorities, however, opposed the king's actions: the bishop of Paris, Eustache du Bellay, and the theological faculty of the University of Paris. On December 1, 1554, the latter issued a formal censure of the Society. The bishop and the doctors gave the Jesuits an early taste of the Gallicanism that would be intimately woven into their history for centuries. Ignatius tried to resolve the conflict but failed. To answer the arguments of the theologians, Fr. Martín de Olave and Fr. Juan de Polanco wrote apologias.[35]

Nadal wrote a third: *Apologia contra censuram Facultatis theologicae Parisiensis* ("Apology against the Censure of the Theological Faculty in Paris"). Strikingly unusual as an apologia, it was in the main a detailed recitation of the events of Ignatius' life from his birth to 1545. Before he began that recitation, however, Nadal tossed to the distinguished doctors of the university some barbed questions. He asked them what impact did they think their rejection of a body founded on the approval of two popes actually had. "Did the Society perish as a consequence? Did it fail in courage? Did it weaken? Was it shaken by the lordliness of your decree? Far from it: it has actually leapt forward, it has grown in strength, it has gathered an abundant harvest in Christ." He then pelted the theologians with a rain of facts: after their blast the Society spread to Ethiopia, led many people in Japan to Christ, built a strong bastion in Prague, founded colleges in Ingolstadt, Cologne, Louvain. He rubbed this point home by repeating the phrase "after your censure." He closed one paragraph with a flourish. "You have therefore done no hurt to the Society, most learned gentlemen, you have done no hurt to the Society. Rather, you have given it a boost."[36] It was quintessential Nadal: sassy and scrappy.

After that audacious sally, Nadal gave a simple recitation of the facts of Ignatius' life. He deliberately confined his story to external events. Rarely did he allude to Ignatius' interior gifts. When he told of Ignatius' experiences at Manresa, he gave not a word to the composition of the *Spiritual Exercises.* Apart from a passing reference to the penetrating vision on the banks of the River Cardoner, he kept silent about other Manresan illuminations, convinced as he was that a simple presentation of Ignatius' external life would provide a solid basis for sound judgment on Ignatius and on the Society. That illation spoke his constant conviction: the life of Ignatius was the authentic blueprint of the Society and of each Jesuit. The life of Ignatius was the best rationale and the best defense of the Society. This apologia Nadal never finished, one of the first of several literary undertakings he would never bring to conclusion.

Curtailed though the *Apologia contra censuram* was, it became the sun of a small galaxy of lesser writings by Nadal on Ignatius at that time. One small document, only three pages in *MHSI,* was what the title said it was, *Chronicon breve ab anno 1521 ad 1543* ("A Brief Chronicle from 1521 to 1543"). In terse sentences Nadal wrote what he may have intended as an outline of the larger, unfinished apologia. A second small document, six pages in *MHSI,* Nadal called *Acta quaedam P. Ignatii* ("A Register of Certain Acts of Our Father Ignatius"). In another small composition, *Patrum Dicta Aliquot* ("Some Sayings of the Fathers"), possibly begun while Ignatius was still alive, Nadal gathered memorable remarks of founding Jesuits, including of course Ignatius.[37] During those years of crisis in Rome, Ignatius was very much on Nadal's mind. All his snippets indicated it and fed the fire of his conviction that in the life of Ignatius the Society could find its best definition. They may have been the first gropings of a desire that found clear articulation seven or eight years later: the desire to write a history of the Society.

13

The Toil of an Exegete

*A certain person perceived that he could possibly do
nothing more worthwhile than edit the Constitutions
and the Rules with utmost exactness, and elucidate
the Constitutions with scholia as well. A full-dress
presentation of the Institute in its entirety, that is the
objective.*

Nadal in his *Orationis observationes*, 1552

One day in early summer of 1557, Nadal posted on an interior
wall of the Roman College a list of suggested mortifications.
This first example of such a public exhortation to religious
discipline illumines the life of the Society of Jesus at that time.
During the academic year, scholastics expended much energy
on study and class. Superiors put a rein on corporal penance.
Lest the desire for mortification grow slack, however, Nadal
suggested that scholastics devote a period of summer vacation
to special works of self-denial.[1] The idea spread rapidly to other
Jesuit colleges in Europe. Nadal's audience, seen and unseen,
soon became a thousand Jesuits engaged in a steady routine of
study, prayer, teaching, counseling, and self-denial. This was the
Society of Jesus of 1557, not the noisy brawl of a few men in
Rome. The poster in the Roman College was a truer reflection
of Jesuit life than brassy communications between Nadal and
Bobadilla.

The poster also confirmed two important traits of Nadal. The
first was his conviction that self-denial must permeate Jesuit life.

Ignatius had often insisted that he had more interest in whether he had more interest in whether a man was mortified than in whether he was prayerful. Despite the powerful attraction prayer had for him personally, Nadal insisted that Ignatius' teaching on self-denial penetrate all aspects of Jesuit life. His placard at the Roman College was the first of many he would post in colleges throughout Europe. They became a distinctive mark of a nadalian visitation.

The second of Nadal's traits that the poster confirmed—a sense of organization that sought to marshal the tiniest details of school life—was apparent in Messina during his tenure as rector there. Nadal had a detective's eye for detail; he had a legislator's yen for codification. The mortifications he listed were suggested, not mandated, but they carried his authoritative touch. In the spiritual regimen as in the academic, Nadal the regulator was emerging.

This placard illumines a significant development in the history of the Society. What had touched most earlier religious institutions now touched the Society: a covering of codification gradually encrusted an early spiritual insight. The first item Nadal suggested on his placard was the making of the Spiritual Exercises. Ignatius had not prescribed any tightly formulated repetition of the Exercises. In the General Examen he directed that the novice, before his vows, "recollect himself for a period of one week," during which "he should make some of the former Exercises or some others." That was all.[2]

In August, two groups of Jesuits undertook modified Spiritual Exercises. The first group did so between August 16 and 23, the second between August 23 and 30. They had contact with other members of the community only in the chapel and the dining room.[3] Nadal's suggestion at the Roman College that the Spiritual Exercises be repeated in brief form spread rapidly to other colleges of the Society. Groups of Jesuits, especially scholastics, received it enthusiastically. In 1559 the scholastics in Prague and Vienna adopted the practice, by 1561 the scholastics in Coimbra, by 1562 those in Cologne, by 1564 those in Lisbon, by 1566 those in Messina. In Rome, the fifty who made a week of the Exercises in 1557 grew to "many" in 1565, to "the greater part" in 1570, and to seventy in 1572.[4]

Nadal's suggestion soon became a common practice. The Sixth General Congregation of 1608 moved further. On March

24 it was prescribed in Decree 29: each year every Jesuit was to spend eight or ten consecutive days in the Spiritual Exercises.[5] The congregation took a basic Ignatian spiritual experience, for which he gave not the slightest intimation of obligatory annual repetition, and encased it in a tight cover of legislation. By its universal application, this legislation offended Ignatius' respect for wide differences among Jesuits in their modes of prayer. It ignored Ignatius' sensitivity to the varied work of the Holy Spirit in hearts. It warped Ignatius' purpose for the Spiritual Exercises, which he never intended to be repeated year after year. To the Spiritual Exercises themselves it did a disservice, since it squeezed them into an annual format that became vulnerable to routine.

The half-century between Nadal's poster of 1557 and the decree of the Sixth General Congregation in 1608 drew the Society into a common experience of earlier religious orders: good men, intent on preserving a spiritual ideal, bound that ideal in tight legalistic thongs. They encased it in a code. Attempting to safeguard it, they endangered it.

Through the spring and summer of 1558, Jesuits turned their eyes toward Rome. They awaited news of the choice of their general superior. Fr. Laínez, after several attempts to set an earlier date, designated May for the opening of the general congregation. Delegates began to arrive in Rome at mid-May. By mid-June, nineteen of the expected twenty-seven had come. News trickled through that Fr. Elpidio Ugoletti (Sicily), Fr. Leonard Kessel (Upper Germany), and Fr. Adrian Adriaenssens (Upper Germany) were delayed by illness. Reports from Spain were discouraging. Fr. Bartolomé de Bustamente (Andalusia), Fr. Antonio Araoz (Castile), and Fr. Francisco Estrada (Aragon) decided not to make the trip. Fr. Juan Bautista Barma (Aragon), however, was due in Rome any day. Fr. Laínez assembled the nineteen who were present and asked their opinion: should they await those who were delayed, or move promptly to the election?[6]

On June 20, Laínez and Salmerón, in the name of the delegates, went to see Pope Paul. Paul received them graciously. He praised the Society; he offered his help for the success of the congregation; he placed two cardinals at their disposal as advisers; he intimated that he would like to see them adopt chanting of the divine office, but assured them that the Society was free in its discussion of its business; he gave them his blessing. Between June 21 and 27, the delegates considered and approved twenty decrees on procedures to be followed in election of their general superior. On the twenty-eighth, Barma arrived. The congregation opened four days of prayer and exchange of information on the aptness of each to be general.[7]

During that inquiry Nadal was profoundly humiliated. Salmerón intimated to Laínez that Nadal might be guilty of ambition for high office. He presented flimsy evidence. He told Laínez that he had heard Fr. Leonard Kessel say that in Flanders Fr. Cornelius Wischaven asserted that Nadal would be the next general. Salmerón's high intelligence certainly lapsed in giving significance to that piece of gossip. Laínez nevertheless was troubled and investigated the insinuations. He questioned men from the Belgian province. They heard nothing. He spoke to Nadal. Nadal said that he did not know, nor did he care, what others were saying about him. With that Laínez dropped the matter.[8]

At nine in the morning of July 2, the twenty electors gathered in the chapel of the Professed House. Laínez offered Mass and gave a sermon. All spent an hour in prayer; then they invoked the Holy Spirit. Under the supervision of Pedro Cardinal Pacheco, vice protector of the Society, each delegate placed his ballot on Pacheco's desk. The result: Laínez received thirteen votes, Nadal four, Broët one, Lanoy one, and Borgia one. For three days, from July 3 to 6, the Jesuits in Rome celebrated. On the sixth Pope Paul received the congregation. Polanco was amazed at the expansive way he spoke of his love for the Society. Paul confirmed Laínez's election. He then invited the fathers to draw closer to him; he praised their order; he reminded them that by their vocation they were called not to enjoy the sweets of this life but to bear the cross.[9]

Two months of dull work followed through the hot summer. The delegates had to decide on day-to-day procedures. They had to review the Castilian text of the Constitutions. They had to check Polanco's Latin translation. They had to resolve many doubts about the correct interpretation of the Constitutions. Some expressed concern for the precise meaning of words; other doubts touched entire passages. Beyond the text of the Constitutions, the delegates had to resolve problems such as the

nature and function of the office of vicar general, a problem
that was fresh in their minds because of Bobadilla's challenges
of the year before. In a short time they realized that by working
as a unit they were doomed to a dead end. One delegate,
probably Polanco, suggested they break into committees and
sub-committees.[10]

The work was tedious and demanding. Nadal served on every
committee save one. Polanco served on all. Despite steady
progress, the delegates realized that they could not handle
within a reasonable time all the questions raised about the
Constitutions. In frustration they gave Nadal and Polanco an
important assignment: to review the constitutional difficulties
and compose commentaries on the Constitutions. In Decree 51,
the congregation called on the Society to esteem what Nadal
and Polanco would compose and to invest their scholia "with
some authority," not however with "the full authority" that flows
from a general congregation. This appointment, which Nadal
fulfilled alone because Polanco had several other demanding
tasks, reflected the recognition other Jesuits gave him as an
especially competent authority on the Constitutions.[11]

The congregation gave Nadal a second serious responsibility.
According to the Constitutions (No. 799, 780, 781), the general
congregation is directed to choose four professed fathers who
should remain close to the general to assist him and observe
him in the performance of his office. The congregation chose
Nadal as one of these assistants. The others were Fr. Cristóbal
de Madrid, Fr. Luis Gonçalves da Câmara, and Fr. Juan de
Polanco. To clarify further their help to the general, the congregation assigned several provinces to each assistant as his
special care. Nadal received the provinces of Germany, Flanders,
and France.[12]

The delegates were eleven weeks into their unglamorous
work when they received a severe jolt. On August 24, Bernadino
Cardinal Scotti appeared at their residence with a message
from Pope Paul. Paul asked that the congregation consider
limiting the term of the general superior. The delegates debated the issue and voted unanimously that the general's life
term be kept. They sent a letter to Paul to inform him that,
ready as they were to obey his direct order, they preferred to
abide by the Society's Constitutions. Paul was miffed. On September 6, Laínez, accompanied by Salmerón, went to explain

to Paul the attitude of the congregation. They met an angry and excited man. Paul unleashed a stormy tirade: Ignatius was a tyrant; failure to chant choir proved a soft attitude toward heresy; the Jesuit general superior should be elected every three years. He envisaged a devil emerging from the Jesuit ranks because they placed study before the chant of the divine office. Paul gradually quieted. He gave the two Jesuits rosaries and Agnus Dei for the members of the congregation. Laínez and Salmerón retreated to their residence.

Two days later, on September 8, Alfonso Cardinal Carafa entered the congregation and ordered it in the pope's name to insert into the Constitutions the two demands made by Paul: a triennial election of the general superior and the chant of the divine office. The congregation complied. Two days later still, the First General Congregation of the Society came to a close. It had passed, after the election of Laínez, 148 decrees.[13]

During the next two-and-a-half years, Nadal remained in Rome, engaged in his threefold responsibility as general's assistant, superintendent of the Roman College, and editor of scholia to the Constitutions. As general's assistant he often fell into spells of self-contempt. Daily he consulted Laínez and the other assistants: Polanco, Câmara, and Madrid. Correspondence from many countries in Europe and overseas kept him alert to the changing features of the Society's experience, but even as his horizon was broadened, moods of severe self-criticism seized him. He pictured himself as a rude bumpkin who grated on the sensitivities of others. He could not see himself as welcome in the circle about the general.[14]

As superintendent of the Roman College he aimed to correct the fuzzy line of command that he found so intolerable when Laínez gave him that position in June of 1557. Initially he kept his peace about parceling authority among five men (Laínez, Polanco, Madrid, Romeo, and Nadal as superintendent), but once the general was elected he could no longer keep silence. He remonstrated with Laínez. Laínez concurred, and corrected the ambiguous situation by placing authority completely in Nadal's hands. Nadal plunged into the life of the college. Each Saturday he engaged in theological disputations. He produced a play of Terence, "The Self-Tormentor" (*Heauton-timorumenos*). He welcomed to the faculty two gifted Spaniards: Francisco de Toledo, who soon gained acclaim for his incisive and lucid lectures on metaphysics, and Fr. Diego de Ledesma, who became one of the Society's finest educational administrators of that era.[15†]

Through the first twenty years of the Roman College's existence, its Jesuits were itinerants in quest of a home. Twice during Nadal's short regime as superintendent, the site of the college was changed. In October 1557, students and faculty moved from their tight quarters near Santo Stefano del Cacco to a larger house on the Piazza Salviati, opposite the Camillian Arch. Between October 21 and 30, Nadal led the way in carrying tables, chairs, beds, and other furniture. Soon, however, this building too became cramped. The number of students grew steadily. Hemmed in as the building was, Nadal had no room for expansion.

In 1560 a wealthy aristocrat, Marchesa Vittoria della Tolfa, offered more ample buildings near the obelisk of San Macuto. Nadal assisted Laínez in the negotiations. In May of that year he moved with his charges to the new complex that included the palace of Marchesa Vittoria's deceased husband Camillo Orsini, the palace that Pope Paul IV had used when he was a cardinal, her own ancestral home, and a site where she had begun to build the Church of Holy Mary of the Annunciation.[16]

Wide as was his involvement in the daily life of the Roman College, Nadal found satisfaction in preparing *Scholia in Constitutiones Societatis Iesu* ("Scholia on the Constitutions of the Society of Jesus") a work commissioned by the recent general congregation. This satisfaction widened its range. Nadal had three other projects tumbling, none officially imposed, all undertaken on his own initiative, all exegetical in nature. The first he had started in Spain, during his retreat, before Francis Borgia's displeasure. He had called that work *Annotationes in Constitutiones* ("Remarks on the Constitutions"). Distinguished from the compact and legal style of the *Scholia*, the *Annotationes* is discursive, fervent, rhetorical. It fills but twenty-two pages of *MHSI*.[17] The second personal undertaking closely resembled

---

†15 *Mon Nad*, II:64–65. Nadal thought that authority should be invested in the rector. In his concept of a Jesuit college he had no place for a superintendent, even though Ignatius set this position in his Constitutions. In 1565, the Second General Congregation (decree 86) abolished the office. Experience had shown that rectors and superintendents usually were not able to work together and therefore troubled the peace of the colleges (*Inst SI*, II:210).

the *Annotationes* in scope and style. He called it *In Examen Annotationes* ("Remarks on the Examen"). It fills seventy-one pages of *MHSI*. In his six chapters of *In Examen Annotationes* Nadal did not get beyond the first chapter of the eight chapters of the General Examen subsection of the Constitutions.[18]

In Examen Annotationes contains what today is probably the most widely known quotation of Nadal. In his fourth, wide-ranging chapter, Nadal reflected on the prayer of Ignatius of Loyola and the prayer peculiar to Jesuits.

> We know that Fr. Ignatius received from God the uncommon grace of untrammeled contemplation and rest in the Holy Trinity. At one moment this grace used to draw him to the contemplation of the Trinity in its fullness, to carry him into the very bosom of the Trinity, to unite him with the Trinity. And all with intense feeling of devotion and spiritual relish. At another moment he used to contemplate the Father, at another the Son, at still another the Holy Spirit. Often did he receive this kind of contemplation at one period or another in his life, but especially in those last years of his pilgrimage, when, you might say, it was his exclusive way of prayer.
>
> As one chosen by God with most exquisite care and endowed by him with a great privilege, did Ignatius receive this mode of prayer. And still more did he receive. To him was given an order of prayer by which he, a contemplative even while active, was led to a sense of God's presence and spiritual reality in all objects, in all activities, in all conversations. He used to clarify it this way: God is to be found in all things.
>
> Much to the intense wonder and consolation of us all, we have seen this interior light-giving grace break in a kind of radiance that enveloped his face and manifested itself in the shining sureness of what he did in Christ. We have an inkling that something of that grace—I do not know exactly what—has been turned toward us. What therefore we understand to be a privilege given Ignatius, we believe has been granted to the entire Society. We feel sure that prayer and contemplation of this mode have been given in the Society for all of us. We affirm that this prayer is tied to our vocation.
>
> Since these things are so, let us place the perfection of our prayer in the contemplation of the Trinity and in the loving union of charity that we extend to our neighbor by our works of service for him. Without question, this way of prayer we prefer to the way of sweetness and relish.[19]

Within that widely known passage lies Nadal's most quoted phrase: "a contemplative even while active (*contemplativus simul in actione*)." It was one of his several efforts to portray Ignatius of Loyola. For the past thirty years it has been in vogue among Jesuits. In Nadal's day it was not so. He never used it again, so far as can be determined from his extensive published works. Nor did other Jesuit authors of the sixteenth century employ it. Within the Church's history it shares a place with other formulas by which authors have tried to capture the essence of a person who was at once intensely active and profoundly prayerful. In the seventh century, an anonymous monk of Lindisfarne in his life of St. Cuthbert described that busy and recollected monk as *vitam contemplativam in actuali agens.*[20] And in our own day, Benedictine Fr. Jean Leclercq entitled a chapter of his life of Peter the Venerable *"Un Contemplatif dans L'Action."*[21]

More important than Nadal's single-phrase description of Ignatius was a wider statement he made, a startling statement: to each Jesuit was granted the same privilege given Ignatius of mystical contemplation of the Trinity and of God's presence in all things. That statement clamored for elucidation but Nadal did not provide it. It raised serious questions but Nadal did not address them. It called for the precise analysis he so admired in scholastic theology but Nadal did not offer one. On his exact meaning he has stirred hesitancy and difference among Jesuit scholars. All agree that Ignatius' privilege informs somehow the vocation of each Jesuit. Their difference seems to be in the measure of intensity and mystical power by which a Jesuit is led by grace to pray as Ignatius prayed. Some think Nadal intended to say that each Jesuit is marked for the intense illumination of mind and heart granted by God to Ignatius. Others say Nadal simply meant that the general direction and character of a Jesuit's prayer is somehow shaped by focal points and objects of Ignatius' prayer. The latter may be closer to the truth, since Nadal introduced his startling statement with reserve. "We have an inkling that something of that grace—I do not know exactly what—has been turned toward us."

For years, as we have noted, Nadal had a persistent preoccupation with his own intense emotional desire for mystical experience of God. Since his entrance into the Society, he had channeled those desires toward the imitation of Ignatius in his prayerful union with God. But he usually checked those desires and reminded himself to stress basic ascetical preparation for gifts of that high order. In this instance grace may have outrun hard intellectual scrutiny, for he formulated a highly charged statement on "an inkling" and not theological reasoning—another one-liner that must not pass unexamined.

Nadal's third project undertaken on his own initiative moved from study of the Jesuit Institute to study of Holy Scripture. He desired to incorporate into a pithy textual exegesis his personal meditations and reflections on the gospels. At this time he felt that he was receiving in prayer a deeper spiritual and mystical understanding of the gospels than he received earlier in life. Somehow the experience of his meditation remained with him. A sense of the subject of his meditation clung to him. This special sense he wanted to communicate. Never did he lose this desire. Until his death he stayed at work. Others saw the work through the press.[22] Of his three personal Roman projects, it was the only one he finished. *Annotationes in Constitutiones* and *In Examen Annotationes* remained incomplete.

Despite his busy pen, Nadal did not relent in keeping his *Orationis observationes* up to date. Throughout 1558 he jotted down a plenitude of reflections. That year he opened and closed the *Orationis observationes* with the same spiritual insight: God at work in his own life and in the life of the Society of Jesus. A sensitive awareness of God's active presence made a handsome set of bookends for his spiritual notes of that year. To God working in him and in the Society was due all success in any spiritual enterprise. Nadal wrote that his experience of the divine action was deep. He felt the proddings of the Holy Spirit that he rely not on his own power in doing the work of the Lord.

As Nadal's understanding of God's supreme power deepened, his distrust of self became keener. He cautioned himself against complacency when God manifested himself in unusual ways. "Even if the Holy Spirit should grant you such notable gifts as deep consolation and striking success, remain fixed in that attitude of personal poverty and misery in which the gifts found you."[23]

Nadal's awareness of his spiritual poverty induced a strong interplay of emotions. When he received graces of sensible consolation, fear descended on him. He faltered at the thought that one so wicked as he should be touched with spiritual delight. One day, as he begged God earnestly for the gift of prayer, he felt drawn to Christ. Then his heart sank before the majesty of Christ. Then dismay that Christ suffered and died for his sins gripped his soul. He turned to the Blessed Virgin Mary, to the angels, to the saints for help. A quiet sense of intimacy with God and Christ Jesus touched the restless waves and calmed them. Such shifts of the emotions were habitual in Nadal's interior life.[24]

Through 1558 the Holy Trinity took a capital place in Nadal's prayer. With thoughts of the Trinity he linked his memories of Ignatius. One day early in the year, as he prayed to his Guardian Angel, "he felt God dwelling within him. In this experience he saw for the first time a living image of the Trinity. Then it seemed as though God was leading him into a thoroughly delightful light, in which he seemed to discover all kinds of lovely things."[25]† On the feast of the Holy Trinity, Nadal met fair wind and foul in his prayer. He first meditated on the qualities that flow from the Divinity. The quality of God's Goodness held him. With ease, delight, and ready faith did he pray. When, however, he turned from the divine qualities to the Divine Being itself, his prayer turned painful and dreary. He even felt repulsed. He seemed to find a glimpse into the meaning of the scriptural passage, "He who searches into the divine Majesty is overwhelmed by glory."[26]

This feast aroused memories of Ignatius' sublime prayer to the Trinity. Nadal felt an ardent desire that Ignatius help him in the way of Trinitarian prayer. Promptly a mighty wave of devotion to Ignatius flooded his being. He felt a powerful sense of reverence for all that Ignatius said and did. "So intense was the impulse that there was no object at the villa on the Aventine or at the house [in Rome] that he was not inclined to embrace with sweet kisses of affection."[27] From time to time through 1558 Nadal visited the room where Ignatius died. "A particular person prayed there. Many sweet tears flowed in his feeling of gentle humility."[28]

---

†25   *Or ob,* 163. The Latin of this passage reads: *Quidam attente orabat Angelum suum custodem; sensit primum in illo Deum inhabitare quasi imaginem vivam videret Trinitatis.* It is a difficult passage to translate because the precise meaning of *primum* is elusive. Nadal had written earlier of devotion to the Holy Trinity, but this entry seems to be the first time that he mentions having seen an *image* of the Trinity. (He does not describe the image.) This translation of *primum* seems therefore to be justified.

As Nadal pondered his spiritual experiences through the years, he often summed his thoughts in an epigram or a tight memorable phrase. One he composed in 1558 was *spiritu, corde, practice,* to signify that a Jesuit served God by his alertness to the inspirations of the Holy Spirit, by his loving and ardent acceptance of his mission, and by the embodiment of his aspirations in solid and practical action. Throughout the *Orationis observationes* of 1558, the makings of that formula were stored in corners of his mind. "Through the Holy Spirit is the Word made clear. In the loving consecration and affection of the heart Holy Scripture is manifest." "From your heart, work with God." "The revelations given in the Scriptures must animate actual life and find fulfillment in action. In action are they at last fully understood." "Truth must be the quest. Truth must be the guide in all things; not just speculatively but practically." The lumber of the future dictum *spiritu, corde, practice* was strewn among the notes Nadal made through 1558. A synthesis was in the making.[29]

Scattered entries in Nadal's journal trace the shifting flow of his interior life.

> On his fifty-first birthday on August 11 he had a perception of his impotence and of God's might.[30]
>
> His sense of faith bolstered him against an old temptation that enticed him to seek visions and apparitions. With such intensity did his faith animate him that it deadened all the force of the former quest for the unusual.[31]
>
> "The faith in God's word resident in the chamber of his heart expelled those thoughts that would trouble prayer and peace of soul. Faith is the key that keeps the door of the heart locked against intruders."[32]
>
> "In Catholic lands the Society is a school for the training of those who are to be sent among the infidels and heretics. This is the way the Society's vocation marked by God's will is accomplished."[33]
>
> "The Church receives its meaning from the Cross of Christ. So also the Society."[34]
>
> "For a particular person a door was opened on a vista of all things invisible wrapped in darkness."[35] Dionysian teaching of this kind still reverberated on occasions within his soul. On the eve of All Saints' he had a sense of the mystical doctrine of the Pseudo-Dionysius.

"Anxiety about being cured must be cast away. One thing only do: openly and humbly show God your sickness and the hidden recesses of your storm-tossed soul. Do as beggars do. They display their sores to those from whom they ask alms."[36]

Then came the last entry, like the first: a sensitivity to the divine power at work in souls. So Nadal closed his spiritual notations for 1558.[37]

On November 6, 1560, Nadal's sojourn in Rome came to an abrupt halt. Laínez named him overall superior (*commissarius*) with a plenitude of power to visit Spain and Portugal. Word had reached Laínez that Spanish Jesuits were snapping at one another. Antonio Araoz and Francis Borgia had serious differences about policy. Jesuits were dividing into two camps, some following Araoz, others Borgia. In Portugal the rapid growth of colleges caused doubts about the grasp of the authentic Jesuit spirit there. Spain and Portugal were the first two stops on an extensive visitation that Laínez conceived for France, the Netherlands, Germany, and Austria.

On November 18, Nadal left Rome for Genoa. With him went a Spanish scholastic whom Laínez assigned to be Nadal's secretary. Diego Jiménez was thirty years old but had been a Jesuit only two years. He was studying rhetoric and Greek when Laínez assigned him as Nadal's aide. In Genoa the two men had a delay because the fleet did not sail until December 18. During that delay Nadal was able to finish the first draft of his *Scholia in Constitutiones.*

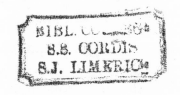
14

Trapped in a
Thicket of Courtiers

I have had it up to my ears with courtiers.

Nadal in his *Ephemerides,* March 1561

Nadal had found the Mediterranean a hostile host. Twice it almost claimed his life. Now once more it awaited him. On December 18, fifteen vessels sailed from Genoa's harbor. Nadal and Jiménez were on the *San Juan.* Two days later they stopped at Nice; then they edged along the coast to Villefranche. A strong wind forced them to take refuge in a small port near Marseilles. There they remained on Christmas and the day after. The captains then mapped their course toward Aigues Mortes. Sandbars off the shore scared the navigators, who then tried to hold course a bit out to sea. A storm scattered the ships across the Bay of Narbonne.

Nadal and Jiménez had a bunk amidships, into which water spilled as waves dashed across the deck. Two or three passengers drowned. Nadal exhorted the soldiers to reform their lives. Some went to confession. Jiménez preached when he was not helping to keep the ship afloat. During the night of December 28, the *San Juan,* which managed to stay with four other ships, made port at El Juncto, a sparsely populated area of the Catalan coast between Cadaqués and Rhoda.[1] The storm at sea adumbrated a storm on land. A turbulent visitation lay ahead.

The twenty-ninth was Sunday. Nadal, concerned about offering Mass, asked the distance to Rhoda. He was told it was a league away, so he and Jiménez left El Juncto at eight in the morning. They walked until Vespers before they reached Rhoda. "A Catalan kind of league (*tan Catalona*)," remarked Nadal.

The two met gracious charity at every turn. Bishop Arias Gallego of Gerona provided a dinner that included two partridges, a capon, four loaves of bread, and two canters of wine. All this, reflected Nadal, made the grim landing on the Catalan coast worthwhile. Abbot Antonio Agullana of the local monastery of San Juan de las Abadesas helped them find mules for their trip across Spain. On January 1, 1561, they reached Barcelona.

Nadal was pleased with what he found at the Jesuit college there. He gave great credit to the rector, Fr. Miguel Govierno, for leadership. Govierno showed notable powers as a preacher and, perhaps for this reason, had earned the responsibility of distributing for the bishop the annual donation from the viceroy of 1500 ducats for the poor. Govierno's aproval was required for any book that was published in Barcelona.[2] The visitation, after such a promising start, went steadily downhill. Three months later Nadal was at Toledo, where he reflected on his experiences and noted in his diary: "I have had it up to my ears with courtiers."[3] In that short time his visitation to Spain unraveled. Men at or near the court had pulled strands that made havoc of his design.

A main reason Laínez had for sending Nadal to Spain was to bring harmony between Francis Borgia (the general's delegate) and Fr. Antonio Araoz (provincial of Castile). The two men differed seriously on basic policy. Borgia advocated a rapid expansion of colleges; he did not let inadequate funding stop him. A shortage of money, he thought, gave Jesuits an opportunity to feel the pinch of poverty and to rely completely on divine providence. Araoz insisted on curbing expansion. Fewer projects would mean higher quality of work. Borgia actively sought alms for the Roman College; he sent Jesuits to needy colleges in France, Germany, and Italy. Araoz, however, insisted on keeping Spanish resources in Spain; he opposed the transfer of money to the Roman College; he argued against dispatch of intellectual luminaries of the Spanish provinces beyond the Pyrenees. Spanish Jesuits divided into two camps, some behind Borgia, others behind Araoz.[4]

Nadal realized he had to speak with both men. But Borgia was 300 miles away in Oporto, Portugal. A year and a half earlier he had quietly slipped across the border. Ugly stories dogged his steps: he was a heretic; he was an adulterer. Men and women at the Spanish court spoke of him with reserve. A troubled year for Francis was 1559. A book that carried his name was placed on the Index by the Spanish Inquisition.

Nine years earlier, in 1550, a printer had published a work entitled *Works of a Christian by the Hand of Lord Duke Francis of Borgia, Duke of Gandía.* The use of Borgia's name was a publicity gimmick. The printer took a leaflet of only eight pages written by Borgia, *A Short Tract on Confusion,* and hemmed it with small works by other authors into a volume of fifty pages. He attributed the entire volume to Borgia. Some ideas of the other authors, thought Araoz, were doctrinally unsound. The mills of the Inquisition ground slowly, but eventually they powdered the *Works of a Christian* and put it on the Index.[5] Francis Borgia was branded a heretic. Still more: in that year, Borgia incurred the anger of Grand Inquisitor Ferdinando de Valdés. In September the Inquisition imprisoned the Dominican archbishop of Toledo, Bartolomé de Carranza, on grounds of heresy.[6] Carranza challenged Valdés's ability to be a fair judge by charging him with the bias of a personal enemy. Francis Borgia, he said, would verify that. Valdés, affronted by the charge, turned his anger on Borgia and debated whether to arrest him.[7]

At the court also Borgia was in trouble. In early September of 1559, King Philip returned to Spain from his brief marriage with Queen Mary Tudor, who died less than a year before. He heard news about Borgia that annoyed him. Against his royal will, Francis' brother, Don Pedro Luis Galcerán de Borja, married Doña Leonor Manuel during Philip's absence from Spain. Behind this match he thought he saw the manipulating hand of Francis. But there was something even more murky. A story was making the rounds of the court about Philip's sister Princess Juana, who governed Spain during his absence in England. The gossips whispered that Francis had lived in concubinage with her. Philip did nothing to squash the story but let it circulate.[8]

In the fall of 1559, therefore, Borgia stood in deep shadows cast by the Spanish Inquisition and the Spanish court. A message from Portugal then changed the course of events. Cardinal Henrique, archbishop of Évora, desiring Borgia's advice, invited him to Portugal, so in early December Borgia quietly left Spain for Évora. Dismay filled many Spanish Jesuits. They did not know what to make of Borgia's action. Some thought he had succumbed to discouragement, others that he was physically and emotionally exhausted. Some non-Jesuits even suggested he was really fleeing the Inquisition.

Nadal faced a vexing problem. To make the visitation worthwhile, he had to speak with Borgia. Should he direct him to return to Spain? He took soundings among local Jesuits; they divided in their counsel. Nadal finally wrote to Borgia and asked him, if he judged it appropriate, to return to Spain. He gave no direct order, but made his preference clear: he would like Borgia to come back for candid talks. Borgia answered that he intended to return.[9] He did not, however, do so, since, as shall be seen, bad health and fresh events in Rome changed his mind.

The other Jesuit superior whom Nadal had to see was Fr. Antonio Araoz. The two met in Alcalá in early January, soon after Nadal arrived there. Araoz gave Nadal a chilly welcome. Evasive and aloof, he made it clear that he resented the visitor's presence in his bailiwick. He was, as Nadal found, untouchable. A bird that flew with the wings of the prince of Éboli, the monarch's closest advisor, and the count of Feria, Spain's chief roving diplomat, was safe from constraining cords of Jesuit superiors. The Spanish aristocracy made the rules. From the beginning Nadal was hobbled. No wonder his exasperation with the power brokers at the court!

The high point of Nadal's contact with the Spanish government came in mid-March. He heard that King Philip was due soon in Toledo. For two reasons he judged that he must speak personally with the monarch. First, he wanted to remove the cloud of misunderstanding hovering over Francis Borgia before Borgia returned to Spain. And second, he wished to deliver letters that he carried for Philip from Pope Pius IV and from Fr. Diego Laínez. He left Alcalá and arrived in Toledo on March 3.[10]

For days before the monarch's arrival, Toledo was astir. Important men of the realm came early to prepare for the royal entry. Several sought Nadal. Gonzalo Fernández de Córdoba, duke of Sesa and viceroy-designate of Lombardy, informed Nadal that he wanted a Jesuit college in Milan.[11] Of Gómez Suárez de Figueroa, count of Feria, Nadal wrote to Laínez: "I do not know how to tell you of his loving concern for the Society's undertakings. . . . Something to see is the way he lectures everybody about the Society."[12†] For Luis Hurtado de Mendoza, marquis of Mondéjar, he had cordial words. "The sweetness of his affection for the Society and our men is a marvel."[13] Not all converse with men in the higher echelons of government, though, was so easy. The prince of Éboli, Rui Gómez de Silva, was the king's closest confidant; wags used to play on his name, slyly turning Rui Gómez into Rey Gómez. He too called on Nadal. Gracious and suave though he was, he once more opened the rift between the court and the Society on admission of New Christians into the Jesuit ranks. Urgently he pressed for exclusion of men of Jewish ancestry. Nadal rejected the request with the familiar arguments against racial barriers.[14]

Among those important visitors to Toledo was a man who stated he knew little about the Society of Jesus. He did not call on Nadal; Nadal went to him. Archbishop Ferdinando de Valdés of Seville, Spain's inquisitor general, remarked that he was astonished that so many Jesuits were preaching in Spain and yet not one had been cited for investigation by the Inquisition. Nadal knew he was dealing with a man hostile to Francis Borgia. He followed a new tack, one he had emphatically rejected in Sicily ten years earlier. He offered the Society's resources to help the Inquisition in its task. Valdés expressed delight. He had great confidence, he said, in the Society and in Fr. Laínez.[15]

Nadal's largesse eventually brought some shameful moments to the Society. Fifteen years later three Jesuits, agents of the Inquisition, grilled Teresa of Ávila for two days about the orthodoxy of her work and her writings. Carmelite friar Jerónimo de

---

†12   The count strove unceasingly to have the Society of Jesus introduced into England after the marriage of Prince Philip and Mary Tudor. He then blamed Reginald Cardinal Pole for the Society's failure to penetrate the kingdom: "I have written to my brother that I have so far been unable to move the Queen or the Cardinal towards letting members of the Society come here, although in my opinion they are people who would do good for this kingdom. But they would have no standing or protection here unless they entered by the Cardinal's door. I will keep at the matter until we see how it turns out. The Cardinal is a good man, but very lukewarm; and I do not believe that the lukewarm go to heaven, even if they are called moderates." R. Tyler, et. al., eds., *Calendar of State Papers, Spanish* (1554–1558) (London, 1862–1954), 370–71.

Gracián recalled that the Jesuits "probed her spirit deeply, as if expecting to find the most dangerous things." They found not even the tiniest "of dangerous things."[16]

The meeting with Philip was memorable. At first Nadal felt nervous, with good reason. The thirty-four-year-old monarch was building about himself a somber, severe etiquette that awed his visitors. He stared, smiled enigmatically, spoke in a hardly audible voice. Teresa of Ávila could not forget the only time she saw him face to face. "I felt deeply disturbed when I began to speak to him because his piercing glance seemed to wound me; it was one of those glances that plumb the very soul, and he had it fixed on me. So I lowered my eyes and as briefly as I could told him what I wanted." Antonio Pérez could never erase the memory of that smile "that cut like a sword."[17] Despite his nervousness, Nadal gave what he later called a good "address to the crown." He explained to Philip that Laínez wished to visit the Jesuits of Spain personally but could not because the pope needed him in Rome; he gave him the letters from Pope Pius and from Laínez; he told him the Society realized that the safety of Christianity depended on the Spanish crown, and that the Society wished to serve him with its own special kind of ministries; he recalled the affection Ignatius had had for Philip when he was a young prince, "in which affection he nurtured all us Jesuits"; he asked Philip to put the seal of his approval on the visitation.[18]

Philip responded most cordially. He told Nadal he was delighted to meet him; he assured him he would read the letters from the pope and the general; he attested to his desire to help the Society; he suggested that Nadal speak to Rui Gómez if anything occurred that could be facilitated by the court.[19†] Nadal was elated. He felt quite pleased that he was learning how

---

†19 *Mon Nad*, I:425. This was the account that Nadal sent to Laínez. A later account in *Ephemerides* told of a much more curt meeting and a far less elaborate conversation with the king. He wrote: "Eventually I was able to give the letters to the king. Araoz had made the arrangements, but he could not have done so in a more slipshod manner. When the king was on his way to mass, I was casually introduced to him. I was nervous. The king replied kindly, 'Welcome. Speak to Rui Gómez.' I have heard nevertheless that the letters from the pope and the general were handed to the Archbishop of Seville [the Inquisitor]." This terse account hardly allows for Nadal's "address to the crown," nor for Philip's rather extended reply. In neither account does Nadal say that he raised the subject of Borgia's reputation at court (II:69).

to deal with Spanish nobility. In the past he had been straight-laced, but now he was relaxed and at ease.

Nadal's elation was not long unspoiled; Araoz quickly deflated him. At Toledo he kept the same haughty mien he had shown at the opening of Nadal's visitation. This weighed on Nadal's mind. "At Alcalá I sensed that I had irritated Araoz, how I do not know. Here [in Toledo], as the days went on, it was clear that more and more was rubbing him the wrong way. I had a major job on my hands to deal with him tactfully. He certainly upset me."[20]

Araoz's resentment went beyond Nadal and reached into Rome. Laínez needed money to keep the Roman College in operation. He begged Pope Pius IV for funds. Pius, for all his high promises, remained niggardly. Polanco remarked that the trickle of money from the papal treasury "keeps us from dying without allowing us to live." He alerted Nadal: "Repeatedly the pope has told our Father [Laínez] that he intends to form a foundation *in perpetuum* for the Roman College. This we shall believe when we see it. So far we have been skeptical. The pope's determination does not seem particularly strong."[21]

Nadal tried to help. He approached Rui Gómez, as King Philip had told him to do if the Society had any need, and asked that the king write to Pope Pius and urge him to continue financial help to the Roman College. Gómez acted promptly. So did King Philip, who wrote not only to the pope but to some cardinals as well. Laínez was shown the letters when they reached Rome. What he read disappointed him; behind the text he saw the baleful pen of Antonio Araoz. A frost lay on the sentences. Laínez's name was not even mentioned. The Spanish ambassador in Rome, who sympathized with the Society's plight, regretted what he thought was a lapse in diplomatic courtesy. Laínez complained to Nadal that he thought "Araoz is failing to do what we expect of him."[22] Laínez should not have expected anything different, however, because Araoz had little sympathy for Jesuit projects outside Spain.

Nadal found some relief from the stiff and chilly style of Araoz in conversation with a secret Jesuit who had acted as regent of Spain during King Philip's recent absence in England. Princess Juana, about whose relationship with Borgia stories had been circulating and who had with Ignatius' permission pronounced the vows of a Jesuit scholastic, had come to Toledo with the court. "So thorough was her trust in me," recalled Nadal, "that I spoke to her as to any member of the Society. There is nothing that we would want for the service of God and the growth of the Society that we cannot hope to obtain from Her Highness."[23]

The entries in Nadal's *Ephemerides* on this visit to Toledo were brief, hardly a page in *MHSI*. Yet the crisp sentences bristle with the tensions that permeated the Society's relations with Spanish officialdom, secular and religious. They describe the heavy burden the Society (indeed, any religious body) had to shoulder in the autocratic air of sixteenth-century Spain. This burden seriously restrained what Nadal explicitly mentioned in his *Ephemerides* as strongly desired by the Society: freedom.[24]

During his weeks in Toledo, concerned with the Society's relations with the court, Nadal pondered other matters. Soon after his arrival in Spain he began to receive from Laínez long lists of tasks. The general's first letter seriously disturbed him. Alert to rumors in Rome about the reopening of the Council of Trent, Laínez urged Nadal to hasten the visitation; he anticipated the possibility that Nadal might be commissioned to attend the council. Nadal demurred. "I find your suggestion to hurry things hard to accept, Father. What must be done in Spain cannot afford to be done superficially. But that will happen if I am constrained to hasten my examination of every college. Until I hear from you I shall proceed as rapidly as I can, without, however, neglecting the problems that a visitor must confront."[25]

Laínez had another reason for urging Nadal to haste in Spain. He wanted him in Portugal as soon as possible. From the Indies he constantly received pleas for more men. And since the main responsibility for providing Jesuits to the Far East burdened the province of Portugal, the general sought a generous response from Portuguese Jesuits. "Portugal must give the necessary help," he advised Nadal. "This is an obligation more grave than that of acquiring new colleges."[26] He instructed Nadal to enter Portugal as soon as he judged he was no longer needed in Spain. "There, on the spot, you will be able to care for the needs of the Indies, to encourage the mission of the Patriarch [Andrés de Oviedo] to Ethiopia, and to dispatch some good men overseas."

Laínez then crossed national boundaries in his appeal for the Indies. He asked Nadal to recruit Spanish Jesuits also; he listed some needs at Goa: a new rector, three Latin teachers, a philosophy teacher, and a theology teacher. The general judged that Castile would not suffer seriously from this call on resources. Laínez even named three Spanish Jesuits who clamored to be assigned to the Indies and urged him to facilitate their trip. Nadal did what he could but later learned that at Lisbon the three men just missed the spring fleet to the Indies.[27]

Pleas for help reached Laínez not only from the Indies. Bishops in central Europe were begging for Jesuit colleges. He had to refuse Bishop John Przerembski of Gniezno and Bishop Andrew IV Noskowski of Plock. To Nadal he lamented, "I do not know how we can provide Dillingen with men, or Innsbruck. The latter college has been putting heavy pressure on us. It is the same story from other places."[28] He asked Nadal to try to send some Spaniards. Nadal tried, and promptly aroused the ire of Antonio Araoz. A scholastic named Álvaro Orive, a member of Araoz's Castilian province, volunteered to work in Germany. Nadal accepted his offer. Araoz protested this raid on his province.[29†] Nadal reported to Laínez, "I am on top of the situation. I hope to settle this squabble gracefully and dispatch him [Orive] northward."[30]

These episodes give a truer picture of Jesuit life in Spain than all Nadal's official business with the nation's rulers. Young

---

†29 Always suspicious that the Society would drain his resources, Araoz did not protest when Nadal added men to his province. The college at Murcia met distressing days: differences had arisen between Jesuits there and the local bishop and founder, Esteban de Almeida, who wanted the Jesuits to teach reading and writing to little boys. The Jesuits contended that this was beyond their contract. Laínez had placed the problem in Nadal's hands. Nadal followed Laínez's suggestion that the college be detached from the province of Aragon and attached to Castile. This transfer made Antonio Cordeses, provincial of Aragon, extremely unhappy. He saw a staff of men, including the competent preacher Miguel Govierno, slipping from his province. He urged Nadal to release his men and to staff the college with Jesuits from elsewhere, and he denounced the spoliation of his province just to keep the bishop happy. But here was the rub: the bishop liked the Jesuits who were working in the college, and so Nadal ordered that none be transferred. He tried to pacify Cordeses by assuring him that he would send to the Aragon province other men just as competent as those Cordeses was losing. Nadal wrote to Laínez that "dealing with this bishop is really a difficult task. With the divine grace, I hope to pass through that city" (*Mon Nad*, I:372–73, 416). Araoz, as provincial of Castile, had, of course, gained by that transfer.

Spanish Jesuits learned in the novitiate that it was their vocation to travel to any part of the world where there was hope of achieving God's greater glory. Those words came alive in the exploits of Francis Xavier and his two companions in Japan, Fr. Cosme de Torres and Br. Juan Fernández, both Spaniards. Reports from and about those men became part of Jesuit lore. A living tradition was being born. Like ivy that rises from the ground to embrace and cover every cranny of a stone wall, this tradition steadily grew and clung to every part of the Spanish provinces.

This tradition mirrored Nadal's own image of the Society: a body carried forward on the wings of Germany and the Indies, the two places on the globe where spiritual needs were most acute. Those were the spots where Jesuits should be. Nadal fed the growth of that tradition. By putting men on board the Indian fleet at Lisbon and on the roads northward over the Pyrenees, he probably did more for Jesuit life in Spain than all his converse with the Spanish aristocracy.

Despite Laínez's wish that Nadal move rapidly, several problems made this impossible. At Cuenca and Alcalá he met local issues that he could not ignore. The college at Cuenca had opened seven years earlier. Nadal had made the initial agreement for the gift of a house and a garden in 1554 with a wealthy canon, Pedro del Pozo. Despite Pozo's inability to provide funds for sustenance of the college, the Society accepted it. By 1561 the need for a steady flow of money became acute. Nadal went from Alcalá to Cuenca to try to relieve the pinch. There he met another canon, Juan de Marquina, who offered to finance the college's foundation and an expansion of the building.[31]

Marquina had known Ignatius in Rome and had carried to Spain a devout respect for the Society. Nadal enjoyed negotiations with him, even though the canon at first made stipulations incompatible with the Society's norms for operation of a college. In a report to Laínez, Nadal assured the general that he hoped to draw up a contract "in completely impeccable form" (*con toda puridad y perfection*). "Forgive me if I seem to have gone too far in my affection for Canon Marquina, but I cannot dissimulate the love I conceived for him during our few business meetings and conversations."[32] Nadal attuned himself to Marquina's spiritual sensitivities and kept conversation to the devout aspirations of the canon. Gradually Nadal drew him to see the Society's point of view. Marquina burst into tears. He realized, he said, that what Nadal was insisting on "was the purer and better thing to do." With two minor exceptions, he heartily agreed with Nadal's formula of the contract. During these negotiations, Nadal suffered seven days of catarrh.[33]

A second problem ended less pleasantly, one involving both Cuenca and Alcalá. Nadal knew the basics of the problem from his earlier visitations in 1554, when he failed to resolve it. Dr. Alfonso Ramírez de Vergara (as was seen earlier) gave generously to the college at Alcalá, but at a price. He demanded and got veto power over assignment of Jesuits to and from the college. He demanded and got a voice in all major decisions on policy. Francis Borgia aggravated the situation by giving Vergara quarters in the college at Cuenca. Antonio Araoz aggravated it more by assigning a brother, listed in the Society's records as Br. Miguel, as Vergara's valet and cook. Br. Miguel let superiors know he was unhappy in his work.

Laínez wanted to break Vergara's hold on the two colleges. Through Polanco he told Nadal to take action. "Many complaints are coming from Castile about good Dr. Vergara's interference in the governance of the Society, especially at the college of Alcalá. You will better picture the problem when you hear oral reports in Alcalá and Toledo. Our father general would be happy if you could break, gently and nimbly, the yoke on the college. Do what you can."[34] A second injunction followed. Laínez wanted Vergara to vacate his quarters at Cuenca and relinquish Br. Miguel. He cautioned Nadal to broach this tricky subject to Vergara "with grace lest we lose his favor."[35] The Society needed his money.

Nadal spoke with Vergara. Earlier his words had touched the emotions of Canon Marquina, who shed tears of devout understanding of the Society's policy. His words also touched the emotions of Dr. Vergara, who loosed self-pitying tantrums. He would quit his canon's post; he would abdicate all other ecclesiastical positions; he would become a hermit. And all the ropes in the Society of Jesus, he warned, could not restrain him. Nadal was cowed by the flowing lava and retreated. He assured Dr. Vergara that for the present nothing would be changed; perhaps they could agree in the future. Laínez approved Nadal's retreat.[36]

By mid-March Nadal had spent two and a half months in Spain. His main purpose, to achieve a resolution of the divergent policies of Borgia and Araoz, eluded him like a wraith. Araoz held him at a distance; Borgia was far away. He had to dance a minuet with high echelons in the state and in the Church. It palled. As he left for Portugal on March 20 he wrote, "I have had it up to my ears with courtiers."[37] He pointed his mule toward Oporto.

From Alcalá Nadal traveled north and west to the valley of the Duero River, hoping to be in Oporto by Easter Sunday, April 7. He followed a route dotted with Jesuit colleges: Ávila, Medina del Campo, Salamanca, and he made a short visit at each.

Nadal's stay at the college of San Gil in Ávila only a day and a half had repercussions in the reform of the Carmelite order. There he met the twenty-six-year-old Fr. Baltasar Álvarez, confessor of Teresa de Cepeda y Ahumada (better known as Teresa of Ávila), then striving to found in Ávila the reformed convent of St. Joseph, a foundation distinct from the Convent of the Incarnation, which she had entered twenty-five years before. Álvarez hesitated about the wisdom of Teresa's formidable project. His doubts added to her distress amid strong opposition from Carmelites who wished no part of her reform.

Nadal unwittingly helped Teresa. He changed the rector of San Gil. Fr. Dionisio Vázquez begged Nadal to be relieved of the burden of the rector's office. Nadal honored his request and summoned Fr. Gaspar de Salazar from Alcalá to be Vázquez's successor. Teresa and Salazar met. For him she immediately felt a "spiritual affinity." Álvarez, noting the harmony between his penitent and his rector, gained confidence in Teresa's venture and encouraged her.[38] His change of heart was one of many helps that carried Teresa to the successful foundation of St. Joseph's.

At Medina Nadal met informally with the founders of the college there, Pedro Quadrado and his wife Doña Francisca. At Salamanca he met the founder of the college in Monterrey, the count of Monterrey, and discussed his foundation. Nadal postponed serious discussion with both until his return from Portugal.[39]

Francis Borgia had played havoc with Nadal's plans in Spain by his absence. In Portugal he would cramp Nadal's schedule by his presence. And all with no breath of malice. Willy-nilly, he could not separate his personal fortunes from the course of Jesuit affairs. In that spring of 1561 he was staying in Oporto.

Before noon on Holy Saturday, April 6, Nadal rode into Oporto on schedule. There he met a community of eight Jesuits, four priests and four brothers, dwelling in a house that had opened nine months earlier, a gift of Don Henrique Gouvea, three of whose sons had entered the Society. And there at last he met Francis Borgia, a tired, sick, perplexed man.[40]

For several months Borgia had been drained of his energies. And for a year he had been wavering at the brink of an important decision. This he explained to Nadal. In the previous summer a serious problem had faced him after a letter from Laínez. The general wanted him in Rome to fill the post of general's assistant vacated by Fr. Luis Gonçalves da Câmara, who had returned to Portugal. Borgia promptly left Portugal, entered Galicia, and headed for Santiago. But gout stopped him. Intensely sick, he returned to Oporto. In October the pressure on him to leave for Rome increased. Laínez enlisted the help of Pope Pius IV. Pope and general both sent messages urging Borgia, if nothing impeded him, to start for Rome.

At this point Borgia doubted the wisdom of going to Rome. Should he not first clear his name at the Spanish court? Should he not, rather, go to Spain and try to dissipate the ugly rumors of heresy and adultery that had followed him into Portugal? Would this not be essential for the Society's well-being in Spain? He confided his quandary to Nadal. Even as the two men tried to solve the problem, more letters arrived from Pope Pius IV and Laínez. Their common message was clear: pope and general preferred that Borgia leave, if possible, for Rome. Borgia's perplexity mounted. Lengthy discussions with Nadal helped not a bit. A week after his arrival at Oporto, Nadal recorded in three Latin words the failure of all his talk with Borgia: "But we reached no decision" (*Sed non definimus*).[41]

During that week Nadal, though, made an important decision about the Oporto community. Borgia had determined— against the advice of the provincial, Fr. Miguel de Torres—that the new residence be a professed house. Nadal reversed Borgia and decided the Society should start a college but retain the possibility of converting the house into a novitiate. Borgia changed and agreed.[42]

Nadal at this time also introduced an innovation of far wider import than his decision about the use of the house. He composed two lengthy questionnaires, which he presented to each of the eight Jesuits in Oporto. The first questionnaire, of thirty questions, was answered in writing. A few of the questions follow:

1. What is your name?
2. Place of birth?
14. What motives and inclinations prompted you to enter the Society; who received you, and where?
18. Have you made the Spiritual Exercises; how much of them; how often, and for what length of time?
19. How many other testings (*probacciones*) have you undertaken?
23. In how many areas of the Society have you been, and what work did you do there?
25. Do you desire to suffer injury and calumny in order to put on the living Christ?
26. Do you desire to mortify your passions and your imperfections, and do you desire the help of your superiors in achieving this objective?
30. With religious indifference presupposed, are you inclined more toward India, or Germany, or some other difficult ministry or mission that gives extensive service and help to the neighbor?

The second questionnaire, of thirty-two questions, was secret. Each Jesuit answered orally. The questions probed such areas as follows:

1. What was the social status of his parents.
2. Whether he was born in or out of wedlock.
3. Whether his forebears were "old Christians."
4. Whether the Inquisition had ever cited any of his relatives.
5. Whether he had any bastards, and, if so, whether he had taken care of the consequences.
6. Whether he had any secret illness or defect.
12. How was he faring in prayer and spiritual things since he entered the Society; whether he was scrupulous.
13. Whether study or other works have weakened, or currently weaken, his spirit; whether these occupations lessen devotion or augment it.

14. Whether he knew anything untoward about his superiors; what was his estimate of them; whether he had grumbled about superiors, or knows of others who had grumbled; whether he has been nosy about others' business.

18. Whether he knew of temptations, especially in the area of vocation, that others had suffered.

21. Whether he had any criticism of the Institute, the Rules, or any other feature of the Society.

28. Whether he had any special friendships, more for one person rather than for another, and so did not love all equally as brothers in the Lord; whether he had an aversion for any persons.[43]

These questionnaires traced the course of the confidential conversations between Nadal and the Jesuits he was interviewing. They gave sharp focus to the inner nature of a nadalian visitation.

Nadal could not let Borgia's predicament, painful as it was, hold him in Oporto. Since he was in the northern part of the country, he was anxious to visit a new college at Monterrey, not far across the Spanish border, in Galicia. And when he left Oporto on April 13 or 14, he prepared to face a problem that had been on his mind during most of his recent stay in Spain. The problem was a provincial, Fr. Bartolomé de Bustamente of Andalusia. For some time respected men of the province had been accusing him of leading them along paths taken by other religious orders and of interpreting the Society's Constitutions in a whimsical and highly personal way. Rectors of the province bypassed him and held an unusual meeting at Montella on handling their rigorist provincial. Bustamente protested to Laínez that, unless the general had given his permission, the session was out of order. In a huff he took off, left Andalusia, traveled to Portugal, and sought Francis Borgia.

Laínez passed the problem to Nadal. "Find how the meeting [of rectors] came about. Then handle the problem as you see fit." Laínez next heard that Bustamente was planning to accompany Borgia to Rome; that he did not want to happen. He told Nadal to keep Bustamente in Spain, even, if were necessary, to remove him from the provincial's post and to appoint him an itinerant preacher. Nadal had found Bustamente in Oporto with Borgia. He took the flinty Andalusian with him to Monterrey and there gave Bustamente his orders: return promptly to your province. He reasoned with him and explained a provincial's responsibilities to his men. Bustamente yielded readily enough, and by early May he was on the road to southern Spain. Nadal hoped to follow him after a few months to visit the Andalusian Jesuit communities.[44]

The college of Monterrey was one of the last schools Ignatius had agreed to open. He did so at the request of the count of Monterrey, Alonso de Acevedo y Zúñiga. Monterrey was not a prepossessing town; nor was the Jesuit venture a prepossessing college. Nadal found Jesuits teaching Latin grammar to 350 boys in cramped quarters, without a church and bereft of a solid financial foundation. The students, many of whom came from outlying hamlets, were extremely poor. On Sundays and feastdays the Jesuits visited nearby hamlets to preach. In Monterrey they taught catechism. Fr. Blasio Rengisio conducted a class in moral theology and supervised the theological disputations that the Jesuits occasionally held for townsfolk.

Nadal inspected all these activities. He observed teachers in classrooms; he listened to preachers; he ordered renovations in the structure of the college until a new building could be erected; he declined an offer of a church two miles from the school. He tried to organize the financial basis of the school but here he met frustration, since the chief benefactor, the count of Monterrey, was away.[45]

A personal meeting with each Jesuit remained the heart of the visit. "I heard the confession of each, covering the period since his last general confession. I received from each an account of conscience. I asked them what sins they had committed before they entered the Society. I asked them what were the sins toward which they were most inclined. I inquired about the quality of their progress since they entered the Society." So did he outline for Laínez his work, which took eight days.[46]

The college next on Nadal's schedule dwarfed tiny Monterrey. Coimbra had the largest Jesuit community in Portugal and one of the largest in the Society. Nadal left Monterrey on May 4; on his way south he again stopped at Orense, Sanfins, Braga, and Oporto.

At Orense, accompanied by the rector of the college of Monterrey, Nadal visited the bishop in whose diocese the college was located. The bishop, who made a good, strong impression on Nadal, received the two Jesuits kindly and made lavish promises that he would assist the troubled college.

The Jesuit residence at Sanfins had caused irritating problems. This remote house, in the area called de Friestas and located on the River Minho, was a monastery that had passed into the hands of the Society. King João III, seeking revenues in 1543 for the Jesuit college he was founding at Coimbra, sought ecclesiastical approval for transferring the monastic institute at Sanfins to the Society. Approval was given in 1546 and confirmed in 1548. Nadal encountered two problems when he visited this residence. Father Borgia had been there earlier and had made arrangements with local farmers about their taxes. The farmers were discontented with the agreements and voiced their complaints to Nadal. He decided nothing and simply forwarded their grievances to Borgia. The second problem was the residence's remote location. This disturbed Jesuits assigned there, because the small community gave them limited companionship. Nadal judged that only the most virtuous should be assigned there.

At Oporto Nadal was forced to make a painful decision. The donor of the Jesuit house and father of three Jesuits, Don Henrique Gouvea, desired to follow his sons into the Society. His wife planned to enter a convent. Nadal had worried about this for some time, but by the time he returned to Oporto he decided to deny Gouvea's request. He could find, he said, no precedent to guide him.[47]

Borgia had also reached a decision. He chose, he told Nadal, to remain in Portugal until Nadal returned to Spain, assessed the political climate there, and advised him whether it would be feasible to return to Spain to clear his name. When Nadal left Oporto for Coimbra, Borgia accompanied him for some two miles. In his recollection of this little journey with Borgia, Nadal penned a tantalizing phrase. He wrote that Borgia "spoke much about Araoz."[48] Not a hint, however, did he give of what things were covered in that simple word *much*. Such phrases suggested a conspiratorial tone that permeated relations among Nadal, Araoz, Borgia, and others who in one way or another were associated with the court. A lack of mutual sympathy in the thicket of courtiers that enveloped Nadal made him react with disgust.

15

A Fine Treasure

I am anxious that you spend much time at that college [Coimbra], much time here [Lisbon], much time in Évora. . . . The time you spend in Portugal can be considered time given to Brazil, India, Japan, the lands of Prester John.

Fr. Luis Gonçalves da Câmara
to Nadal in May 1561

Nadal arrived in Coimbra probably on May 20 or 21. Awaiting him were 170 Jesuits, most of whom were scholastics in their studies, divided among three communities. The first, the Colégio de Jesus, located in the highest part of the city, Nadal knew from his visit eight years earlier. The second college, Colégio Real (or Colégio des Artes), located in the lower area of the city, had been entrusted to the Society by King João III in 1555. The third community, of sixty novices, was situated near Colégio de Jesus. The rector of Colégio de Jesus was Fr. Miguel de Sousa; the rector of the Colégio Real was Fr. Cipriano Soares.[1]

In the presence of this large body of men, Nadal set for himself a clear objective: to know each of them personally. In a private dining room he had dinner each day with a few members of the community. In a relaxed atmosphere he chatted easily about the history and works of the Society. He drew on a fund of anecdotes about Jesuits he had known. These he recounted, observed Fr. Miguel Venegas, a member of the audience, "delightfully and prudently" (*iocunde et prudenter*). Venegas thought Nadal excelled as a raconteur and that his stories taught some fine lessons about the Society in an intensely inspiring way. Nadal heard each man's general confession from the time of his entrance into the Society. Fr. Manuel Álvarez remembered especially the gentleness with which he heard the confessions.[2]

Within the community Nadal strove for a friendly and joyful atmosphere. He ran contests in the form of community draws. To the winners he distributed holy pictures and other keepsakes. On feast days he challenged the scholastics with riddles; to the riddle breakers he gave little prizes. Several points of the external regimen of the two colleges he altered according to the model of the Roman College. He set a schedule for the ordinary occupations of the scholastics: study, prayer, class, recreation. He designated Thursday as the weekly holiday; he visited the classrooms, observed the teachers; he engaged in the philosophical disputations; he attended the ceremonies for the distribution of prizes; he admitted eighteen young men into the novitiate.[3]

Nadal's propensity for directing the minutiae of Jesuit life blossomed at Coimbra. Some of his instructions follow:

> In the two colleges, pictures were to be hung on the four walls of the dining rooms. One picture was to be of the Last Supper.
>
> At supper each evening a scholastic was to give a sermon. The scholastic was to be appointed only an hour before supper, when the theme of the sermon was to be given him. He was to be excused from the regular repetition to prepare his sermon.
>
> On alternate Fridays, either the superintendent or the rector or another qualified priest was to give an exhortation to the community. On the next Friday a discussion (*collocutio*) was to be had on the same subject. The exhortations were to be given before supper for about an hour.
>
> For the sick a special table in the dining room was to be designated. Members of the community were to be assigned to help those who were not able to eat on their own.[4]

Nadal esteemed a code of etiquette among Jesuits. He drew up a list of directives on correct forms of address within the Portuguese Society. All were to address the general as Your Paternity. All were to address provincials as Your Reverence. Among themselves the provincials were to call one another

Your Reverence, but to others they were to say You (in its formal form). Local superiors, rectors, and novice masters were to address one another as Your Reverence, all others as You (in its formal form). Priests were to call one another Your Reverence. Others they were to address as You (in its formal form). Brothers were to say to priests Your Reverence, among themselves You (in its formal form). Although each should treat the other with respect, it was not to be exaggerated.[5]

Nadal also introduced a practice Fr. Miguel Venegas liked very much. It was a ceremonial built about the renewal of simple vows by the scholastics. According to the Constitutions the scholastics were to renew their simple vows twice a year, at Easter and Christmas or on two other principal feasts, "for greater devotion, and to refresh the meaning of the obligations they are under, and to confirm themselves more solidly in their vocations." Nadal expanded that simple directive. He devised a triduum of special prayer and recollection that would precede the renewal of the vows. Each scholastic was to make a general confession for the period since his last general confession; each was to take the discipline. Litanies were to be recited before the Blessed Sacrament.

This triduum Nadal had introduced three years earlier at the Roman College, when, on December 28, 1557, he opened a series of conferences over a three-day period before renovation of vows. This nadalian innovation spread to other Jesuits houses, largely by impulses of Nadal himself. The themes of the conferences concentrated on central themes and meditations of the Spiritual Exercises. This annual evocation of the Exercises probably exerted the most potent influence in creating a disposition for the later legislation that would impose the obligation on Jesuits to make the Spiritual Exercises each year.[6]

Nadal brought to Portugal another innovation he had introduced at the Roman College. In various parts of the two Coimbra colleges, he posted placards on which he listed fifteen to twenty suggested mortifications for the scholastics to practice during summer months when they were free of study and class. He remained insistent on one of his first insights into the Jesuit vocation: self-denial is rooted deeply in the Society's life. Some of his suggestions: making the Spiritual Exercises for a week or so, fasting, taking the discipline in the dining room, working in a hospital, making a pilgrimage, teaching catechism to boys,

wearing shabby clothes, requesting superiors to impose mortifications in those things for which the most repugnance was felt.
These and the other suggestions remained basically the same as
those Nadal had suggested at the Roman College.[7]

Nadal's stress on self-denial meshed with the conviction of
one of the most influential spiritual leaders of the province. Fr.
Luis Gonçalves da Câmara wrote long letters to Nadal, at least
three, each a plea for rigor and a rule of iron. Nadal had known
this forty-two-year-old native of Madeira since 1554, when Ignatius
made Câmara minister of the Roman Professed House and
dictated to him his autobiography. He had also worked closely
with him in Rome after both were elected assistants by the First
General Congregation in 1558. Compelled to leave Rome a year
later, when Queen Catherine wanted him to be tutor for young
King Sebastião, Câmara emerged as a moral leader of a group
of Portuguese Jesuits who, in the name of Ignatius' teaching,
took to the field against any show of softness or mildness in
Jesuit life. On the alert against humankind's evil inclinations
and the human aversion to sustained heroic asceticism, these
martinets identified the Jesuit ideal with self-denial and subju-
gation of the passions. In his joyless and apprehensive letters to
Nadal at Coimbra, Câmara poured out his anxieties for the
Portuguese province.[8]

The rectors of the province, reported Câmara, were a spine-
less lot. Timid, cautious, diffident, they were a soft spot in the
province. Greater care must be taken to find qualified men. Yet,
oddly enough, in the presence of those weaklings, members of
the communities cringed in fear, looking on them as judges,
not fathers. The spirit of servile fear must be removed. Câmara
had other worries. He found the Portuguese Jesuits, his own
countrymen, listless and lazy. Compared with the Italian Jesuits,
who worked with zest and who were ever on the lookout for
other tasks beyond their own assignments, they made a poor
showing. The Italian Jesuits got more work done. Portuguese
Jesuits lacked the spiritual stamina of the Italians. A decline of
fervor among the Portuguese Jesuits also troubled Câmara.
Despite the high promise in learning and devotion of a large
number of men, he detected a cooling in their love of the cross
and a dampening of the flame of their charity.

The prospect of heresy's taking root in the Portuguese province also profoundly worried Câmara. He had heard reports

that heresy was on the move in Spain, and that the Spanish Inquisition was having an unusually busy season arresting culprits. Portugal was not far away. Contagion was possible. The Portuguese Jesuits must be kept free of heretical blemish. Câmara urged Nadal to scrutinize closely any attitude among the Portuguese Jesuits that might leave the door ajar for the infiltration of doctrinal error. He confessed he had forebodings. "I hope to God that such a thing will not come to pass. But if it does, it will not dismay me. Yet I take great comfort in the belief that all the necessary preventive steps will be taken. The Lord knows that this is one reason why I look forward so intensely to your presence among us."[9]

Câmara urged Nadal to tarry long in Portugal, so that "you will get a full view of the defects and disorders peculiar to us. . . . I am anxious that you spend much time at that college [Coimbra], much time here [Lisbon], much time in Évora." Time would be necessary for Nadal "to plant the Society's way of life not only by the spoken and written word but also by the active and practical implementation of that word." Câmara offered a broader reason to keep Nadal in Portugal. No other province in the Society touched the expanding world to the extent that the Portuguese province did. Jesuit missions in Brazil and the entire Orient were the responsibilities of the Portuguese. Any impact Nadal had on Portugal's Jesuits would be reflected eventually in lands far away. "The time you spend in Portugal can be considered time given to Brazil, India, Japan, the lands of Prester John."[10]

Nadal replied to Câmara at least twice, but those letters have been lost. By conviction Nadal himself leaned decidedly toward a stress on self-denial in Jesuit life, but he did so with the conviction that self-denial produces a deep interior joy and freedom of spirit. His "Theology of the Heart" animated his asceticism with a spiritual relish. Whether in his answers to Câmara he tried to drain off the latter's grim attitudes is unknown. If he did so he failed, for Câmara became the leader of a group of Portuguese Jesuits who identified Ignatius' spirit with severity and penance, humiliations and reproaches, all in the main external.

Câmara's personal knowledge of Ignatius while minister of the Professed House in Rome and as scribe of Ignatius' autobiography gave him a special authority among men of the province. He brought back from Rome an image of Ignatius the martinet. At first hand he had seen Ignatius give Nadal a severe reprimand. As minister he had most likely himself felt the sting of Ignatius' reprimand, as had Nadal during his tour as minister. He quoted Ignatius as saying that the desire to be guided by charity was the worst signal of a person's interior spirit. This was the Ignatius who impressed him; the rounded Ignatius whom Nadal appreciated he did not perceive. Baleful indeed was his later influence in Portugal. Did Nadal have any perception of this? The answer may lie in his lost letters.

In two ways, though, Nadal agreed with Câmara. Câmara insisted on the need for an extended stay by Nadal in Coimbra. Nadal spent two months there; it could well have been eight, he said.[11] Câmara stressed the need for more men, to ease the burden of the Portuguese Jesuits in the farflung missions in Brazil and the Orient. Nadal concurred and wrote Laínez an urgent request for help. He suggested a norm in the choice of missionaries that almost surely raised eyebrows in Rome. "In this province, Father, I find a glaring shortage of men to care for the Indies and Brazil. From what Fr. Luis Gonçalves [da Câmara] tells me, the need for men in Brazil is especially acute. If, with those vast regions in mind, you should have on hand men of mediocre talent, not quite sharp enough to be sent to Germany but gifted with good hearts and strong backs, do assign them [to Brazil and the Orient]. They would be a great boon to the task of converting the heathens. Besides, the monarchs of this realm would be pleased. Feel free to dispatch them right away. And as many as you can. If you are able to act promptly, do so, since it would be preferable to have the men arrive [in Lisbon] before the winter sets in."[12]

At Coimbra Nadal took action on a letter he had received from Laínez. The Spanish provinces were being forced to turn away many promising young men because their houses were poor and could not sustain the great influx of vocations. Lest these young men be lost to the Society, Laínez instructed the Spanish provincials to send some to Rome, where they could be trained and dispatched to countries north of the Alps. Nadal received the same instructions from Laínez. From Portugal he sent Pedro Jean Perpinyà, who would later distinguish himself as a humanist. Nadal also wrote to Castile instructions that Juan de Mariana, Diego de Acosta, Diego Páez, and Juan Ramírez should be sent to Rome. When the inquisitor general,

Ferdinando de Valdés, heard that these men were leaving Spain he tried to stop them but they had crossed the border.[13]

About midpoint in Nadal's stay at Coimbra, Borgia once more burst into his life with a sackful of worries. Reversing his previous plan to await Nadal's study of the lay of the land in Spain, he had now decided to go to Rome. To avoid a collision with Spanish authorities, he planned to take ship at Oporto, sail northward a short distance to Bayonne in France, and then travel across southern France, through the Alps into Italy, and on to Rome. He came to Coimbra in early June to tell Nadal personally.

Nadal immediately foresaw dire consequences. Before him rose dismal portents for his own future work in Spain. He sensed that Spanish officials, resenting Borgia's escape from their clutches, would readily conclude that Nadal had conspired in the flight. For the sake of his own credibility in Spain, it therefore became imperative that Nadal cleanse his hands of any complicity in Borgia's actions. He had to make it clear that he had no authority to stop Borgia. He and Francis discussed how to achieve those objectives.[14]

From their conversations emerged two documents. Borgia wrote one, stating clearly that the decision to go to Rome was his alone, prompted as it was by a Jesuit's sensitivity to the least wish of the pope. Pointedly he said that Nadal had no part in the decision. He signed the document. Nadal countersigned it. Nadal wrote the second document. He clearly stated that he personally disapproved of Borgia's action. He signed it. Borgia countersigned it. Both documents bore the date of June 7, 1561.[15]

Borgia left Coimbra, turned northward, and embarked for the short sail to Bayonne. Almost immediately the sea churned heavily under strong winds. The ship had to turn back to port; Borgia rested at Sanfins. He then recast his plans and gave Nadal a severe fright. He decided to go by land, cutting across northwestern Spain into France, and then to Rome. He wrote Nadal about his change, posted the letter, and promptly set out.

Nadal received the letter three or four days later and it filled him with dismay. Borgia was flouting the Spanish government. Nadal envisaged Philip's court rising to higher levels of wrath against the Society. In his diary he noted that Borgia's conduct emphatically (*vehementer*) displeased him and the Jesuits of Coimbra. He turned to others for advice, then hastily wrote to

Borgia. "With utmost firmness (*constantissime*)" he argued against the trip through Spanish territory. He bluntly expressed his disapproval. He kept a copy of this letter, signed by himself and other Jesuits, as a proof to show the Spaniards that he and the Society had nothing to do with Borgia's escapade. His message to Borgia failed, however, to cut him off at the Portuguese-Spanish border. Francis had a start of several days, and when the courier reached Sanfins, Borgia was safely on the other side of the Pyrenees.[16]

The "Borgian incident" would haunt Nadal through his remaining nine months in the Iberian peninsula. At times he seemed to shake off his dread; at other times he seemed on the brink of despair. One of the first bits of news he received reported that Borgia had gone safely through Spanish territory and arrived unscathed in France. For this the Jesuits at Coimbra recited prayers of thanksgiving. As further news dribbled in, Nadal began to wonder a bit about the alleged tensions generated around the person of Borgia. During "the flight" through Spain, Borgia had taken sick with fever and had to stop at a small village called Villalpando. At that moment the Spanish court was resting not far from Villalpando, and with the court was Inquisitor General Ferdinando de Valdés. Valdés heard Borgia was in the area but made no move to apprehend him. This puzzled Nadal. He wondered whether reports on Spain's displeasure with Borgia were blown out of proportion.[17]

Fr. Antonio Araoz had no such doubts. In letters to Laínez and Nadal he strongly denounced Borgia's flight and said that Borgia had lost credit in the eyes of all Spaniards;[18] friends and foes alike denounced his action. Anger swept through Spanish officialdom. Other reports confirmed Araoz's dire picture. Inquisitor General Valdés was especially incensed. "All of Castile was in flames in its contempt for his [Borgia's] stealing away." Yet Nadal took a slack attitude. He decided to pay no heed "to the Castilian din and the Araozian roar. We gave thanks to God for the good father's escape from danger."[19] Nadal miscalculated; a few months later, back in Spain, he would discover how wrong he was. The Spaniards took the Borgia family seriously.

Nadal gave twenty conferences at Coimbra, the first on May 25, 1561. He began by stating that Fr. General Laínez had wished to conduct the visitation personally, because he desired to strengthen the union between himself and the members of the Coimbra communities. Fr. Laínez judged that he would be helped in his office by meeting each Jesuit and talking intimately with him about his personal problems in Jesuit life. Pope Pius IV, however, refused to allow Fr. Laínez to leave Rome, since he wanted the general's theological expertise immediately at hand. Fr. Laínez was forced then to send a substitute. So did Nadal explain to the Coimbra Jesuits his presence in Portugal.[20]

Next he described his approach to the visitation by outlining his personal dispositions and detailing the dispositions he would like to find in the Coimbra communities. For the first time, three ideas he had been talking about for several years jelled into a formula: *spiritu, corde, practice.* He intended to present his conferences *spiritu, corde, practice,* and he asked his fellow Jesuits to hear the conferences *spiritu, corde, practice.*[21] This formula became one of his favorites.

Nadal promptly gave a brief exegesis of his three terms. *Spiritu* he explained in terms of Ignatius' injunction that Jesuits walk in the way of the Holy Spirit. This meant that a Jesuit's life, his speech, his actions, all take shape under the molding influence of God's grace. The guidance of the Holy Spirit assures a Jesuit's fidelity to the peculiar grace of his vocation. *Corde* he explained by what he called "the true heart" (*el verdadero corazon*), which he defined as "charity and the affective love of God." "The affective love of God" fashions all that a Jesuit does— study, cooking, preaching—with a joyful ease, a growth in grace, a mounting desire to serve. The "true heart" is also "a most gentle heart" (*suavisimo corazon*). Joyful animation, Nadal stressed, was what the scholastics should feel in their studies and in the practice of obedience.

Nadal expounded *practice* by describing a Jesuit's external works as the extension of his interior life. Between a Jesuit's contemplation and his labor stretched an unbroken cord. Nadal warned against halting at speculation; to do that, he said, was "a very grave error," especially when Protestants were depicting the role of works in our salvation. Nadal esteemed the work in hospitals required of the novices, because it tested their ability to carry into their labor among the sick the prayerful attitudes they learned in the Spiritual Exercises. He recalled for the Coimbra Jesuits the memory of Francis Xavier, who skillfully united prayer and hospital work.

Nadal recalled a man whom Ignatius hesitated to admit into the Society. The novice could not bring himself to work among the sick. With counseling, however, he changed little by little until he moved with assurance into the wards. Nadal emphasized *practice.* He insisted that a Jesuit must carry his life of prayer into the streets, the classrooms, the pulpits, the confessionals. Grievous indeed was the error of the Jesuit who knew a great deal about the Society of Jesus yet shared but little in the Society's life. Repeatedly Nadal brought up in his conferences the theme of *practice.*[22]

Nadal's style was personal and intimate. He drew widely on his own experiences. He shunned the abstract and the abstruse. As he expounded the theological base of the Society's purpose and character, he sprinkled his doctrinal teaching with anecdotes from the lives of the first Jesuits and with stories of his personal experiences in the Society. He invited his hearers to match their experiences with his. He insisted, for example, on the need that each Jesuit comprehend the meaning of what he called "the grace of the Society." As a step toward an intellectual grasp of that essential idea, he asked each Jesuit to compare his life since he entered the Society with what had gone before. What each would recall would be a life of sin yielding to a life of spiritual consolation, inspiration, and pious desires. "Certainly then," he said, "there is no one here who does not experience some first stirrings of this grace of the Society of Jesus and a taste for it."[23]

Nadal used the same approach in the hard task of explaining obedience as the supreme guide toward union with Christ. As though intellectual arguments left something unsaid, he promised the obedient Jesuit a happy experience. "I believe that you yourselves will have the personal awareness of God Our Lord giving you the spiritual help you need to bring to perfection the virtue of obedience."[24]

Nadal called on their memories of local history. The Jesuit foundation at Coimbra was identified from its origins with a flow of young men readying themselves for apostolic labor in the Far East. The University placed in its store of memories scenes of Jesuit scholastics, unselfish and zealous, setting out for Lisbon and the Indies. Nadal told his hearers that in them he saw worthy followers of those who broke ground there. "Nowhere else have I had the abundant consolation that God Our Lord has given me here [in Coimbra]. I say this because I am a witness to the desire all of you have to move forward and distinguish yourselves in the service of God Our Lord. You radiate what, in the early years of the Society, took place here, the jumping-off point for our venture in the Indies."[25]

Nadal recited details from his own life. He told his fellow Jesuits that, in the wide range of teaching positions in the colleges, he had always preferred the lowest classes of grammar. Teachers in those classes do not enjoy the natural gratification of the professors of theology, who can grow in the deep appreciation of their subject, but they have students at an age when they are malleable and can be formed in truth and holiness. God helps those in such lowly work, "as I know is the case with the coadjutor brothers, for whom I have deep affection."[26] He even pulled the veil back a little on his personal prayer. He revealed that he found devotion in the simple method described by Ignatius as "The Third Method of Prayer," a measured and rhythmical recitation with each breath of a single word of a particular formula of prayer.[27]

Some of Nadal's extended incursions into autobiography recounted his dealings with Ignatius. In the ninth exhortation, a wide-ranging talk on several subjects, Nadal described two incidents. He recalled the day he pressed Ignatius to give him the key to progress in the spiritual life. Ignatius somewhat solemnly answered that the key was the desire to be identified with Christ despised, insulted, and criticized. "Master Nadal, desire insults, failure, injuries, reproaches; desire to be regarded as a dunce, to be contemned by every one, to have everything about you stamped with the cross, and all this for love of Christ Our Lord."[28]

On another day, when Ignatius and Nadal were chatting, Ignatius explained his way of regarding his brethren in the Society. He turned, he said, his interior gaze not on their defects but on the gifts that God had given them. This he did because he believed that God so looked on him. Nadal then told the Coimbra Jesuits why he recalled this incident: it was to illumine a certain practice in the Society, a practice called fraternal correction. Fraternal correction included two facets: a Jesuit's willingness to have his errors and defects made known to superiors, and a Jesuit's willingness to aid in correction of defects of others. Ignatius called it "manifesting one another with due love and charity, to help one another more in the spiritual life."[29] Ignatius did not design this practice, recalled Nadal, to make a Jesuit feel miserable but to help him remove obstacles to God's grace. Defects obtrude themselves. Jesuits, even as they aid one another in conquest of those defects, should not allow them to blur the vision of the gifts given by God to each. Ignatius set the example: he did not allow defects to distract attention from the attractive qualities and endowments of others. Harshness departs from fraternal correction practiced in the Ignatian way.[30]

Personal recollections, therefore, gave color and life to Nadal's presentation. This his hearers found attractive, enjoyable, and memorable. Such was the manner in which he presented several ideas of importance in the formation of young Jesuits. Many of these were discussed at Alcalá in 1554. Some of these ideas follow, each under its own heading.

The Import of the Life of Ignatius

Nadal did more than recall his conversations with Ignatius. He rehearsed episodes from Ignatius' life that demonstrated how Ignatius wove the fruit of his experiences into the spirit and structure of the Constitutions. Nadal told the Coimbra Jesuits about Ignatius discovering, during his Latin classes in Barcelona, that a devotion that intrudes itself on study is an illusion; about Ignatius learning from the hodgepodge he made of his studies at Alcalá the mistake of an education without system and order; about Ignatius deciding, because of the damage that bad health and a financial pinch inflicted on his studies at Paris, that Jesuit scholastics should care for their health and should live in financially secure houses; about Ignatius, so distressed at times by desolation that he felt he could carry on no longer, receiving strength in his conformity to God's will; about Ignatius, conscious of the constraint that a lack of education put on his apostolic desires, prescribing an exacting intellectual program for the Society's scholastics; about Ignatius, during a walk one day in the garden, gazing on an orange tree and receiving insights into the mystery of the Holy Trinity; about Ignatius banking on three principles to guide his decisions: conformity to God's will, to the Church, to right reason.[31]

Nadal therefore tied the style of life that the Jesuits at Coimbra were leading with the personal experiences of their founder.

They were living a wisdom that was acquired in the crucible of Ignatius' setbacks and conquests. By his roll call of Ignatian episodes, Nadal lit lamps that illumined "our way of doing things."

Nadal's recollections of Ignatius inevitably evoked Manresa and La Storta. To the Coimbra Jesuits he spoke of these two episodes as memorable in the history of the Jesuits. At Alcalá in 1554, Nadal stated that Ignatius at Manresa had foreseen the future Society of Jesus in the meditations on the kingdom and the two standards. He again presented this idea at Coimbra. He presented the familiar picture of Christ calling angels and saints and, through them, all people to the Banner of the Cross. Nadal believed that Christ placed Ignatius in that company of saints, and that Ignatius, in turn, specifies "our" style of conduct in preaching, lecturing, and doing all that superiors propose. This is a Jesuit's daily warfare. It is in this that Christ asks a Jesuit to follow him and to advance on the enemy. "With this meditation," said Nadal, "I think Our Lord gave Ignatius to understand the obligation that he [the Lord] placed on the Society and the good he wants us to strive for." The hearers could too readily understand Nadal to mean that Ignatius saw the actual lines of an organized religious order in that meditation. How detailed was it? Did it include constitutional features? Or was it broad and general: did it include only the fundamental élan?[32]

Intentionally or not, Nadal was one of those who started an oral tradition in the Society that Ignatius learned through God's special grace the structure of the Society that he was to found. Despite reservations of the Society's first historian, Nicholas Orlandini, who qualified the tradition as *pia ac probabilis conjectura* ("pious and probable conjecture"), the tradition gained certitude among Jesuits. Through the centuries, Jesuits learned of Ignatius as a man who had been gifted with knowledge of the structure of the Society eighteen years before he presented his request for papal approval. Meticulous modern historians have since dismantled what Nadal constructed.[33]

In his presentation of the vision at La Storta, Nadal confused the issue. In his fourth exhortation he discussed the name of the Society and the significant role of Ignatius' religious experience at La Storta in confirming him in his desire to call it the Society of Jesus. He told his hearers of the trip made in October of 1537 by Ignatius, Favre, and Laínez to Rome. At the crossroads of La Storta—Nadal did not mention a chapel—"he [Ignatius] felt very consoled, and God the Father appeared to him, showed him his Son with the Cross on his shoulders, placed him with the Son in a show of his love, and said to him 'I will be with you'" (*Ego vobiscum ero*). Here Nadal deviates from his exhortations of 1554 in Spain. There he placed the spoken words in the mouth of the Son. He deviated also from an earlier account of the words. In his *In Examen Annotationes,* he quoted the words as "I shall be propitious to you" (*Ego vobis ero propitius*). Nadal is on surer ground when he attributes the words to the Father. Ignatius himself recommended to Câmara that he consult Laínez for an ample and accurate account of what happened, and Laínez always attributed what was said to the Father. Yet Laínez used a longer formula, which Nadal never presented: "I shall be propitious to you in Rome" (*Ego ero vobis Romae propitius*).[34]

For Nadal the vision at La Storta remained through the years a significant event in the life of Ignatius. Its main import was clear enough: a show of divine predilection for Ignatius and of Ignatius' closeness to Christ. Yet it is troubling that the accuracy of the significant details was not established for transmission of a clear and precise tradition in the Society.

The Special Grace of the Jesuit Vocation

Early in the Coimbra conferences, Nadal spoke about the Society's "grace of vocation." Here he combined several ideas on this theme he had put forward in previous years. The heart of the visitation he identified with "the renewal of the special grace and spirit" that is peculiar to the Society. That grace he defined as a divine gift, as a higher life, as a call, as a combat. A divine gift: God, taking the initiative, placed in the Church a distinctive grace that shaped certain men of the sixteenth century according to the Jesuit way of life. He alone began this fresh religious impulse; it was his gift to the Church. A higher life: guided by this special gift, Jesuits aim to evolve from a union of the active life (asceticism, mortification) and the contemplative life (prayer, meditation) "a higher life," by which they imitate bishops in the labor of leading souls to God. A call: this special divine gift sounds "a call" to labor with Christ, a call that echoes through the *Spiritual Exercises.* "In our day the

Lord raised up our least Society, popularly called a company, to aid him achieve victory. He first called Fr. Master Ignatius, then through him he called us, giving us the grace to make our promises and live up to them." A combat: the Jesuit's special grace delineates for him a combat in which two strategies, Christ's and Satan's, vie for the souls of humankind. By this gift "did Our Savior give Fr. Ignatius to understand what the Society is about and what is its aim."[35]

A gift, a higher life, a call, a combat, like so many spokes of a wheel leading toward the hub: all point to the central grace of vocation. Good teacher that he was, Nadal used all of them in his pedagogy. He deeply desired that each Jesuit understand the meaning of the grace that led him to the Society. He urged each to pray for it daily.

Love, the Way to Knowledge

At this stage in his life, Nadal described his heart as the workshop in which the Holy Spirit forged for him a deeper understanding of God. This was the *leitmotiv* of his *Orationis observationes* just before he left Rome for Spain and Portugal. At Coimbra he told his fellow Jesuits of this personal conviction: "The more one loves God by conforming to his divine will, the more one comes to know him. There is no other way. St. John tells us this" (1 John 2:3–5).[36] In accord with the doctrine, Nadal took the measure of a Jesuit's growth in his understanding of the Society. From a wholehearted acceptance of the Society's Institute in love springs a surer intellectual grasp of its nature. "Out of this all-embracing love will arise," said Nadal, "God's guidance toward a deeper understanding of the Society."[37]

Purpose of the Society

At Coimbra Nadal presented, as he had done years before, the story of the Society's foundation as a part of the Church's history in the mid-sixteenth century. It was a historical event with a divine purpose. To clarify that purpose, Nadal approached the subject under two rather unusual headings. The Society came into being, he said, first to care for social outcasts, and secondly to imitate Christ in his death for humankind. In his third conference Nadal posed a question: in view of the many

religious orders that existed in Ignatius' day, why the foundation of the Society of Jesus? Were not the Dominicans,
Franciscans, and others enough? Nadal replied to his own question: despite the labor of bishops, secular priests, and religious
orders, the Church failed to reach all people. The unreached
are the Society's concern. The Jesuit mission is the universal
one of reaching those most in need, among whom were the
heretics and infidels of the day. "Because among the religious
orders we are the lowest on the totem pole, we take the work of
helping the ones who are left at the end of the line of those in
need of help." Jesuits do not minister to religious, men or
women, since they are being cared for. "We are on the lookout
for none save the left-out."[38]

Nadal digressed a bit. He introduced here the basic historical
reason for the Society's special vow of obedience to the pope.
How did the early Society determine who and where were the
left-out, those spiritually most abandoned? The first Jesuits recognized that the pope, as universal pastor, carried the cares of
the entire world. He knew where the spiritually most destitute
of the world lived. He had the knowledge to make a sound
judgment. They decided, therefore, to pledge themselves to go
wherever the pope might choose to send them. This pledge
gave them the assurance they desired: that they would be working with the most indigent. Ignatius, explained Nadal, evolved
his concept of a Jesuit-on-mission bound by a vow of obedience
to the pope out of his conviction that the Society was designed
by God for the spiritually bereft.[39]

Using glowing colors, Nadal painted a noble ideal for his
fellow Jesuits. But reality cast some shadows over these colors.
To work among the most needy in the world could not be the
real expectation of every Jesuit; many would be sidetracked into
less exacting avenues. The priests in the Professed House in
Lisbon, for example, worked amid a population that had more
ample spiritual resources than many other areas in the world.

After that digression, Nadal moved to his second heading on
the Society's purpose: the imitation of Christ in his death for
humankind. Here again he kept within the historical experience
of the sixteenth century. He reminded the Coimbra Jesuits of
the Society's commitment to Germany and India, two areas of
the world most pertinent to Jesuits in view of Christ's mission to
the world to ward off the eternal loss of souls. There is no Jesuit,

said he, who is not ready to set out for Germany or the Indies and there lay down his life "lest the blood of Christ be spent in vain. . . . This is what every Jesuit is called to do." The imitation of Christ in his dying for souls, that is what the Society is about. That defines its purpose.[40]

To go among the Protestants of Germany or the infidels of India would indeed be to work among the world's spiritually poor, but Nadal in this exposition gave a rather distorted picture of these regions. He seems to suggest that these areas have been neglected, and in so doing he ignores the challenge made to the Protestants by other religious orders, and of the overseas missions initiated decades before the appearance of the Society. Nadal's broad strokes reflect the animated style of his delivery but such a rhetorical style often blurs exactness.

Self-abnegation

To no subject in his exhortations did Nadal give more attention than self-abnegation. Self-abnegation he placed at the heart of a Jesuit's identity, his spiritual growth, his apostolic effectiveness. It was the marrow of the Jesuit style of imitating Christ. He recalled the key to the secret of holiness Ignatius had given him: likeness to Christ insulted, contemned, reproached. To each of the Coimbra Jesuits that key was offered. Each should take it and make it his own. Each was obliged to be true to this Ignatian conviction. "It comes to this: the living of our vocation is in carrying the Cross. If we fail here, we are quitting the road that leads to the purpose of our vocation."[41]

In his tenth exhortation, on the function of the Jesuit novitiate, Nadal listed ten virtues the novices were expected to develop. He put mortification first. Nadal urged the novices to love mortification, and for one reason only (*unicamente*): it invests them with the power to give full and uninhibited service to God's greater glory. Remissness in mortification spells failure in holiness. Self-abnegation cannot be allowed to rest in the mind. "Get this straight: the humility I am talking about is not the humility that stops in speculation. It is rather an interior taste of a truth about one's self, a truth that exposes one as evil, lost, deserving hell. This truth we should keep stamped on our practical judgment and our conduct. It is the way to eject such contrary thoughts as self-esteem."[42]

Nadal linked mortification with a special office Ignatius set into the structure of the Society. In each house he wanted a man designated to observe and assess the external decorum of the men and the physical condition of the structures. This official he called a "syndic." According to the measure of authority given him, the syndic would either inform the rector of deficiencies he observed or directly admonish the erring persons. This procedure, Nadal realized, a Jesuit could find distasteful. But, he argued, this need not be. If the syndic's admonitions were well founded, a Jesuit should welcome the chance to relieve his fellow Jesuits of his offensive conduct. If the syndic's charges were groundless, a Jesuit should embrace this opportunity to experience humiliation.[43]

Nadal told a story about Ignatius. Even before he finished the Constitutions, Ignatius wanted a syndic installed at the Professed House in Rome. He assembled the community and explained to them what he planned to do. All save one concurred. The dissenter, an older man and an important figure in the early Society (Nadal did not identify him), spoke strenuously against the idea. Ignatius, nevertheless, without delay assigned a syndic. All went well. Within a few days even the dissenter accepted Ignatius' viewpoint.[44]

Nadal's story meshed easily with Ignatius' teaching on the Jesuit desire for perfection: this desire takes each Jesuit to the point where he is willing to have his errors and defects revealed to superiors by anyone who knows them outside confession. That desire also prompts him, in his concern for fellow Jesuits, to disclose their defects and errors to superiors. Ignatius himself, insisted Nadal, placed fraternal correction firmly within the Jesuit way of life. This practice, Nadal realized, projected on the Society an appearance of harshness. His lists of suggested mortifications confirmed that appearance. He therefore took his fellow Jesuits behind the harsh and forbidding mien of mortification and opened to them a vista fair and lovely. He called it an interior freedom of spirit. "This freedom of spirit is nothing other than an ease (*suavidad*) in all that one does: an ease in detecting what here and now is more fitting, what is more in harmony with the Lord's service; an ease in jettisoning every compromise in that service."[45] It frees a Jesuit from anxiety, annoyance, and vexation in his work, be it with the lowly or the lordly. It is a light, an illumination, that guides the mind in its judgments.[46]

Harsh though self-abnegation might be in its aspect, Nadal never ceased to talk about it. With the relentless hammering of a woodpecker, he drove his conviction home. Mortification did not stop with the novitiate. What held for the novices held for all. "Either we have these virtues [self-abnegation and humility] or we don't. If we don't, we in fact remain novices, and with novices' obligation to get them."[47]

Obedience

From the start of his conferences, Nadal placed obedience within the framework of mystical theology. He cited the Pseudo-Dionysius—God is known in darkness. In the darkness of self-denial and surrender of personal judgment to the judgment of a superior, the Jesuit gains the true light of understanding. Amid this darkness he finds his capacity to discover the true light. "The denial of personal judgment and understanding in obedience," Nadal told the Coimbra Jesuits, "opens to the possession of true light and comprehension."[48] To guide them to the shore of growth in obedience, he indicated a landfall. The landfall had three promontories: divine providence, the Jesuit vocation, the presence of Christ in superiors. Each promontory is a gift from God. Each is a sign of God's action and initiative in a Jesuit's life. Each is an invitation to Jesuits to respond in obedience to God's guiding grace, not in gloom but in gladness. "With lightsome hearts, not with low and heavy spirits, do we go forward."[49]

In this ideal of perfect obedience a Jesuit has a steady reminder of his apostolic vocation. Called to give his life for the salvation of souls, he has at hand the most apt means to achieve this goal. Perfect obedience could carry him to Germany or to the Indies, indeed anywhere. The splendor of this ideal, Nadal thought, should inspire a Jesuit to free himself through mortification to be perfectly obedient. Failure in perfect obedience spells failure in the wholehearted acceptance of gifts offered them by God (it means "falling from the grace that is given us") and it spells failure in our mission.[50]

Studies

Nadal devoted his tenth conference almost entirely to the intellectual formation of a Jesuit. He reminded the Coimbra Jesuits that the Society had been founded only twenty years earlier and already the people of Europe, Catholic and Protestant, had formed a distinct image of the order. To them it was a body of men highly skilled in intellectual disciplines. Before large audiences of bishops, abbots, clergy, and laypeople, Diego Laínez and Alfonso Salmerón enriched debates at the Council of Trent with their theological expertise. In Rome, leading clergy sought the counsel of Jesuits. Protestants identified them as a body of especially learned people. Within two decades the Society had found a special mission in the Church. The Coimbra Jesuits, by their entry into the Society, had become part of a solid pillar of learning within the Church. It was their responsibility to be true to that special mission.[51]

Nadal developed his apologia for studies along pragmatic lines. He took his cue from St. Jerome. Simplicity, observed Jerome, is a lovable trait. But simplicity on its own cannot cope with the practical demands of life. Learning must complement it. Nadal elaborated. Pious intentions, said he, will not carry a Jesuit far in his apostolic work. To preach, to explain the Catholic faith, to dialogue with Protestants, he must become a learned man. This lesson, recalled Nadal, Ignatius learned from personal experience, and then supplemented his profound spiritual experience with university training. Ignatius passed this lesson to other Jesuits in his Constitutions and his correspondence.

Nadal also raised his argument for education in the Society above the level of practicality; he elevated it to imitation of the apostles. The apostles distinguished themselves by their command of languages, their prophecy, their holding the doctorate in the Church (*el doctorado en la Iglesia*). All were gifts from God. Jesuits, Nadal advised, since they are servants of the apostles, should seek to imitate them. They study languages, philosophy, and theology so that, like the apostles, they will be equipped to be "interpreters of the scriptures."

With such arguments, Nadal defined the task of each Jesuit scholastic as the formation within himself of a harmony of learning and devotion. To his quest for knowledge (*scientia*) a Jesuit links his quest for wisdom (*sapientia*), which is knowledge steeped in compassion. "This each scholastic should make his goal: a broad grasp of knowledge and wisdom." Behind these ideas sounded Nadal's personal experiences of his theology of the heart, that workshop in which the Holy Spirit brought knowledge to the spiritual unction and light of wisdom.[52]

Nadal then told the young Jesuits of Coimbra that their first great opportunity to employ the force of their personal union of learning and wisdom was their regency, that period of three years or so during which they would teach in the schools. He recalled a letter of Ignatius on this point. In December of 1551, Ignatius had sent a general letter to the Society, endorsing the acceptance of colleges as an apostolate proper to the Society.[53] Nadal repeated the three points that Ignatius made. First, the scholastic tries to lead his young students toward his own ideal of creating a personal fusion of learning and religious devotion; second, the scholastic, by the force of his example, attracts young men to the Society; third, the scholastic in his teaching deepens his own grasp of the subjects he teaches.

Throughout his long talk on studies, Nadal maintained a practical level. He did not speculate on the meaning of Christian Humanism, nor did he speak as an educational theorist. He posited what would become a mark of much Jesuit learning through the centuries: "a supernatural pragmatism." At that moment, seeing the Catholic Church locked into a peculiar period of history, he conceived learning as a way of service by refutation of heretics and winning of infidels. His attitude adumbrated the Society's readiness to adapt its learning to demands of a historical moment. It also intimated a strain of utilitarianism and of susceptibility to, in Erich Przywara's words, "scholarship by command."[54]

Jesuits and Apostles

In his explanation of the Society's institutional structure to the young Jesuits of Coimbra, Nadal resorted to some ideas he first formulated eight years before in his *Annotationes in Constitutiones*.[55] He wanted to clarify, for example, the difference between the Jesuit's first and second probation. This led him to forge some odd and artificial divisions. He explained the difference in terms of the apostles' growth in closeness to Christ. Just as the apostles first became acquainted with Christ at their call, so the Jesuits come to have an introductory knowledge of the Society in their first probation. The apostles then grew in their familiarity with Christ, learned how to pray, did lowly chores, traveled, taught—and all this before they were ordained priests and bishops. Jesuits, too, within their first probation, grow in their familiarity with Christ, learn to pray, teach catechism, make pilgrimages, and help the sick in hospitals. The crown of these experiences is leaving all and following Christ.[56]

Nadal worked out still another schema. To explain the differences between the professed fathers and the spiritual and temporal coadjutors, Nadal again proposed an odd example. The Jesuit professed fathers correspond to the apostles, the spiritual coadjutors to the disciples, and the temporal coadjutors to the deacons who served table. Christ chose priests and sent them forth under Peter, the universal pastor. In similar manner, Jesuits, walking in the way of the apostles and the disciples, go forth. But the apostles and disciples went forth *ex officio;* the Jesuits, as their servants and ministers, are sent by the successor of Peter, the universal pastor. Nadal pushed the comparison further: Jesuits, like the apostles, wore no distinctive habit and did not chant in choir.[57]

Prayer

Nadal devoted conferences eighteen and nineteen almost entirely to prayer.[58] Knowing that the majority of his hearers were in the Society but a few years, he tried to be practical. With his pedagogical instinct for order, he divided his material into a series of blocks, each given to a particular form of prayer: vocal, mental, eucharistic, petitionary, meditative, and contemplative. He explained each. A mass of ideas about prayer poured forth; the sheer number was intimidating.[59] Realizing that he had put together a large and unwieldy cargo of ideas, he saw the need of tight bands to secure the cargo from breaking apart, shifting loosely, and tilting the ship. He looked for cords of unity. He found them in the special marks of Jesuit prayer.

One cord was the image of a circle. For the Jesuit, prayer points to work and work points to prayer. Prayer feeds a Jesuit's work; work feeds a Jesuit's prayer. He knew that this ideal could elude some scholastics. With sympathy he spoke as one who understood their problems in working toward a smooth integration of learning and devotion in their lives. The scholastic who found his religious devotion chilled by his studies should, he advised, every now and then turn from the books, say a little prayer, recall that he is doing God's will, then return to the books, "moving from one into the other as one making the round of a circle."[60]

Nadal gave this illustration a wider scope than prayer and a scholastic's study of his books. He applied it to the prayer of any Jesuit and his apostolic work. Prayer animates labor for one's neighbor; labor for one's neighbor enriches prayer. They move on the circle's rim, each into the other. Nadal was emphatic: a Jesuit advances in personal charity by his work for others; prayer that fails to inspire an increase in work for souls in need means that a Jesuit is marking time, is stalled in his growth in charity.[61] A broken circle means a failed Jesuit.

A second cord and characteristic of Jesuit prayer Nadal always linked intimately with Ignatius. "Take note of this," he told the Coimbra Jesuits. "An excellent way to pray, indeed a special way, is to find God readily in all things and to let one's thoughts dwell in him. Our Father Ignatius had a grasp of this particular way. That is what he told me. I hope that all [of the Society], if they put their minds to it, will with the divine grace do the same."[62]

A third cord and characteristic of Jesuit prayer was the unity of spiritual experience. He had coined a phrase to express it: *reliquiae cogitationum* (the lingerings of my thoughts, the afterglow of my thoughts). It was a fruit of his personal experience. Nadal noted that a central thought or thoughts of his morning meditation lingered through the day. They clung to him; they remained with him; they colored his day; they gave continuity to his experience. The past left a residue and became part of the present.

Nadal applied the *reliquiae cogitationum* to several aspects of a Jesuit's life. One aspect was a Jesuit's prayer on the life of Christ. On Pentecost Sunday, May 25, he spoke to the Coimbra Jesuits on the mystery of Christ's sending the Holy Spirit to the apostles. This mystery, Nadal insisted, is not isolated. The Christ of Pentecost is the Christ who suffered, died, rose, and ascended into heaven. He is the one Christ. On Pentecost Sunday a Jesuit should enter his prayer with his remembrances of the spirit of penance he felt during Lent, the joy he experienced in the presence of the risen Lord, the happiness he knew as he gazed on Christ ascending into heaven. Past prayer feeds present prayer. Past prayer shapes present prayer. Christ's life is a unity of past and present; so too is a Jesuit's prayer to Christ. The *reliquiae cogitationum* embrace a Jesuit's inner life.[63]

Nadal also invoked his formula of "lingering thoughts" in another context. He discussed the experiments of the Jesuit novitiate. During his month in the Spiritual Exercises, the novice arouses in his heart the spiritual ideals of the Society of Jesus. He then serves in hospitals, undertakes a pilgrimage, begs food, teaches catechism. These works test the viability of the novice's grasp of the Spiritual Exercises, measure the durability of his ideals, gauge the staying power of the *reliquiae cogitationum* from his retreat.

And in another way Nadal employed his formula: to help young Jesuits who found that success in seeing God in all things was eluding them. He suggested that they recall their experiences of God's closeness to them. From those recollections could arise a fresh, joyful awareness of God's presence. "I urge the Jesuit who fails to find God in all things to summon his memories of past consolation. I urge him to take the fragments of those earlier thoughts (*reliquiaes cogitationum assumat*), link them to the present moment, tie one experience with another, and then, humbly and simply, enter [this way of prayer] and with the conviction that God will help him."[64]

Nadal invoked his doctrine of *reliquiae cogitationum* to explain contemplation. He did not explicitly quote the formula, but he made the doctrine a strong underpinning of this part of his conference. Nadal conceived contemplation as a growth in knowledge and love of God, a growth achieved by the cumulation of ideas about God. Contemplation of the present starts from earlier contemplation. It is like the gradual and prolonged grasp of the details of a landscape. "One is contemplating when he joins what his mind is now looking upon with what it looked upon in the past. It is like gazing at a landscape. One stands before it until ultimately one sees it in its totality. Contemplation reaches its full meaning when every facet of a subject is perfectly grasped to the extent that our intelligence can do so." The present and the past of a Jesuit's prayer compose an object for the mind's gaze. Thoughts of past prayer linger and merge with the thoughts of this moment. Together they bring contemplation to a fullness. So did Nadal apply his doctrine of *reliquiae cogitationum* to a Jesuit's contemplative prayer.[65]

With those three cords: the swing around the rim of a circle, the perception of God's presence in all things, and the impact of *reliquiae cogitationum,* Nadal tried to bind into a unity his abundant, even diffuse, ideas on prayer in the Society of Jesus. They gave a concentrated firmness to his teaching that there is a Jesuit way of prayer that Jesuits should honor and pursue.

That concentrated firmness made him apprehensive, however, as he perceived that he sounded dogmatic, rigid, or parochial. He decided therefore to soften and nuance his blunt statements. For all his stress on the Jesuit way, he respected the freedom of each Jesuit to follow the guidance of the Holy Spirit in his style of prayer. Jesuits do not pray in lockstep. God determines the road proper to each.

Nadal outlined for the Coimbra Jesuits the methods of prayer traditionally associated with the purgative, illuminative, and unitive ways of spiritual growth but promptly capped them with this caution: "We must not fail to note that an individual is free to disregard what we have here presented, and to follow still another way, the way taught him by the Lord." Nadal alerted confessors to be careful in this area. They must yield to God's way of leading a person in prayer; they must not presume to instruct God. Nadal's respect for God's guidance in prayer resonated with his favorite theological teaching on God's action in the world and on humankind's complete dependence on the divine initiative.[66]

These are some of the salient ideas Nadal presented at Coimbra. There are many others scattered helter-skelter throughout his text.

Fr. Pedro da Silva probably spoke for all the Coimbra Jesuits in a long report he sent to Rome. "In his talks he [Nadal] threw a wide and bright light on the various aspects of our Society. He did this by expounding the peculiar grace of the Society, the Society's way of doing things, its works, its persecutions. He also clarified the nature of the Society by discoursing on the conversion, the life, the traits of our Father [Ignatius] of glorious memory." Nadal's manner enhanced the power of his talks. "To see and ponder his deep humility and simplicity, his ease and admirable cheerfulness amid his excessive and unending work, to ponder his charity, his zeal for the honor of God and for the advancement and continuing growth of the Society, all this leaves us truly amazed." Coimbra Jesuits made copies of the talks. They thought that they had acquired "a rich treasure" (*un gran tesoro*). [67]

Nadal left Coimbra on July 14. The time until October 2 he devoted in the main to the Jesuit communities in Évora and Lisbon. Each visit resembled on a smaller scale his stay at Coimbra, yet each had its own quirks. At Évora he found a university of 750 students and a community of sixty-six Jesuits. Startling changes had taken place since he was there eight years earlier. Under the lavish patronage of Cardinal Henrique, archbishop of Évora, a tiny college had grown into a university, modest but impressive. Nadal arrived there on July 17. He promptly began a busy round of interviews, conferences, inspections, and lists of mortifications. Within a few days fever leveled him. On the advice of doctors that he escape Évora's sultry heat for Lisbon's salty breezes, he left Évora and on July 31 arrived in Lisbon.[68]

At Lisbon Nadal met twenty-six Jesuits stationed at the Colégio São Antoão for boys and fifty at the Professed House of São Roque. Because of his tight schedule he asked the São Antoão community to join the São Roque community for the conferences.[69] With them he left a list of minute directives. A few follow:

> They were to wear a habit of rough woolen material, black if possible, like that worn in Rome.
>
> For duties peculiar to the novices, a handbell was to be used. For duties common to the whole community, the house bell was to be rung.
>
> Letters of Jesuits from the Indies were to be printed, corrected, then presented to the Inquisition for approval.
>
> Oddly shaped or spectacular buildings were to be shunned. In construction, rough bricks, not polished ones, were to be used.
>
> In areas of the novice master's responsibility, superiors should honor his opinions unless certainty about an opposite view persists.

Handbells and house bells, rough wool and black wool, rough bricks and polished bricks: Nadal's attention to things of that kind began to distract from his inspirational teaching of Jesuit spiritual doctrine. Some Jesuits had misgivings. Domesticity was winning a place next to broad vision.[70]

Early on, Nadal found himself in a delicate position in regard to the court: he could not evade the need to move an important

Jesuit. For five years Fr. Miguel de Torres had been juggling two positions, superior of the province and confessor of Queen Catarina. Nadal disapproved. Torres's obligation to be at the beck and call of the queen constrained his freedom to move among the communities of the province. This must be corrected. Major shifts at the court gave Nadal a chance to do what he would have hesitated to do earlier under King João III. João had died four years before, leaving a three-year-old son, Sebastião, as the new king. Queen Catarina had become coregent with Cardinal Henrique, Sebastião's uncle and the queen's deadly opponent (she apparently was hoping that her son's failure as a monarch would pave the way for her Spanish nephew Philip), who assumed an important voice in the care of the child-monarch. Nadal made a daring move. In a bid for freedom to run the Society's internal affairs without outside interference, he decided to appoint a new provincial without first checking with the queen and the cardinal.[71]

For some time Nadal had been observing Fr. Gonçalo Vaz de Melo. Impressed by this thirty-five-year-old native of Vilar, he appointed him as the new provincial. Torres he made rector of Lisbon's Professed House, where he would be easily available to the queen. No cry of dismay arose from Queen Catarina or from Cardinal Henrique. Henrique in fact applauded Nadal's pluck. Catarina, her generosity undiminished, gave Nadal 500 gold coins for traveling expenses. Sebastião, now seven years old, radiated friendship. Nadal was quite taken by the youngster's charm (*Placuit mihi vehementer puer rex*). When he left Lisbon for Évora on September 10, he carried pleasant memories of the key figures at the Portuguese court.[72]

Before Nadal left Lisbon, one of the Society's greatest friends boxed him into an awkward corner. Leonor Mascarenas, the noble governess of Philip II during his boyhood, earnestly asked a difficult favor of Nadal. On the other side of the Tagus, with a view of Lisbon, she had a home and some land. On the land she wished to build a church to which she wanted a Jesuit assigned as chaplain. Nadal had problems in reconciling such an assignment with the Society's Constitutions and their prohibition of this kind of task. He wished not to offend Doña Leonor and so he looked for a legal loophole. He conceived the idea of attaching the Mascarenas estate to Colegio São Antoão as a villa or recreational house for the members of the community. In this way he could avoid saying "no" to a gracious lady. After Nadal worked out the problem, Doña Leonor changed her mind. Nadal was delighted. "So it worked out," he wrote, "that we respected her to whom the Society owed so much, and at the same time we were relieved of a burden."[73]

The journey of two days to Évora was unpleasant. Queen Catarina had purchased for Nadal a mule of fine pedigree (*mulam egregiam*). But the *mula egregia* was pesky and obdurate. Even as the animal performed its antics, Nadal's two companions, Fr. Vaz and the province's treasurer, Fr. Francisco Henriques, badgered him with questions about governance in the Society. The treasurer's questions he found more thorny than the provincial's. On September 12, he and his companions reached Évora and he promptly got rid of his churlish mule. A noblewoman and mother of a future Jesuit martyr bought it from him for the amount Queen Catarina had paid for it. Doña Maria, wife of Pedro Álvarez de Carvalho and mother of Fr. André Álvarez de Carvalho, who would die in Africa the next year as a prisoner of the Turks, not only bought the balky mule but purchased for Nadal another, not indeed pedigreed (*vilem quidem illam*) but one that did its work without fuss. Sometime later, reflection on this deal stirred scruples in Nadal's mind. "I should not have accepted."[74]

Amid the usual routine of the Évora visitation, Nadal dealt with an exasperating situation. Some noblemen had been loitering in the college grounds, making pests of themselves. Nadal devised a simple tactic to remove them. He advised the community to pick one of their members skilled enough to engage the noblemen in conversation on exclusively spiritual subjects. If this tactic should fail to expel the loiterers, he was to limit the conversation solely to such sobering subjects as the Last Judgment. It worked; the idle noblemen quit their haunt.[75]

As the time approached for his departure from Portugal, Nadal gave Fr. Vaz minute instructions on how to insure the gains of the visitation. Vaz was to return promptly to other communities of the province and check observance of the rules Nadal had promulgated. If he detected negligence, he was to take action. In drawing general lines of policy, Nadal gave Vaz little latitude. Vaz was to alter none of Nadal's regulations without first consulting either the general or Nadal.

Vaz could delay the execution of a regulation only after receiving the opinion of his consultors, and then Nadal was to be informed. In the event of a serious doubt about the feasibility of a regulation, Vaz should delay its implementation until he asked Nadal for further clarification. These general guidelines Nadal supplemented with suggestions to help Vaz mold his style of governance. He urged him to be universal in his charity and to forestall any suggestion of favoritism; to avoid all show of aversion for anyone; to see in each member of the province the Christ-given endowments of goodness and grace; to work with the men of the province, especially the tempted, in the conquest of their imperfections; to strive to build unity among the older men of the province, a unity that could become a source of strength to others; to aim for that special mark of good governance, the impeding temptation and complaint among the men.

Beyond the explicit instructions he received from Nadal, Vaz made his personal list of other points he remembered from his conversations with Nadal. He called the list "Points That Father Master Nadal Gave Me At Évora." The points read as follows:

- Do all things to God's greater glory.
- Love the Institute.
- Love the [Society's] purpose.
- Love and desire to work for this purpose.
- Perfect obedience.
- Prayer that is practical reaches out to work.
- Humility.
- Simplicity.
- Love of mortification.
- Love of suffering.
- Modesty and edification in conversation.
- Diligence in the observance of daily religious duties.
- Walk ever before God and in his presence.
- Hold always the living principle of God's grace.
- Acquire an ease in your grasp of the reality of God's love, so that your every action will be informed by every virtue, charity, of course, being supreme.

There were also specific instructions about a number of Jesuits. Fr. de Torres, the royal confessor, was to moderate his

engagement in secular affairs as much as possible. Br. Gil
Barreto was to be moved to Coimbra and assume the posts of
buyer, sacristan, and porter. Fr. Pais was to work in a hospital
to get this experience required of Jesuits. Fr. Lobo was to be
sent on a pilgrimage to Lisbon and then, if Vaz thought it wise,
he was to be sent to India. Pedro Álvarez was to be allowed to
spend half a year in the area around his home in order to
recoup his physical and spiritual energies. An aspirant to the
Society named Cristóbal Díaz was not to be admitted. Nadal
thus left Vaz well stocked and at least a little smothered with
dos and don'ts. Nadal's anxiety to safeguard his work by legislation became increasingly manifest.[76]

Nadal closed his visit to Évora by attending the ceremonies
inaugurating the new academic year on October 1. The next
day, on his *mula vilis,* he left for Spain. Fr. Vaz accompanied him
part of the way.[77] A year and a half had passed since he had
arrived in Portugal. Never again was he to see that country.

The reaction to his visitation among the Jesuits was mixed.
Most who recorded their feelings told of the renewal of religious
spirit that Nadal inspired, a spirit of self-abnegation, of dedication to the service of those in need, of industry in study, of
fidelity to the Constitutions and the Rules. Fr. Pedro da Silva of
Coimbra said that he looked on Nadal as God's special instrument for the communication of many blessings to the community. Fr. Blasio Gómez wrote to Laínez from Évora. "Abundant is
the fruit Our Lord brought forth in this college through Fr.
Nadal. A fresh fervor of charity is felt here, a new love of
obedience and the other virtues, a new desire to serve the
neighbor, a fresh urge for mortification. Whenever an opportunity opens during their studies, they give themselves to other
work." Another Jesuit at Évora stressed the gentle and intelligent way Nadal conducted his visit there. In the round of talks
on the Society's Institute, the general confessions he heard, the
discipline he enforced, the renovation of vows he supervised,
the nadalian style stood out: the pleasant manner, the wisdom,
the humility, and the cultivated speech dotted with polished
phrases.[78]

Nadal also had his critics. Fr. Miguel de Sousa wrote Laínez
from Lisbon that Nadal was too facile and trigger-happy in his
decisions, too hurried in his interviews, too minute in his regulations, too lavish in his directives. At times, rarely however, he

gave disedification by a show of crankiness.[79†] Fr. Diego Mirón complained that Nadal left so many directives that superiors could not attend to the Society's Constitutions and Rules, mired as they were in nadalian minutiae. Even Fr. Pedro da Silva, ardent devotee of Nadal, mentioned, although in admiration, Nadal's concern "for the tiniest things" of the house. Fr. Francisco Rodrigues, the best modern authority on the Portuguese province, agreed with Diego Mirón. He thought that Nadal's preoccupation with minutiae was the chief defect of the visitation, and that by legislating on insignificant details he ran the danger of turning religious life into a mechanical observance of the picayune.[80] This was the burgeoning of Nadal the Fussbudget. The bud was beginning to blossom.

Nadal's own estimate of the stay was optimistic. He wrote Laínez from Évora on September 20, little more than a week before he left for Spain: "I am very happy and consoled with this province, Father. Glory be to the Lord, I am brought to this feeling by the alertness prevalent among superiors as well as by what is commonly seen in all members of the province: a desire to walk the road of perfection with fervor and vivacity of spirit. Many mortifications of every kind have been the order of the day during vacation periods, especially in Coimbra but in Évora and Lisbon as well."[81] It was a cheerful note on which to leave Portuguese soil.

---

†79 Sousa's strictures probably merit a little tempering. Sousa had a propensity to see the bleak side of things. Eight months after he wrote his strictures of Nadal, Sousa came in for criticism by his provincial, Fr. Gonçalo Vaz de Melo. In June of 1562 he was minister at the Professed House in Lisbon. Vaz wrote to Nadal, "I have conducted the visitation of São Roche. I received, according to your instructions, the manifestation of conscience of each man in the community. I put in order some things that called for action. One was the removal of the minister [Fr. de Sousa]. Since he was in the grip of depression, I used the pretext of sending him to Évora to get a break for a few days. He has practically no comprehension of what his work is. He does not apply himself to it. As a consequence, a certain amount of disorder has appeared in the house. Practically everybody notes this" (*Mon Nad,* I:699–700).

16

Spain

*The Society wants men who, as far as possible, are
consummate experts in every area that contributes to
the purpose of the Society. Do you have it in you to be a
fine logician? Go to it. Or an accomplished theologian?
Go to it. Or an outstanding humanist? Or a master of
any other discipline that can advance the Jesuit way
of doing things? According to your ability and talent,
refuse to settle for mediocrity.*

Nadal in a conference to the community of
the Alcalá college in November 1561

The first sentence in the section of Nadal's *Ephemerides* that
records his return to Spain in early October of 1561 reads as
follows: "Before I reached Alburquerque [a Spanish city near
the Portuguese border] I had a presentiment of troubles brew-
ing in Castile."[1] The next seven months proved his presentiment
to be accurate.

Alburquerque, sixty miles northeast of Évora, was the first
town of some size in Spain at which Nadal stopped. There he
encountered his first task. Fr. Bartolomé de Bustamente, the
recently returned provincial of Andalusia, sent a Jesuit to seek
Nadal's permission to open a school in Seville. Bustamente was
most insistent with his request. Behind the request stood the
city's inquisitors, who were earnest about having a Jesuit school
in their city. The pressure on Nadal was heavy. Ferdinando de
Valdés, archbishop of Seville, was the grand inquisitor of Spain.

Nadal had earlier offered to him the Society's resources in the work of the Inquisition. In his diary Nadal wrote: "I could not say No." He therefore gave Bustamente permission to open negotiations.[2]

From Alburquerque Nadal planned to go fifty miles northeast to Plasencia and then to turn east to the area of Madrid, Alcalá, and Toledo. On the road between Alburquerque and Plasencia, a Jesuit brother, Hernando Tello, met him carrying letters from Antonio Araoz and Antonio de Córdoba. The letters warned Nadal that the Spanish court seethed with anger because of Borgia's escape to Rome and Nadal's impending visitation to the Jesuit houses in Spain. Br. Tello also brought a copy of a decree of the royal council, recently sent to the college at Plasencia, forbidding the export of money and the assignment of men abroad. Hard on those letters came others carried by another brother named Avendaño. They included more letters from Araoz and Córdoba, advising Nadal not to travel east to the court at Madrid but rather to go north to Salamanca, as well as letters from Fr. Manuel López, rector of the Alcalá college, and Fr. Alfonso Ramírez de Vergara, a generous benefactor, warning that a split was developing between the court and the Society. The advice from Araoz and Córdoba to go to Salamanca vexed Nadal; he resented their presuming to tell him how to map his plans.[3] Underlying these messages throbbed a clear warning for Nadal: he was in danger of becoming just one more puppet in the vast show operated by the court of Philip II. As other Spaniards had come to know, he was to feel the pull of the strings now this way, now that. Nadal, however, never became a docile puppet. Indeed, he often tried to clip the cords that tugged at him.

At Plasencia an even more troubling message awaited him. The rector told him that the city's magistrate was holding a secret message for him from the crown. On October 7, Nadal presented himself to the magistrate who, in the presence of witnesses, handed a document to Nadal. Its message was that Nadal, within fifteen days of receipt, was to appear at the royal court in Madrid and present the documents that invested him with power to conduct the visitation. Until then he was to refrain from opening the visitation. The crown informed him that it found especially irritating the fact that he, a foreigner, was exercising authority on Spanish soil.[4]

Nadal wondered who inspired that document from the crown, and he tried to dismiss the thought that it was Antonio Araoz. He refused to yield an inch to the dark suggestion "that so heinous a deed, so vicious a betrayal had been carried out by so fine a Father." Indeed, so successfully had he conquered that suspicion that he felt able to swear that Araoz was not guilty. He went even further, convinced that he had to rule out any Jesuit as the perpetrator, since such a deed "could not possibly be done by anyone who had given his name to the Society."[5]

For all his mighty effort to reject any suspicion of Araoz, Nadal could not avoid wondering who actually inspired the documents. He reviewed the grievances felt at court against the Society: the marriage of Borgia's brother, a marriage that aroused the anger of the king; Borgia's slipping out of Spain into Portugal and then to Rome; the assignment of Spanish Jesuits to posts outside Spain; the forwarding of Spanish money to the Roman College; anger with Fr. Diego Laínez because he was traveling on a papal mission to France with a legate known to be hostile to Spain;[6] the cancellation of Pope Paul IV's decree that the Jesuit general be elected every three years, which also canceled a chance to remove Laínez, a man known to be of Jewish stock. Nadal analyzed all those irritants and concluded that the man who was closest to Philip II guided the pen that wrote the constraining orders. He finally held the prince of Éboli responsible. Nadal discerned another reason that linked the prince with the suspension of the visitation: he saw the visitation as a threat to his friend Araoz and therefore he must undercut it. So reasoned Nadal.[7]

On October 13 Nadal arrived in Alcalá. The next day Araoz and Córdoba came from Madrid. They confirmed the gloomy news Nadal had heard on his travels. Araoz darkened the skies still more. Inquisitor General Ferdinando de Valdés, he reported, held Nadal responsible for Borgia's escape to Rome. This accusation Nadal promptly challenged with a lengthy apologia that told the story of his personal disapproval of Borgia's design and his inability to stop Borgia.[8] This apologia did not completely satisfy Nadal; he wished to confront the inquisitor general personally. He preferred this, not only to give a personal exegesis of the apologia but also to defend Borgia's innocence of any wrongdoing. And a key question Nadal planned to throw at the Inquisitor was this: since you had Borgia within your range and you had a chance to seize him, why did you not stop his trip? Nadal was, of course, referring to the incident at the small town of Villalpando, where Borgia was halted by sickness within a short distance of the Spanish court.[9]

Nadal spoke of reporting to the court as he had been ordered. the desire to speak with Valdés was accompanied by another desire: to see Philip and plead the Society's cause. Araoz, Córdoba, and other Jesuits at Alcalá persuaded him to refrain from going to Madrid; Araoz could better handle the official conversations between the crown and the Society. In an act of trust, Nadal commissioned Araoz to return to Madrid and present his case to the crown under two headings: his innocence in the Borgia episode and his right to make a free and uninhibited visitation of the Jesuit communities. For the next ten days Araoz shuttled back and forth between Madrid and Alcalá, mediating between Nadal and the court. Nadal insisted on the Society's right to conduct its affairs in freedom. The court maintained that Nadal's activities must be supervised by the government.

Araoz was back in Alcalá on October 19, bringing what James Brodrick has called "a rose and a thistle for his superior."[10] The rose was the inquisitor general's acceptance of Nadal's defense of his conduct during the Borgia affair. The thistle was a continued restriction on Nadal's travel. He received approval to visit Old and New Castile briefly; he was to avoid Aragon and Andalusia. The royal puppeteer was pulling the strings of his new toy.[11]

Nadal was angered by the denial of access to two blocs of Jesuit communities. With Araoz, Córdoba, López, and Gil González Dávila, Nadal analyzed the message carefully. He bridled at the denial of freedom to travel in Aragon and Andalusia, where several important Jesuit communities were located. To his consultants he presented a strategy he had formulated when he first heard the ominous reports two weeks earlier. This strategy had three points: first, to avoid any show of resistance to, or disapproval of, the judgments of the king or the royal council on the visitation; second, to uphold, nevertheless, the Society's freedom from the jurisdiction of any secular tribunal and to avoid any semblance of submission to any such institution; and third, in the event that the king and the royal council posed no obstacle, to conduct the visitation entirely by reason of the

Society's rights, avoiding any semblance of acting by reason of royal sufferance. Nadal reasoned with moderation and prudence. Firm though he was, he had no intention of playing the gallant toreador taunting the royal bull with a red cloth of inflammatory rhetoric. After the consultation, Araoz returned to Madrid with Nadal's more refined position.[12]

In Madrid, Araoz once more presented to the council Nadal's arguments for the freedom of the Society from interference by a secular institution. The council refused to yield in its decision forbidding Nadal to enter Andalusia and Aragon but agreed to lengthen by fifteen days Nadal's freedom to visit the Jesuit communities in Old and New Castile. In two days Araoz was back in Alcalá with the disappointing news.[13]

Nadal began to lose his battle against suspicious thoughts about Araoz. Araoz had a privileged position at court; he was a personal friend of Rui Gómez, prince of Éboli. Why had he not done more for the Society? Why had he not obtained permission for Nadal to visit all the Jesuit communities? And Nadal's exoneration by the inquisitor general of complicity in Borgia's escapade? Was that Araoz's sly way of making Nadal feel indebted to Araoz for help rendered?

During conversations with Araoz, Nadal discovered that Antonio was convinced Laínez was not the general of the Society. Araoz held that the edict of Pope Paul IV that limited the general's term to three years remained in effect despite canonical developments since Paul's death in 1559. In order to do so, he ignored the vote by the professed members of the Society to return to a life term for the general as prescribed in the Society's Constitutions. He likewise ignored the decree of Pope Pius IV that canceled Paul's decree.[14] Nadal came to the harsh conclusion that Araoz honored the machinations of the Spanish court more than he did the Institute of the Society.

Face to face Nadal challenged Araoz: either clear away the impediments to the visitation or state openly where he stood in relation to the Society. Was Araoz's heart more in the court than in the Society? Araoz gave an evasive answer. Nadal surrendered. He concluded he could expect no assistance from Araoz. Either Araoz did not want to help, or he really had no power to do so.[15] "I did not care to decide that one," wrote Nadal in his diary.[16] His hopes to visit Aragon and Andalusia were dashed. He rethought his strategy. The hinge on which swung his new approach was simple: avoid any show of resistance to the king and his council. Lie low.[17]

The Araoz shuttle continued between Nadal and the court. Each time Araoz returned to Alcalá, it was with a small concession. The court continued to lengthen his permitted stay in Castile. As we have seen, it had at first given him thirty days to make the round of Jesuit houses, then stretched it by fifteen days more, then twenty days more. During one of his conversations with Araoz, Nadal mentioned a plan he had weighed for some time: to divide the Castile province in two, one to cover the southern area and to be called the province of Toledo, and the other to cover the northern area and to retain the title province of Castile. He also made Araoz an offer. Since the office of overall superior was vacant after Borgia's departure for Rome, Araoz could have the post or, if he preferred, he could have the position of provincial in either of the two new provinces.[18]

One day, about three weeks after Nadal had come to Alcalá, the prince of Éboli came from Madrid and paid Nadal a visit. The usually suave and gracious prince was angry and agitated. He told Nadal to summon two priests to act as witnesses to some extremely grave business. Nadal asked Antonio de Córdoba and Bartolomé de Bustamente to join the group. Éboli then produced a letter sent from France by Laínez to Nadal. He had intercepted it. He read it to Nadal. What he read were instructions from Laínez that directed Nadal to get Araoz out of the Spanish court by hook or by crook. Dispatch him to the Council of Trent, directed Laínez, or give him a direct order to quit the court and go to one or other Jesuit community. Do anything to extract him from Madrid. The Society was caught red-handed. Éboli salted the evidence with his personal exegesis of the event: behind this plot Nadal's jealousy was at work. He proclaimed to Nadal that he would not abandon Araoz. Breathing threats, he stormed out of the house.

Within a short time, Éboli was back. Meanwhile, Nadal had studied Laínez's letter and found an escape hatch. In the conclusion of the letter Laínez had written that he left the ultimate disposition of Araoz to Nadal, since he was on the scene. Nadal grasped that. He assured Éboli that Araoz had nothing to fear, that Araoz would not be touched. Éboli kept repeating: "He [Araoz] is my friend, Father." Again Nadal tried to calm the prince, once more asserting that Araoz would not be moved.

Éboli kept up his chant: "He is my friend, Father." Nadal then told the prince of the offer he had made to Araoz some days earlier: choose the post he preferred, to be overall superior or to be provincial of either of the two new provinces. Éboli's reply startled Nadal: the prince said that he saw through Nadal's words of peace; behind his posture of reconciliation lurked a trap. The post of overall superior, charged Éboli, exists at the discretion of the general; shortly after Araoz was installed, Laínez would abolish the office. This charge silenced Nadal. Éboli pressed his advantage and tried to extract a promise from Nadal that the position would not be abrogated. Nadal replied that he would do what he could.

So concluded a series of painful interviews. During all of them Gómez Suárez de Figueroa, count of Feria, a loyal friend of the Society, stood by, saying not a word because the Society's foes had tied his hands. Nadal looked at the situation realistically: Éboli would go to any lengths to keep Araoz in Madrid. The Jesuits at Alcalá preferred to have it that way, since they thought the Society would benefit from the court's benevolence shining through the person of Araoz. Nadal yielded to the hard facts and reaffirmed his earlier decision to avoid all confrontation and shun all argument.[19]

Through those last few difficult weeks, Nadal was in surprisingly high spirits. His natural bent toward depression had become submerged. "I experienced," he wrote, "a joyful confidence such as I cannot recall ever before having in the Society."[20] He puzzled some Jesuits. They thought that he might be a bit balmy, out of touch with reality.[21] In this elated mood, Nadal decided to proceed with the visit of the Castile province. He chose to start with Alcalá. To the Jesuit communities in Aragon and Andalusia, closed to him by order of the court, he sent his questionnaires. He directed the two provincials to collect the completed forms and bring them to Alcalá, where he intended to review with them in time those documents. On October 24 or 25 he formally opened his inspection of the Alcalá college.[22]

On October 26 Nadal delivered his first conference to the Alcalá community. Through three weeks he gave fourteen talks in Spanish, six fewer than he had given at Coimbra. Fr. Gil González Dávila copied them. He caught, as the Coimbra copyist did not, the verve, the élan, the intellectual keenness, the easy mingling of doctrine and anecdote, and the rhetorical questions with which Nadal peppered his addresses. Some sixty Jesuits heard Nadal at Alcalá.[23]

The content of these talks was basically the same as the content of the talks he had been giving since his first visits to Portugal and Spain in 1552: the purpose and character of the Society of Jesus, the meaning of the life of Ignatius, the stages in Jesuit formation, the import of the vows. Theology, history, and law intertwined in the talks.[24]

In his first talk Nadal explained why Laínez, held at Rome by the pope, was unable to come to Spain. He confided to the Alcalá Jesuits that he tried to evade Laínez's appointment of him as visitor by pleading ineptitude and lack of talent. The general, however, insisted, and that, basically, was why Nadal at that moment was addressing them. He asked their patience and indulgence. He would speak to them—and here he used the formula he had unwrapped at Coimbra—*spiritu, corde, practice.* He hoped that they would listen *spiritu, corde, practice.*[25] Some of his main headings follow.

The Society: A Grace

Nadal defined the purpose of his visitation in terms of divine grace. The Society is a singular and distinctive grace: he now nuanced this familiar idea with a fresh perception. Under the pope, the general is the head and font though which God diffuses this grace of the Society to individual Jesuits. The closer a Jesuit's union with the general, the greater his disposition to receive a rich influx of divine grace. The more secure the union with the font [the general], the more potent the power received from that font. Nadal told the Alcalá Jesuits he hoped he could help them weld that kind of intimate and firm union with their general and thereby intensify their disposition to receive the grace of the Society.

On this positive bent of his visitation Nadal insisted. He had come to Spain, he said, not to listen to gripes and grumblings, not to hear about defects, not to punish knaves. He had come rather to animate awareness of the grace given by God to and through the Society. If this were achieved, any needed reforms would follow naturally. He promised that his admonitions would be few, that his stress would be on fidelity to the traditions and customs of the Society. He would, he continued, check implementation of the decrees of the First General Congregation, and try to get a grasp of the Spanish scene, all with a view to briefing the general.[26]

The Import of Ignatius' Life

The story of Ignatius was the compass Nadal always employed in his conferences. At Alcalá he once again guided his fellow Jesuits in their quest for the identity of the Society of Jesus. He indicated landmarks that traced the route: Loyola, Montserrat, Manresa, Jerusalem, Barcelona, Alcalá, Paris, Rome. He guided them to a precious personal discovery: Ignatius' life is the form of the Society of Jesus. The Manresa period especially drew distinctive lines in the molding of that form. In his meditations on the Kingdom of Christ and the Two Standards, Ignatius delineated the future Society's distinctive way in the service of Christ and of the Catholic Church. The impact of those two meditations, thought Nadal, "led Fr. Ignatius to arrange as he did the ministries and divisions of the Society."[27]

An integral element of Ignatius the founder was his theological acumen; Nadal used the expression: "our father the theologian." One of the doctors at the Sorbonne, Martial Mazurier, recalled that never had he encountered one who showed such penetration and mastery of theological questions.[28] The secret of Ignatius' theological perception was locked within the interior illuminations God granted him. God had opened the eyes of Ignatius' soul to see truth in a depth and breadth that converted him into a new man. Nadal encouraged his listeners to realize, in their aspirations to follow the Jesuit way of life, that they could find nourishment in the high spiritual gifts of their founder. "In those revelations we find strength."[29]

Nadal tried to portray the unity within the person of Ignatius of natural endowments and supernatural gifts. Ignatius the courtier and soldier showed a personal magnanimity, generosity, nobility. In turning to God under the attraction of divine grace, he directed his human qualities to the greater glory of God. "And this was his prime principle," a principle enunciated in each chapter of the Constitutions. Grace had seized Ignatius' natural magnanimity and endowed it with a shining spiritual beauty.[30]

For the Jesuit students at Alcalá, as elsewhere, Nadal knew that a constant problem was how to hold a balance between study and devotion. He recalled for them Ignatius' own sensitivity to this problem and the lessons he learned from his experience. Ignatius looked for two marks among the scholastics: first, that their devotion aroused in the novitiate perdure; and second, that this devotion not impede their study. Nadal centered his resolution of this issue on the principle that in all things the scholastic seeks his growth in charity, therefore in study too. To advance in study a Jesuit's devotion is an aid. "The prayer practiced in the Society moves into the practical order. . . . The scholar's prayer must therefore be geared to helping him in the work assigned him by the Society, namely study."[31]

These guidelines Nadal traced back to Ignatius' experience at Paris. There Ignatius learned that his devotion was impairing his academic progress. He therefore tempered his austerities and his prolonged prayer to the demands of the university.[32] In his work with the books he found God and grew in his love. With recollections of this kind, Nadal tried to complete for other Jesuits the picture of "our way of doing things."

The Society's Apostolic Character

To the Society's men who were laboring in India and Germany Nadal gave an emotional accolade. "They do more work, gain more merit, give more service to the Lord [than other Jesuits]. They are absorbed in virtues of superlative worth. They gather more fruit from their labors. On these two wings [Germany and the Indies] does the Society fly."[33]

The Jesuit is turned outward toward his fellow human beings. Within him there is a drive for action (*inclinatio efficax ad praxim*); he goes beyond the call of the contemplative. The Jesuit is therefore never idle, is always on the alert, is sprightly in his quest for work. "Do you not see," asked Nadal of the Alcalá community, "that we are at war?" The Jesuit is therefore ever ready with his arms. Each day he grows in learning the Society's battle plans.

In one of his pungent rhetorical flourishes, Nadal ventured another definition of the Society: "If you take the Society in its entirety, its Institute, and its Spiritual Exercises, you will see that the whole thing is a bundle of vivacious love." Nadal worried that he might be giving the wrong impression. A Jesuit's dynamic energy did not make him abrasive. Tractable and agreeable, the Jesuit conveys conviction but does not irritate. His words pierce but do not anger his hearers. "Our vocation is to be on the lookout for workers of this caliber." The Society, therefore, was not established for Jesuits alone. "If it [the Society] were set up for its members only, there would be no need for its coming into existence. Nor would it be heard of."[34]

In the grace of the Jesuit vocation Nadal perceived an internal unity, which bound into a single endeavor the Jesuit's search for growth in personal charity and in his work for his fellow human beings. The same grace permeated the Jesuit's personal and apostolic life. "The grace that God gives you for yourselves and for helping your neighbor is one and the same. Your obligation toward both is the same." With this *inclinatio ad praxim* Nadal tied a sense of modernity. The Jesuit must be alert to the needs of the modern world. In the sixteenth century, insisted Nadal, the Jesuit had to know the minds of the Protestants, *alumbrados, dejados,* and others who taught doctrines alien to the Catholic Church. He should address those people in the language of the contemporary world. More was needed than speaking in the medium of St. Augustine or St. Jerome. Modernity should be a distinctive mark of Jesuit performance.[35]

Adversity

Nadal closed his first talk at Alcalá with these words: "It is especially worthwhile to note that from its origins the Society came to realize that whenever the Lord has in mind some unusual gift for us, buffets and troubles always come first. This is what took place at the foundation of the Society. I get much comfort and strength in reflecting that, in this age of setbacks and blasts against religion from one quarter or another, the Lord has raised the Society and given it so notable an increase. This is his special mercy and blessing. By it, all of us are consoled. Ask the Lord to bless me with the grace, the competence, the vigor to know how to open to you the meaning of our Institute."[36]

Adversity, stressed Nadal, is an ingredient of Jesuit history. It is also a harbinger of divine blessings. Nadal gave an example: Bartolomeo Cardinal Guidiccioni tried to thwart Ignatius' aspirations in 1539–1540 by having a papal ban on all new religious orders. Guidiccioni's opposition was God's way of preparing the Society for special graces. It was the novitiate of the Society of Jesus.

Adversity, continued Nadal, is an important component of the Jesuit novitiate. The Jesuit novice is assigned to work in a hospital, to beg, to teach children catechism, to make a pilgrimage—all tailored to probe his virtue. In these difficult probings, called experiments, a novice's virtue stands or falls. The aspirations aroused during the thirty days of the Spiritual Exercises are brought face-to-face with challenge and resistance. The power of resolutions made during retreat (*reliquiae cogitationum*) to survive is actively tested throughout the novitiate. The Jesuit novice is schooled for the way of adversity, the Jesuit way of life.[37]

Pungent, Personal, Practical

During the fifteen years Nadal had been giving conferences to his fellow Jesuits, he consistently dipped into the well of his own life to exemplify principles he was trying to illumine. This practice he continued at Alcalá. He told the Jesuits there, for example, of a certain habit he had developed: endeavoring to find Christ in the author of the book and in the speaker in the lecture hall. "I make a point of shaping this attitude: it is Christ, in the person of this doctor, whom I am reading or to whom I am listening." Christ was his teacher in the volume and at the lectern.[38]

At Alcalá, Fr. Gil González Dávila, perhaps better than any other copyist, caught the pungency of Nadal's words. "The Society wants men who, as far as possible, are consummate experts in every area that contributes to the purpose of the Society. Do you have it in you to a be a fine logician? Go to it. Or an accomplished theologian? Go to it. Or an outstanding humanist? Or a master of any other discipline that can advance the Jesuit way of doing things? According to your ability and talent, refuse to settle for mediocrity."[39]

Nadal had an ear for laments of young and inexperienced men in learning the Jesuit way of life, especially in prayer. He gave much time to practical hints on prayer. He insisted first of all that there is a distinctly Jesuit mode of prayer. A Jesuit novice learns to discard not only evil habits but also those forms of virtue that do not mesh with the Jesuit Institute. The same holds for prayer. One of the first obligations of a new Jesuit is to make the Spiritual Exercises of Ignatius, in which "we have indicated to us our road of prayer."

Our road of prayer: Nadal sensed that this phrase sounded severely restrictive. A rigid application of what would become a leaden cliché, "the kinds of prayer in the Spiritual Exercises," as enforced by Fr. General Everard Mercurian ten years later, Nadal shunned. Within the Society, God is the supreme guide in prayer. Ignatius recognized this. With God as guide, Nadal told the Alcalá community, "you will find the door [of prayer] opening wide for you. This was Fr. Ignatius' experience. He used to say that he found prayer in everything." Nadal explained one of his favorite approaches, the *reliquiae cogitationum*. He suggested they recall a past consolation in prayer and note how it moves them along "and sprinkles devotion" on their hearts and minds. These were a few of the hints Nadal proposed to Jesuit fledglings during his conferences at Alcalá.[40]

Two younger Jesuits were especially impressed by this theme. Br. Alfonso Bravo, who ten years later would be one of eight Jesuits with the fleet of Don Juan of Austria at the battle of Lepanto, hailed Nadal's insistence that Jesuits walk the way of the Society's Constitutions.[41†] José de Acosta, a twenty-one-year-old scholastic, reported that the community was realizing more each day the blessings that flowed from fidelity to directives given by Nadal. All now shared his single-minded purpose: observance of the Constitutions and Rules. All now manifested a strong intellectual conviction about their vocation. And all this Nadal did with a smile.[42]

Nine years earlier, in 1553, when he gave his first conferences in Alcalá, Nadal had written a short synopsis on Jesuit prayer entitled *Orden de oración* ("An Instruction on Prayer"). It contained eighteen terse, lapidary statements. Now, nine years later, he supplemented his conferences, again at Alcalá, with a longer work entitled *De la oración, especialmente para los de la Compañia* ("On Prayer: Especially for Those of the Society"). It contained

---

†41 *Mon Nad*, I:538 n 1. Unfortunately he himself wandered from that path. After Lepanto he became restless, wanted to become a Jesuit priest, was denied, and was eventually dismissed from the Society. He later passed himself off as an expert in moral theology to an unsuspecting bishop.

forty compact paragraphs. Nothing he wrote in that work was new; he had said it all before. But here he brought several ideas on prayer together. The result was not a treatise distinguished for a gracefully executed literary unity. A unity it had indeed, but one that resembled the unity of a delta, a wide range of islets washed by the flow of the same mighty river running to the ocean. *De la oración* was a delta of forty-eight islets.[43]

In *De la oración* Nadal laid out familiar ideas: the link between relish in prayer and the desire to follow Christ in humiliation, rejection, and poverty; a warning that pursuit of devotions alien to the Jesuit spirit can lead to an obstinate distancing of self from the Society; a caution against curiosity about mystical graces; advice to rest at that point in prayer where spiritual relish attracts; an exhortation to stretch contemplation to active ministries. He also proposed some of his familiar definitions of Jesuit prayer: a gift, a way of life, a mystical understanding of spiritual reality, a finding of God in all things.

This work gave a measure of Nadal's expanding grasp of his "specialty," Jesuit prayer. In 1553, in *Orden de oración,* he had listed eighteen items. In 1562, in *De la oración,* he listed forty. That increase, although impressive, suggests a slightly troubling development. As he became more diffuse, he retreated somewhat from the priority Ignatius gave to self-denial. Not that he overlooked self-denial's important role in a Jesuit's life—indeed he continued to affirm it—but the sheer force of prayer as a central absorbing subject made it "king of the hill." Ignatius had been chary of those who professed their fascination with prayer. He had kept his guard. Nadal was letting his slip. Only three years later, in a general congregation, he would take a step away from Ignatius' legislation on prayer in the Society. The disposition to make that move had been gradually building. *De la oración* was part of that buildup.

It was probably during this visitation that Nadal composed a small work called *Tractatus de traditionibus et consuetudinibus Societatis Iesu* ("A Tract on the Traditions and Customs of the Society of Jesus").[44] Juridical in tone and objective, *Tractatus* was filled with definitions and distinctions. Nadal did not concern himself with the speculative nature of tradition; he focused rather on single and specific forms of action, to each of which he applied the term tradition. He bundled them, used the plural form, and called them *traditions*: thus the plural form in the title of *Tractatus*.

Nadal opened his *Tractatus* by making a distinction between a tradition and a custom. He defined a tradition as a practice whose authority did not derive from either the Society's Constitutions or Rules, but from its being handed down from Ignatius. A custom he defined as a practice whose origin was uncertain, but which attained its authoritative state by usage. He promptly raised his guard lest every action of Ignatius be interpreted as reason for a tradition; this would result in a mass of traditions giving shape to Jesuit life. Certain practices of Ignatius he cut from what should be imitated: his infrequent offering of Mass and his substitution of a short part of the rosary for the reading of the divine office. So overwhelming was Ignatius' devotion that it made daily celebration of Mass and recitation of the breviary impossible for him. Since such overpowering devotion was not the usual experience of a Jesuit, he should not adopt those practices of Ignatius.

Nadal listed twenty instances of Jesuit traditions in the sense he defined. A few examples are abstinence on Fridays, prayer in private rather than in common, undertaking the moral and doctrinal training of poor orphans, maintaining a vineyard or a garden for recreation and play of the community, avoiding easy converse with women save those of social status, keeping on file a copy of communications from the father general, administering public reprehensions, singing Matins on the vigil of Christmas. Customs Nadal divided into those that pertained to the Society as a whole and those that concerned individual provinces. He made an extended list of those applicable to the Society as a whole. Some follow: reading of the martyrology at supper, renewal of vows at or close to Christmas and the feast of St. Peter, introduction to use of the discipline immediately on a novice's entry into the first probation or whenever he could be gently persuaded to adopt this custom, confessing from the pulpit faults committed, daily offering of Mass by priests, delivery of a weekly exhortation on spiritual subjects in the communities, undertaking of mortifications during school vacations, especially during hot summer days.

The substance of *Tractatus* reflected Nadal's fifth exhortation at Alcalá in 1561, and it imbued his *Dialogi de Instituto S.I.*

("Dialogues"), which were written over the next few years.[45] Earlier, in 1554, during his exhortations in Spain, he had spoken of tradition in a much broader way; he was then explaining various reasons for writing the Society's Constitutions. Not to write constitutions, said he, would among other things have been to tempt God, for to be without constitutions would risk uncertainty of direction. With the passage of time, he explained, tradition gradually became weakened, became diverted into meanings other than the basic one. Here he was arguing from a certain assumption: initially the Society lived a fundamental understanding of its spirit and aim that was the common possession of its first members. It held in hand "a unity and conformity in all things." With the increase of numbers, however, came a danger of losing that unity and conformity. That fundamental tradition must be preserved. That was the burden of the Society's Constitutions.

In his earlier years as visitor, therefore, Nadal wrote of tradition in a sense broader than the restricted meaning he intended in the 1560s. The wider sense he never really explored, nor ever made a personal venture to plumb the theological depth of tradition. He turned his concern rather toward certain practices in the Society, their foundations, their value, their authority. Here Nadal the administrator ran ahead of Nadal the theologian.

His visitation of the Alcalá college completed, Nadal started his tour of the southern area of the Castile province. On November 14, he left Alcalá for nearby Ocaña. Dogging him on the way was an admonition from the royal council: make your stop at each community as brief as possible. He spiced his diary: "With Araoz prodding them, that's the way the satraps lean on me." But he did what he was told: he kept moving.[46]

In driving rain and against strong winds, Nadal and Jiménez plodded for four weeks through deep mud—Jiménez recalled that never had he seen so much mud—to eight towns and villages: Ocaña, Toledo, Ocaña again, Villarejo de Fuentes, Belmonte, Cuenca, Mondéjar, Guadalajara, Jesús del Monte, stopping not only at Jesuit houses, most of which were small, but also calling on friends of the Society. Two benefactors, high on Spain's social staircase, would not be denied visits. Doña Maria de Mendoza, the marquesa de Mondéjar, and the marquesa de Cenete insisted that Nadal interrupt his circuit and visit them. Nadal's sober comment was: "In both places [Mondéjar and

Cenete], with the divine grace, I obtained some fruit." Even as he plodded the muddy highways, the eyes of King Philip's court followed him. At Cuenca he received a crisp order from Madrid: keep moving. "I received word that the satraps were pressuring me to move on."[47]

Cuenca gave Nadal what was perhaps the most gratifying triumph of the entire tour. Once more he faced the explosive Dr. Ramírez de Vergara, who, it may be recalled, in return for generous gifts to the Society, insisted on living quarters in the Cuenca college, the service of a brother as cook and valet, and a say in the assignment of Jesuits at the Alcalá college. In his earlier visitations of 1556 and 1561, Nadal lost two strenuous rounds in his effort to break Vergara's grip on the Society. This time he won. Vergara surrendered his Jesuit cook and valet, gave up his voice in the assignment of Jesuits, and agreed that his quarters in the Cuenca college be apart from the rooms of the Jesuits, although he was allowed to live there for the rest of his life. In return for his surrender, he was permitted the use of the Jesuit villa at Jesús del Monte in Loranca da Tajuña, and was assured he would receive the suffrages given to founders of Jesuit colleges.[48]

Nadal arrived back in Alcalá on December 9. He found waiting for him the Jesuits he had summoned from Aragon and Andalusia: Fr. Antonio Cordeses, provincial of Aragon; Fr. Alonso Román, rector in Granada; Fr. Juan Suárez, rector in Córdoba; and Fr. Bartolomé de Bustamente, provincial of Andalusia, who actually had come to Alcalá before Nadal started his tour. Nadal planned this assembly as a substitute for the visit to Aragon and Andalusia that the government denied him.[49]

For three weeks, Nadal and these men toiled through a tedious routine of paper work and conferences. With his guests he read sheaves of answers to questionnaires and reviewed major problems in their two provinces. For the Jesuits whom he could not meet he penned letters of advice and encouragement. He tailored the general directives and regulations he had issued in Portugal to the regional characteristics and local customs of the eastern and southern areas of Spain. With his insistence that uniformity should prevail in essentials, he nevertheless aimed at flexibility in his legislation. He also made some shifts in personnel. Bustamente he relieved of the provincial's post and replaced him with Juan de la Plaza;

Bustamente was named superintendent of the college in Seville. Cordeses remained provincial of Aragon. Suárez, whom he was thinking of making provincial of the proposed new province of Old Castile, he planned to take with him on his further visitations. Before he ended the consultations, Nadal asked the others their opinions about various men then being considered for provincials elsewhere, and about who should be named *comissarius* in Spain. Shortly after Christmas he dispatched the group to their provinces with general letters Nadal had written to their communities as a whole. He wanted to send to Laínez, who was then still in France, a report on all these developments but he feared interception of his correspondence by the Spanish authorities. He therefore summoned Fr. Manuel Godinho from Portugal, gave him the letters, and sent him to Fr. Laínez.[50]

At least one of the conferees left Alcalá with misgivings. Fr. Antonio Cordeses, provincial of Aragon, carried some thirty packets of Nadal's directives, enough to make a hefty volume. Sections of these included titles such as "The Relations of the Superior with His Consultors," "An Instruction on the Examination of Applicants to the Society," "An Instruction on Forbidden Books," "Procedures in the Dining Room and in Waiting on Table," "A Directive on Reading in the Dining Room." Cordeses complained to Diego Laínez that Nadal had gone too far. He lamented that he could not cram so much material into his head, already filled with the Constitutions, Rules, declarations on the Constitutions, and decrees of the First General Congregation. "Although he [Nadal] did not place his regulations on the level of the latter in importance, in reality they carry the force of the Rules, since he ordered that they be exactly observed, no change being allowed save by you [Laínez] or himself."[51]

Cordeses' discontent spread. Other Jesuits chafed under the wide net of regulations such as those Nadal imposed at Ocaña about the kinds of dessert, antipasto, and postpasto that could be served. Five months after Nadal left Spain, Fr. Jerónimo Doménech reported to Laínez that feelings were simmering against what Nadal left behind. He advised the general: "Until you yourself look them over, and either give your approval or quash what you think should be quashed, I think the unrest will continue unabated. This situation will be relieved, I feel, if, with Nadal out of the country, someone comes along who will temper things a bit." Doménech made a correct diagnosis. Nadal's fussiness was running out of control. He had woven a coat of many colors for the Spanish Jesuits, but some did not care to wear it. It was too tight.[52]

These early laments in Spain and Portugal were the first rumblings of a widening opinion that Nadal was essentially a regulator and a man of cramped spirit. His propensity for regulations was strong. Yet it may not have been as strong as it appeared at first glance, for many of his points were responses to questions and doubts raised by rectors and provincials. This was a period when Jesuit communities were groping towards the Jesuit way of life. Many of these communities were only two or three years old when Nadal appeared on the scene. The work of the community had been parceled out to cooks, buyers, sacristans, teachers, porters, and superiors; all had to be instructed in the minutiae of their posts. Nadal had the responsibility of setting in motion customs that in years to come would make communities run on their own. Yet, despite this demand for precise directives, Nadal did at times become ridiculously specific. At Ocaña, as we have seen, he even itemized what desserts and antipastos might be served.[53]

With his consultants on their way home from Alcalá, Nadal lost no time in starting his round of the northern part of the province. He felt the royal council hounding his heels; they would brook no delay. Yet he started on a note of confidence inspired by "the word and assurance of one of the key men in the King's entourage" (the prince of Éboli? the count of Feria?). Nadal outlined his route for Araoz: Segovia, Ávila, Salamanca, Medina del Campo, Burgos. From Burgos he intended to enter France. He ordered Araoz to meet him in Burgos in a month, where together they would recapitulate all that Nadal had done. Araoz grimaced. He rarely took orders from above gracefully, but he gave the impression he had been given a dose of gall and wormwood. That was ominous. To speed the visitation, Nadal sent Fr. Gil González Dávila ahead with the questionnaires; he wanted them completed by the time he arrived. He took seriously the royal admonitum: do not tarry. On January 3, 1562, in the heart of winter, he left Alcalá with Jiménez and Fr. Juan Suárez, whom he planned to make provincial of the area they were visiting once he had formally divided the Castile province. For two grim days they fought heavy snow and bitter winds as they climbed the twisting road through the Sierra de Guadarrama to Segovia. The frightened mules balked and often backtracked.[54]

On the fifth, the thoroughly shaken travelers rode into Segovia, where a community of twelve men awaited them. The Segovia college had its peculiar problem: the main benefactor, Canon Hernando Solier, hedged his promise of financial surety with conditions Nadal found unacceptable. Nadal refused to sacrifice the Society's freedom to run the school in a Jesuit way and declined Solier's money. The college would seek other sources of income.

Other colleges along the way had their special problems. At Ávila, Nadal learned that the rector, Fr. Gaspar de Salazar, whom he had appointed on his earlier trip, had, on the advice of a layman, taken the pulpit and admonished the bishop for acting "suspiciously." The bishop did not take kindly to such public admonition. Nadal moved Salazar out of town. Fr. Baltasar Alvares, Teresa of Ávila's confessor, enjoyed Nadal's presence and regretted his leaving.

At Salamanca, Nadal met a large community of thirty-six men who still needed a fixed and steady source of income. During his stay of twelve days, the usual round of conferences, confessions, and questionnaires filled the time. But the most difficult problem Nadal encountered in Salamanca did not concern that college. The count of Monterrey again came to see Nadal about a foundation the count had promised for the college at Monterrey. The count was a hard bargainer, however, and tied his gift with so many strings that Nadal found it incompatible with the Jesuit Institute. Yet by the time Nadal concluded his visitation, he had basically succeeded in bringing the count to his point of view. The few loose ends that remained Nadal left for the provincial.

At Medina del Campo he encountered more problems with the Society's benefactors. Pedro Quadrado and his wife were extremely generous. They had built an ample residence and commodious church, and they continued to supply an annual revenue of 600 ducats. But Nadal discovered that the rector, without permission of the general, had made agreements with Quadrado that were incompatible with the liberty the Society emphasized in its Institute. Nadal corrected these arrangements with difficulty, and he issued a strong directive that rectors were not to act on their own in agreements with benefactors. There were other problems. Some Jesuits were entertaining the school's generous benefactress, Doña Quadrado, in the community's garden. This he stopped. He also calmed the waves churned within the community by a priest, a favorite of Doña Quadrado, who was piqued because he had not been appointed rector of the school.[55]

At Medina Nadal received several letters that threw his plans into disarray. Araoz wrote that he was sick and could not meet Nadal at Burgos as he had been directed. The prince of Éboli wrote and ordered Nadal to return promptly to Alcalá; he explained that the royal council was incensed Nadal was still making the visitation. Éboli insisted that he could no longer hold the ire of the king's counselors at bay. Nadal must return to Alcalá immediately. Besides, wrote Éboli, he himself wished to discuss with Nadal some serious business about the Society and its relations to the crown. "Nothing new in this," wryly remarked Nadal, yet he held his policy of avoiding confrontation. He wrote Éboli that he would hurry back to Alcalá. First he did a bit of corner-cutting, however. The Valladolid college, with thirty Jesuits, was a half-day's journey from Medina del Campo, so to Valladolid he rode and stayed there two days. He made a claim that can only excite wonder: he did "everything I did in the other colleges." How much time could he have given to each of thirty men in two days? On February 7 he left Valladolid with Jiménez. Five days later they were back in Alcalá.[56]

The prince of Éboli, true to his word, went to Alcalá and discussed with Nadal several issues that had soured the court in it dealings with the Society. Araoz participated in at least a few of the meetings. Nadal was surprised, though, to find Éboli friendly and conciliatory; Araoz was cooperative and obliging. Something mysterious had taken place in Madrid. What propelled the change is unknown. Éboli abandoned a number of his hard and intractable positions, and from the talks emerged some practical and moderate adjustments. The crown, for example, made a distinction in its application of the ban on exportation of money to the Roman College; the interdict now referred to inheritances, not to alms. Nadal was content. He estimated that the ban on inheritances did not materially affect what financial aid the Roman College might expect from Spain, since most inheritances were meagre and local needs were so acute that little could be spared for the Roman College.

The crown also made a distinction in its embargo on sending Jesuits outside the country: it did not affect those residing in Rome. With this too Nadal was satisfied. He thought that in time bad feelings at the court would abate and the ban would be eased. He noticed, too, that the early fury over Francis Borgia had almost completely dissipated. "Nothing—or very little—is said about it any more." One serious restraint, however, remained: Nadal was not permitted to visit Aragon and Andalusia. At the meeting he told Araoz he intended to appoint him superintendent "of all Spain and the Indies." He then outlined the duties of the new office and cautioned Araoz that, although the provincials depended on the superintendent, he should allow them to carry out their work without interference.

Nadal finished his meetings with Éboli and Araoz in an optimistic mood. He remarked that, after all, the court had not closed all doors. Some remained open and gave hope of better times to come. He thought his policy of shunning confrontation was succeeding.[57]

To Alfonso Salmerón, acting as vicar general during the absence of Diego Laínez in France, Nadal reported his delight with the meeting, with the agreements made, and especially with Éboli's new attitude. The Society's Institute remained unimpaired. The court had indeed showed hostility to his visitation but, as a matter of fact, he had visited many Jesuit houses. The court had not stopped him "as indeed they have halted other [religious]." The court had put pressure on him to rush his work, but his speed not only had not vitiated the visitations but had been consonant with Laínez's directives to finish as soon as possible with a view to a quick departure for the imminent convening of the Council of Trent.

"Of all those at the court," he wrote Salmerón, "Rui Gómez, the prince of Éboli, has most clearly shown himself to be an outstanding friend and patron of the Society. I have spoken to him a number of times. Our last conversation took place when he came posthaste to Alcalá to see me. He came with a single-minded love and concern for the Society's welfare. He offered to back us in every way." Even Araoz was shifting with the changing tide. Nadal informed Salmerón that Araoz "has been my chief, practically my sole help in all these negotiations. On every point he has given me great comfort, indeed supreme satisfaction. So true is this that I am ready to affirm that in him our father general and our Society have an outstanding man for the service of God Our Savior."

Nadal's elation carried him into a spell of euphoria. His usual capacity for calm and objective judgment slipped away. Only a week and a half after that outburst of praise of Araoz, he returned to the same theme. Three times in a short letter he told Salmerón that the Jesuits had a fine brother in Fr. Araoz, that the Society should deal with him in complete confidence and love as though he had never caused any trouble, "as indeed he never intended to do." The last line of that letter read: "Show total trust in Fr. Araoz. This is for us an obligation." Possibly Nadal's judgment was influenced by the general attitude of satisfaction with Araoz's appointment that he found at Alcalá. This widespread satisfaction, thought Nadal, made it appear "that Our Lord has, with his great and gentle providence, brought this about." But never had Nadal been more wrong. He thought the leopard had changed his spots; through his rose-tinted glasses he failed to see they were still there.[58]

The results of his conversations with the prince of Éboli convinced Nadal of the wisdom of his policy of avoiding confrontation with the court. At least one influential Jesuit, however, differed. Jerónimo Doménech accused Nadal of timidity. Before the ire of the court, said Doménech, Nadal had shilly-shallied. Events, however, were on the side of Nadal. If he had flouted Éboli's order to return to Alcalá and had continued through Burgos into France, the royal council certainly would have flared in a rage at his decamping à la Borgia. Nadal's submission led to conciliatory conferences at Alcalá and a notable easing of tensions between the crown and the Society.[59]

During the five weeks after his return to Alcalá, Nadal found time to compose more directives for the Spanish provincials. He dispatched orders on things great and small. One especially evoked cries of protest from three of the four provincials. Nadal had instructed Antonio Cordeses that, save in the case of novices, he should consult the newly named commissary, Father Antonio Araoz, before he used his constitutional powers and dismissed anyone from the Society. "If the judgment of Fr. Araoz has to be sought on the dismissal of men unsuited for the Society," Cordeses wrote to Laínez, "either dismissal will come late in the game or no one will ever be sent away. Rarely does he [Araoz] ever make up his mind on points of business. A result will be the considerable damage done by restless men before they are let go."

Cordeses ventured to identify the cloven hoof: Araoz was first a courtier, then a Jesuit. The court, its feuds and its fiefs, pushed his Jesuit responsibilities into a corner. With right did Cordeses contest one of the most ill-advised appointments Nadal ever made. Laínez initially backed Nadal, but he intended to look into the issue thoroughly. He advised Cordeses to carry out Nadal's instructions for the time being and promised to discuss the problem of dismissals with Nadal when the latter arrived at Trent. Meanwhile he asked Cordeses to write in specific detail what instructions of Nadal were impracticable in the light of experience and also to explain his reasons for making these judgments.[60]

Nadal set March 10 as the day of his departure from Alcalá for France. On the evening before, he served table at supper. He then gathered the community, announced the appointments of Araoz as general's delegate, of Fr. Juan de Valderrábano as superior of the new province of Toledo, and of Fr. Juan Suárez as superior of the province of Castile. He gave a final exhortation that stressed obedience and prayer. On his knees he begged pardon for his defects. He embraced each of the community. He wept. They wept. The next day, on newly purchased mules, Nadal rode eastward toward Zaragoza, and Jiménez went north for a brief visit with his relatives in Logroño before rejoining Nadal.[61]

Even in those last days in Spain, though, unfinished business harried Nadal. Juan de Marquina, the benign canon and founder of the college at Cuenca, wanted Nadal to stop at Cañaveras for a discussion of the contract between himself and the Society; certain phrases in the contract left him uncomfortable. Nadal therefore halted at Cañaveras and worked over with Marquina the text, forging a new wording that satisfied the canon without changing the substantial components of the contract.[62]

Nadal arrived in Zaragoza on March 19. Jiménez joined him three days later. The corpus of official papers Nadal had gathered during his visitation—correspondence, reports, questionnaires—made a heavy load that filled two large traveling bags. These he shipped to Rome by the Barcelona-Genoa route. At Zaragoza he met a young man named Bertrand, a native of Béarn of the Kingdom of Navarre and a university student who had known the Jesuits for four years. Bertrand asked to be received into the Society and Nadal decided to take the young Béarnais with him and eventually leave him at some French Jesuit college to do his novitiate. He was also happy to have with him someone who could speak French and the patois of Gascony.[63]

On April 6, Nadal, Jiménez, and Bertrand rode northward to Jaca at the foothills of the Pyrenees. They reached Ayerbe by nightfall. There they encountered a team of muleteers and a detachment of soldiers with a cargo of gold destined for Lyons. These they joined, and the next day they rode to Jaca and then started the ascent into the Pyrenees to the village of Confranc. On the eighth they moved through the charming valley of the Aspe to Oloron in the duchy of Foix.[64] Nadal had seen the last of Spain: he was never to return. In his last report to Rome, Nadal sounded a high note of optimism and confidence in God's support of the Jesuit enterprise: "It is, when all is said and done, the work of his divine and generous hand. He does it. May he ever be glorified in all."[65]

17

Conclusion

[Nadal] remained with us three weeks and helped and heartened us enormously by his counsels and daily addresses on the Constitutions. He spoke to our boarders also warm words of encouragement. He was so well while he was here that he said he had never felt better since he left you [Laínez] in Rome for his travels, and this happy state of affairs he attributed to our Cologne beer.

Leonard Kessel, rector at Cologne, to the general

Once Nadal and Jiménez arrived in France in 1562, they traveled through countryside patroled by bands of Huguenots to their first destination, the Jesuit college at Pamiers.[1] In 1559 Robert de Pellevé, bishop of Pamiers, had persuaded the Society to open a college in his see after he heard glowing reports about the Jesuit college at Billom. Pamiers was in the heart of a Calvinist enclave, and the bishop hoped the college would detract from the appeal of the reformed religion. Unfortunately, the bishop did not translate his religious fervor into financial support, and the college was not adequately endowed.

The continual warfare between the Huguenots and the Catholics added to the Society's woes. In September of 1561 the college at Pamiers shut down in the face of a Huguenot attack. Its Jesuits retreated to Toulouse and the college remained closed until 1630. Nadal learned about the Society's expulsion and journeyed to Toulouse to see the Jesuits there. At Toulouse the

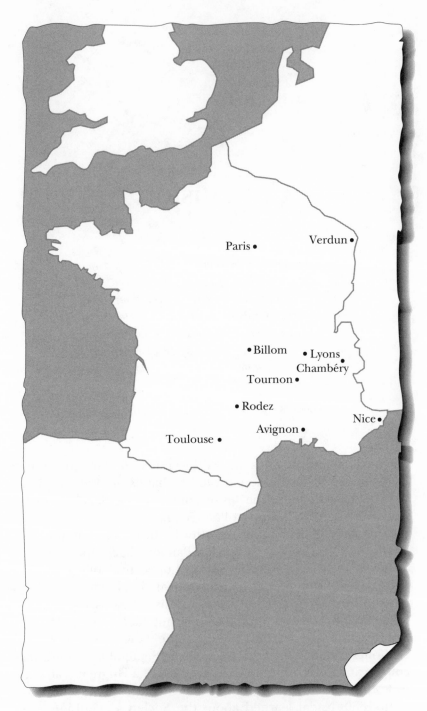

Cities in France visited by Nadal

refugees were the guests of the Benedictines. The fury of the Calvinists raged around the city during his six days there, yet Nadal's negotiations with the Jesuits led not only to the establishment of more colleges and residences but, eventually, to the creation of the province of Aquitaine in 1564.

On an excursion to the residence of Georges Cardinal d'Armagnac in Rodez, Nadal, Jiménez, and Bertrand encountered a roving band of Huguenot soldiers. For three hours the soldiers debated what to do with their captives. When they discovered that their captives were Spaniards and Jesuits, they threatened them with the gibbet. But their captain observed the law, and turned them over to the local magistrate on a charge of spying for the Spanish king. The judge dismissed the case.[2]

The visit to Rodez was a successful one, for Cardinal d'Armagnac was eager to endow Jesuit colleges in Rodez and Toulouse. Nadal accepted the foundations subject to the approval of the general, whom he hoped to see in Paris. A college was opened in Rodez in 1562 and in Toulouse in 1563. The cardinal, too, was about to depart for Paris and invited Nadal to join his well-armed entourage for the journey. Not wishing to repeat his experiences with the Huguenots, Nadal was tempted by the offer. To accept it, however, meant not visiting the colleges at Tournon and Billom, and Nadal was determined to visit the men there despite the dangers. Plans to head first to Tournon and then to Billom were altered when an unknown Benedictine monk suggested that, if the order were reversed, the journey would be much easier. This change saved the Jesuits from visiting a Tournon controlled by the cruel Baron des Adrets.[3]

The college at Billom had been the first run by the Society in France. Founded in 1556 by Guillaume du Prat, bishop of Clermont, it had grown to approximately 1200 lay students, with 25 Jesuits on the staff. Only the Jesuit college at Coimbra was larger. It had been transferred to the Society in 1561 by François Cardinal de Tournon because of his fear of Calvinist influence.[4†]
The community's numbers increased with the arrival of the

---

†4 A traditional interpretation of the Society's educational policy in France stressed the conflict with heresy. It was claimed that that struggle determined the location of the colleges. Lynn Martin and others have noted, and Bangert's study confirms, that the initiative was rarely the Society's. The establishment of a college was the response to an offer made by some dignitary. Sometimes the offer was prompted by a concern for heresy. See A. Lynn Martin, *The Jesuit Mind: The Mentality of an Elite in Early Modern France* (Ithaca, N.Y., 1988), 15–17.

Jesuits from Tournon, forced to abandon their college for a year when the town was threatened by the Huguenots.

Paschase Broët, provincial of France, walked from Paris to Billom to greet the general's visitor. Nadal spent twenty days in Billom. He visited the Jesuits of both colleges, accepted fifteen novices, and arranged the acceptance of a second college from the bishop of Clermont, which opened at Mauriac in 1563. A third foundation would be opened in Paris in 1564. In mid-May, with Broët and Jiménez as his companions, Nadal left for Paris on foot.[5]

The journey was not easy. Nadal laconically remarked that the path was infested with rebellious heretics. At Moulins they were advised to detour through Burgundy, then safely controlled by Catholics, because Huguenots were in possession of the country-side between Moulins and Paris. In danger for the entire journey because of rebellions, the three safely reached Paris on May 28, 1562. There Nadal found Frs. Polanco and Laínez, about to embark for the Council of Trent at the pope's command.

Broët, Laínez, and Nadal briefly reviewed the Society's prospects in France. At the time they were surprisingly good. The Jesuits had not been as welcome in Paris as they were in the provinces. Since the death of Ignatius, Broët and Ponce de Cogordan had sought official recognition of the Society's existence within the kingdom against opposition from the university and Parlement. Despite royal confirmation by Henry II in 1551, Francis II in 1560, and Charles IX in 1561, Parlement delayed the registration of the documents. The conflict was even discussed at the Colloquy of Poissy in 1561. Admirers of the Society such as the cardinals of Tournon, Bourbon, Lorraine, and Armagnac forced Parlement and Gallicans such as Eustache du Bellay, bishop of Paris, to compromise in late 1561. The conditions were the use of a title other than the Society of Jesus; ("Society of the College of Clermont") recognition of episcopal jurisdiction; subjection to the common law without any privileges; the renunciation of any papal privileges contrary to the jurisdiction of Parlement.

The three discussed how the "Society of the College of Clermont" could take advantage of its limited freedom. Laínez accepted the agreements negotiated by Nadal at Toulouse, Rodez, and Billom. The bishop of Clermont's third foundation opened its doors in Paris in 1564. Their discussions were brief, however, because Laínez had to set off for Trent. Nadal and Laínez traveled together into Flanders. At Tournai they parted. Laínez resumed his journey to Trent and Nadal began his visitation of the Belgian colleges.[6]

Legal recognition of the Society in the Netherlands had only been obtained through the skillful diplomacy of Pedro de Ribadeneira at the court of Philip II after he succeeded his father, Charles V. The first Jesuit college opened at Tournai in 1562. The endowment was provided by the bishop, the cathedral chapter, and the city itself. Nadal participated in the organization of its program of studies. Initially reluctant to accept boarding students because of the extra expense, he conceded that it might be necessary to protect the students from heretical influences. Nonetheless he tried to pass responsibility for the temporal welfare of the boarders either to the chapter or to some layperson. He was unsuccessful in both cases.

After fifteen days in Tournai, Nadal moved to Antwerp to hunt religious books, both Catholic and Protestant, among the city's many booksellers. These were sent to Trent for the use of Laínez and other theologians. Having spent very freely the money left by Laínez, Nadal journeyed to Louvain, where the Jesuits had been barely tolerated by the university since 1542. The scholasticate there was poorly funded and poorly governed. The rector was Adrian Adriaenssens, one of Bobodilla's original backers in the earlier constitutional struggle.

What Nadal discovered at Louvain disgusted him. The scholasticate attracted no students from the university and produced "little fruit." The rector magnified the problem. Adriaenssens refused to recognize Nadal's authority and denied the visitor's request for an account of the state of the scholasticate. Because the Constitutions did not bind under sin, the rector asserted that it was his prerogative to adapt them as he saw fit to the particular circumstances of Louvain. Nadal perhaps naively attributed the rector's unfriendliness to bad health, but for the sake of the community he advised Laínez to appoint a new rector in a way to avoid hurting the former's feelings.

While Nadal was in Louvain he continued negotiations initiated by Laínez with the duke-archbishop of Cambrai, Maximilien de Berghes, for the establishment of a college in his see. The archbishop promised to provide enough annual support for ten Jesuits, and the agreement was sealed. A college opened at

Cities in Central Europe visited by Nadal

Cambrai in May of 1563. With the completion of this transaction, Nadal departed for Germany.[7]

The Jesuit college in Cologne had been founded by Peter Canisius in 1543 as a residence for Jesuits. Between its foundation and Nadal's visitation in 1562, the community had grown from two to fifty-seven Jesuits. There were 495 students, of whom 51 were boarders. Despite the growth and success of the college, the institution remained financially unstable: it lacked a single founder and depended on the generosity of many persons for its continuation. Its problems were aggravated by hostility from other colleges in the university that were threatened by the Society's success.

During the three weeks Nadal spent in Cologne, he could not resolve the college's financial and educational problems. He did, however, fortify it internally. He threw himself into this visit with the same vigor that had characterized his Iberian visitations. Each day he addressed the community, as he sought to bring their practices into harmony with the Constitutions. Many made the Spiritual Exercises, some for the first time. Censors and admonitors were introduced into the college to aid each one's spiritual growth. The improvements were so great, one Jesuit testified, "that it might be called a new college altogether. I have never known it in so flourishing a state, blessed be God."

In a letter to the general, the rector of the college, Leonard Kessel, echoed these sentiments: "He [Nadal] remained with us three weeks and helped and heartened us enormously by his counsels and daily addresses on the Constitutions. He spoke to our boarders also warm words of encouragement. He was so well while he was here that he said he had never felt better since he left you in Rome for his travels, and this happy state of affairs he attributed to our Cologne beer. Indeed, the great charity wherewith he is consumed for the conversion of Germany makes him now in his old age take on the nature of Germans." From Cologne, Nadal and Jiménez detoured to Spa before moving to the next Jesuit college in Trier.[8] They took the waters for ten days before heavy rains made them undrinkable. Refreshed nonetheless, they journeyed to Trier.

The Jesuit college at Trier had been founded by Archbishop Johann von der Leyen and opened in 1561. At the time of Nadal's visitation, there were approximately 200 students and twenty Jesuits. By 1564 there would be 550 students. After a stay of about ten days, Nadal continued to another newly established college. The archbishop of Mainz, Daniel Brendel von Homburg, had invited the Society to establish a college in his see. Supported by the archbishop, the college opened in 1561. Enrollment was 150 students, with a Jesuit staff of nineteen. Nadal spent most of September in Mainz. After a stop in Frankfurt to purchase more Protestant books, he traveled to Augsburg via Würzburg.[9]

There was no Jesuit college in Augsburg at the time, but only a small residence of five men. During Nadal's brief stay there he secured enough financial support from Otto Cardinal Truchsess von Waldburg of Augsburg to arrange for its elevation from residential to collegiate status. Because of the plague, Nadal did not visit the college Peter Canisius had opened in Munich in 1559–60; instead he traveled to Ingolstadt in late October. The Society had been active in Ingolstadt since the mid-1540s.

By the end of that decade, Peter Canisius, Claude Jay, and Alfonso Salmerón were exhorting Duke Wilhelm of Bavaria to establish a Jesuit college as the best means for the prevention of Protestant influence at the university in Ingolstadt. Despite the support the Society received from some of the duke's advisors, Wilhelm hesitated. The duke's death in March of 1550 postponed the project. But the Jesuits persisted, and appealed to the new duke, Albrecht V, who eventually proved a generous benefactor to colleges established at Ingolstadt and Munich. His generosity, however, was not without strings. Even before he provided funds for a Jesuit college, the duke had vehemently protested the removal of individual Jesuits from the university. Then, shortly after Albrecht succeeded his father, he complained to the pope about the removal of Claude Jay. Now that he had invested money in the Society, his complaints were more vociferous.

When Nadal met Duke Albrecht to discuss financial arrangements, the duke refused to permit Nadal to make any changes among the personnel of the college. Attempts to explain to his highness that the establishment of new colleges demanded the transfer of more experienced men to them left the duke unmoved. Because the Society could not afford to alienate one of its most powerful supporters in Germany, Nadal did not press the matter.[10]

The next stop was Landsberg. There Nadal, Peter Canisius, Theodoric Canisius, Peter's half-brother and rector of the college in Munich, and Nicolas Lanoy, rector of Ingolstadt, met Duke Albrecht's chancellor, Simon Thaddeus Eck, to discuss an increase in the endowment of the colleges at Munich and Ingolstadt. After the departure of Eck, the four Jesuits discussed the Society's prospects in Bavaria. Their decision was a strategy of prudence. In the years immediately before the arrival of Nadal, the Society had opened colleges at Mainz, Trier, Munich, Innsbruck, and Dillingen. Henceforth expansion would be more controlled.

This caution may have resulted from a fear that mediocrity would follow more rapid growth, or because of an unwillingness by benefactors such as the duke of Bavaria to allow the transfer of experienced teachers. There were too few competent instructors. The immediate need was filled by importation of Jesuits from the south. A number of scholastics were taken from the Roman College in the middle of their studies and sent to Germany for a few years. Nonetheless these scholastics had little or no preparation. Growth was slower, and only two more colleges were established in Germany in the 1560s: Würzburg and Speyer, both in 1567.[11]

On November 10, 1562, Nadal arrived in Innsbruck. The Jesuit college there had opened its doors in December of 1561, even though it still lacked a solid financial base. The Holy Roman Emperor had not yet provided a permanent foundation. The Jesuits there numbered twenty and the students 150. For three weeks, Nadal reorganized the college and introduced updated rules and regulations forwarded from Rome. Because he was still unable to travel to Munich, he decided to visit Trent to see Laínez at the council. He arrived there on December 15 and remained for two months.[12]

The third and final session of the Council of Trent had opened on January 18, 1562, and was adjourned on December 4, 1563. Nadal became the fourth Jesuit—the others were Salmerón, Peter Canisius, and Juan de Polanco—to hold a consultative vote: they could participate in all theological deliberations but could not cast a vote for the final decree. There is no record of either the conferences attended by Nadal or of the deliberations in which he participated. Historians such as Batllori and Pate think, however, that his involvment can be detected in the removal of Ramón Lull's name from the Index of Prohibited Books.

Involvement at the council was not Nadal's only occupation. During the sojourn he continued to write on the Society's Institute and to compose defenses of the new order against the attacks of Lutherans. In discussions with Laínez, plans for the German provinces were formulated and approved. And Nadal's links with the Spanish and Portuguese provinces continued as the two men reviewed the promotion to final vows of Jesuits from those areas.[13]

Nadal departed for Vienna on February 10, but his journey was interrupted at Innsbruck by a dispute that threatened to destroy the council at Trent. The topics for this session of Trent had been chosen with care. Afraid of both the emperor and the French, the delegates had decided to limit the council's initial concerns to twelve articles of reform.

A deceptively innocent question regarding episcopal residence (the requirement that bishops live in their diocese) ignited the powder keg. Was episcopal residence required by divine law or by ecclesiastical law? Lurking behind the question were two opposed concepts of the very nature of the Church. Did bishops hold their power of jurisdiction directly from God? If so, what of the papal claims of universal jurisdiction in the Church? On the other hand, if the plenitude of power had been given to Peter and his successors, all episcopal authority must flow from it; bishops, therefore, received their jurisdiction immediately from the pope and only mediately from God. The French and Spanish factions at the council forged an alliance in favor of divinely ordained episcopal powers. Their opponents were curial cardinals who opposed any challenge to papal authority. Holy Roman Emperor Ferdinand I flirted with the Franco-Spanish faction. His opposition to the curia, however, stemmed not from the theological nature of episcopal authority but from the pragmatic realization that all real reform was blocked by vested interests in the curia.[14]

The dispute threatened to paralyze the proceedings. In an attempt to refocus the council, Ferdinand's ambassadors at Trent submitted the emperor's *Libellus Reformationis,* which detailed the abuses then plaguing the Church. Any correction of these abuses must begin with the reform of the papacy and the curia. Echoes of conciliarism vibrated among the assembly: the papacy was to be subjected to reformation by the council. Efforts to persuade Ferdinand to withdraw the document failed.

In the beginning of February 1563, the emperor summoned four theologians to Innsbruck to discuss the next step. Peter Canisius was the only one of them opposed to stronger imperial intervention. Cardinal Delfino, papal nuncio to the emperor, sought support for Canisius' minority report and it was he who co-opted Nadal upon his arrival in Innsbruck. The two Jesuits had the unenviable task of trying to convince the emperor that the reform of the papacy and the papal curia was the work of the pope and the cardinals, and that—despite recent contrary evidence such as the elevation of an eighteen-year-old Gonzaga and a twelve-year-old de Medici to the purple—there were sincere attempts to reform.[15] They failed.

Two letters were sent to the pope by the emperor in early March. He protested his loyalty but insisted that his program for reform be placed before the council and that the pope prevent the curia from interfering with the activities of the council. Shortly thereafter Cardinal Morone was dispatched from Rome to discuss the matter with Ferdinand. Through this personal intercession, Ferdinand was convinced of the pope's good intentions for reform and, as a result, the emperor abandoned his plan to visit Trent. The future of the council was left in the hands of the papal legates.[16]

The opposition of Canisius and Nadal to the emperor's proposed reforms did not harm the relationship between Ferdinand and the Society. He could have destroyed the Society's efforts in Germany with one command, but he did not, despite various rumors of his displeasure, and he continued to favor the Society. The emperor met Nadal before the Jesuit's departure from Innsbruck. He promised to continue his annual contribution to the Roman College and added that he had written to the pope to urge that the multiplication of Jesuit colleges was the most effective means for the reformation of Germany. As proof, the negotiations for a Jesuit college in Innsbruck were completed: Ferdinand provided an endowment and a building large enough to accommodate twenty-five to thirty men.[17]

Nadal's next destination was the Jesuit college in Vienna. Opened in 1552 with Claude Jay as its first superior, the Viennese college had approximately four hundred students by 1565. The college possessed a large church and the Jesuits lived in a former Carmelite monastery. Ferdinand provided the greater part of the endowment, but a community of twenty-four poor students were supported by Spanish merchants. These students were permitted to attend the college if they promised to become priests.[18]

Over three separate stays, Nadal spent nearly fourteen weeks at this college. Besides his usual concerns, Nadal instructed the college to use its press to print 1500 correct Latin editions of the *Spiritual Exercises*. Although they had been printed earlier in Rome, the few copies that remained did not satisfy the demand. The new edition would be distributed equitably among the provinces.[19]

The emperor's absence from Vienna prevented a necessary discussion of the Viennese college's foundation. Until the arrival of Ferdinand from Innsbruck, Nadal decided to visit the other Jesuit colleges in the area. A small college had been established in Tyrnau in Hungary (now Trnava, Czechoslovakia) on the Turkish frontier in 1561. The ten Jesuits there conducted classes for a hundred students. The archbishop of Esztergóm, Miklós Oláh, had invited the Society to erect the college. He, the emperor, and the local Catholics provided the alms that kept the college's doors barely open.[20] During his visit from April 21 to May 4, Nadal corrected the curriculum and attempted to improve the finances. He then returned to Vienna but, since the emperor was still in Innsbruck, he continued to Prague.

The emperor was responsible for this college also. It was he who had originally proposed that the Society open one in a city that was no longer Catholic but predominantly Lutheran and Hussite. And it had been Nadal who was instrumental in the implementation of the emperor's wishes when he sent Canisius to open the college in 1555. The Society received from the emperor a large abandoned Dominican monastery and an endowment sufficient for fifty men. There were, however, only thirty Jesuits in the college in 1563. Non-Catholics were accepted in the college on the condition that they participate in all catechetical classes and religious services. Nadal was astonished how many parents agreed to these stipulations for the sake of their children's education. He changed the rector and gave various exhortations during his stay in Prague from May 18 to June 16 and then returned once more to Vienna.[21] He was finally successful in arranging a meeting with the emperor on this third visit.

For two months, Nadal conducted a thorough visitation of the college and was impressed with the work done there in the preservation of Catholicism and the battle against heresy. Among the college's students were many boys of noble birth, especially Poles. Besides their work in the college, a few members of the community lectured on Thomas Aquinas at the university. Yet, despite the good work being done, Nadal found many in the college depressed because of the plague, the threat of the Turks, and the seasonal eastern wind. He also thought the community's own excessive austerities were factors in the depression. In one exhortation to moderation, Nadal explained that because they were Germans he did not wish to burden them with such ascetical practices as hairshirts and disciplines— practices that were more natural to Italians and Spaniards than to the Germans. This injudicious comment agitated many, who then claimed that they were as stalwart as any in the Society. Generally, however, the Jesuits testified to the skill with which Nadal handled the community: he could console, encourage, exhort, and restrain.[22] One problem, however, could not be solved easily: the rector, Juan de Vitoria. Vitoria's eccentricities predated his entrance into the Society. In Rome in 1549, shortly after Vitoria made the Spiritual Exercises but before he joined the Society, he was distracted by the carnival outside his window. The sounds of lewd songs and the sights of drinking and dancing mobs filled him with righteous anger. Stripping naked, he ran through the streets, lashing himself with a heavy scourge so badly that he left a trail of blood.

In Vienna, Vitoria's activities were more subdued but no less zealous. His energy was boundless, but in his missionary zest he was often insensitive to others. A fiery preacher, Vitoria was the darling of many nobles and and in danger of becoming another Araoz. Moreover, his austere regulations and his constant longing for Italy made life unbearable for his community. Since Vitoria could not be in Italy, he would introduce as many Italian customs as he could into Vienna. Despite the poverty of the Jesuit colleges, he arranged for part of their income to be sent to the colleges in Italy. He even demanded that eggs and vegetables be prepared in the Italian way, and that the weaker

German and Hungarian wines be diluted as was the custom with the stronger Italian wines.

Peter Canisius had tried to deal with Vitoria; it was left to Nadal to solve the problem. Because of Vitoria's character and high-placed friends, any solution must be diplomatic. Nadal's resolution was similar to that used in Spain for Araoz. He elevated Vitoria to a new position that oversaw the temporal administration of the colleges in whose improvement Vitoria's influential friends could assist. But he was dethroned as rector, and Nadal judged he should never again have that type of jurisdiction.[23]

Nadal made a number of administrative changes also. He had received a promise from the emperor that his endowment of the Viennese college would be increased and made permanent. Laínez approved at this time Nadal's proposal for a division of the province of Upper Germany. The colleges of Ingolstadt, Munich, Innsbruck, and Dillingen remained in the province of Upper Germany. The new province of Austria consisted of the colleges in Vienna, Tyrnau, and Prague. Peter Canisius remained provincial of Upper Germany and Nicolas Lanoy was named provincial of Austria. The plague in Munich had finally abated, so Nadal left Vienna for Bavaria on September 4.[24]

The small college in Munich opened by Canisius in 1559–60 had grown to an institution that educated two hundred students with a Jesuit staff of twenty-four. Because of the increase in vocations, a novitiate had been erected nearby. Nadal was pleased with the Society's efforts. By means of their sermons and lectures, the Jesuits preserved Catholicism in a pivotal area. So pleased was Albrecht V that he added to the foundations of the colleges in Munich and Ingolstadt. He bequeathed annual rents to each of the colleges, sufficient for the maintenance of twenty-five Jesuits. Nadal stayed in Munich three weeks. Besides his usual chores, during this stay he had the added duty of preparing the Belgian Olivier Mannaerts for the post of visitor to France. Not surprisingly, Nadal gave the new man a number of detailed instructions concerning the execution of the visit, and pedagogical regulations for implementation in the Jesuit colleges in France.

Nadal traveled from Munich to Innsbruck in early October. Here he found the fresh recruits sent from Rome to work in the Jesuit colleges. The presence of the plague had made their passage even more difficult, because a strict watch was kept to prevent the entry of anyone from infected areas. A number of Jesuits reached Innsbruck only to be denied access to the college by a fearful rector. Nadal met the men and distributed them to the colleges in Flanders, Germany, and Austria, especially to the new foundation in Dillingen.[25]

Otto Cardinal Truchsess von Waldburg, who had earlier rebuffed Jesuit requests to endow houses for the Society, had recently approached the Society with an important proposal. He had founded a college at Dillingen in 1549 and had arranged for its elevation to university status in 1554. Because of the persistent problem of finding qualified professors, the cardinal considered the possibility of asking the Society to establish a college in the university, and of turning the university itself over to the Society for management. A few months before he made the proposal, the cardinal had written to King Sigismund of Poland: "It is plain and obvious to everybody that the brethren of the Society of Jesus are the most diligent and skillful of all laborers in the vineyard of the Lord. I am therefore consumed with longing past belief to establish a college of that Society in Dillingen, in order thus to protect the flock committed to me from the wolves around them. Poverty, at present, is the chief obstacle to my hopes and the chief danger to my people. I would, then, beg and beseech Your Majesty to favor with royal bounty an excellent design which will bring glory to God and salvation to my flock."[26]

Nadal was sent by Laínez to accompany Canisius investigating the site at Dillingen and discussing the proposal. Neither Laínez nor Canisius was impressed by the offer. Laínez wondered where the men would come from; Canisius was all too familiar with the cardinal's extravagant promises. What Nadal and Canisius found at Dillingen confirmed these suspicions. The house intended for the Jesuit community was small and incommodious, without a garden or a chapel. Such omens were inauspicious, but the project continued because of the importance of Germany. After further negotiations, the cardinal promised to bestow upon the university annual rents totaling 3000 florins. There were eight Jesuits, recent arrivals from Rome, on the staff when the college opened its doors in October. Upon his arrival from Innsbruck, Nadal supervised the opening sessions and organized the college's program of studies.[27]

From Dillingen, Nadal returned to Munich and to Ingolstadt for brief visits before continuing to Trent in early December. He arrived in Trent a few days after the council finished. Laínez's original desire to have Nadal visit the Italian colleges was altered. Because of the number of regulations and instructions Nadal had left in Germany and throughout the Jesuit world, the general realized it was important that Nadal return to Rome with him and prepare definitive editions of these regulations. The party of Salmerón, Laínez, Polanco, and Nadal arrived in Rome on February 12, 1564.

In a letter to Araoz, Nadal summarized his impressions: "Each province and each college I stayed in seemed to me at the time the one I loved best of all. But I can say now that Germany comes first with me, because its need is so great. I find myself moved with pity for that noble nation, so miserably deceived by pestilent and infernal impostors. Other nations in which the Society exists have alternative means of spiritual assistance, but in Germany we are practically the only ones to help, and, if we fail, there is, humanly speaking, no remedy left. It is not only the Catholics who say this. The heretics say it too in their own fashion by atrocious libels against us and threats of our extermination. . . . For the love of God our Lord I beg all of you in Spain to help the reviled and persecuted Church in Germany with your holy desires and prayers and sacrifices; and I entreat superiors by their regard for the Constitutions of the Society which bind us to render most assistance where the need is greatest to use every means in their power for the succor of Germany. So will the good God help us and the whole Society, increasing in it His holy gifts unto the greater service and glory of His Divine Majesty."[28]

Nadal had set out from Rome for his visitation to Spain, Portugal, France, Germany, and Austria on November 18, 1560. He spent more than three years in the execution of this commission. He was prevented, as we have seen, from visiting all the Spanish colleges, but he made extended stops at the colleges in Portugal. At each of the colleges he promulgated the Constitutions and drafted more specific instructions whose implementation he left to the Spanish and the Portuguese provincials. These instructions, resented by many, introduced a uniformity throughout the Society based on a Roman model. Throughout Spain and Portugal, Nadal brought a stability to provinces that were expanding rapidly. No subsequent visitor to this area had to introduce such sweeping institutional structures; they had only the simpler task of overseeing the observation of Nadal's reforms.[29]

Nadal encountered different problems north of the Alps. Many benefactors sought Jesuit assistance and wished to endow colleges. Institutional expansion had to be restricted because of a lack of Jesuits. Offers had to be refused until the Society had an adequate supply of personnel. North of the Alps the Society risked spreading itself too thin, a problem that not even the importation of Jesuits from the south could stem. In the haste to produce a sufficient number of Jesuits to fill the colleges, many did not complete a proper period of training; as a result, there were problems with obedience, competence, and apostasy. Tighter control had to be established over formation.

The proliferation of colleges created another problem: there were few experienced rectors in the north. As provincial, Peter Canisius should have visited the colleges under his jurisdiction and supervised the efforts of the rectors. Cardinal Truchsess, however, had chosen him as cathedral preacher in Augsburg, which often prevented him from leaving the city and exercising such authority. As a result, the inexperienced rectors lacked supervision and men such as Vitoria governed idiosyncratically. Much more work was needed to regularize practices in Germany and to implement more fully the Institute. Nadal would have to make one more visit.[30]

Nadal remained in Rome for two years. Once again he was superintendent of the Roman College. During his stay he was also assistant to the general for Germany and Austria and, for a time in July of 1564, visitor of the German College. In the midst of these activities, he still found time to write a defense of the Society against the accusations of the bishop of Oppido Mamertina, Ascanio Cesarini, and to continue work on two dialogues on the Society's Institute.[31]

On January 19, 1565, Laínez died. On the twentieth, the professed fathers in Rome gathered and elected Francis Borgia vicar general despite his previous problems with Nadal. The Second General Congregation opened on June 21. On July 2, *dies meae crucis* ("the day of my crucifixion") as Borgia himself described it, he was elected third general of the Society by a majority of thirty-one votes out of the thirty-nine cast.[32] With the general's election completed, the congregation turned to other business, much of which involved problems that Nadal had addressed.

Worried by the rapid expansion of the Society's commitments, the congregation recommended more moderation in the future. Instead of opening new colleges, the current ones should be strengthened. Although the congregation conceded the general's right to accept any new college proferred, the fathers suggested that any accepted "should be of such quality and location and circumstance that they would appear to have great promise for the good of the Church." So concerned were the fathers about this problem that they refused the honor of assuming control of the University of Valencia. Another decree authorized the establishment of a novitiate in each province, where the novices could be "well tested for two years, not in literary studies, but in the pursuit of mortification and spiritual progress."

Questions were raised in the congregation about the rules and regulations left by Nadal. A committee of six men, including Nadal himself, was appointed to study the issue. After their deliberation, the committee decided that the more general rules that had been extrapolated from the Constitutions be kept intact. Nadal was asked to reduce these to a single edition. All others would be examined by Borgia and, if possible, abbreviated. It was also decided that these general rules be considered directives and not obligations. Borgia and Nadal finished their edition of the specific rules by April of 1568, but Nadal was still working on his edition of general regulations when he died some twelve years later.[33] The congregation ended on September 3. A few months later Cardinal Truchsess was asking Borgia to send a few theologians to assist him at the important imperial Diet of Augsburg. Nadal was chosen.

The generalate of Borgia was one of cautious consolidation. An ascetic himself, Borgia established strict regulations for every office in the Society. Nadal's earlier suspicions that Borgia did not fully understand the Institute of the Society were shared by many. Complaints that he was too much of a rigorist were common, as customs more applicable to the monastic life were introduced into the Society. The spiritual freedom established by Ignatius was reduced through the requirement of longer periods of prayer. The flexibility valued by Loyola was vanishing.

To oversee the whole Society more carefully, Borgia introduced a new type of congregation into the Society's institutional structure: the congregation of procurators. It was to be a triennial meeting of representatives from every province. Its primary role was discussion of the need for a general congregation, but it was also a valuable way for the general to ascertain the practices of his men throughout the world.[34]

Consolidation was also the concern of Nadal's second trans-Alpine visitation. The regularization of northern practices Nadal had initiated on his first visit was to continue. He was to introduce more approved procedures and to strengthen the practices he had earlier established. The near occasion of Nadal's visit was Truchsess' request. Another important imperial diet had been scheduled for Augsburg in 1566 to discuss the implementation of the decrees of the Council of Trent. In a letter to Cardinal Truchsess, Peter Canisius urged him to petition the pope to send both a legate and also theological advisors to the diet. "I am afraid," Canisius wrote, "that if we neglect the opportunity offered by the diet there will not be another chance of commending the council to these lands. I can see a struggle coming, prepared by the devil to weaken the authority of the council at Augsburg, and I fear, and have good reason for fearing, that some so-called Catholic princes may put forward fresh proposals of conciliation between Catholics and Protestants."[35]

The new pope, Pius V, did send a papal legate, Giovanni Francesco Cardinal Commendone, and also asked Borgia to send six Jesuit theologians to assist the legate. The general could not spare that many but he did offer three: Canisius, Diego de Ledesma, and Nadal as their superior. Nadal was also appointed visitor to the provinces of Austria, Upper Germany, Belgium, and the Rhine (the last two erected in 1564). The provinces of France and Aquitaine were later added to the list. Interestingly, the authority granted by Borgia's letter of appointment was less than that given to Nadal by his predecessors, Ignatius Loyola and Laínez; although Nadal was allowed to use his discretion, important decisions should be relayed to Rome.[36]

Ledesma and Nadal, accompanied again by the loyal Jiménez, left Rome on February 7, 1566; Peter Canisius welcomed them to Augsburg on March 6. The next day the three theologians began a series of meetings with Cardinal Truchsess, the apostolic delegate, the Spanish ambassador, and the Catholic princes. Despite his fondness for the Society, Emperor Maximilian tried to prevent the arrival of the Jesuits and, having failed, did not appreciate their activity in the city. For the presence of Catholics, Lutherans, and Calvinists in the city created an atmosphere of religious rivalry that often bordered on the absurd. The Lutheran Duke Christoph of Württemberg and his entourage rented a house across the street from the residence of the Jesuit theologians. Some of the duke's retinue took to throwing bricks into the Jesuits' garden whenever they saw a Jesuit walking there. This led to a fight between a German Jesuit laybrother and the duke's cook. Some Lutherans sabotaged the cathedral's holy water font with coal-dust; Catholics left Mass with darkened faces. During Lent, Protestants gathered outside the cathedral with meat and sweets, which they devoured as the Catholics entered for Mass. Both the duke of Württemberg and the duke of Saxony ended such harassment through strict control of their retainers.[37]

There were two major issues the emperor wanted addressed when the diet opened on March 23: the renewed threat of the Turks on his eastern borders and the religious peace of Augsburg of 1555. The second had to be reexamined because of recent changes. In light of the recent decrees of the Council of Trent, could Catholics continue to assent to this treaty as they had done in 1555, 1557, and 1559? The conversion of Friedrich III, elector of Palatine, from Lutheranism to Calvinism raised a problem of the legal status of Calvinism. The Peace of Augsburg had legal force between Roman Catholics and adherents of the Confession of Augsburg. No recognition had been granted to Calvinism.

Before the religious topics were addressed, however, the diet discussed funds for a new war against the Turks. Nadal took advantage of the diet's discussion of military expeditions to excuse himself from Augsburg and to visit the Jesuits at Dillingen on April 16. Before his departure he promised to return to the diet whenever the legate needed him, so his stay in Dillingen was brief. As Nadal was hearing the confession of one of the Jesuits, he received word that Commendone demanded his presence in Augsburg as soon as possible. Obedient "to the letter," Nadal did not even complete the sacrament but returned immediately. The diet had approved funds for the Turkish war;[38]† now it would address religious questions.[39]

The elector Palatine agitated for an extension of the religious peace to include the Calvinists. He failed. The diet confirmed the religious settlement but refused to draw the legal implications of Friedrich's stand. Nevertheless, a fundamental question remained: could Catholics accept the peace? The papacy had consistently attacked the peace as a recognition of heresy. One of Commendone's charges from Pope Pius was rejection of the peace by the Catholic princes. But because the Catholic princes, both ecclesiastical and secular, did not want the civil disorder that would result from the repudiation of the religious peace, they were reluctant to follow the pope's wishes. The pope compromised: if renewal of the Peace of Augsburg harmed any of the doctrinal decrees of the Council of Trent in any way, the papal legate was to lodge an official protest and leave the diet. The entire issue rested on a possible conflict between Trent and the Peace of Augsburg. Commendone asked his theological advisers to analyze the issue.

Nadal hastily returned from Dillingen to debate the matter with Canisius, Ledesma, an auditor of the Rota, Scipione Lancillotti, and an English theologian, Nicolas Sander. The issue was debated for fifteen days and nights. The Jesuits argued that the Peace of Augsburg, although it damaged religious discipline, did not conflict with any doctrinal decrees, simply because the peace said nothing at all about doctrine. Sander agreed with them, but Lancillotti hesitated. The legate forwarded both opinions to Rome for the pope to judge. The three Jesuits then wrote to Borgia to present their case to the pope. All sides begged the pope to accept this solution. Pius finally agreed, as long as the Catholic princes formally recognized the decrees of Trent. This they did. The diet ended at the end of May, with the German Catholics in a stronger position insofar as they had successfully resisted all Protestant attempts to repeal the "ecclesiastical reservation" in the Peace of Augsburg.[40]

---

†38 Canisius and Nadal wrote to Rome to urge Borgia to beseech the pope to subsidize the Turkish war. The emperor's agents in Rome learned that the Jesuits were secretly promoting his interests. This knowledge, of course, kept him well disposed toward the Society. See Brodrick, *Peter Canisius*, 646–47.

The experience at Augsburg affected Nadal's outlook. His letters to Borgia repeat the necessity of moderation and charity in any dealings with the northern nations because of their great affliction and extreme need. The rigor of the law must be tempered for them. In any future negotiations with such nations, Nadal suggested, the pope should seek the advice not of the curial Roman officials but of those who resided in those countries and "who knew from practical experience the dispositions of their rulers and peoples, and who bore a special love to them." The extent of the transformation would become apparent during his visitation. On May 30, 1566, he left Augsburg for Munich.[41]

There were twenty-five Jesuits in the college at Munich with approximately 350 students. During the sixteen days Nadal was there, he heard the confessions of all the Jesuits, presided over the renovation of vows, and examined all aspects of life. The detailed instructions left upon his departure varied from suggestions for the sermons of Jesuit preachers to prohibitions against dining outside the community unless it was clear that such a dinner would produce spiritual fruit. Individual Jesuits were given specific assignments and exemptions. Among the most curious instruction was the command that the "magical apparatus" in the room of Fr. Georg Schorich be destroyed because "we should not use that sort of thing."[42]

Other guidelines were more significant. Nadal wanted the preachers to exhort their congregations to frequent confession and communion, and to more prayer in general. Since it was customary in Munich to abstain on the vigils of a number of feasts, Nadal wished that the Jesuits follow that local tradition regardless of the customs of their own countries. Among practices he wanted started were the introduction of the Spiritual Exercises and domestic experiments for the novices, and the establishment of lectures in cases of conscience. Indeed, he recommended that the duke should be approached with a suggestion that attendance at these lectures be made a prerequisite for ecclesiastical promotions and benefices.

The last is a most interesting suggestion, especially in view of the problems the duke was already causing. As benefactor, Duke Albrecht took an active interest in the affairs of the college and especially in the selection of the court preachers. One attempt by the Society to change a preacher was resisted by the duke. Nadal again encountered a danger he had first faced in Sicily: the Society's loss of freedom in the face of secular interference. All Nadal could do at this stage was hope that the duke would gradually learn the Society's Institute and, as a result, leave the governance of the Society's institutions alone.[43]

Ingolstadt was Nadal's next stop. The Jesuit college there was comparable in size to that in Munich, but its government was much more difficult because Jesuits from the college served on the philosophical and theological faculties of the university. Since these men were obliged to observe the regulations of the university, a common discipline was difficult. Nonetheless, Nadal instructed the Jesuits there to observe the one-and-a-half hours of daily prayer—a requirement recently introduced by Borgia.[44] He also advised the rector to propose a catalogue of mortifications to be practiced outside of term. Many of the other instructions left by Nadal concerned the spiritual welfare of the community and its members.

A Welshman, Vincent Powell, had been in the Society since 1562 but had never made the Spiritual Exercises.[45] Nadal instructed that Powell be given the Exercises in an abbreviated form, both for Powell's spiritual development and so that he could give others the Exercises in the future. Perhaps prompted by complaints about the food, Nadal insisted on better, more sanitary preparation. He especially drew the rector's attention to beer left in the refectory overnight. As a result of this neglect the beer became warm and could harm the men.[46]

On June 27, after a stay of ten days, Nadal left Ingolstadt for Dillingen. On the way he called at the Jesuit residence in Augsburg. The community of seven men exercised various spiritual ministries in the city. Though the community was not a college, Nadal introduced into it the regular daily routine common to Jesuit colleges. He wanted grace at meals, reading at table, and regular times for meals and prayers. Priests were to celebrate Mass daily; nonpriests were to receive communion at least weekly. No Jesuit was to leave the residence without the permission of the superior and without a companion. No one outside the Society was to reside in the house, and no woman was to be admitted into the house. Nadal also urged caution whenever a preacher spoke on usury; a few years earlier, the strict teachings of a few Jesuits against usury sparked a controversy, and he did not want a repeat performance. The crowning achievement of the short visit was Canisius' replacement as cathedral preacher. Freed from the obligations of that office, Canisius could now visit the Jesuit colleges and residences under his jurisdiction.[47]

Nadal continued his journey to Dillingen in early July. The Jesuit college there had grown from its inauspicious foundation to a community of twenty-eight men with a student body between 350 and 400. Despite its apparent prosperity, the college remained a problem. Ever since the foundation, Peter Canisius had sought to stabilize the college's foundation, a task made almost impossible by the evasiveness of Cardinal Truchsess. Nor were finances the only problem. One master at Dillingen devoted much time and energy to arguing against the Immaculate Conception. The remainder of his time he devoted to the collection of amorous poems of ancient writers, which he then used to shock his brethren. There was much work for Nadal at Dillingen.

The first job he tackled was the creation of a permanent financial contract to solve the college's and the university's debts. The cardinal was the problem. Because of his own financial problems, he was very reluctant to grant rents permanently to the Jesuit college. And the continuous opposition of his cathedral chapter to his transfer of the university to the Society aggravated the cardinal's grief. A third reason for the ongoing failure to reach a definitive financial settlement was the cardinal's unwillingness to relinquish his right to intervene directly in the institutions. At length, however, an agreement was finally reached between the cardinal, Nadal, and Canisius. The Society assumed unconditional control of the college and the university, but the Society was not allowed to move either institution. The cardinal promised a total of 3000 florins in annual rents—as his earlier agreement had stipulated—but the Jesuits would settle for 2000 florins until the cardinal's financial position improved.

Nadal insisted that the spiritual and academic dimensions of the Jesuit community received equal attention. The spiritual prefects of the college should not only hear confessions but also instruct the students in prayer and the spiritual life, lest the Society be accused of impeding their spiritual progress and disposition toward the Society. The students ought to be instructed in Christian doctrine and obliged to attend daily Mass; they should also make a monthly confession. They should be taught the importance of a daily examination of conscience and daily recitation of the rosary or of the Marian hours. Every fifteenth day there should be an exhortation to piety. No one was to possess heretical books. Indeed, Nadal demanded that Borgia's recent decree on novel opinions in philosophy and theology be observed. Two theologians, Jerónimo de Torres and Alfonso de Pisa, were assigned the task of writing against Lutheran attacks on Catholicism. The former had been cooperating with Canisius in the composition of *Confessio Augustiniana,* a refutation of the Lutheran *Confessio Augustana,* based on the writings of Augustine. Nadal authorized the completion of this work, which was printed at Dillingen the following year.[48]

Before his departure, Nadal arranged a meeting with Canisius and the rectors of the colleges at Munich and Ingolstadt, Paul Hoffaeus and Martin Lebenstein, to discuss the Society's prospects. Two major problems loomed: the paucity of novices and scholastics, and the continued interference of college founders. The lack of men resulted in a frequent reshuffling of professors, which neither pleased the founders nor furthered the education of the students. In this context the distribution of the Jesuits coming from Rome had to be determined. The importation of Jesuits, however, was only a temporary solution: more students had to be attracted to the Society. Each Jesuit should advertise the Society to any student who seemed suited to its style of life. Nadal was not simply looking for the most intelligent students; he thought even men of inferior ability could play an important role in the Society's work in Germany. If vocations improved, though, there would be a lack of money for the support of novices. Nadal and Canisius approached the Dominican archbishop of Sorrento, Giulio Pavesi, who was visiting Dillingen. They begged him to assist their efforts to persuade the pope to endow a Jesuit novitiate, so that these vocations would be saved.

The second problem was even more difficult. Nobles such as Duke Albrecht, and cardinals such as Truchsess, assumed involvement in their foundations as a prerogative of the benefactor. The Jesuits saw it as interference, and sought ways to liberate their colleges without insulting their benefactors. On July 22, Nadal and Jiménez departed Dillingen for the Austrian province. They were accompanied by six Jesuits sent to teach in the eastern colleges.[49]

The trip down the Danube was uneventful in comparison with Nadal's first journey to Vienna in 1555. The travelers arrived on the twenty-seventh and remained there sixteen days. Vienna was an exotic city. Besides Germans, Hungarians, Bohemians, and Poles, there were Spanish, French, and Italians. Since the community usually provided men for the spiritual needs of each nationality, there was great diversity among the forty Jesuits in the community. Nadal again followed his customary routine of general confessions and exhortations, meetings with each man, and a renovation of vows. He was generally satisfied with what he saw. Nonetheless he had a number of instructions for the college's improvement.

With regard to the community, Nadal reminded the Jesuits of the Society's Rules, especially of the prohibition of one Jesuit entering the room of another without the superior's permission. Benediction should be shorter and grace at meals uniform with the rest of the Society. Major feasts should be celebrated by the community alone, without externs. As to dinners with non-Jesuits, Nadal permitted the occasional meal with a friend or a nobleman as long as the superior's approval had been obtained. It was better, however, not to dine with women, even nobles. The absence of frequent conferences on cases of conscience distressed Nadal and he wanted that corrected. During his first visitation, Nadal had been distressed by the chanting of the divine office; church services continued to concern him. For the sake of simplicity he ordered that no organs, trumpets, and so forth be used to accompany singing in church. And because the performance of marriages and the administration of extreme unction were the ministries of parish priests, Nadal did not want any member of the Society to perform them.

Nadal's interest in the religious formation of the students was likewise obvious. The colleges were intended for Catholics, but a non-Catholic might be admitted for a time if he promised to observe the rules and to participate in all religious services. More diligent care should be taken that pious religious habits were inculcated in the students. To be more effective teachers, Nadal wanted the Jesuits who did not know the language of the region to learn it. A number of men were reassigned during Nadal's stay. Nicolas Lanoy completed his three-year term as provincial and was named rector of the college at Innsbruck. The rector of the Viennese college, Lorenzo Maggio, succeeded

Lanoy and was instructed to start his own visitation of the province.[50]

Nadal left Vienna with the new provincial on August 13, 1566. Their destination was Tyrnau. The small community of eight or nine faced a bleak future there. Because of irregular rents, finances were precarious; the Jesuits also lacked adequate housing and a church. Few students attended the college, and there was unceasing rivalry between the Jesuit school and the other colleges in the city. During the three or four days Nadal was there, he held out hope to the men that the situation would improve. He exhorted them to greater fidelity to the Institute, and he heard their confessions. Because their vows had been renewed only recently, he did not repeat that ceremony. The newly appointed rector, Peter Hernáth, was directed to approach Miklós Oláh, the archbishop of Esztergóm, about the college's foundation. Apparently he had no success, because Borgia dissolved the college in June of 1567.[51]

Nadal's and Maggio's next destination was Olmütz in Moravia (now Olomouc, Czechoslovakia); on their journey they encountered numerous soldiers on the way to the eastern wars. Bishop Wilhelm Prusinowsky had invited the Society to establish a college in Olmütz in 1565. Because of the shortage of men, the Austrian provincial could send only three to start a few classes. Nadal's visit would decide the future of the inchoate college. Neither he nor Maggio was predisposed to its continuation. Their reluctance vanished upon their reception. The bishop, the cathedral canons, the parents, and the students were so enthusiastic that they won over the two Jesuits.

Nadal was torn between popular demands and official restrictions. Eventually he agreed that the Society would transform the two grammar classes into a regular school, but he would not yet commit the Society to the establishment of a large college. The bishop promised an annual revenue for the initial endowment, and Nadal promised to send seven more Jesuits from Vienna and Prague.

Even before the college was in full swing Nadal was instructing the Jesuits on its operation. He repeated regulations he had established at other colleges. Male visitors to the college were to be controlled and women were not to pass beyond the college's doors. Each Jesuit was charged with supervision of the students in Christian piety, moral probity, and sound learning—for the greater glory of God; anything that impeded progress in these areas was to be removed. Nadal set the new college firmly within the educational traditions of the Society. Despite Borgia's customary hesitation to accept new colleges, he approved Nadal's initiative in Olmütz. A few years later, in 1570, the bishop increased the endowment. Four days after his arrival, Nadal left for Prague.[52]

On October 14, 1555, Peter Canisius had written to Ignatius Loyola that Ferdinand, then king of the Romans and later Holy Roman emperor, wanted to introduce the Society into Bohemia. At the suggestion of Bishop Weber of Laibach, the king wanted the Jesuits to found a college in Prague like the one in Vienna. Arrangements were made for the transfer of a Dominican priory in the center of the city to the Society. Canisius was impressed with the apostolic opportunity Prague provided: "Neither in Austria nor in Bavaria have I seen circumstances as favorable as those here for the return of schismatics to Catholic unity."[53]

The college opened on July 8, 1556, with an invitation: "All persons, without respect to nationality, age, or condition, may freely attend the lectures of this College, or Royal and Catholic School, there to be educated and trained without charge, to participate in scholastic disputations and exercises, and to be taught all the varieties of arts, letters, and languages of the curriculum."[54]

Still accompanied by the Austrian provincial, Nadal visited Prague from September 2 to 19. In addition to the college, the Society now had a novitiate in Prague. In the two institutions, there were forty Jesuits. After exhortations and confessions, the vows of the Jesuits were not renewed because this had been done just two months earlier. The visitor found a number of practices not compatible with the Institute and corrected them. To better organize the novitiate, a new novice master, called from Olmütz, was installed. Various Jesuits were appointed to supervise the college's discipline.

Despite the transfer of the Dominican priory to the Society, the college's finances were a source of great concern. Moreover, some confusion remained about the sources of this income. And the Dominican priory had had various pastoral responsibilities; Nadal wondered if their transfer violated the Society's Institute. He could only hope this whole situation would be clarified with the return of the emperor from the Turkish wars.

Nadal and Maggio parted at Prague, and Nadal returned to Innsbruck to assign eleven more Jesuits who had just arrived from the Roman College.[55] The college at Innsbruck, however, had been a cause of concern to Peter Canisius. The rector, Joannes Dyrsius, had so mismanaged the college that he had allowed it to degenerate into an "absolute Babylon." Neglect, more than malice, was the cause of the deterioration. The "five Queens"—the daughters of the emperor—resided at Hall near Innsbruck. They took a fancy to Dyrsius and asked that he be their chaplain, even though another Jesuit had been assigned that role. Their official chaplain, Hermes Halbpaur, did not appreciate the rector's poaching and both appealed to Canisius.

With the first signs of the reappearance of the plague in April of 1564, the five queens decided to migrate to Merano. Dyrsius immediately sought to accompany them. Canisius would not permit it: he did not approve of the displacement of their regular chaplain and the desertion of the community. The queens were not to be denied, however, and they finally compelled Canisius to consent to allow both Dyrsius and Halbpaur to travel with them: the men were needed for confessions, sermons, and counsel. The ladies' status prevented any disagreement. Both Canisius and Laínez concurred. Dyrsius was lost to the college just when he began to show some talent as a rector.

As we have seen, Nadal replaced Dyrsius with the former Austrian provincial, Nicolas Lanoy. The new rector would later cause problems because of his strict discipline, but now both he and Nadal sought to reintroduce some order. The recent arrivals from Rome were redirected to the colleges that most needed help, those in the Upper German province. During the three weeks he was there, he followed his usual routine with the 18 Jesuits and the 130 students. In order to restore domestic tranquility, Nadal was obliged to reassign a few Jesuits. Then, after short stays at the colleges in Munich, Ingolstadt, and Dillingen to see how his instructions were being implemented, Nadal left for Würzburg in the Rhine province.[56]

In 1564 Friedrich von Wirsberg, bishop of Würzburg, had approached Peter Canisius about opening a Jesuit college in his episcopal seat. "The City is gravely infected with heretical opinions, and the clergy, sunk in their vices, are more like soldiers than saints," Canisius reported, and the Society, if it opened a school, "may well expect as difficult and varied a species of opposition [from them and from the people] as they will find anywhere in Germany."[57] Because of the apostasy of many parish priests, the diocese was in tatters. The bishop saw the Society as his salvation and would require a great deal of ministerial work from the Jesuits to reverse his diocese's decline.

The need was great, Canisius argued, but what of men and money? The province had few extra men, and the religious foundation offered by the bishop, a convent still occupied by the Poor Clares, needed extensive and expensive renovation. The bishop was notoriously stingy. Various problems—presumably one was the shortage of Jesuits—delayed the project, but the bishop never abandoned hope. Shortly before his death, Laínez promised the bishop that the next college the Society opened in Germany would be in Würzburg. In late November, Nadal and Canisius departed for Würzburg to conclude the discussions.[58]

After an initial delay, Nadal and Canisius concluded an agreement with the chancellor of the diocese. The bishop gave his approval later. In return for an initial annual income of 1500 rhenish florins, which would be supplemented as the college grew, the Jesuits promised nine instructors, two of whom would be philosophers and two theologians. Because of the paucity of Jesuits and especially such educated ones, the Society rarely granted requests for more than five Jesuits. This petition was exceptional.

Nadal and Canisius had tried to dissuade the bishop with no success. The bishop also demanded that the Society provide a German-speaking preacher for the cathedral. This was a clear violation of the Society's Institute, which stipulated that ministries be gratuitous. The bishop would not be denied. A compromise was reached that followed the letter if not the spirit of the Society's Institute; the promise to supply a preacher would not be included in the foundation charter but instead in an accompanying letter. It would be an obligation the Society imposed on itself, and not one that was legally binding.

Nadal and Canisius were more successful with their refusal to commit the Society to writing books against the heretics, assisting in episcopal visitations, and singing in choir whenever the bishop wanted. Even so, Nadal was not happy about the final agreement. Although he had preserved the integrity of the Institute in some areas, he was uncertain about others. In addition to the constitutional issue, Nadal was not enthusiastic about the foundation. He considered the endowment too small for a major college. Nonetheless, he forwarded the agreement to Borgia for his approval. The general rejected it.[59]

Times had changed. Nadal and Borgia had disagreed earlier on acceptance of colleges. Nadal had tried to curb Borgia's acceptance of any small foundations with too many strings attached. Now, as general, Borgia rejected a foundation negotiated by Nadal. The Constitutions, Borgia argued, were clear: "Since it is so proper to our profession not to accept any temporal remuneration for the spiritual ministries in which we employ ourselves according to our Institute to aid our fellowmen, it is not fitting for us to accept for a college any endowment with an atached obligation of supplying a preacher or a confessor."[60]

Even if the agreement were constitutionally sound, Borgia did not approve the large number of Jesuits promised to the bishop when there were already other colleges with comparable needs.[61] Nadal was not ignorant of the Constitutions when he negotiated the college's foundation with the bishop of Würzburg; he knew the stipulations conflicted with the Society's Institute, but he knew also that the Society had granted exemptions for the sake of the greater glory of the Lord. We have noted Nadal's concern for Germany ever since his first visit: "In no part of the world is the Society, supported of course by God's grace, more needed." There was so much to be done in Germany that the apostolate should take precedence over the Institute.[62]

Nadal was no longer in Würzburg when Borgia rejected the offer. It was Canisius' task to renegotiate it. Anton Vinck, provincial of the Rhineland, accompanied him. Canisius explained the general's decision as carefully as he could. It was not the wish of the Society to avoid sending preachers and theologians to Würzburg; the problem was the clear prohibition of the Constitutions of any contractual arrangement for them. The bishop was furious and at one point left the room to regain his composure. Canisius' fabled eloquence soothed the ruffled episcopal feathers. If only the bishop would trust the Society, it would not fail him.

Bishop von Wirsberg wanted a college so badly he eventually agreed to Borgia's conditions in June of 1567. The new foundation still had an annual income of 1500 rhenish florins, but the

Society committed itself only to providing six professors. Nor did it assume any responsibility for providing philosophers, theologians, or preachers. The college opened its doors in the following October. The community numbered seventeen and the student body 160.[63]

Between December 5 and 7, 1566, Nadal journeyed from Würzburg to Speyer, the seat of the *Reichskammergericht* or Supreme Court of Justice. The city was a thriving center of Protestantism. Probably for that reason, the cathedral canons and the bishop petitioned the Society for a college. Nadal was not eager to accept another college and tried to postpone acceptance, but Borgia thought the time was convenient for a serious discussion. He commissioned Nadal to negotiate a foundation. The catch in the discussions was a provision, similar to that at Würzburg, that the Society provide theologians and a preacher. Because these negotiations were carried out before Borgia rejected the Würzburg agreement, the Speyer charter was similarly phrased: the obligations were not contractual but moral.

By the time Borgia also rejected the contractual arrangements for this college, Nadal had gone. It was left to the provincial of the Rhineland, Anton Vinck, to explain the general's rejection to the chapter and, if possible, to negotiate a new charter. The bishop and the canons, however, did not want the Society to remain without legally binding stipulations. Even though Vinck and the chapter could not reach a mutually acceptable agreement, a college was opened in May.

Until a settlement could be concluded, the college was supported by rents freely given as alms. A year later the college, still without a permanent endowment, had five classes and approximately two hundred students. Throughout this period of discussion, Borgia permitted a Jesuit to function as the cathedral preacher and granted a theologian to the college. He repeated, though, that these men were freely provided by the Society. The Society and the chapter did not conclude a definitive charter until 1571. In return for 700 rhenish florins per annum and other material support, the Society agreed to provide Jesuits to teach six classes of grammar and one of theology, and a preacher for the cathedral.

Borgia, in a curious reversal of his earlier decision, accepted the renegotiated charter and declared that the preacher and the theologian differed from the teachers of humanities, in that the Society was contractually obliged to supply the latter but the former were given voluntarily. Dennis Pate, perhaps rightly, interprets Borgia's concessions to a realization that providing theologians and preachers so desperately needed in Germany took precedence over his customarily rigorist interpretation of the Institute.[64]

A Jesuit college had been founded in Mainz in 1561. Archbishop Brendel von Homburg, elector of Mainz and Lord Chancellor of the Empire, was the benefactor. From the revenues of his see he sought to endow both the college and a seminary for poor students under supervision of the Jesuits. The endowment was significant and supported a large college; at the time of Nadal's visitation the Jesuit community numbered approximately forty and there were about five hundred students. Nonetheless there were still important details Nadal had to discuss with the archbishop. Because of these negotiations and because of the revolt in the Netherlands, Nadal's next destination, he remained in Mainz and Aschaffenburg, the site of the archbishop's residence, for two months.

Finances were not the only concern. There were numerous practices and customs that needed correction. For four weeks Nadal threw himself into the life of the college. He questioned all the Jesuits, heard their general confessions, and exhorted them to spiritual growth. The usual regulations regarding silence and cloister were promulgated. Externs were to be invited into the community rarely, and then only if there was hope that great spiritual fruit would result. The library was to be purged of all prohibited books. These would be stored in a locked closet whose key was in the possession of the rector; only the rector would grant the necessary permission to read these works. The rector was also granted full constitutional power for governing the college, including the right to dispense from the regulations when it was appropriate. One of his tasks was a weekly exhortation to the community on the Society's Institute.

Nadal also structured more clearly the lives of the novices. During the novitiate, after the novices had made the Exercises (and Nadal wanted the rector to arrange that not only the novices but also the older men who had not yet done so should make the Spiritual Exercises), they spent a few months in domestic chores. They could study later. In the college, there was to be religious instruction and periodic admonitions to greater piety.[65]

These negotiations between Archbishop Brendel and Nadal took place at the episcopal residence in Aschaffenburg in late January. Nadal was prepared to concede to the archbishop what he had earlier granted in Würzburg, but final agreement was not easy. Because the endowment was for both a college and a residence for boarders, Nadal wanted the agreement to be very clear regarding how much income went to each establishment. The archbishop insisted that he must seek the counsel of the cathedral chapter in Mainz before he would permit any changes. A final charter was not signed until September of 1568. The Jesuits received 1600 rhenish florins in rents, and their college became a part of the University of Mainz with the right to issue degrees in philosophy and theology.[66]

Nadal returned to Mainz from Aschaffenburg at the end of January 1567, and concluded his visitation. On February 20 he departed for Cologne by way of Frankfurt. He arrived in Cologne on the twenty-fourth and remained there until April 2. The situation had not improved since his last visit. The Cologne college continued to grow but its foundations were still precarious. Despite their efforts the Jesuits were never able to secure an endowment that was independent of the university. As a result, the university senate could demand that the Society govern its college no differently from the other colleges in the university. The university also regulated the courses taught by the Jesuits. Since November of 1564, the Society had been forbidden to teach, among other subjects, metaphysics, ethics, mathematics, and Greek syntax. Also forbidden to the Society were separate catalogues of courses and the presentation of dramatic works.

Especially troublesome was the university's insistence that the Jesuits charge the students for their education and promotion to graduation. Even the archbishop of Cologne, Friedrich von Wied, opposed the Society; he was convinced they had delated him to the pope. There was nothing Nadal could do. He conducted the usual interviews, gave exhortations, and heard confessions, but there could be no serious attempt to regularize the college until it had gained its independence. On April 2 he left for Trier.[67]

The college at Trier, too, continued to grow. By this time there were more than thirty Jesuits in the community and more than five hundred students in the college. Among the students

were scions of many illustrious families. Although the archbishop was quite generous, especially with the revenues of the
monastery of Saint Barbara, the college's endowment had not
been properly negotiated and secured. The time was not ripe,
however, for further discussions: Jakob von Eltz was newly elected
archbishop, and he had more pressing issues. These negotiations Nadal left to the provincial, Anton Vinck—with complete
instructions for their execution.

His other instructions again ranged from the practical to the
spiritual. Common recreation was important. The hours of
prayer and examen were to be observed. The rector should see
to it that all could speak some German. Common life dictated
that all eat the same food unless, for medical reasons, they were
permitted to substitute other food. No students were to be
accepted without permission of their parents.

Nadal had planned to establish a novitiate in Trier—he still
hoped to do this—but he was unable to find a suitable spot and
decided to concentrate on the establishment of the college's
endowment before embarking on another expensive project.
At Trier, Nadal met Olivier Mannaerts, the Belgian whom Nadal
had earlier prepared for his visitation of France, and the
provincials of the Rhineland, Anton Vinck, and of Lower Germany, Frans de Costere. All three sought his advice. On May 9
Nadal left Trier for Liège.[68]

Germany again made a deep impression on Nadal. His concern for the preservation and perhaps restoration of Catholicism softened his outlook. Through the mediation of Borgia,
Nadal petitioned the pope for a number of concessions to
strengthen German Catholicism. He proposed giving the communion cup to the laity in Jesuit churches under certain circumstances. Likewise he urged that educated, reform-minded,
and orthodox clergy be permitted to hold more than one
benefice—despite Tridentine regulations—to prevent the other
benefices from going to less reliable clergy.

More practical requests concerned burial and absolution
from heresy. With respect to the first, Nadal begged that Catholics be allowed to be buried in Catholic cemeteries, even though
they had been "desecrated" by the burial of Protestants, because
Catholics had no other locale. Regarding the second, the visitor
urged that the demand for a public abjuration be dropped, so
that Protestants could be absolved from their heresy privately.

Three of these requests were granted by Pius V: the cup, the benefices, and private absolution.[69]

Nadal was not so successful with Borgia. The issue was a simple one: religious dress. The Jesuits coming into Germany from Rome wore the cassock of the Roman clergy. Now that they were working in colleges throughout the north, Nadal asked Borgia if they could exchange their Roman cassock for the attire of the local clergy. This change would establish a style more harmonious with the injunctions of the Constitutions: "The clothing too should have three characteristics: first, it should be proper; second, conformed to the usage of the region where one is living; and third, not contradictory to the poverty we profess."[70]

In Spain, Portugal, and France Jesuits dressed like other priests. They should do the same in Germany. An added reason for the change was the Germans' dislike of foreigners, especially those from the south; the cassock just made the Society's work that much harder. Before Borgia made a decision, he solicited the views of the three German provincials. Canisius, Vinck, and Costere agreed with Nadal but, despite the unanimity, Borgia would not grant the request. His reason: since there was a great variety of local clerical dress in the north, unity within the Society demanded standardization.[71]

One of the immediate results of the consult at Trier was a proposal for a college at Liège. Bishop Gerard van Groesbeck was the potential benefactor. Initial negotiations lasted about a week, and the result was auspicious. The bishop promised an annual revenue of 1500 talers besides a house for the Jesuits, the college itself, and a church. The Jesuits would provide a preacher but, as was the custom of the Society, without obligation. In the midst of his visitation of Louvain, Nadal returned to Liège to complete the negotiations. To his dismay, the bishop introduced a new condition: he insisted that the Jesuit college be combined with the other schools in the city. Nadal would not accept this new arrangement and the proposal was withdrawn.[72]

The return to Liège was not the only interruption of Nadal's visitation of Louvain. A chronic sufferer from catarrh, Nadal and his faithful companion Diego Jiménez went to take the waters at Spa in late June. They stopped at Liège on their way. On the same trip Nadal visited Saint-Omer. Situated on the frontier with France, Saint-Omer periodically suffered the devastation of war. With its few natural defenses, any institution was vulnerable to attack. Nadal thought the site inconvenient—indeed dangerous—for a Jesuit college. Even if there were no war, the town was too small either to support a college or to attract students from France. Thus he would not approve a college.

Nadal was therefore surprised and angry to discover that a college had opened its doors in April. He demanded an explanation. Frans de Costere gave it: Borgia had allowed classes to begin even though the foundation had not been completed. Once Nadal inspected the college, his disapproval dissipated. Gérard d'Haméricourt, bishop of Saint-Omer, had endowed the college with an annual income of 1200 rhenish florins, more than sufficient for the college. The bishop even promised to increase the endowment in the future. Construction of a new building had begun as soon as Borgia granted his permission. Nadal completed the arrangements. The bishop fulfilled his promise: a few years later he increased the annual revenues to 1600 florins.[73]

On his return from Spa in mid-August 1567, Nadal visited the college at Dinant. The Jesuit community there numbered fifteen. The college presumably was not well endowed by the city, because Nadal permitted the Jesuits to seek alms from various potential benefactors if annual revenues were not sufficient. His other instructions for the college repeated Nadal's concern for proper religious and spiritual formation of the students. The visitor ordered that certain obscene books, such as those by Martial and Terence, be held by the rector; he might allow others to read them but not the obscene sections. Certain books must be purged of their obscenities. No one was to read or possess the books of heretics.

Within the community, Nadal reminded the men of the importance of common recreation. Foreigners within the community should practice their French as often as possible. Nadal left it to the provincial to ask the general whether the fathers should add water to their wine at meals. If anyone was unable to wash his own feet, the rector should appoint someone to do so: the rest of the community could take care of themselves. The question of religious dress again surfaced. Those who did not wear the "habit" should dress decently and simply according to the clerical customs of the country.[74]

From Dinant Nadal returned to Louvain in early September to complete his visitation. His previous visit had not been a happy occasion; the second augured better. Although the college was still only a poor scholasticate for Jesuits, there was a new, more congenial rector, Jacobus Schipman. Since there was no longer a hostile rector to undermine the visitor's authority, Nadal investigated the community thoroughly.

Although it was the custom of the Society that the fathers and brothers relax after dinner and supper, certain forms of recreation were forbidden to Jesuits. They should not bowl unless the green was private. Football should not be played except with the approval of a doctor. Heretical and prohibited books were forbidden to Jesuits unless they had received the rector's permission. The community library should not contain any such books, nor should it possess any by Erasmus or other suspected authors. Nadal also imposed restrictions on the books read at table: Cochlaeus's *Commentaria de actis et scriptis Martini Lutheri* was specifically forbidden in both the Jesuit and the students' refectories.

Religious discipline was to be observed. Jesuits should recite the office of the Blessed Mother unless some other prayer was found to be more beneficial. Masses were to be celebrated according to the Roman Rite. Nadal suggested that a room be set aside separated from the community for private mortifications.

Boarding students were forbidden to have any money on their persons and must deposit everything with the prefects. Nadal reformed the drinking habits of the boarders. Beer was no longer to be readily available. Whoever wanted a drink had to report to the janitor, who would dispense the beer. If he noticed frequent and excessive drinking, he was to notify the prefects.

The Society did not have the custom of receiving guests; in fact, it had a rule that prohibited it. Nonetheless, friends might be invited to dinner or supper in the refectory for reasons of edification or spiritual benefit. One wonders if any visitors would have wanted to stay at the community after Nadal decided that it was not necessary to build heating stoves, since it was not the custom of the region!

The novices were to be separated from the rest of the community if possible. Nadal also forbade acceptance of any assistance from the parents of novices upon their entrance. The

Society was to demand nothing from them. If, however, parents wished to make a voluntary contribution, it could be accepted as alms. This prohibition was especially important in view of the college's financial need. Nadal still hoped to augment the endowment. He hoped himself to discuss the matter with the king. If he were unable to do so, he delegated the provincial.[75]

In early October, Nadal departed for Antwerp to visit the Jesuits who ministered to the Spanish in the city. Nadal's detailed instructions reminded them of the importance of spiritual conversation. They were to be especially concerned about this. In their work with the Spanish, they were not to discrimate: they were to converse with all without favoring any class or province. If they happened to converse with the Flemish, the Jesuits must give no offense. Similarly, the men should take care not to offend the heretics in their sermons; a simple exposition of Catholic doctrine was sufficient.

From Antwerp Nadal proceded to Brussels. There he was well received by the duke of Alba. Though the duke was favorably disposed toward the Society, according to Nadal, he still insisted that it pay a special tax from which he had exempted the other religious orders. The next stop was the college at Tournai, where the Jesuits had been expelled by Dutch rebels in August of 1566. The rebels were now evicted, but the college had not reopened. Until the college was again in operation, Nadal wanted some form of education for the students. Detailed instructions were left for this. In his observations for the Jesuit community, Nadal was concerned about religious decorum and the Jesuits' work with women religious.

From Tournai Nadal returned to Saint-Omer to supervise the progress of the new college. In early November, he visited the Jesuits at Cambrai and investigated the possibility of erecting a Jesuit college at Douai. Cambrai remained Nadal's base for nearly three months, because civil war prevented him from entering France. On February 3, 1568, he returned to Louvain for the provincial congregation.[76]

In the Constitutions, Ignatius stipulated that each province send a man to Rome every three years to inform the general of the state of the province.[77] The Constitutions, however, did not demand that all procurators come at the same time. This condition was added by the Second General Congregation in 1565.[78] The newly elected general wished general congregations to

convene on a regular basis. At first the general congregation
agreed with him, but strong interventions resulted in a compromise. It was decided that provincial procurators would come to
Rome at the same time, and there, with the general and his
consultors, they would discuss common issues and the possibility of a general congregation. The first congregation of procurators would meet in October of 1568. At the preceding provincial congregations, the assembled professed fathers of each
province would elect a procurator and decide on the issues they
wanted addressed in Rome. During the generalate of Francis
Borgia, congregations of procurators were an effective instrument for an increase of uniformity throughout the Society and
of unity within it. The periodic presence of procurators also
reduced the importance of official visitors. Their work could
now be done through the procurators.[79]

Nadal returned to Antwerp after the provincial congregation. From there he moved to Louvain, where he received a
letter from Borgia that authorized him to visit the provinces of
France and Aquitaine as soon as this was safe and convenient.
On June 8 he left Brussels for Paris and arrived at Clermont
College in Paris on the fifteenth. Nadal was quite impressed
with what he found.

In the four years since its foundation, the college had grown
in size and influence. The work of the forty Jesuits at the college
was producing tremendous fruit. This was especially true of the
sermons of Émond Auger, whose influence with the royal family
allowed him to desert his post as the provincial of Aquitaine for
the pulpits of Paris, and of the lectures of the theologian Juan
Maldonado. Both were most effective in the fight against heresy.
Nadal spent only a month in Paris, too short a period, Mannaerts
protested, to examine the institution thoroughly. But because
Borgia was exhorting Nadal to quicken his pace in order to
return to Rome in time for the congregation of the procurators
in October, the visitor could not linger longer. Nadal left for
Verdun on July 15.[80]

The college at Verdun had been founded by Bishop Nicolas
Psaume in 1564. The endowment, however, still required some
negotiation. During the five or six days Nadal was able to spend
with the sixteen men in the college, he attempted to resolve the
foundation with the bishop. The latter, however, was reluctant
to make a definitive settlement: he was convinced he could

obtain even better buildings for the college and the community if he were given more time. Nothing definitive was concluded.

The college at Chambéry, Nadal's next stop, was founded in 1565 by Emmanuel-Philibert, duke of Savoy. Nadal arrived there on August 6 and remained for eight days. Although the community there lacked adequate accommodation, it does not appear Nadal did anything to correct that during his brief stay. From Chambéry he journeyed to Lyons, where he remained from the seventeenth until the end of August. There he visited the college community and supervised the provincial congregation of Aquitaine.

The college, founded in 1565 by Antoine d'Albon, Archbishop of Lyons, was staffed by twenty Jesuits, who had good accommodations. Their work in the college and against the heretics had generally been successful. Because of the provincial's involvement in Paris, he was unable to attend the congregation and consequently Nadal was not able to discuss with him his general impressions of the province. Indeed, those impressions remained incomplete. The fathers assembled at Lyons, moreover, persuaded Nadal to cancel his proposed visitations of the colleges at Tournon, Billom, Mauriac, Rodez, Toulouse, and Avignon because Huguenots made the journey hazardous. In 1569 Everard Mercurian was named to complete the visitation. Accompanied by the recently elected procurator from Aquitaine, Nadal left Lyons on September 1 for Rome, where he arrived on the twenty-second.[81]

Nadal had been on the road for nearly two and a half years. During his visitations of France, Flanders, Germany, and Austria he oversaw implementation of the Institute, the establishment of colleges, and the formation of Jesuits. No detail was too insignificant to elude his detection. What he discovered was often surprising; what he left was astonishing. As he had done earlier in Spain and Portugal, he introduced order based on a sympathetic understanding of the Institute. Few were as familiar with the Society's Institute as he was; fewer still could rival him in its interpretation. Sacred as the unity of the Society and its Institute was to him, the apostolate took precedence. The work in Germany was essential, and the Society should adapt to it. Whether the issue was religious dress or the endowment for a college, however, Borgia did not always agree with his approach.

Everard Mercurian

Nadal remained in Rome for the next six years. At the congregation of procurators, the representatives from Spain protested the de facto absence of a Spanish assistant. Araoz, of course, had been elected to that position by the general congregation in 1565, but he never left Spain. Protesting his undying affection for the Society and his willingness to serve it in any capacity, Araoz blamed Philip II and Rui Gómez for his failure to comply with Borgia's summons. He shed "tears of blood" when he heard that Borgia was grieved with him. "To imagine that there ever had been or could be in the Society," Araoz asserted, "a man more truly and sincerely devoted to our Father's [Borgia's] very shadow than I, Antonio Araoz, would be to lay hands on the *sancta sanctorum,* the apple of my eye, the fibres of my heart."[82]

The prince of Éboli believed, and Araoz concurred, that Araoz was elected assistant in order to remove from Spain a person "feared by some as a plotter and by others as an obstacle to the despoiling of the country for money for Rome and of men for Italy." Prayers and pleas moved neither the Jesuit nor his backers.[83] Someone else had to be named, insisted the Spanish procurators. Borgia appointed Nadal to the post and he held it until 1571.[84]

In 1571, Pope Pius V sought to create a grand alliance against the Turks. To obtain support of the Spanish, Portuguese, and French courts, the pope sent Michele Cardinal Bonelli to negotiate with their kings. He ordered Borgia to accompany the cardinal. Borgia named Nadal as his vicar during his absence from Rome. Because Borgia would be in Spain and Portugal for most of his travels, he retained authority over the Jesuit provinces there. Nadal oversaw the remainder. He demurred that he was too old and too inept for this responsibility, but Borgia did not relent. Full authority, however, was not delegated to Nadal. When Nadal had visited the northern provinces, the general had insisted that all major decisions be referred to himself; he did so again now. All major decisions were reserved for the general. Indeed, so conscientious was Nadal that he informed Borgia of even the smallest decisions.[85]

During his tenure as vicar general, Nadal was much involved in governance of the communities in Rome. He met daily the rectors of the Roman and German colleges, visited the novitiate weekly, and monitored administration of the Professed House. Issues of major concern—but not important enough to refer to the general—Nadal discussed with the professed fathers. With the approval of the general, Nadal accepted new colleges in Milan, Fulda, and Pont-à-Mousson, novitiates at Arona and Brno, and a Professed House in Milan. He also rejected a seminary/ college in Bruges because of the small foundation and the stipulations attached.[86]

Nadal's concern for the integrity of the Institute and the uniqueness of the Society's spirituality can best be seen in his negotiations with the pope to lift papally imposed practices. In 1566–67, Pius V ordered two changes in the practice of the Society: introduction of communal recitation of the office and profession of solemn vows by all Jesuit scholastics before ordination. The first change was prompted by Pius's fears that the Society's failure to chant the office would result in a spiritual deterioration. As a Dominican, he knew the value of the office and considered it a necessity for an order such as the Jesuits so involved with the world. Borgia had tried unsuccessfully to convince the pope that such alterations were unnecessary. Upon the succession of Pope Gregory XIII in 1572, Nadal made another attempt. The pope referred the matter to a commission headed by Carlo Cardinal Borromeo. Nadal submitted a defense of the traditional practices of the Society to Borromeo, and the cardinal was convinced of the case. So was the pope, and the Society returned to its former practices.[87]

Illness cut Borgia's futile embassy short, and he returned to Italy in 1572.[88] At Ferrara he became too ill to travel any farther. In May he extended Nadal's authority as vicar general over the entire Society. Borgia lingered at Ferrara for four months, preferring the company of other Jesuits to the comforts offered by his friend and kinsman Duke Alfonso d'Este. In September he asked to be carried to Loreto to visit the Holy House. From Loreto he returned to Rome on September 28. There he died on October 1. Nadal's delegated authority expired with the death of the general. On October 2, the professed fathers in Rome elected Juan de Polanco vicar general.[89]

The Third General Congregation convened in Rome on April 12, 1573, for the election of a new general. Even before the congregation opened there were problems. Fearful of the

VENITE AD ME OMNES QVI
LABORATIS ET ONERATI ESTIS
ET EGO REFICIAM VOS.

EVANGELICAE HISTORIAE IMAGINES
Ex ordine Euangeliorum, quæ toto anno in Missæ sacrificio recitantur,
In ordinem temporis vitæ Christi digestæ.
Auctore Hieronymo Natali Societatis IESV Theologo
Antuerpiæ Anno Dñi M.D.XCIII.
SVPERIORVM PERMISSV.

Frontispiece

increased "hispanization" of the Society (the first three generals had been Spanish and a number of Spaniards dominated major offices within the Society), Pope Gregory XIII questioned the election of yet another. When Polanco and others visited the pope to receive his blessing on the congregation, Gregory asked how many Spaniards there were in attendance. Half of the forty-six men in attendance were Spanish. He suggested that a non-Spaniard be elected this time and even recommended Everard Mercurian as a good candidate. The Belgian received twenty-seven votes on the first ballot and was duly elected. For reasons probably of age as well as nationality, Nadal was retired.[90]

Nadal remained in Rome and Tivoli a year after the close of the congregation. In April of 1574, he was invited by the general to retire to his beloved Germany. In May he departed for Hall, near Innsbruck. He was delighted to be there. Freed from the burdens of administration, Nadal returned to many of his un-finished manuscripts and completed final revisions of the *Scholia in Constitutiones* and the *Apologia contra censuram Facultatis theo-logicae Parisiensis*. He also wrote two books of meditation that were not published until the 1590s: *Evangelicae Historiae Imagines ex ordine Evangeliorum quae toto anno in Missae sacrificio recitantur, in ordinem temporis vitae Christi digestae* (Antwerp, 1593) and *Adnotationes et Meditationes in Evangelia quae in sacrosancto Missae sacrificio toto anno leguntur; cum Evangeliorum concordantia historiae integritati sufficienti* (Antwerp, 1594).[91]

Nadal's enthusiasm upon his return to Germany soon waned. By 1575 Peter Canisius, Nadal's friend and associate, was com-plaining to the general about the disedification caused by Nadal's depression. He had become old and peevish. His mo-rose behavior and his finicky appetite bothered many.[92] He constantly pestered the rector, Mathias Lackner, who later apostatized (some thought there was a connection). In June of 1575, Paul Hoffaeus, the German provincial, wanted to send Nadal back to Rome. By December of 1576, Nadal himself was asking to return to Rome because his health had become so bad. Mercurian granted him permission to return to Rome in February of 1577. In August he departed for Venice. He re-mained there for a few months before he continued to Rome, where he spent his final years at the novitiate of Sant' Andrea and died on April 3, 1580.[93]

 za za za za za

In an essay on Jesuit spirituality prompted by the English translation of Joseph de Guibert's *The Jesuits: Their Spiritual Doctrine and Practice,* John O'Malley criticized the "bookish" nature of de Guibert's approach to spirituality. De Guibert, he thought, failed to examine the nature of Jesuit spirituality as exemplified in the lives of Jesuits and in the institutions of the Society: "To be sure Aloysius, Stanislaus, and John Berchmans receive their due, but today one would like to ask why Matteo Ricci, John de Britto, and Robert de Nobili, for example, cannot be discussed in relationship with the Ignatian ideal." [94] One could add Nadal's name to O'Malley's litany of omitted apostles.

Nadal was an acknowledged expert on Ignatian spirituality, and this expertise should be sought not simply in his exhortations but in his life. Nadal himself preferred the image of the circle: a Jesuit's prayer flows into his work and his work into his prayer. In Nadal, theory and practice merge. In a eulogy written in 1607, Pedro de Ribadeneira adequately summarized Nadal's life: "His qualities were very great, especially his obedience and his esteem and zeal for our Institute and the welfare of the Society, for which he worked so much."[95]

Abbreviations

AHSI	*Archivum Historicum Societatis Iesu*
Cons	*The Constitutions of the Society of Jesus*
Epp Can	*Beati Petri Canisii Societatis Iesu epistulae et acta*
Epp Mixt	*Epistolae Mixtae ex variis Europae locis, 1537–1556*
FN	*Fontes narrativi de S. Ignatio de Loyola et de Societatis Iesu initiis*
Inst SI	*Institutum Societatis Iesu*
Lit Quad	*Litterae Quadrimestres*
Mon Broet	*Epistolae PP. Paschasii Broëti, Claudii Jaji, Joannis Codurii, et Simonis Rodericii, S.I.*
Mon Bob	*Bobadillae Monumenta*
Mon Borg	*Sanctus Franciscus Borgia*
Mon Ign	*Sancti Ignatii de Loyola Societatis Iesu Fundatoris Epistolae et Instructiones*
Mon Nad	*Epistolae et Monumenta P. Hieronymi Nadal*
Mon paed	*Monumenta paedagogica Societatis Iesu*
Or ob	*Orationis observationes*
Pol Chron	*Vita Ignatii Loiolae et rerum Societatis Iesu historia auctore Joanne Alphonso de Polanco* [*Polanco Chronicon*]

Notes

Preface

1 *Mon Ign,* V:109. I have used John O'Malley's translation ("To Travel to Any Part of the World: Jerónimo Nadal and the Jesuit Vocation," *Studies in the Spirituality of Jesuits* 16 [1984]: 3).

2 *Mon Nad,* I:144 (translation of O'Malley, "Jerónimo Nadal").

3 James Brodrick, *The Origin of the Jesuits* (London, 1940), 211.

4 Mario Scaduto, S.J., *Storia della Compagnia di Gesù in Italia,* vol. 3, *L'Epoca di Giacomo Lainez 1556–1565* (Rome, 1964), 196.

5 (Madrid, 1949).

6 Dennis Pate, "Jerónimo Nadal and the Early Development of the Society of Jesus, 1545–1573" (Ph.D. diss., UCLA, 1980).

Chapter 1

1 Miguel Nicolau, S.J., "Nadal (Jérôme), Jésuite, 1507–1580," in *Dictionnaire de Spiritualité,* vol. 11, col. 3; Miguel Batllori, S.J., "Jerónimo Nadal y el Concilio de Trento," in *Mallorca en Trento* (special edition of *Boletin de la Sociedad Arqueológica Lulliana* 29, nos. 714–715 [Sept.–Dec. 1945]), 14.

2 *Mon Nad,* I:1; *FN,* I:446; Georg Schurhammer, S.J., *Francis Xavier, His Life, His Times,* vol. 1, trans. M. Joseph Costelloe, S.J. (Rome, 1973), 241–42.

3 *Mon Nad,* I:1; Schurhammer, *Francis Xavier,* 1:204–7; Paul Dudon, S.J., *Saint Ignatius of Loyola* (Milwaukee, 1949), 103–18; Cándido de Dalmases, S.J., *Ignatius of Loyola* (St. Louis, 1985), 93–105.

4 José Luis González Novalín, "La Inquisición Española," in *La Iglesia en la España de los siglos XV y XVI,* ed. José Luis González Novalín, vol. 3, part 2 of *Historia de la Iglesia en España,* ed. Ricardo García-Villoslada, S.J. (Madrid, 1980), 147–51.

5 Melquiades Andrés Martín, "Pensamiento Teológico y Vivencia Religiosa en la Reforma Española (1400–1600)," in *La Iglesia en la España de los siglos XV y XVI,* ed. González Novalín, 279–80; *Mon Nad,* I:3.

6 Schurhammer, *Francis Xavier*, 1:204–7; Ricardo García-Villoslada, S.J., *La Universidad de Paris durante los Estudios de Francisco de Vitorias, O.P. (1507–1522)* (Rome, 1938), 413; *Mon Nad*, I:2.

7 *Mon Nad*, I:2.

8 *Ibid.*; Dalmases, *Ignatius*, 106–25.

9 Dudon, *Saint Ignatius*, 128–57

10 *Mon Nad*, I:2–3.

11 *Ibid.*, I:3.

12 *Ibid.*

13 William V. Bangert, S.J., *To the Other Towns: A Life of Blessed Peter Favre, First Companion of St. Ignatius* (Westminster, Md., 1959), 36–38.

14 *Ibid.*, 40–41; *Mon Nad*, I:3, 29.

15 Gabriel Codina Mir, S.J., "La ordenación y el doctorado en teología de Jerónimo Nadal en Aviñón (1537–1538)," *AHSI* 36 (1967): 247.

16 Armand Mossé, *Histoire des Juifs d'Avignon et du Comtat Venaissin* (Paris, 1934), 81, 96–97; Philippe Prévot, *Histoire du Ghetto d'Avignon: A Travers la Carrière des Juifs d'Avignon* (Avignon, 1975), 143.

17 Mossé, *Histoire*, 7–8; *Mon Nad*, I:29.

18 *Mon Nad*, I:29–30.

19 *Ibid.*, I:30.

20 *Ibid.*, I:4–5, 30–31.

21 *Ibid.*, I:4–5, 31.

22 *Ibid.*, I:5; Codina Mir, "La ordenación," 250–51.

23 *Mon Nad*, I:4–5.

24 *Ibid.*, I:4.

Chapter 2

1 *Mon Nad*, I:5.

2 *Ibid.*, I:5–6.

3 *Ibid.*, I:6.

4 *Ibid.*, I:7 and n 1.

5 *Ibid.*, I:7–9.

6 *Ibid.*, I:9–10; *Or ob*, 265.

7 Juan Vich y Salom, "Miscelánea tridentina maioricense," in *Mallorca en Trento* (special edition of *Boletin de la Sociedad Arqueológica Lulliana* 29, nos. 714–715 [Sept.–Dec. 1945]), 189–94, 267–72; Miguel Batllori, S.J., "Jerónimo Nadal y el Concilio de Trento," in *Mallorca en Trento* (special edition of *Boletin de la Sociedad Arqueológica Lulliana* 29, nos. 714–715 [Sept.–Dec. 1945]), n 42 on 21–22.

8 *Mon Nad,* I:10; Miguel Nicolau, S.J., "La vocación del P. Jerónimo Nadal y sus relaciones con el V. Padre Antonio Castañeda," *Manresa* 53 (1981): 163–65.

9 *Mon Nad,* I:10–11; Nicolau, "La vocación," 165.

10 *Mon Nad,* I:10.

11 *Ibid.,* I:11, 32.

12 *Ibid.,* I:11–12; Nicolau, "La vocación," 165–66.

13 *Mon Nad,* I:12–13.

14 *Ibid.,* I:13, 33–34.

15 Many Catholic reformers were involved in apostolic work with prostitutes. On this, see Christopher F. Black, *Italian Confraternities in the Sixteenth Century* (Cambridge, 1989), 206–13.

16 *Mon Nad,* I:13.

17 *Ibid.,* I:14.

18 *Ibid.*

19 *Ibid.,* I:15.

20 *Ibid.,* I:15–16.

21 *Ibid.,* I:16.

22 *Ibid.,* I:16, 21.

23 *Mon Nad,* I:16–17; Ignatius Loyola, *The Spiritual Exercises of St. Ignatius, S.J.,* translated by Louis J. Puhl, S.J. (Westminster, Md., 1951), 25–33.

24 Ignatius Loyola, *Spiritual Exercises,* 43–78.

25 *Ibid.,* 43–45, 60–63; *Mon Nad,* I:17.

26 *Mon Nad,* I:17; Ignatius Loyola, *Spiritual Exercises,* 71–73; Roger Cantin, S.J., "L'Élection de Jérôme Nadal: Des ténèbres jaillit la lumière," *Cahiers de Spiritualité Ignatienne* 4 (1980): 269–70.

27 *Mon Nad,* I:17; Ignatius Loyola, *Spiritual Exercises,* 74; Ignacio Casanovas, S.J., "La Vocación del Padre Jerónimo Nadal en las Elecciones de los Ejercicios," in *Comentario y Explanación de los Ejercicios Espirituales de San Ignacio de Loyola,* ed. Ignacio Casanovas, S.J. (Barcelona, 1945), 335–36.

28 *Mon Nad,* I:17–18; Casanovas, "La Vocación," 337–41.

29 *Mon Nad,* I:17–18.

30 *Ibid.,* I:19.

Chapter 3

1 *Mon Nad,* I:19–20.

2 *Ibid.,* I:22–23.

3 *Ibid.,* I:19, 23.

4 *Ibid.,* I:20, 23–24.

5   *Ibid.*, I:19–20.

6   *Ibid.*, I:20

7   *Ibid.*, I:20–21.

8   *Ibid.*, I:23.

9   *Mon Nad,* I:24, n 2 on 74–75. Here Ignatius was playing on words in an old idiom, *hecharle un hechardizo.* Basically it means to toss to him someone useless or worthy of rejection. In the context of the incident it means to toss to Nadal (or match him up with, or fix him with) someone who deserves dismissal from the Society because of disobedience. Two Jesuits have helped me unearth the meaning of this sixteenth-century phrase, Fr. José Sanchez and Fr. Fernando Picó. *Mon Nad,* V:75.

10   *Mon Nad,* I:24, 34–35, n 2 on 74–75.

11   Jerónimo Nadal, S.J., *Pláticas espirituales del P. Jerónimo Nadal, S.J., en Coimbra (1561),* ed. Miguel Nicolau, S.J. (Granada, 1945), 108–9. In this conference in Coimbra, Nadal illustrated his point by this recollection of his years in Rome with Ignatius.

12   *Or ob,* 73–95.

13   *Mon Ign,* I:390–94.

14   *Mon Nad,* I:50–53.

15   *Mon Ign,* I:450–53.

16   William V. Bangert, S.J., *Claude Jay and Alfonso Salmerón* (Chicago, 1985), 89–94.

17   Hugo Rahner, S.J., ed., *Saint Ignatius Loyola: Letters to Women* (New York, 1960), 282–83.

18   *Ibid.*, 283–87; *Mon Nad,* I:22.

19   Rahner, *Ignatius Letters,* 287–93; Jerónimo Nadal, S.J., *Scholia in Constitutiones S.I.,* ed. Manuel Ruiz Jurado, S.J. (Granada, 1976), 168–69.

20   *Or ob,* 32–33.

21   *Ibid.*, 32–34. In his autobiography eight years later, Ignatius made somewhat the same point. Ignatius Loyola, *St. Ignatius' Own Story as Told to Luis González de Cámara,* translated by William J. Young, S.J. (Chicago, 1956), 27.

22   *Or ob,* 68.

23   *Ibid.*, 72.

24   *Ibid.*, 61.

25   William V. Bangert, S.J., *To the Other Towns: A Life of Blessed Peter Favre, First Companion of St. Ignatius* (Westminster, Md., 1959), 93.

26   *Or ob,* 34–35.

27   Bangert, *Peter Favre,* 148–55.

28   *Epp Can,* I:252 and n 4.

29   *Mon Ign,* I:533–35, 634–35; *Epp Can,* I:230 and n 1; Bangert, *Peter Favre,* 178–79.

30 *Mon Nad*, I:22.

31 James Brodrick, S.J., *Saint Peter Canisius, S.J. 1521–1597* (Baltimore, 1950), 104–7; [Society of Jesus] *Documents of the 31st and 32nd General Congregations of the Society of Jesus* (St. Louis, 1977), 404–5.

32 *Mon Nad*, V:195. On this topic, see John W. O'Malley, S.J., "To Travel to Any Part of the World: Jerónimo Nadal and the Jesuit Vocation," *Studies in the Spirituality of Jesuits* 16 (1984): 1–20.

33 Antonio de Aldama, S.J., "La Composición de las Constituciones de la Compañía de Jesús," *AHSI* 42 (1973): 207–21.

Chapter 4

1 *Mon Nad*, I:24–25; Miguel Nicolau, S.J., "La vocación del P. Jerónimo Nadal y sus relaciones con el V. Padre Antonio Castañeda," *Manresa* 53 (1981): 166.

2 *Mon Nad*, I:25; Nicolau, "La vocación," 167.

3 *FN*, I:644–45.

4 *Or ob*, 66.

5 *Ibid.*, 44, 52, 56–58, 61.

6 *Ibid.*, 43–44, 49, 58, 62, 69.

7 *Ibid.*, 43, 52, 59, 63.

8 *Ibid.*, 43–44, 60, 62, 73.

9 *Ibid.*, 34.

10 The roots of the terminology Nadal adopted go back into medieval Franciscan tradition. Nadal chose this terminology rather than the one associated with St. Thomas Aquinas, who made a threefold division of the active life, the contemplative life, and the mixed life. Despite the difference of nomenclature, the two schemas were not very far apart. St. Thomas did not always identify the active life with business and mere external action; sometimes he put under that heading "the ordering of the soul's passions" and the development of the moral virtues. At other times St. Thomas divided the active life into two classes: the one that consists totally in external occupations, such as showing hospitality and giving alms; the other that flows from contemplation into preaching, teaching (*contemplata aliis tradere*). Nadal's terminology never became widespread in the Society. See Miguel Nicolau, S.J., *Jerónimo Nadal: Obras y Doctrinas Espirituales* (Madrid, 1949), 327–38. Other quotations of Nadal in this section are in *Mon Nad*, IV:646.

11 *Mon Ign*, I:373–74.

12 *Or ob*, 69.

13 *Ibid.*, 44.

14 *Ibid.*, 55.

15 *Ibid.*, 59, 65.

16   *Ibid.,* 54.

17   *Ibid.,* 57.

18   *Ibid.,* 53.

19   *Ibid.,* 60.

20   *Ibid.,* 66.

21   *Ibid.,* 72.

22   *Ibid.,* 59.

23   *Ibid.,* 71.

24   *Ibid.,* 66.

25   *Ibid.,* 63.

26   *Ibid.*

27   *Ibid.,* 62.

28   *Ibid.,* 57.

29   *Ibid.,* 62, especially section 134.

30   Ricardo García-Villoslada, S.J., *La Universidad de Paris durante los Estudios de Francisco de Vitorias, O.P. (1507–1522)* (Rome, 1938), 218–20; Nicolau, *Jerónimo Nadal,* 428–29.

Chapter 5

1   *Mon Ign,* II:51–52, 74–77; *Mon Nad,* IV:875–77; *Lit Quad,* I:91–99.

2   Ladislaus Lukács, S.J., "The Origin of Jesuit Colleges for Externs and the Controversies about their Poverty, 1539–1608," translated by George E. Ganss, S.J., *Woodstock Letters* 91 (1962): 129–33 (reprinted in Thomas H. Clancy, S.J., *An Introduction to Jesuit Life* [St. Louis, 1976], 283–326); Mario Scaduto, S.J., "Le origini dell'Università di Messina," *AHSI* 17 (1948): 102–59.

3   *Lit Quad,* I:91–99; James Brodrick, S.J., *Saint Peter Canisius, S.J. 1521–1597* (Baltimore, 1950), 111–12.

4   *Epp Can,* I:275, n. 3; Scaduto, "Le origini," 105.

5   Scaduto, "Le origini," 106; Allan P. Farrell, S.J., *The Jesuit Code of Liberal Education* (Milwaukee, 1938), 27–30.

6   Farrell, *The Jesuit Code,* 29, 35. For the best recent study of the influence of the Parisian method on the Jesuit philosophy of education, see Gabriel Codina Mir, S.J., *Aux Sources de la Pédagogie des Jésuites le "Modus Parisiensis"* (Rome, 1968).

7   Farrell, *The Jesuit Code,* 27; *Mon Nad,* I:59–60.

8   *Mon Nad,* I:97–98, 121.

9   Brodrick, *Peter Canisius,* 112; *Mon Nad,* I:56–58.

10   *Mon Nad,* I:57–58.

11   William A. Christian, Jr., *Local Religion in Sixteenth-Century Spain* (Princeton, 1981), 137.

12 *Mon Nad,* I:54, 92.

13 *Ibid.,* I:54.

14 *Ibid.,* I:66.

15 *Ibid.,* I:92.

16 *Ibid.,* I:76–77 and n 3 on 76.

17 *Ibid.,* I:123.

18 *Ibid.,* I:96.

19 Because of the current interest in popular religion, sodalities and confraternities have become popular subjects of research. For their role in the devotional life of Catholic Europe see Christopher F. Black, *Italian Confraternities in the Sixteenth Century* (Cambridge, 1989) and Louis Châtellier, *The Europe of the Devout: The Catholic Reformation and the Formation of a New Society* (Cambridge, 1989).

20 *Mon Nad,* I:69, 108, 123.

21 William V. Bangert, S.J., *To the Other Towns: A Life of Blessed Peter Favre, First Companion of St. Ignatius* (Westminster, Md., 1959), 249; *Mon Nad,* I:69–70.

22 *Mon Nad,* I:123.

23 *Ibid.,* I:123.

24 *Ibid.,* I:125.

25 Scaduto, "Le origini," 107–8.

26 *Ibid.,* 107; *Mon Nad,* I:62.

27 Scaduto, "Le origini," 109; *Mon Nad,* I:71–74; *Pol Chron,* I: 372.

28 Scaduto, "Le origini," 109, 132–33, n 10; *Mon Nad,* I:74.

29 Scaduto, "Le origini," 111; *Mon Nad,* I:84.

30 Scaduto, "Le origini," 111; *Mon Nad,* I:86.

31 Scaduto, "Le origini," 111–12.

32 *Ibid.,* 112–13; *Mon Nad,* I:125, 127–28.

33 Scaduto, "Le origini," 132–33.

34 *Mon paed,* I:15*.

35 *Ibid.,* I:19–29.

36 *Ibid.,* I:22*–3*, 94–106.

37 R. R. Bolgar, *The Classical Heritage and its Beneficiaries. From the Carolingian Age to the End of the Renaissance* (New York, 1964), 360.

38 Christopher Dawson, *The Crisis of Western Education* (New York, 1961), 38.

39 *Mon Nad,* I:93.

40 *Ibid.,* I:81–82, 120.

41 *Ibid.,* I:61–62.

42 *Ibid.,* I:74–75 and n 2.

43 *Lit Quad,* I:425–26.

44 *Mon Nad,* I:70–71.

45 *Ibid.*, I:63–64, 71, 84, 94; Manuel Ruiz Jurado, S.J., *Orígenes del Noviciado en la Compañía de Jesús* (Rome, 1980), 61–62, 69–70, 125–26.

46 *Mon Nad*, I:88–89, 94–95; Hugo Rahner, S.J., ed., *Saint Ignatius Loyola: Letters to Women* (New York, 1960), 459.

47 *Pol Chron*, II:219.

48 Mario Scaduto, S.J., *Storia della Compagnia di Gesù in Italia*, vol. 3, *L'Epoca di Giacomo Lainez 1556–1565* (Rome, 1964), 151, 310.

49 *Mon Nad*, I:100, 107; *Pol Chron*, II:233.

50 *Mon Nad*, I:103; *Pol Chron*, II:232, 235.

51 *Pol Chron*, II:243; *Lit Quad*, I:317.

Chapter 6

1 *Mon Nad*, I:108.

2 Roger B. Merriman, *The Rise of the Spanish Empire in the Old World and in the New*, vol. 3 (New York, 1925), 341; Hugo Rahner, S.J., ed., *Saint Ignatius Loyola: Letters to Women* (New York, 1960), 457.

3 Rahner, *Ignatius Letters*, 457; *Mon Nad*, I:118; *Pol Chron*, II:237.

4 *Pol Chron*, II:237–38.

5 *Mon Nad*, I:114–16.

6 *Ibid.*, I:114.

7 *Ibid.*, I:116.

8 *Ibid.*, I:118–19.

9 *Ibid.*, I:118.

10 *Pol Chron*, II:239.

11 *Mon Nad*, I:755–56. The editors of the *MHSI* have put this editorial heading over the text of Vinck's letter: "On the Progress of the Society's Scholastics under Fr. Nadal." The bulk of the letter, however, is concerned with lay students. Fr. Miguel Nicolau (*Mon Nad*, I:755–56) was misled by this faulty caption, for in using this text of Vinck's letter, he identified the program of the lay students as the program of the Jesuit scholastics (*Mon Nad*, V: 25 and n 22).

12 *Mon Nad*, V:26–30.

13 *Ibid.*, V:28–29.

14 Miguel Batllori, S.J., "Jerónimo Nadal y el Concilio de Trento," in *Mallorca en Trento* (special edition of *Boletin de la Sociedad Arqueológica Lulliana* 29, nos. 714–715 [Sept.–Dec. 1945]), 24–25.

15 *Pol Chron*, II:552–53.

16 William V. Bangert, S.J., *Claude Jay and Alfonso Salmerón* (Chicago, 1985), 204–7.

17 *Mon Nad*, I:129–30; II:6–7 and n 1; *Or ob*, 146; *Pol Chron*, II:553; *Cons*, no. 511.

18 *Or ob,* 97–98, 100.

19 *Mon paed,* I:25*–27*, 133–35.

20 *Pol Chron,* II:553–54; Arthur L. Fisher, "A Study in Early Jesuit Government: The Nature and Origins of the Dissent of Nicolás Bobadilla" *Viator* 10 (1979): 428–30.

21 *Pol Chron,* II:554.

22 Rahner, *Ignatius Letters,* 459–64.

23 *Mon Nad,* I:133; *Pol Chron,* II:555.

24 *Mon Paed,* I:25*–27*, 133–60; *Cons,* 490–509.

25 *Pol Chron,* II:556.

26 In 1552 Ignatius established the German College for secular seminarians from Germany who did their studies at the Roman College. Their presence resulted in the drawing up of an ordered regime of higher studies (*Mon Paed,* I:134).

27 *Mon Nad,* I:137; *Pol Chron,* II:557–58.

28 *Mon Nad,* I:132.

29 *Ibid.,* I:133.

30 *Pol Chron,* II:558–59.

Chapter 7

1 *Mon Nad,* I:143–45.

2 Antonio Astráin, S.J., *Historia de la Compañía de Jesús en la Asistencia de España,* vol. 1 (Madrid, 1902), 389.

3 *Mon Nad,* I:774.

4 William V. Bangert, S.J., *To the Other Towns: A Life of Blessed Peter Favre, First Companion of St. Ignatius* (Westminster, Md., 1959), 221–24; Astráin, *Historia,* 1:588–92.

5 *Mon Ign,* V:270–71.

6 Astráin, *Historia,* 1:599.

7 Francisco Rodrigues, S.J., *História da Companhia de Jesus na Assistência de Portugal,* vol. 1, part 2 (Porto, 1931), 137–41.

8 *Mon Nad,* I:148–50 and nn 2, 3, 4 on 149.

9 *Ibid.,* I:159.

10 *Ibid.,* I:176.

11 *Ibid.,* I:774.

12 *Ibid.,* I:175–76.

13 *Ibid.,* I:178, 197; Rodrigues, *História,* 1:2:294–95.

14 *Mon Nad,* I:184, 194; Rodrigues, *História,* 1:2:304–6.

15 Astráin, *Historia,* 1:629–33.

16   *Ibid.*, 1:634–35. Nadal recalled one negative aspect of the highly charged occasion. Yielding to the importunate requests of the Jesuits present, he gave a sermon. He said it fell flat and was roundly criticized. This was an early indication of a theme that would recur: Nadal's lack of talent as a pulpit orator. *Mon Nad*, II:18.

17   *Mon Nad*, I:194–95, 221; II:18; Astráin, *Historia*, 1:636.

18   Rodrigues, *História*, 1:1:302–7; 1:2:222; *Mon Nad*, I:200–201; *Pol Chron*, II:701–2; III:431–32; Manuel Ruiz Jurado, S.J., *Orígenes del Noviciado en la Compañía de Jesús* (Rome, 1980), 127–28.

19   Astráin, *Historia*, 1:400–401.

20   *Pol Chron*, III:418–19.

21   *Mon Nad*, I:205–6; Rodrigues, *História*, 1:1:439–40 and 1:2:210–12; Hugo Rahner, S.J., ed., *Saint Ignatius Loyola: Letters to Women* (New York, 1960), 68–74.

22   *Mon Nad*, I:207–8; Rodrigues, *História*, 1:2:212.

23   *Mon Nad*, I:193–212.

24   Rahner, *Ignatius Letters*, 68–74.

25   *Mon Nad*, I:194; II:20; III:828–29.

26   *Cons*, no. 161.

27   *Cons*, no. 734.

28   James W. Reites, S.J., "St. Ignatius of Loyola and the Jews," *Studies in the Spirituality of Jesuits* 13 (1981): 19–20.

29   *Ibid.*, 20.

30   Promising as Antonio was, his appointment brought Nadal face to face with a vexing problem that he would deal with many times in Spain: the shallow reservoir of experienced Jesuits. Not all the inexperienced rectors had the admirable characteristics of Antonio, and their tenure often ended unhappily. Francisco de Rojas was rector of Zaragoza. A Castilian, Rojas knew Ignatius and his companions as early as 1538 in Rome. He seems to have joined the Society around 1540. He was ordained in 1544 with little or no theology. In 1547 Ignatius appointed him rector of the new college in Zaragoza. During his visitation, Nadal noted Rojas's instability. He found him shaky in his vocation and flawed by "a streak of Spanish moodiness and pride." Rojas left the Society in 1556, two years after Nadal's visitation and diagnosis, because Ignatius refused to grant him the ardently desired solemn profession of four vows unless he devoted four years to theological study. See Georg Schurhammer, S.J., *Francis Xavier, His Life, His Times*, vol. 1, trans. M. Joseph Costelloe, S.J. (Rome, 1973), 447; *Mon Nad*, I:238; *Pol Chron*, III:347–48, 367.

31   *Mon Nad*, I:223–24; Rahner, *Ignatius Letters*, 382–90. Antonio's brothers attained distinction. An older brother, Gómez Suárez de Figueroa, count (later duke) of Feria, became celebrated in the service of King Philip II as Spanish ambassador to the courts of Queens Mary and Elizabeth of England. A younger brother, Don Lorenzo Suárez de Figueroa, became a Dominican bishop of Sigüenza (Rahner, *Ignatius Letters*, 382–83).

32 Rahner, *Ignatius Letters*, 382–90; *Pol Chron*, V:527. This emotional issue, aggravated by gossip, lingered long in Córdoba. On September 1, 1572, Fr. Juan Ramírez wrote to Fr. General Borgia, "More than 600 students attend our college in Córdoba. Among them are the sons of the noblemen of Córdoba, gentlemen of the utmost purity of blood. Many of them feel attracted to the religious life and to our Society, but, because of our sins[the acceptance of the New Christians], not one of them comes to us. All join the Dominicans at their convent of Saint Paul. The reason is this: the story among the nobility is that only Jews enter the Society. These are their words. San Paulo is the place for noblemen. This opinion is as strong as if it were built of lime and stone (*cal y canto*). So strong is this sentiment that if someone has the misfortune of entering the Society, he is regarded as having been garbed in a sanbenito" (Astráin, *Historia*, 3:591).

33 Araoz, a native of Vergara and a nephew of Ignatius, was the first Jesuit to enter Spain after the Society was approved. He entered the Society in 1540 and pronounced his final vows on February 19, 1542, scarcely two years after his admission. From the beginning, Araoz received wide freedom from Ignatius to preach throughout Spain, a task that showed his gifts as a preacher. When he was not even seven years in the Society, and much of that time spent as a free-lance preacher, he was appointed the first provincial of Spain. Araoz became the darling of the Spanish court, and in his cultivation of those connections he neglected the government of the province. Despite Araoz's grave defects, Ignatius kept him in authority. Ignatius drew back from a possible offense to the Spanish court in the hope that Araoz would be a good connection at the center of the Spanish government. As we shall see, Araoz was another example of aristocratic connections leading to the corrosion of Jesuit ideals.

34 *Mon Ign*, V:335.

35 *Ibid.*, V:24; *Pol Chron*, V:527 and n 5.

36 *Mon Nad*, II:21.

37 *Ibid.*, I:226–27.

38 *Ibid.*, II:21.

39 *Ibid.*, I:224, 227. Ávila, Juan de, *Obras Completas del Santo Maestro Juan de Ávila*, vol. 1, ed. Luis Sala Ballust (Madrid, 1952), 73, 164 and nn 155–156.

40 *Mon Nad*, I:221–22; *Pol Chron*, III:364–65.

41 Ignacio Iparraguirre, S.J., *Historia de la Práctica de los Ejercicios Espirituales de San Ignacio de Loyola*, vol. 1 (Bilbao and Rome, 1946), 91–92; Astráin, *Historia*, 1:351–53.

42 *Mon Nad*, II:22.

43 Astráin, *Historia*, 1:209, 259, 264–65.

44 *Ibid.*, 1:397.

45 *Cons*, nos. 342, 582, 583.

46 Astráin, *Historia,* 1:397.

47 Pedro de Leturia, S.J., "La Hora Matutina de Meditación en la Compañía Naciente (1540–1590)," in *Estudios Ignacianos,* vol. 2, ed. Ignacio Iparraguirre, S.J. (Rome, 1957), 210–14, 251–53. The published text of the *Orden de oración* is scattered. The first part is in Leturia, "La Hora," 251–53. The sequel is in *Mon Nad,* IV:670–72.

48 *Mon Nad,* I:250.

49 *Ibid.,* I:236.

50 *Ibid.,* I:250.

51 *Ibid.,* I:236; Astráin, *Historia,* 1:398.

Chapter 8

1 *Mon Nad,* V:31–32 and n 1 on 31; 36–105.

2 *Ibid.,* V:37, 48–49.

3 *Ibid.,* V:83.

4 *Ibid.,* V:36–37.

5 *Ibid.,* V:37.

6 William V. Bangert, S.J., "The Second Centenary of the Suppression of the Jesuits," *Thought* 48 (1973): 186–88.

7 *Mon Nad,* V:37. In a recent article Philip Endean, S.J., argues for a critically sound biography of Ignatius Loyola from the perspective of Nadal's spirituality: "If one accepts what Nadal and Vatican [Council] II say about the theology of religious life, it follows that religious can live out their vocations authentically and healthily only if they have, in some sense, reliable knowledge of the life and teachings of their founders." See Philip Endean, S.J., "Who Do You Say Ignatius Is? Jesuit Fundamentalism and Beyond," *Studies in the Spirituality of Jesuits* 19 (1987): 8.

8 *Mon Nad,* V:40–42.

9 On this theme see Thomas H. Clancy, S.J., "The Proper Grace of the Jesuit Vocation According to Jerome Nadal," *Woodstock Letters* 86 (1957): 107–18 (reprinted in Thomas H. Clancy, S.J., *An Introduction to Jesuit Life* [St. Louis, 1976], 271–82).

10 *Mon Nad,* V:94–95.

11 *Ibid.,* V:51–52. For a minute textual examination of Nadal's corrections of Manuel Sá's notes and for his account of the vision in contrast to the accounts given by Ignatius himself, Diego Laínez, and Pedro de Ribadeneira, see *Mon Nad,* V:n 16 on 51, and *FN,* I:n 37 on 313.

12 *Mon Nad,* V:41–45.

13 *Ibid.,* V:45–46.

14 *Ibid.,* V:85–86.

15 *Ibid.,* V:57–58, 60–63.

16 *Ibid.*, V:89–98.

17 *Ibid.*, V:52–53.

18 *Ibid.*, V:93.

19 *Ibid.*, V:92.

20 *Ibid.*

21 *Ibid.*, V:95.

22 *Ibid.*, V:97–98.

23 *Ibid.*, V:96–97.

24 *Ibid.*, V:90–91.

25 *Ibid.*, V: 38.

26 Nadal was not only instrumental in defense of the *Spiritual Exercises* but was also important in their practice. Under Nadal's direction, the college at Messina was a center for dissemination of the Exercises. It was the first college to give the Exercises to adults. See Dennis Pate, "Jerónimo Nadal and the Early Development of the Society of Jesus, 1545–1573" (Ph.D. diss., UCLA, 1980), 83–84.

27 *Epp Mixt,* III:665–66.

28 *Mon Ign,* II:649–50; *FN,* I:315–16.

29 Louis Cognet, *Post-Reformation Spirituality* (New York, 1959), 27–29.

30 Ignacio Iparraguirre, S.J., *Historia de la Práctica de los Ejercicios Espirituales de San Ignacio de Loyola,* vol. 1 (Bilbao and Rome, 1946), 92–95.

31 *Ibid.*, 95–96 and n 36 on 95.

32 *Ibid.*, 97.

33 *Ibid.*, 98; *Pol Chron,* III:503–10.

34 Ignatius Loyola, S.J., *The Spiritual Exercises of St. Ignatius,* trans. Louis J. Puhl, S.J. (Westminster, Md., 1951), 6.

35 *Pol Chron,* III:509–10.

36 *Mon Nad,* I:243–44; II:23–24.

37 Angelo Walz, O.P., *I Domenicani al Concilio di Trento* (Rome, 1961), 273.

38 *Epp Mixt,* IV:162–63.

39 *Mon Nad,* II:25–26; Antonio Astráin, S.J., *Historia de la Compañía de Jesús en la Asistencia de España,* vol. 1 (Madrid, 1902), 402–3.

40 *Mon Nad,* II:25.

41 Astráin, *Historia,* 1:401.

42 *Mon Nad,* I:252.

43 Astráin, *Historia,* 1:401–3.

44 *Mon Nad,* I:254; II:25–26, 30.

45 *Ibid.*, I:253–54.

46 In light of Borgia's subsequent legislation on prayer and his continual attraction to excessive prayer, and of Nadal's fears that Borgia was not

sufficiently familiar with the Society's ways of proceeding, it is important to note that at Borgia's profession of vows in February of 1548 was the controversial Fray Juan Texeda. He and the Jesuits Andrés de Oviedo and Francisco Onfroy, influenced by the reformist prophetism that Texeda espoused, threatened the spiritual orientation of the newly founded order. See Manuel Ruiz Jurado, S.J., "Un Caso de Profetismo Reformista en la Compañía de Jesús: Gandía 1547–1549," *AHSI* 43 (1974): 217–66.

47 A few months later Nadal's misgivings were confirmed. In Murcia, the rector, Juan Bautista Barma, showed Nadal the hermitage, in a secluded spot, that he prepared for Borgia (*Mon Nad,* II:30). Within two years, Borgia's strong leaning to the contemplative life led to a confrontation with Nadal.

48 *Mon Nad,* I:254.

49 *Ibid.,* I:256; II:25.

50 *Ibid.,* I:758–61; II:27–28; *Pol Chron,* V:429.

51 *Mon Nad,* II:27.

52 *Ibid.,* I:255; II:8–9, 19; Astráin, *Historia,* 1:413.

53 Astráin, *Historia,* 1:392–93.

54 *Mon Nad,* II:26; *Pol Chron,* IV:494–95 and n 1 on 495.

55 Pedro de Leturia, S.J., "La Prima Misa de San Francisco de Borja en Loyola," in *Estudios Ignacianos,* vol. 2, ed. Ignacio Iparraguirre, S.J. (Rome, 1957), 412–13; *Mon Ign,* I:255–57, 283–85.

56 *Mon Nad,* II:26. Ignatius Loyola, *Obras Completas,* 3rd ed., ed. Cándido de Dalmases, S.J. (Madrid, 1977), 826–27.

57 *Mon Nad,* I:265–67.

58 *Ibid.,* I:267–68.

59 *Mon Ign,* VI:713–14 and n 3 on 714.

60 *Cons,* no. 817.

61 *Mon Borg,* III:174–75 and n 1 on 174; *Pol Chron,* IV:492, 494–95 and n 1 on 495.

62 *Mon Nad,* I:261–62; Astráin, *Historia,* 1:405–6. See Joseph F. Crehan, S.J., "Saint Ignatius and Cardinal Pole," *AHSI* 25 (1956): 72–98 on Loyola's efforts to get his men into Marian England.

63 *Mon Nad,* II:28.

64 *Ibid.,* II:30–31.

Chapter 9

1 *Mon Nad,* II:31.

2 *FN,* I:54*–55*.

3 *Mon Nad,* II:31–32; *Mon Ign,* VIII:42–43; *FN,* II:216. Francisco J. Egaña, S.J., *Orígenes de la Congregación General de la Compañía de Jesús* (Rome, 1972),

166. The several sources differ slightly in recording the number who participated in this meeting as well as the precise total of the majority vote.

4   *Mon Nad,* II:32.

5   *Ibid.,* II:32; *FN,* I:644–45, 676–77.

6   *Mon Nad,* II:32. This remark conflicts with another he made in the same paragraph. "Afterwards he [Ignatius] dropped me completely from his service." This is one of the inconsistencies that crop up occasionally in Nadal's recollections.

7   *FN,* I:354–63. Ignatius took a little over two years to complete his story. Nadal tells in his diary of his efforts to persuade Ignatius to tell the history of his soul (*Mon Nad,* II:33–34). His chronology differs from Câmara's. The editors of *MHSI* judge that Câmara's account, the older of the two, is the more accurate one (*FN,* I:327–30).

8   Jean Leclercq, O.S.B., "La Paternité de S. Benoît," in *Recueil d'études sur Saint Bernard et ses écrits,* vol. 3, ed. Jean Leclercq, O.S.B. (Rome, 1969), 279–84.

9   Erwin Iserloh, "The Reform in the German Principalities," in *History of the Church,* vol. 5, ed. Hubert Jedin (New York, 1980), 295–96.

10 *Mon Nad,* I:279–82. See also William V. Bangert, S.J., *Claude Jay and Alfonso Salmerón* (Chicago, 1985), 173–74.

11 *Mon Nad,* I:282; II:34; *Mon Ign,* VIII:493; 9, 443.

12 *Mon Nad,* II:34.

13 *Ibid.*

14 *Ibid.*

15 *Pol Chron ,* V:263–66; *Mon Nad,* I:293.

16 *Mon Nad,* I:286–87, 296–97.

17 *Ibid.,* I:289, 292, 295.

18 *Ibid.,* I:296; *Pol Chron,* V:36, 234, 246, 264–65.

19 *Mon Nad,* I:290–91; *Pol Chron,* V:264–65.

20 *Mon Nad,* I:290–91.

21 *Ibid.,* I:290; *Cons,* no. 338.

22 *Pol Chron,* III:262; *Mon Nad,* I:291. Ignatius liked the idea of boarding facilities at Vienna, but he replied slowly, deliberately, and eventually favorably. After four months, in mid-July 1555, Polanco assured Nadal that the consultation in Rome on his suggestion was moving smoothly but that Ignatius had not decided. Three months later, Ignatius gave permission to provide facilities at Vienna for boarders (*Mon Ign,* IX:317; X:72–73).

23 *Mon Nad,* I:298; *Pol Chron,* V:267–69.

24 *Mon Nad,* I:298.

25 *Ibid.,* I:304; II:34–35.

26 *Ibid.,* I:311–12; *Pol Chron,* V:228; James Brodrick, S.J., *Saint Peter Canisius, S.J. 1521–1597* (Baltimore, 1950), 171.

27 *Mon Nad,* I:312.

28 *Ibid.,* 311; *Cons,* no. 451. Adler's mental suffering overwhelmed him. He went from Vienna to Prague. There he left the Society. He then traveled to Rome and was readmitted. Sent to Trier, he again left the Society. He became a court preacher for the Elector of Trier. Again he went to Rome and asked to be received into the Society. This time superiors refused. Twice he attempted suicide (*Mon Nad,* II:35 and n 5).

29 *Mon Nad,* I:312–13.

30 *Ibid.,* I:309–11; *Pol Chron,* V:271–72.

31 *Mon Nad,* I:310.

32 *Ibid.,* I:305, 309.

33 *Ibid.,* I:301.

34 *Ibid.,* I:302, 308; II:35.

35 *Ibid.,* II:35; James Brodrick, S.J., *The Origin of the Jesuits* (London, 1940), 248–51; *Mon Broet,* 652–55.

36 *Mon Nad,* I:321–24; II:35.

37 *Ibid.,* I:321–24; II:37; *Mon Broet,* 663–64.

38 Dennis Pate, "Jerónimo Nadal and the Early Development of the Society of Jesus, 1545–1573" (Ph.D. diss., UCLA, 1980), 210–12; Thomas H. Clancy, S.J., *An Introduction to Jesuit Life* (St. Louis, 1976), 302–3; *Mon Nad,* I:315–19.

39 *Mon Nad,* I:305–31; II:35–38; *Pol Chron,* II:429; V:135, 142, 151–53, 163–70; *Mon Ign,* IV:496–97; Paul Dudon, S.J., *Saint Ignatius of Loyola* (Milwaukee, 1949), 362–63.

40 Hastings Rashdall, *The Universities of Europe in the Middle Ages,* vol. 1, ed. F. M. Powicke and A. B. Emden (Oxford, 1936), 3.

41 *Mon Nad,* II:37.

42 *Ibid.,* II:38.

43 *Or ob,* 108.

44 *Ibid.,* 111–12.

45 Miguel Nicolau, S.J., *Jerónimo Nadal: Obras y Doctrinas Espirituales* (Madrid, 1949), 240–45.

46 *Or ob,* 111, 115–16.

47 *Mon Nad,* IV:677–78.

48 *Or ob,* 114. This is not the place to discuss the debate among scholars about the essence of St. Ignatius' "Application of the Senses" in his *Spiritual Exercises.* There are, as Fr. Hugo Rahner shows, two schools on this subject. One holds that Ignatius had nothing more in mind "than a means of allowing the imagination to work spontaneously on the simplest

points of the contemplated mysteries." This is a simple, even primitive, form of prayer that anyone can use. A second school holds "that the senses are no longer being simply applied to the object of contemplation; what happens is that the soul moves outward and upward until it finally comes to visualize and touch divine things directly." To attempt to adjudicate this dispute between scholars is beyond the province of this work. Hugo Rahner, S.J., *Ignatius the Theologian* (New York, 1968), 190–98.

49 *Or ob,* 117–18.

50 *Ibid.,* 110, 119.

51 *Ibid.,* 110.

52 *Ibid.,* 121.

53 *Ibid.,* 122.

Chapter 10

1 During this brief stay, Nadal aided Ignatius with some administrative business and participated in a meeting of several priests that reached conclusions about the Society's Constitutions. The stay may have been brief, but it was long enough for Nadal's impetuous tongue to get him in trouble again. Ignatius mentioned that he wanted a document written on obedience and that he intended to give this commission to Fr. Cristóbal de Madrid, a Spanish secular priest who was still a novice. Nadal blurted out: "What novice could carry that assignment off?" Ignatius nevertheless commissioned Madrid (*Mon Nad,* II:38–39).

2 *Mon Ign,* X:14–17; Antonio Astráin, S.J., *Historia de la Compañía de Jesús en la Asistencia de España,* vol. 2 (Madrid, 1905), 2–3. From his analysis of Borgia's position in the Society, Astráin concluded "From the moment that the Duke of Gandía was received into the order, our holy patriarch [Ignatius] contrived that no one of Ours would be superior of so outstanding a person."

3 *Mon Ign,* X:17–18.

4 *Ibid.,* XII:271; *Mon Nad,* II:39–40; *Pol Chron,* VI:552, 560.

5 *Mon Nad,* I:331–41; II:40–41; *Pol Chron,* VI:636.

6 *Mon Nad,* I:342; II:41; *Pol Chron,* VI:552.

7 *Cons,* no. 398; *Mon Nad,* II:41, 48; *Pol Chron,* VI:641.

8 *Mon Nad,* II:43–44.

9 *Ibid.,* II:43.

10 *Ibid.*

11 *Ibid.,* II:48.

12 *Ibid.,* II:43.

13 *Ibid.,* II:42.

14 *Ibid.,* II:43.

15   *Ibid.,* II:44.

16   *Ibid.,* II:42–43.

17   *Ibid.,* V:108–30.

18   *Ibid.,* V:108–9.

19   *Ibid.,* V:122–23.

20   *Ibid.,* V:123–24.

21   *Ibid.,* V:124–25. On the emphasis of the ministry of the word in the early Society, see John W. O'Malley, S.J., "Priesthood, Ministry, and Religious Life: Some Historical and Historiographical Considerations," *Theological Studies* 49 (1988): 223–57. See Thomas H. Clancy, S.J., *The Conversational Word of God* (St. Louis, 1978) for an exposition of one ministry of the word that is too often overlooked: spiritual conversation.

22   *Mon Nad,* V:126–27.

23   *Ibid.,* V:126.

24   See John W. O'Malley, S.J., "To Travel to Any Part of the World: Jerónimo Nadal and the Jesuit Vocation," *Studies in the Spirituality of Jesuits* 16 (1984): 1–20, for this dimension of Nadal's spirituality.

25   *Mon Nad,* V:127.

26   *Ibid.,* V:124–25.

27   *Ibid.,* I:345–46; II:48.

28   *Ibid.,* II:48–49. When Nadal planned to leave Spain immediately he had not heard that twenty days earlier, on September 1, the duke of Alba abruptly reopened hostilities by marching out of Naples toward Rome with 12,000 troops.

29   *Mon Nad,* II:48–49.

30   *Ibid.,* II:49.

31   *Ibid.,* II:48. The sequence of events at this point is most difficult to ascertain. On September 20, when Nadal wrote to Polanco from Valladolid, he had not yet heard about Laínez's election as vicar general. He told Polanco that he intended to leave Valladolid the next day, the twenty-first. Yet in his diary he wrote that a few days after learning on September 17 of Ignatius' death, "we heard that Fr. Laínez had been made vicar general." In the context "we" seems to indicate that Nadal was still with Borgia and the three provincials. This, however, is impossible to reconcile with his intention to leave Valladolid on the twenty-first, at which point he had not heard the news of Laínez's election. Nadal must have received the news about Laínez somewhere after he left Valladolid, perhaps at Burgos. At this point in the diary, Nadal's memory played tricks on him.

32   Franciso J. Egaña, S.J., *Orígenes de la Congregación General de la Compañía de Jesús* (Rome, 1972), 168–70. On this crisis see André Ravier, S.J., *Ignatius of Loyola and the Founding of the Society of Jesus* (San Francisco, 1987), 275–317.

33   *Pol Chron,* VI:638; *Mon Nad,* II:47.

Chapter 11

1   *Mon Nad,* II:49; Ludwig von Pastor, *The History of the Popes from the Close of the Middle Ages,* vol. 14, trans. Ralph E. Kerr, E. F. Peeler, and Ernest Graf, O.S.B. (St. Louis, 1924), 138–45.

2   Francisco J. Egaña, S.J., *Orígenes de la Congregación General de la Compañía de Jesús* (Rome, 1972), 187–88.

3   *Ibid.,* 191; Mario Scaduto, S.J., *Storia della Compagnia di Gesù in Italia,* vol. 3, *L'Epoca di Giacomo Lainez 1556–1565* (Rome, 1964), 36–37.

4   Scaduto, *Storia,* 3:36–37

5   On this crisis see André Ravier, S.J., *Ignatius of Loyola and the Founding of the Society of Jesus* (San Francisco, 1987), 275–90, and Arthur L. Fisher, "A Study in Early Jesuit Government: the Nature and Origins of the Dissent of Nicolás Bobadilla," *Viator* 10 (1979): 397–431.

6   Scaduto, *Storia,* 3:25–26; Egaña, *Orígenes,* 191.

7   *Or ob,* 129–30.

8   *Mon Nad,* II:13.

9   Scaduto, *Storia,* 3:30.

10   *Ibid.,* 3:31.

11   *Mon Nad,* II:55.

12   *Ibid.,* II:15–16.

13   *Or ob,* 144–45.

14   *Ibid.,* 145.

15   *Ibid.,* 145–46.

16   *Ibid.,* 146.

17   *Ibid.,* 155.

18   *Mon Nad,* IV:729–32.

19   Scaduto, *Storia,* 3:36–37.

20   Egaña, *Orígenes,* 194–95; *Mon Nad,* II:51–57; IV:98–103.

21   *Mon Nad,* II:52–53.

22   *Ibid.,* II:54.

23   *Ibid.,* IV:104–6.

24   *Ibid.,* IV:121–23. Bobadilla forgot that he himself had voted in the election of the vicar general, placing his notes in the hands of Juan de Polanco.

25   *Mon Nad,* IV:732–34.

26   *Ibid.,* IV:734–35.

27   *Ibid.,* II:55–56.

28   *Ibid.,* II:53.

29   *Cons,* no. 3.

30   *Ibid.,* 2, 3.

31   *Mon Nad,* IV:130.

32 D. Fernández Zapico, ed., *Ignatii de Loyola Constitutiones Societatis Jesu* (Rome, 1934), I:376–77. The phrases as they appear in the original Latin of *Exposcit debitum* are the following: *Qui quidem Propositus de consilio consociorum constitutiones ad constructionem hujus propositi nobis fines conducentes condendi.* And second: *Consilium vero necessario convocandum ad condendas vel immutandas constitutiones et alia graviora.* It is difficult to capture in English the precise meaning of *condendi* and *condendas.* "Produce, frame, forge, put together, compose, write, establish, institute, set in place?" In this context the word has two basic implications: (1) composing the Constitutions; (2) setting them in place within the Society. Fr. Ganss chose the word establish. But does one really establish Constitutions? I prefer either "frame" or "forge."

33 *Mon Nad,* IV:130.

34 *Ibid.,* IV:131–47.

35 This paragraph is based on two documents that complement each other. The first includes the last few sentences of Nadal's reprimand to Bobadilla (*Mon Nad,* IV:133). The second is from Nadal's *Ephemerides* ("Diary") (*Mon Nad,* II:59).

36 *Mon Nad,* IV:134–35.

37 *Ibid.,* IV:142.

38 *Ibid.,* IV:141–42.

39 *Ibid.,* IV:137–38. Nicolás Bobadilla was invited to come from Tivoli. He excused himself. Later Ignatius gave him the text for review. Bobadilla read but a little, saying that he found the document difficult to comprehend. Eventually Nadal recognized that Bobadilla had a strong point in his contention that *Exposcit debitum* called for approbation of the Constitutions by a general congregation. He tried to fill that gap with the meeting of the professed fathers called by Ignatius in January 1551. He spoke of that meeting as "like a general congregation." But of course it was not a general congregation in the real sense of the words. Ignatius had not convened the meeting as a general congregation. The procedures for the convocation of a general congregation were not followed. Its likeness to a general congregation did not make it a general congregation. Jozef de Roeck, S.J., "La Genèse de la Congrégation Générale dans la Compagnie de Jésus," *AHSI* 36 (1967): 283. For Salmerón's role at this gathering, see William V. Bangert, S.J., *Claude Jay and Alfonso Salmerón* (Chicago, 1985), 204–7.

40 *Mon Nad,* IV:140.

41 *Ibid.,* IV:729–34; see Ravier, *Ignatius of Loyola,* 285.

42 *Mon Nad,* IV:99.

Chapter 12

1 *FN,* II:3–10; *Mon Nad,* II:50.

2 Mario Scaduto, S.J., *Storia della Compagnia di Gesù in Italia,* vol. 3, *L'Epoca di Giacomo Lainez 1556–1565* (Rome, 1964), 23; *Mon Nad,* II:50.

3   *Or ob,* 150.

4   *Ibid.*

5   *Mon Nad,* II:56.

6   Scaduto, *Storia,* 3:44.

7   *Mon Nad,* II:56–57; IV:110–11.

8   *Ibid.,* II:57–58; Scaduto, *Storia,* 3:45.

9   *Mon Nad,* II:57–58.

10   *Ibid.,* II:58.

11   *Mon Bob,* 185–87.

12   Francisco J. Egaña, S.J., *Orígenes de la Congregación General de la Compañia de Jesús* (Rome, 1972), 196.

13   *Mon Nad,* II:59.

14   *Or ob,* 129.

15   *Mon Nad,* II:12, 54; Egaña, *Orígenes,* 193–94; *Or ob,* 130.

16   *Or ob,* 72, 127, 137.

17   *Ibid.,* 127.

18   *Ibid.,* 153–54.

19   *Ibid.,* 155–57.

20   *Ibid.,* 126.

21   *Ibid.,* 127; *Mon Nad,* V:322.

22   *Mon Nad,* V:322; *Or ob,* 133.

23   *Or ob,* 139.

24   *Ibid.,* 130.

25   *Ibid.,* 129.

26   *Ibid.,* 159.

27   *Ibid.,* 128, 134, 156–57.

28   *Ibid.,* 127–28, 133.

29   *Ibid.,* 138.

30   *Ibid.,* 126–27.

31   *Ibid.,* 126–28.

32   *Ibid.,* 136, 139.

33   *Ibid.,* 131, 141.

34   *Ibid.,* 157, 160.

35   See James Brodrick, S.J., *The Progress of the Jesuits* (London, 1946), 32–65, and more recently A. Lynn Martin, *The Jesuit Mind: The Mentality of an Elite in Early Modern France* (Ithaca, 1988).

36   *FN,* II:45–113.

37   These can be found in *FN,* II:116–19, 121–27, 314–17.

Chapter 13

1 Ignacio Iparraguirre,S.J., *Historia de la Práctica de los Ejercicios Espirituales de San Ignacio de Loyola*, vol. 2 (Bilbao and Rome, 1955), 305–7.

2 *Cons.*, 98.

3 Iparraguirre, *Historia*, 2:305–7.

4 Iparraguirre, *Historia*, 2:307 and n 67.

5 *Inst SI*, II:302–3.

6 Francisco J. Egaña, S.J., *Orígenes de la Congregación General de la Compañía de Jesús* (Rome, 1972), 216–17.

7 *Ibid.*, 217.

8 *Ibid.*, 217–18; *Mon Nad*, II:61.

9 Egaña, *Orígenes*, 255–57.

10 *Ibid.*, 270–71.

11 *Inst SI*, II:168 Decree 51; Mario Scaduto, S.J., *Storia della Compagnia di Gesù in Italia*, vol. 3, *L'Epoca di Giacomo Lainez 1556–1565* (Rome, 1964), 109.

12 Scaduto, *Storia*, 3:115.

13 William V. Bangert, S.J., *Claude Jay and Alfonso Salmerón* (Chicago, 1985), 242–43; André Ravier, S.J., *Ignatius of Loyola and the Founding of the Society of Jesus* (San Francisco, 1987), 290–307.

14 *Mon Nad*, II:65.

15 *Ibid.*, II:64–65. Nadal thought that authority should be invested in the rector. In his concept of a Jesuit college he had no place for a superintendent, even though Ignatius set this position in his Constitutions. In 1565, the Second General Congregation (decree 86) abolished the office. Experience had shown that rectors and superintendents usually were not able to work together and therefore troubled the peace of the colleges (*Inst SI*, II:210).

16 Ricardo García-Villoslada, S.J., *Storia del Collegio Romano dal suo Inizio (1551) alla Soppressione de la Compagnia di Gesù (1773)* (Rome, 1954), 49–55; *Mon Nad*, II:65–66. For all her religious devotion, Marchesa Vittoria della Tolfa drove a hard bargain. For her practical and business sense see García-Villoslada, *Storia*, 54–55.

17 *Mon Nad*, V:108–30.

18 *Ibid.*, V:134–205.

19 *Ibid.*, V:162–63.

20 James Anselm Wilson, D.D., *The Life of Bishop Hedley* (New York, 1930), viii.

21 Jean Leclercq, O.S.B., *Pierre Le Vénérable* (Abaye S. Wandrille, 1946), 299–322.

22 Jerónimo Nadal, S.J., *Adnotationes et Meditationes in Evangelia quae in sacrosancto Missae sacrificio toto anno leguntur; cum Evangeliorum concordantia historiae integritati sufficienti* (Antwerp, 1594).

23 *Or ob*, 162.

24 *Ibid.*, 171.

25 *Ibid.*, 163. The Latin of this passage reads: *Quidam attente orabat Angelum suum custodem; sensit primum in illo Deum inhabitare quasi imaginem vivam videret Trinitatis.* It is a difficult passage to translate because the precise meaning of *primum* is elusive. Nadal had written earlier of devotion to the Holy Trinity, but this entry seems to be the first time that he mentions having seen an *image* of the Trinity. (He does not describe the image.) This translation of *primum* seems therefore to be justified.

26 *Or ob*, 168.

27 *Ibid.*

28 *Ibid.*, 169.

29 *Ibid.*, 162, 166–67.

30 *Ibid.*, 170.

31 *Ibid.*, 172.

32 *Ibid.*, 164.

33 *Ibid.*

34 *Ibid.*, 171.

35 *Ibid.*

36 *Ibid.*, 175.

37 *Ibid.*

Chapter 14

1 *Mon Nad*, I:363–64.

2 *Ibid.*, I:364–65.

3 *Ibid.*, II:69.

4 Antonio Astráin, S.J., *Historia de la Compañía de Jesús en la Asistencia de España*, vol. 2 (Madrid, 1905), 130.

5 *Ibid.*, 2:110.

6 Carranza had been in England with Philip. His record there, as John Lynch noted, showed that "he was no sympathizer with Protestantism." His case became a "struggle for ecclesiastical power between pope and king." See John Lynch, "Philip II and the Papacy," *Transactions of the Royal Historical Society* series 5, 11 (1961): 23–42.

7 Astráin, *Historia*, 2:115–16.

8 *Ibid.*, 2:116.

9 *Mon Nad*, II:67–68.

10 *Ibid.*, I:398; II:68–69.

11 *Ibid.*, I:423.

12 The count strove unceasingly to have the Society of Jesus introduced into England after the marriage of Prince Philip and Mary Tudor. He then blamed Reginald Cardinal Pole for the Society's failure to penetrate the kingdom: "I have written to my brother that I have so far been unable to move the Queen or the Cardinal towards letting members of the Society come here, although in my opinion they are people who would do good for this kingdom. But they would have no standing or protection here unless they entered by the Cardinal's door. I will keep at the matter until we see how it turns out. The Cardinal is a good man, but very lukewarm; and I do not believe that the lukewarm go to heaven, even if they are called moderates." R. Tyler, et. al., eds., *Calendar of State Papers, Spanish (1554–1558)* (London, 1862–1954), 370–71.

13 *Mon Nad*, I:424.

14 *Ibid.*, II:69.

15 *Ibid.*, I:424.

16 Stephen Clissold, *St. Teresa of Avila* (New York, 1962), 189–90.

17 Gregorio Marañón, *Antonio Pérez, "Spanish Traitor"* (London, 1954), 19–20, especially n 1 on 20.

18 *Mon Nad*, I:424–25.

19 *Ibid.*, I:425. This was the account that Nadal sent to Laínez. A later account in *Ephemerides* ("Diary") told of a much more curt meeting and a far less elaborate conversation with the king. He wrote: "Eventually I was able to give the letters to the king. Araoz had made the arrangements, but he could not have done so in a more slipshod manner. When the king was on his way to mass, I was casually introduced to him. I was nervous. The king replied kindly, 'Welcome. Speak to Rui Gómez.' I have heard nevertheless that the letters from the pope and the general were handed to the Archbishop of Seville [the Inquisitor]." This terse account hardly allows for Nadal's "address to the crown," nor for Philip's rather extended reply. In neither account does Nadal say that he raised the subject of Borgia's reputation at court (II:69).

20 *Mon Nad*, II:69.

21 *Ibid.*, I:437; Mario Scaduto, S.J., *Storia della Compagnia di Gesù in Italia*, vol. 3, *L'Epoca di Giacomo Lainez 1556–1565* (Rome, 1964), 280.

22 *Mon Nad*, I:469–70; II:69.

23 *Ibid.*, I:425. See Hugo Rahner, S.J., ed., *Saint Ignatius Loyola: Letters to Women* (New York, 1960), 52–56.

24 *Mon Nad*, II:69.

25 *Ibid.*, I:418–19.

26 *Ibid.*, I:367.

27 *Ibid.*, I:367–68, 370, 403–10. For a full history of the mission to Ethiopia, see Philip Caraman, S.J., *The Lost Empire* (New York, 1985).

28 *Mon Nad*, I:379.

29 Always suspicious that the Society would drain his resources, Araoz did not protest when Nadal added men to his province. The college at Murcia met distressing days: differences had arisen between Jesuits there and the local bishop and founder, Esteban de Almeida, who wanted the Jesuits to teach reading and writing to little boys. The Jesuits contended that this was beyond their contract. Laínez had placed the problem in Nadal's hands. Nadal followed Laínez's suggestion that the college be detached from the province of Aragon and attached to Castile. This transfer made Antonio Cordeses, provincial of Aragon, extremely unhappy. He saw a staff of men, including the competent preacher Miguel Govierno, slipping from his province. He urged Nadal to release his men and to staff the college with Jesuits from elsewhere, and he denounced the spoliation of his province just to keep the bishop happy. But here was the rub: the bishop liked the Jesuits who were working in the college, and so Nadal ordered that none be transferred. He tried to pacify Cordeses by assuring him that he would send to the Aragon province other men just as competent as those Cordeses was losing. Nadal wrote to Laínez that "dealing with this bishop is really a difficult task. With the divine grace, I hope to pass through that city" (*Mon Nad*, I:372–73, 416). Araoz, as provincial of Castile, had, of course, gained by that transfer.

30 *Mon Nad*, I:418.

31 Astráin, *Historia*, 1:422–32; 2:131–32.

32 *Mon Nad*, I:381–83.

33 *Ibid.*, II:68.

34 *Ibid.*, I:388.

35 *Ibid.*, I:393.

36 *Ibid.*, I:399.

37 *Ibid.*, II:69.

38 Clissold, *Teresa of Avila*, 79; *Mon Nad*, I:428, 465, 615–18.

39 *Mon Nad*, I:429–31.

40 *Ibid.*, I:427, 432; II:70; Francisco Rodrigues, S.J., *História da Companhia de Jesus na Assistência de Portugal*, vol.1, part 2 (Porto, 1931), 409–10.

41 Astráin, *Historia*, 2:120–32; *Mon Nad*, II:70.

42 *Mon Nad*, I:432; II:70.

43 A collection of answers Nadal received to questions of the first questionnaire is given in *Mon Nad*, II:527–89. In n 1 on 527–28, there is an explanation of changes gradually made in numeration of the questions and in the Latin and Spanish versions of the questions.

44 Astráin, *Historia*, 2:135–36; *Mon Nad*, I:372, 388–89, 417, 457.

45 Astráin, *Historia*, 1:437; 2:135; *Mon Nad*, I:452–55.

46 *Mon Nad*, I:455; II:71.

47 *Ibid.*, I:466; II:72–73; Rodrigues, *História*, 1:2:460–63.

48 *Mon Nad*, II:72–73.

Chapter 15

1 *Mon Nad,* I:448, 451; Francisco Rodrigues, S.J., *História da Companhia de Jesus na Assistência de Portugal,* vol.1, part 2 (Porto, 1931), 366, and vol. 2: part 1: 4, 139–40.

2 *Mon Nad,* I:804, 811–12.

3 *Ibid.,* I:805; *Lit Quad,* VII:438.

4 *Mon Nad,* IV:199–200.

5 *Ibid.,* 200.

6 *Cons,* nos. 346–47; *Pol Chron,* II:615–16; Ignacio Iparraguirre, S.J., *Historia de la Práctica de los Ejercicios Espirituales de San Ignacio de Loyola,* vol. 2 (Bilbao and Rome, 1955), 301.

7 *Lit Quad,* VII:437; *Mon Nad,* IV:447–48.

8 *Mon Nad,* I:445–51, 471–74; Josef Franz Schütte, S.J., *Valignano's Mission Principles for Japan,* vol. 1 (St. Louis, 1980), 65–66.

9 *Mon Nad,* I:449–50.

10 *Ibid.,* I:446.

11 *Ibid.,* II:74.

12 *Ibid.,* I:492–93.

13 Antonio Astráin, S.J., *Historia de la Compañía de Jesús en la Asistencia de España,* vol. 2 (Madrid, 1905), 352–23; *Mon Nad,* II:76–77.

14 Astráin, *Historia,* 2:126–27.

15 *Mon Nad,* I:485–87.

16 *Ibid.,* II:75; Astráin, *Historia,* 2:126.

17 *Mon Nad,* II:78–79.

18 *Ibid.,* II:79.

19 *Ibid.*

20 Jerónimo Nadal, S.J., *Pláticas espirituales del P. Jerónimo Nadal, S.I., en Coimbra (1561),* ed. Miguel Nicolau, S.J. (Granada, 1945), 40–41.

21 *Ibid.,* 43–44.

22 *Ibid.,* 44–45, 85–86, 101, 125, 178.

23 *Ibid.,* 46–47.

24 *Ibid.,* 167.

25 *Ibid.,* 179.

26 *Ibid.,* 131–32.

27 *Ibid.,* 195.

28 *Ibid.,* 108–9.

29 *Cons,* no. 63.

30 Nadal, *Pláticas,* 108–9.

31 *Ibid.,* 71, 94, 121.

32 *Ibid.*, 81.

33 Paul Dudon, S.J., *Saint Ignatius of Loyola* (Milwaukee, 1949), 452–55.

34 Nadal, *Pláticas,* 72, especially n 5; *Mon Nad,* V:51, 136–37; *FN,* II:133–34; Ignatius Loyola, S.J., *St. Ignatius' Own Story as Told to Luis Gonzalez de Câmara,* ed. and trans. William J. Young, S.J. (Chicago, 1956), 67. See [Herbert Alphonso, S.J., ed.] *The Vision of La Storta* (Rome, 1988) on the history and spirituality of this vision.

35 Nadal, *Pláticas,* 79, 81, 85.

36 *Ibid.*, 82.

37 *Ibid.*, 86–87.

38 *Ibid.*, 69.

39 *Ibid.*, 148. See John W. O'Malley, "To Travel to Any Part of the World: Jerónimo Nadal and the Jesuit Vocation," *Studies in the Spirituality of Jesuits* 16 (1984): 1–20.

40 Nadal, *Pláticas,* 73–74.

41 *Ibid.*, 109.

42 *Ibid.*, 117.

43 *Ibid.*, 205; *Cons,* no. 271.

44 Nadal, *Pláticas,* 204–5.

45 *Ibid.*, 107–8, 207–9; *Cons,* no. 63.

46 Nadal, *Pláticas,* 207–9.

47 *Ibid.*, 116.

48 *Ibid.*, 170.

49 *Ibid.*, 166–67.

50 *Ibid.*, 172–73.

51 *Ibid.*, 124–25.

52 *Ibid.*, 124, 126, 128.

53 *Mon Ign,* IV:5–9.

54 Nadal, *Pláticas,* 130–32; Avery Dulles, S.J., "St. Ignatius and the Jesuit Theological Tradition," *Studies in the Spirituality of Jesuits* 14 (1982): 17.

55 *Mon Nad,,* V:108–30.

56 Nadal, *Pláticas,* 81.

57 *Ibid.*, 80–81.

58 On Nadal's contribution to Jesuit prayer, see Joseph F. Conwell, S.J., *Contemplation in Action: A Study in Ignatian Prayer* (Spokane, Wash., 1957).

59 Nadal, *Pláticas,* 179–81.

60 *Ibid.*, 127.

61 *Ibid.*, 76.

62 *Ibid.*, 195–96.

63   *Ibid.*, 46–48.

64   *Ibid.*, 196–97.

65   *Ibid.*, 183–84.

66   *Ibid.*, 194–95.

67   *Lit Quad*, VII:435–36.

68   Rodrigues, *História*, 1:2:283; *Mon Nad*, I:803, 807, 811.

69   *Mon Nad*, I:807–8.

70   *Ibid.*, IV:202–5.

71   *Ibid.*, II:80.

72   *Ibid.*, II:78; *Cons.*, 324, 325, 588; Hugo Rahner, S.J., ed., *Saint Ignatius Loyola: Letters to Women* (New York, 1960), 417–20.

73   *Mon Nad*, II:78.

74   *Ibid.*, I:536, 808; II:78, 80; Rodrigues, *História*, 1:1:466.

75   *Mon Nad*, II:80. This was a technique suggested by Ignatius as a way of getting rid of troublesome visitors. See Conwell, *Contemplation in Action*, 8; *Mon Nad*, IV:663–64.

76   *Mon Nad*, IV:192–94, 206–9.

77   *Mon Nad*, I:537.

78   *Lit Quad*, VII:436, 716.

79   Sousa's strictures probably merit a little tempering. Sousa had a propensity to see the bleak side of things. Eight months after he wrote his strictures of Nadal, Sousa came in for criticism by his provincial, Fr. Gonçalo Vaz de Melo. In June of 1562 he was minister at the Professed House in Lisbon. Vaz wrote to Nadal, "I have conducted the visitation of San Roche. I received, according to your instructions, the manifestation of conscience of each man in the community. I put in order some things that called for action. One was the removal of the minister [Fr. de Sousa]. Since he was in the grip of depression, I used the pretext of sending him to Évora to get a break for a few days. He has practically no comprehension of what his work is. He does not apply himself to it. As a consequence, a certain amount of disorder has appeared in the house. Practically everybody notes this" (*Mon Nad*, I:699–700).

80   *Mon Nad*, I:809; Rodrigues, *História*, 2:1:285.

81   *Mon Nad*, I:537.

Chapter 16

1   *Mon Nad*, II:81.

2   *Ibid.*

3   *Ibid.*, I:539–40, n 3 on 539; IV:738–39.

4   *Ibid.*, II:81–82; IV:738–39.

5   *Ibid.*, II:82.

6 The papal legate was Ippolito Cardinal d'Este and their goal was the Colloquy of Poissy. On this attempt to reach a religious understanding within France, and on Laínez's role, see Donald Nugent, *Ecumenism in the Age of Reformation* (Cambridge, Mass., 1974).

7 *Mon Nad*, II:82.

8 *Ibid.*, IV:764–70.

9 *Ibid.*, II:79, 83.

10 James Brodrick, S.J., *The Progress of the Jesuits* (London, 1946), 135.

11 *Mon Nad*, I:538; II:83–84; IV:740; Antonio Astráin, S.J., *Historia de la Compañía de Jesús en la Asistencia de España*, vol. 2 (Madrid, 1905), 141.

12 *Mon Nad*, IV:741

13 *Ibid.*, IV:740–41.

14 Willam V. Bangert, S.J., *Claude Jay and Alfonso Salmerón* (Chicago, 1985), 242–43; William V. Bangert, S.J., *A History of the Society of Jesus* (St. Louis, 1972), 72.

15 *Mon Nad*, II:84; IV:740–41.

16 *Ibid.*, II:85.

17 *Ibid.*, II:85–86; IV:741.

18 *Ibid.*, II:85.

19 *Ibid.*, II:85–86; IV:741.

20 *Ibid.*, II:84.

21 *Ibid.*

22 *Ibid.*, IV:742–43.

23 *Ibid.*, V:206–7.

24 *Ibid.*, V:213–14; besides the Spanish text, there is a Latin text of the first three conferences done fifteen years later, in 1576, and edited, revised, annotated, and amplified by Nadal himself. Although this Latin text provides a richer source of Nadal's maturing thought, we confine this analysis to the Spanish text, since this chapter is concerned with Nadal as he was in 1561.

25 *Mon Nad*, V:224–27.

26 *Ibid.*, V:222–25.

27 *Ibid.*, V:288–91.

28 *Ibid.*, V:280–84; Hugo Rahner, S.J., *Ignatius the Theologian* (New York, 1968), 1–2.

29 *Mon Nad*, V:228–29.

30 *Ibid.*, V:270–71.

31 *Ibid.*, V:455–56.

32 *Ibid.*, V:280–84.

33 *Ibid.*, V:322.

34 *Ibid.*, V:230–31, 296–303, 312–13, 324–29, 456.

35 *Ibid.,* V:337, 460–61.

36 *Ibid.,* V:246–54.

37 *Ibid.,* V:252, 368, 381.

38 *Ibid.,* V:453.

39 *Ibid.,* V:452.

40 *Ibid.,* V:484, 486.

41 *Ibid.,* I:538 n 1. Unfortunately he himself wandered from that path. After Lepanto he became restless, wanted to become a Jesuit priest, was denied, and was eventually dismissed from the Society. He later passed himself off as an expert in moral theology to an unsuspecting bishop.

42 *Mon Nad,* I:810–11. Acosta became in time a fine missionary in Peru, and then, back in Spain, a conspirator in the plot to undermine the authority of Fr. General Claudio Acquaviva (Bangert, *History of the Society,* 100).

43 *Mon Nad,* IV:670–72, 672–81 (translation of this may be found in L. Schillebeeckx, "On Prayer: Especially for Those of the Society," *Woodstock Letters* 89 [1960]: 285–94).

44 *Mon Nad,* IV:619–25.

45 *Ibid.,* V:524–774.

46 *Ibid.,* II:87–88.

47 *Ibid.,* I:553, 647; II:88.

48 *Ibid.,* I:581; II:68, 88, 325.

49 *Ibid.,* I:648.

50 *Ibid.,* I:635, 648–49; II:88.

51 *Ibid.,* I:816; IV:59–92; Astráin, *Historia,* 2:432.

52 *Mon Nad,* I:815.

53 Miguel Nicolau, S.J., *Jerónimo Nadal: Obras y Doctrinas Espirituales* (Madrid, 1949), 54.

54 *Mon Nad,* I:635–49; II:88–89.

55 *Ibid.,* I:615–16, 649–50, 653–54; II:89–90.

56 *Ibid.,* I:655; II:90.

57 *Ibid.,* I:672–74.

58 *Ibid.,* I:671–74, 677–79. Araoz was later influential in a move to restrict the power and authority of the general in Rome in favor of the local provincials. Guenter Lewy does not provide a very accurate or perceptive anaylsis of this movement in his "The Struggle for Constitutional Government in the Early Years of the Society of Jesus," *Church History* 29 (1960): 141–60. Nonetheless, it is the only discussion available in English. For more detail see Astráin, *Historia.*

59 *Mon Nad,* I:815.

60 *Ibid.,* I:816–17; Astráin, *Historia,* 2:487 n 2.

61 Astráin, *Historia,* 2:146.

62 *Mon Nad,* I:675; II:91.

63 *Ibid.,* I:675.

64 *Ibid.,* II:92.

65 *Ibid.,* I:674.

Chapter 17

1 Throughout this conclusion, I shall rely for dates on Manuel Ruiz Jurado, S.J., "Cronología de la Vida del P. Jerónimo Nadal S.I. (1507–1580)," *AHSI* 48 (1979): 248–76.

2 *Mon Nad,* I:40–46, 728–36; II:92–93; William V. Bangert, S.J., *A History of the Society of Jesus* (St. Louis, 1972), 65–66; James Brodrick, S.J., *The Progress of the Jesuits* (London, 1946), 141–42.

3 *Mon Nad,* I:736–38; II:93; Brodrick, *Progress,* 142.

4 A traditional interpretation of the Society's educational policy in France stressed the conflict with heresy. It was claimed that that struggle determined the location of the colleges. Lynn Martin and others have noted, and Bangert's study confirms, that the initiative was rarely the Society's. The establishment of a college was the response to an offer made by some dignitary. Sometimes the offer was prompted by a concern for heresy. See A. Lynn Martin, *The Jesuit Mind: The Mentality of an Elite in Early Modern France* (Ithaca, N.Y., 1988), 15–17.

5 *Mon Nad,* I:738–44; II:93–94; Bangert, *History of the Society,* 65; Brodrick, *Progress,* 142–43; Martin, *Jesuit Mind,* 16–17.

6 *Mon Nad,* I:745–46; II:94–95; Brodrick, *Progress,* 143; Bangert, *History of the Society,* 67–69.

7 *Mon Nad,* I:746–48, II:95–96, 608–9; Brodrick, *Progress,* 143–47.

8 *Mon Nad,* II:96–97, 611, 613–14; Brodrick, *Progress,* 146, 171–73. The exhortations given at Cologne are in *Mon Nad,* V:775–800.

9 Dennis Pate, "Jerónimo Nadal and the early Development of the Society of Jesus, 1545–1573" (Ph.D. diss., UCLA, 1980), 298–99.

10 *Mon Nad,* II:138, 139, 491; William V. Bangert, S.J., *Claude Jay and Alfonso Salmerón* (Chicago, 1985), 111–18.

11 *Mon Nad,* II:141–44, 408–9, 492–93; Pate, "Jerónimo Nadal," 300–302.

12 Pate, "Jerónimo Nadal," 302–3.

13 *Ibid.,* 303–4; Miguel Batllori, S.J., "Jerónimo Nadal y el Concilio de Trento," in *Mallorca en Trento* (special edition of *Boletin de la Sociedad Arqueológica Lulliana* 29, nos. 714–715 [Sept.–Dec. 1945]), 11–58 . On the meaning of this promotion, see Ladislaus Lukács, S.J., "De gradum diversitate inter sacerdotes in Societate Iesu," *AHSI* 37 (1968): 237–316; a summarized translation is in Ignatius Loyola, S.J., *The Constitutions of the Society of Jesus,* trans. George E. Ganss, S.J. (St. Louis, 1970), 349–56. Around this time Nadal also composed a few smaller spiritual treatises. See *Mon Nad,* V:494–774.

14 James Brodrick, S.J., *Saint Peter Canisius, S.J. 1521–1597* (Baltimore, 1950), 472ff.

15 Around this time Nadal composed two treatises on the reform of the curia. Presumably they were intended to dissuade Ferdinand from his course. They were published in Diego Laínez, *Disputationes Tridentinae*, vol. 2, ed. Hartmann Grisar (Innsbruck, 1886), 74–88, 89–93. See Hermann Josef Sieben, S.J., "Option für den Papst," in *Ignatianisch: Eigenart und Methode der Gesellschaft Jesu*, ed. Michael Sievernich, S.J., and Günter Switek, S.J. (Freiburg, 1990), 245–46.

16 Brodrick, *Peter Canisius*, 522–65.

17 *Mon Nad*, II:494–95; Pate, "Jerónimo Nadal," 307; Brodrick, *Peter Canisius*, 291–94.

18 On the establishment of this college, see Bangert, *Jay and Salmerón*, 129–46.

19 *Mon Nad*, II:404, 496, 641–42; Pate, "Jerónimo Nadal," 308.

20 *Mon Nad*, II:498; Pate, "Jerónimo Nadal," 308–9; Bangert, *History of the Society*, 72.

21 *Mon Nad*, II:499–501; Pate, "Jerónimo Nadal," 309–10.

22 *Mon Nad*, II:499–504, 622; Brodrick, *Progress*, 172–75; Pate, "Jerónimo Nadal," 310.

23 *Mon Nad*, IV:278–83; Brodrick, *Peter Canisius*, 307–33; Brodrick, *Progress*, 173–74.

24 *Mon Nad*, II:502–4; Pate, "Jerónimo Nadal," 310.

25 *Mon Nad*, II:335, 368–69, 392, 423–24, 504–6; *Mon Paed*, II:85–133; Pate, "Jerónimo Nadal," 310–11; Brodrick, *Peter Canisius*, 289–91, 450–51, 566–67. On Mannaerts in France, see Martin, *Jesuit Mind, passim*.

26 Quoted in Brodrick, *Peter Canisius*, 567–68.

27 *Mon Nad*, II:413–24; 430–37; 466–67; 506–9; Brodrick, *Peter Canisius*, 567–79; Pate, "Jerónimo Nadal," 311–12.

28 *Mon Nad*, II:509–10, translated in Brodrick, *Progress*, 175; Pate, "Jerónimo Nadal," 312.

29 Pate, "Jerónimo Nadal," 312–14.

30 *Ibid.*, 314–15; Brodrick, *Peter Canisius, passim.*

31 *Mon Nad*, IV:148–65; V:524–774; Pate, "Jerónimo Nadal," 314–15.

32 The congregation elected Antonio Araoz the general's assistant for Spain. On the subsequent controversy, see Brodrick, *Progress*, 176–79.

33 *Inst SI*, II:195–96; 197–98; 199; 201, 204, 206–7; Brodrick, *Peter Canisius*, 176–77; Pate, "Jerónimo Nadal, 315–17.

34 Mario Scaduto, S.J., "Il governo di S. Francesco Borgia (1565–1572)," *AHSI* 41 (1972): 136–75.

35 Quoted in Brodrick, *Peter Canisius*, 639.

36 *Mon Nad*, III:1–2, 4, 324; Pate, "Jerónimo Nadal," 331–35.

37 *Mon Nad,* IV:773–74; Brodrick, *Peter Canisius,* 641–42.

38 Canisius and Nadal wrote to Rome to urge Borgia to beseech the pope to subsidize the Turkish war. The emperor's agents in Rome learned that the Jesuits were secretly promoting his interests. This knowledge, of course, kept him well disposed toward the Society. See Brodrick, *Peter Canisius,* 646–47.

39 *Mon Nad,* IV:772; Pate, "Jerónimo Nadal," 336.

40 *Mon Nad,* III:130–32, 152; Pate, "Jerónimo Nadal," 335–37; Brodrick, *Peter Canisius,* 646–48.

41 *Mon Nad,* III:146–47; Pate, "Jerónimo Nadal," 339–40; Brodrick, *Progress,* 179–80.

42 Schorich was the court preacher in Munich. He seems to have been sensitive and easily disturbed. See Brodrick, *Peter Canisius, passim.*

43 *Mon Nad,* III:181–82; IV:230–41, 777–78; Pate, "Jerónimo Nadal," 340–41.

44 Borgia argued that the period of prescribed prayer must be lengthened to preserve the Ignatian legacy. See Scaduto, "Il governo," 155–62. As we have seen, Borgia's preference for prolonged meditation caused a conflict with Nadal. One wonders, therefore, what Nadal thought of this requirement.

45 See *Mon Nad,* II:589.

46 *Mon Nad,* III:183–84; IV:248–53, 778; *Mon Paed,* III:113–16; Pate, "Jerónimo Nadal," 341–42.

47 *Mon Nad,* IV:254–57, 778–79; Pate, "Jerónimo Nadal," 341–42. For the controversy surrounding Jesuit teachings on usury, see Brodrick, *Peter Canisius,* 591ff.

48 *Mon Nad,* III:185–90; IV:779–80; *Mon Paed,* III:102–13, 383–85; Brodrick, *Peter Canisius,* 649; Pate, "Jerónimo Nadal," 342–44.

49 *Mon Nad,* III:185, 243, 255, 272, 472, 241–42; IV:780; Brodrick, *Peter Canisius,* 650; Pate, "Jerónimo Nadal," 344–46.

50 *Mon Nad,* III:256–58; VI:266–311, 780–82; *Mon Paed,* III:116–21; Pate, "Jerónimo Nadal," 346–47.

51 *Mon Nad,* III:258–60; IV:782–83; Pate, "Jerónimo Nadal," 347.

52 *Mon Nad,* III:150, 173, 260–63; IV:783; *Mon Paed,* III:121–26; Pate, "Jerónimo Nadal," 348.

53 Quoted in Brodrick, *Peter Canisius,* 260.

54 *Ibid.,* 256–79.

55 *Mon Nad,* III:263–66; IV:783–84; Pate, "Jerónimo Nadal," 348–49.

56 *Mon Nad,* III:270, 274–76; IV:784–85; Brodrick, *Peter Canisius,* 577–79, 649; Pate, "Jerónimo Nadal," 349.

57 Quoted in Brodrick, *Peter Canisius,* 628.

58 *Mon Nad,* III:175; IV:785; Brodrick, *Peter Canisius,* 628–29, 653.

59 *Mon Nad,* III:336–38; IV:320–26, 785; Brodrick, *Peter Canisius,* 653–54; Pate, "Jerónimo Nadal," 350–51.

60 *Cons,* no. 398.

61 *Mon Nad,* III:414–15, 478.

62 *Mon Nad,* III:338–39. For a sympathetic understanding of Nadal's plight, see Pate, "Jerónimo Nadal," 351–54.

63 Brodrick, *Peter Canisius,* 660; Pate, "Jerónimo Nadal," 355.

64 *Mon Nad,* III:117, 352–54, 464, 473, 769–71; IV:786–87; Brodrick, *Peter Canisius,* 640, 661; Pate, "Jerónimo Nadal," 355–57.

65 *Mon Nad,* III:381–84, 390–91; IV:326–38, 787; *Mon Paed,* III:127–37; Brodrick, *Peter Canisius,* 448, 629, 766; Pate, "Jerónimo Nadal," 357–58.

66 *Mon Nad,* III:383–84, 390–91; IV:787; Pate, "Jerónimo Nadal," 358–59.

67 *Mon Nad,* III:427–31; IV:788; Pate, "Jerónimo Nadal," 359–60.

68 *Mon Nad,* III:467–70; IV:339–40, 789–90; Brodrick, *Peter Canisius,* 631; Pate, "Jerónimo Nadal," 361.

69 *Mon Nad,* III:316–18, 343–45, 595, 644; Pate, "Jerónimo Nadal," 340.

70 *Cons,* no. 577.

71 *Mon Nad,* III:355, 400, 433–34, 493, 789–90; Pate, "Jerónimo Nadal," 361–62.

72 *Mon Nad,* III:501–2; IV:790; Pate, "Jerónimo Nadal," 362–63.

73 *Mon Nad,* III:496–500, 503; IV:791; Pate, "Jerónimo Nadal," 363.

74 *Mon Nad,* IV:355–58, 790; *Mon Paed,* III:137–41.

75 *Mon Nad,* IV:341–52, 790; *Mon Paed,* III:141–47.

76 *Mon Nad,* III:535–38, 801; IV:358–63, 790–92; *Mon Paed,* III:147–61; Pate, "Jerónimo Nadal," 364–65.

77 *Cons,* no. 679.

78 *Inst SI,* II:199 (d. 19).

79 Scaduto, "Il governo," 162–71.

80 *Mon Nad,* III:564, 579, 808; IV:792–94; Pate, "Jerónimo Nadal," 365–66; Martin, *Jesuit Mind, passim.*

81 *Mon Nad,* III:621, 631–32, 639–40; IV:794–96; Pate, "Jerónimo Nadal," 366–67; Martin, *Jesuit Mind,* 17, 19, 52. For Nadal's general instructions to the provincial of France, see *Mon Paed,* III:161–63.

82 Quoted in Brodrick, *Progress,* 178.

83 *Ibid.,* 176–79.

84 Pate, "Jerónimo Nadal," 369.

85 *Mon Nad,* III:648; Pate, "Jerónimo Nadal," 369.

86 *Mon Nad,* III:654–55, 815; Pate, "Jerónimo Nadal," 370–71.

87 Bangert, *History of the Society,* 51–52; Pate, "Jerónimo Nadal," 371. Nadal's defense is in *Mon Nad,* IV:165–81.

88 On this trip, see Brodrick, *Progress,* 265–67.

89 *Ibid.,* 267–68; *Mon Nad,* III:815–16; Pate, "Jerónimo Nadal," 371–72. On the state of the Society at Borgia's death, see Cándido de Dalmases, S.J., "Estado de la Compañía al final del generalato de San Francisco de Borja," *AHSI* 53 (1984): 55–83.

90 Bangert, *Jay and Salmerón,* 330; Pate, "Jerónimo Nadal," 372–73.

91 *Mon Nad,* III:667, 734–35; Pate, "Jerónimo Nadal," 373. On the competance of these works see Miguel Nicolau, S.J., *Jerónimo Nadal: Obras y Doctrinas Espirituales* (Madrid, 1949), 114–32.

92 It will be recalled that Ignatius had earlier worried about Nadal's disposition: "This fellow is going to be a problem for us. He carries a large dose of melancholy within him. You can see it in his eyes. I am afraid that, if God does not give him a vocation to the Society, he will slide into an out-and-out depression and lose his mind. Right now he wants to serve God. But he is really a crippled person" (above, p. 22). I thank Fr. John O'Malley for drawing this to my attention. Perhaps, as Fr. O'Malley suggested, Nadal had controlled this depression through his activity. When that ceased, the depression returned.

93 *Mon Nad,* III:731, 736, 750–51; Thomas H. Clancy, S.J., *An Introduction to Jesuit Life* (St. Louis, 1976), 136; Pate, "Jerónimo Nadal," 373–74; Nicolau, *Jerónimo Nadal,* 62–63.

94 John W. O'Malley, S.J., "De Guibert and Jesuit Authenticity," *Woodstock Letters* 95 (1966): 109.

95 *Mon Nad,* III:852 (translation in Pate, "Jerónimo Nadal," 374).

Bibliography

Primary Sources: *MHSI*

The following are the volumes in the *Monumenta Historica Societatis Iesu* to which I refer. This historical series, which began in 1894, now numbers more than 140 volumes.

Bobadillae Monumenta. 1 vol. Edited by D. Restrepo, S.J. Madrid, 1913.

Epistolae et Monumenta P. Hieronymi Nadal. 6 vols. Edited by F. Cervós, S.J., and M. Nicolau, S.J. Vols. 1–4, Madrid, 1898–1905. Vols. 5–6, Roma, 1962–64.

Epistolae Mixtae ex variis Europae locis, 1537–1556. 5 vols. Edited by V. Agusti, S.J. Madrid, 1898–1901.

Epistolae PP. Paschasii Broëti, Claudii Jaji, Joannis Codurii, et Simonis Rodericii, S.I. 1 vol. Edited by F. Cervós, S.J. Madrid, 1903.

Fontes narrativi de S. Ignatio de Loyola et de Societatis Iesu initiis. 4 vols. Edited by D. Fernández Zapico, S.J., C. de Dalmases, S.J., and P. Leturia, S.J. Rome, 1943–65.

Litterae Quadrimestres. 7 vols. Edited by M. Lecina, S.J., and D. Fernández Zapico, S.J. Madrid and Rome, 1894–1932.

Monumenta paedagogica Societatis Iesu. 5 vols. Edited by L. Lukács, S.J. Rome, 1965–86.

Orationis observationes. Edited by M. Nicolau, S.J. Rome, 1964.

Sancti Ignatii de Loyola Constitutiones Societatis Jesu. 4 vols. Edited by D. Fernández Zapico, S.J., Rome, 1934–1948.

Sancti Ignatii de Loyola Societatis Iesu Fundatoris Epistolae et Instructiones. 12 vols. Edited by M. Lecina, S.J., V. Agusti, S.J., and D. Restrepo, S.J. Madrid, 1903–11.

Sanctus Franciscus Borgia. 5 vols. Edited by I. Rodriguez, S.J., V. Agusti, S.J., and F. Cervós, S.J. Madrid, 1894–1911.

Vita Ignatii Loiolae et rerum Societatis Iesu historia auctore Joanne Alphonso de Polanco [*Polanco Chronicon*]. 6 vols. Edited by J. M. Velez, S.J., and V. Agusti, S.J. Madrid, 1894–98.

Other Primary Sources

Ávila, Juan de. *Obras Completas del Santo Maestro Juan de Ávila.* 3 vols. Edited by Luis Sala Ballust. Madrid, 1952.

Canisius, Peter, S.J. *Beati Petri Canisii Societatis Iesu epistulae et acta.* 8 vols. Edited by Otto Braunsberger, S.J. Freiburg-im-Breisgau, 1896–1923.

Laínez, Diego. *Disputationes Tridentinae.* 2 vols. Edited by Hartmann Grisar. Innsbruck, 1886.

Loyola, Ignatius, S.J. *The Spiritual Exercises of St. Ignatius.* Translated by Louis J. Puhl, S.J. Westminster, Md., 1951.

———. *St. Ignatius' Own Story as Told to Luis Gonzalez de Câmara.* Edited and translated by William J. Young, S.J. Chicago, 1956.

———. *The Constitutions of the Society of Jesus.* Translated with an introduction and commentary by George E. Ganss, S.J. St. Louis, 1970.

———. *Obras Completas.* 3rd edition, rev. Edited by Cándido de Dalmases, S.J. Madrid, 1977.

Nadal, Jerónimo, S.J. *Evangelicae Historiae Imagines ex ordine Evangeliorum quae toto anno in Missae sacrificio recitantur, in ordinem temporis vitae Christi digestae.* Antwerp, 1593.

———. *Adnotationes et Meditationes in Evangelia quae in sacrosancto Missae sacrificio toto anno leguntur; cum Evangeliorum concordantia historiae integritati sufficienti.* Antwerp, 1594.

———. *Pláticas espirituales del P. Jerónimo Nadal, S.I., en Coimbra (1561).* Edited by Miguel Nicolau, S.J. Granada, 1945.

———. *Scholia in Constitutiones Societatis Iesu.* Edited by Manuel Ruiz Jurado, S.J. Granada, 1976.

———. "On Prayer: Especially for Those of the Society." Translated by L. Schillebeeckx. *Woodstock Letters* 89 (1960): 285–94.

[Society of Jesus]. *Institutum Societatis Iesu.* 3 vols. Florence, 1892–93.

———. *Documents of the 31st and 32nd General Congregations of the Society of Jesus.* St. Louis, 1977.

Tyler, R. et al., eds. *Calendar of State Papers, Spanish (1554–1558).* London, 1862–1954.

Other Works

Aldama, Antonio de, S.J. "La Composición de las Constituciones de la Compañía de Jesús." *AHSI* 42 (1973): 201–45.

[Alphonso, Herbert, S.J., ed.] *The Vision of La Storta.* Rome, 1988.

Andrés Martín, Melquiades, "Pensamiento Teológico y Vivencía Religiosa en la Reforma Española (1400–1600)." In *La Iglesia en la España de los siglos XV y XVI,* edited by José Luis González Novalín, 279–80, vol. 3, part 2 of *Historia de la Iglesia en España,* edited by Ricardo García-Villoslada, S.J., Madrid, 1980.

Astráin, Antonio, S.J. *Historia de la Compañía de Jesús en la Asistencia de España.* 7 vols. Madrid, 1902–1923.

Bangert, William V., S.J. *To the Other Towns: A Life of Blessed Peter Favre, First Companion of St. Ignatius.* Westminster, Md., 1959.

———. *A History of the Society of Jesus.* St. Louis, 1972.

———. "The Second Centenary of the Suppression of the Jesuits." *Thought* 48 (1973): 165–88.

———. *Claude Jay and Alfonso Salmerón.* Chicago, 1985.

Batllori, Miguel, S.J. "Jerónimo Nadal y el Concilio de Trento." In *Mallorca en Trento* (special edition of *Boletin de la Sociedad Arqueológica Lulliana* 29, nos. 714–715 [Sept.–Dec. 1945]), 11–58.

Black, Christopher F. *Italian Confraternities in the Sixteenth Century.* Cambridge, 1989.

Bolgar, R. R. *The Classical Heritage and its Beneficiaries: From the Carolingian Age to the End of the Renaissance.* New York, 1964.

Brodrick, James, S.J. *The Origin of the Jesuits.* London, 1940.

———. *The Progress of the Jesuits.* London, 1946.

———. *Saint Peter Canisius, S.J. 1521–1597.* Baltimore, 1950.

Cantin, Roger, S.J. "L'Élection de Jérôme Nadal. Des ténèbres jaillit la lumière." *Cahiers de Spiritualité Ignatienne* 4 (1980): 263–73.

Caraman, Philip, S.J. *The Lost Empire.* New York, 1985.

Casanovas, Ignacio, S.J. "La Vocación del Padre Jerónimo Nadal en las Elecciones de los Ejercicios." In *Comentario y Explanación de los Ejercicios Espirituales de San Ignacio de Loyola,* edited by Ignacio Casanovas, S.J., 297–352. Barcelona, 1945.

Châtellier, Louis. *The Europe of the Devout: The Catholic Reformation and the Formation of a New Society.* Cambridge, 1989.

Christian, William A., Jr. *Local Religion in Sixteenth-Century Spain.* Princeton, 1981.

Clancy, Thomas H., S.J. *An Introduction to Jesuit Life.* St. Louis, 1976.

———. "The Proper Grace of the Jesuit Vocation According to Jerome Nadal." *Woodstock Letters* 86 (1957): 107–18 (reprinted in Clancy, Thomas H., S.J. *An Introduction to Jesuit Life,* 271–82. St. Louis, 1976).

———. *The Conversational Word of God.* St. Louis, 1978.

Clissold, Stephen. *St. Teresa of Avila.* New York, 1962.

Codina Mir, Gabriel, S.J. "La ordenación y el doctorado en teología de Jerónimo Nadal en Aviñón (1537–1538)." *AHSI* 36 (1967): 247–51.

———. *Aux Sources de la Pédagogie des Jésuites le "Modus Parisiensis."* Rome, 1968.

Cognet, Louis. *Post-Reformation Spirituality.* New York, 1959.

Conwell, Joseph F., S.J. *Contemplation in Action: A Study in Ignatian Prayer.* Spokane, 1957.

Crehan, Joseph, S.J. "Saint Ignatius and Cardinal Pole." *AHSI* 25 (1956): 72–98.

Dalmases, Cándido de, S.J. "Estado de la Compañía al final del generalato de San Francisco de Borja." *AHSI* 53 (1984): 55–83.

————. *Ignatius of Loyola*. St. Louis, 1985.

Dawson, Christopher. *The Crisis of Western Education*. New York, 1961.

Dudon, Paul, S.J. *Saint Ignatius of Loyola*. Milwaukee, 1949.

Dulles, Avery, S.J. "St. Ignatius and the Jesuit Theological Tradition." *Studies in the Spirituality of Jesuits* 14 (1982): 1–21.

Egaña, Francisco J., S.J. *Orígenes de la Congregación General de la Compañía de Jesús*. Rome, 1972.

Endean, Philip, S.J. "Who Do You Say Ignatius Is? Jesuit Fundamentalism and Beyond." *Studies in the Spirituality of Jesuits* 19 (1987): 1–53.

Farrell, Allan P., S.J. *The Jesuit Code of Liberal Education*. Milwaukee, 1938.

Fisher, Arthur L. "A Study in Early Jesuit Government: The Nature and Origins of the Dissent of Nicolás Bobadilla." *Viator* 10 (1979): 397–431.

García-Villoslada, Ricardo, S.J. *La Universidad de Paris durante los Estudios de Francisco de Vitorias, O.P. (1507–1522)*. Rome, 1938.

————. *Storia del Collegio Romano dal suo Inizio (1551) alla Soppressione de la Compagnia di Gesù (1773)*. Rome, 1954.

González Novalín, José Luis, ed. *La Iglesia en la España de los siglos XV y XVI*. Vol. 3, part 2 of *Historia de la Iglesia en España*. Edited by Ricardo García-Villoslada, S.J. Madrid, 1980.

Iparraguirre, Ignacio, S.J. *Historia de la Práctica de los Ejercicios Espirituales de San Ignacio de Loyola*. 3 vols. Bilbao and Rome, 1946, 1955, 1973.

Iserloh, Erwin. "The Reform in the German Principalities." In *History of the Church*, vol. 5, edited by Hubert Jedin, 208–300. New York, 1980.

Leclercq, Jean, O.S.B. *Pierre Le Vénérable*. Abaye S. Wandrille, 1946.

————. "La Paternité de S. Benoît." In *Recueil d'études sur Saint Bernard et ses écrits*, vol. 3., edited by Jean Leclercq, O.S.B., 279–84. Rome, 1969.

Leturia Pedro de, S.J. "La Hora Matutina de Meditación en la Compañía Naciente (1540–1590)." In *Estudios Ignacianos*, vol. 2, edited by Ignacio Iparraguirre, S.J., 189–268. Rome, 1957.

————. "La Prima Misa de San Francisco de Borja en Loyola." In *Estudios Ignacianos*, vol. 2, edited by Ignacio Iparraguirre, S.J., 411–18. Rome, 1957.

Lewy, Guenter. "The Struggle for Constitutional Government in the Early Years of the Society of Jesus." *Church History* 29 (1960): 141–60.

Lukács, Ladislaus, S.J. "The Origin of Jesuit Colleges for Externs and the Controversies about their Poverty, 1539–1608." Translated by George E. Ganss, S.J. *Woodstock Letters* 91 (1962): 123–66 (reprinted in Clancy, Thomas H., S.J. *An Introduction to Jesuit Life*, 283–326. St. Louis, 1976).

————. "De gradum diversitate inter sacerdotes in Societate Iesu." *AHSI* 37 (1968): 237–316.

Lynch, John. "Philip II and the Papacy." *Transactions of the Royal Historical Society* series 5, 11 (1961): 23–42.

Marañón, Gregorio. *Antonio Pérez, "Spanish Traitor."* London, 1954.

Martin, A. Lynn. *The Jesuit Mind: The Mentality of an Elite in Early Modern France.* Ithaca, 1988.

Merriman, Roger B. *The Rise of the Spanish Empire in the Old World and in the New.* New York, 1925.

Mossé, Armand. *Histoire des Juifs d'Avignon et du Comtat Venaissin.* Paris, 1934.

Nicolau, Miguel, S.J. *Jerónimo Nadal: Obras y Doctrinas Espirituales.* Madrid, 1949.

———. "Nadal (Jérôme), Jesuite, 1507–1580." In *Dictionnaire de Spiritualité* vol. 11, cols. 3–15. Paris, 1982.

———. "La vocación del P. Jerónimo Nadal y sus relaciones con el V. Padre Antonio Castañeda." *Manresa* 53 (1981): 163–69.

Nugent, Donald. *Ecumenism in the Age of Reformation.* Cambridge, Mass., 1974.

O'Malley, John W., S.J. "De Guibert and Jesuit Authenticity." *Woodstock Letters* 95 (1966): 103–10.

———. "To Travel to Any Part of the World: Jerónimo Nadal and the Jesuit Vocation." *Studies in the Spirituality of Jesuits* 16 (1984): 1–20.

———. "Priesthood, Ministry, and Religious Life: Some Historical and Historiographical Considerations." *Theological Studies* 49 (1988): 223–57.

Pastor, Ludwig von. *The History of the Popes from the Close of the Middle Ages.* 40 vols. Translated by Ralph E. Kerr, E. F. Peeler, and Ernest Graf, O.S.B. St. Louis, 1891–1953.

Pate, Dennis. "Jerónimo Nadal and the Early Development of the Society of Jesus, 1545–1573." Ph.D. diss., UCLA, 1980.

Prévot, Philippe. *Histoire du Ghetto d'Avignon: A Travers la Carrière des Juifs d'Avignon.* Avignon, 1975.

Rahner, Hugo, S.J., ed. *Saint Ignatius Loyola: Letters to Women.* New York, 1960.

———. *Ignatius the Theologian.* New York, 1968.

Rashdall, Hastings. *The Universities of Europe in the Middle Ages.* 3 vols. Edited by F. M. Powicke and A. B. Emden. Oxford, 1936.

Ravier, André, S.J. *Ignatius of Loyola and the Founding of the Society of Jesus.* San Francisco, 1987.

Reites, James W., S.J. "St. Ignatius of Loyola and the Jews." *Studies in the Spirituality of Jesuits* 13 (1981): 1–48.

Rodrigues, Francisco, S.J. *História da Companhia de Jesus na Assistência de Portugal.* 4 vols. in 7 parts. Porto, 1931–1950.

Roeck, Jozef de, S.J. "La Genèse de la Congrégation Générale dans la Compagnie de Jésus." *AHSI* 36 (1967): 267–90.

Ruiz Jurado, Manuel, S.J. "Un Caso de Profetismo Reformista en la Compañía de Jesús: Gandía 1547–1549." *AHSI* 43 (1974): 217–66.

———. "Cronología de la Vida del P. Jerómino Nadal S.I. (1507–1580)." *AHSI* 48 (1979): 248–76.

———. *Orígenes del Noviciado en la Compañía de Jesús.* Rome, 1980.

Scaduto, Mario, S.J. "Le origini dell'Università di Messina." *AHSI* 17 (1948): 102–59.

———. *Storia della Compagnia di Gesù in Italia.* Vol. 3, *L'Epoca di Giacomo Lainez 1556–1565.* Rome, 1964.

———. "Il governo di S. Francesco Borgia (1565–1572)." *AHSI* 41 (1972): 136–75.

Schurhammer, Georg, S.J. *Francis Xavier, His Life, His Times.* Vol. 1. Translated by M. Joseph Costelloe, S.J. Rome, 1973.

Schütte, Josef Franz, S.J. *Valignano's Mission Principles for Japan.* 2 vols. St. Louis, 1980, 1985.

Sieben, Hermann Josef, S.J. "Option für den Papst." In *Ignatianisch: Eigenart und Methode der Gesellschaft Jesu,* edited by Michael Sievernich, S.J., and Günter Switek, S.J., 235–53. Freiburg, 1990.

Vich y Salom, Juan. "Miscelánea tridentina maioricense." In *Mallorca en Trento* (special edition of *Boletin de la Sociedad Arqueológica Lulliana* 29, nos. 714–715 [Sept.–Dec. 1945]), 155–299.

Walz, Angelo, O.P. *I Domenicani al Concilio di Trento.* Rome, 1961.

Wilson, James Anselm, D.D. *The Life of Bishop Hedley.* New York, 1930.

Index

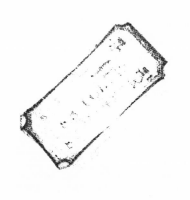